THE ENVIRONMENTAL ARCHAEOLOGY OF INDUSTRY

Symposia of the Association for Environmental Archaeology No. 20

Edited by Peter Murphy and Patricia E. J. Wiltshire

Oxbow Books

Published by
Oxbow Books, Park End Place, Oxford OX1 1HN

© Oxbow Books and the individual authors 2003

ISBN 1 84217 084 8

A CIP record for this book is available from The British Library

This book is available direct from
Oxbow Books, Park End Place, Oxford OX1 1HN
(Phone: 01865–241249; Fax: 01865–794449)

and

The David Brown Book Company
PO Box 511, Oakville, CT 06779, USA
(Phone: 860–945–9329; Fax: 860–945–9468)

and

via our website
www.oxbowbooks.com

Typeset by Oxbow Books
Produced by Bookchase (UK) Ltd.
Printed in Great Britain

Contents

Industry and human health

Preface

The 20th conference of the Association for Environmental Archaeology was held at the University of Surrey, Guildford on 14th–16th April 2000, with the title of 'The Environmental Archaeology of Industry'. Many of the papers presented over that weekend are published in this volume, together with one supplementary paper from Dr Simon Mays.

The environmental impacts of industry are obviously profound and far-reaching yet, as Prof. Frank Chambers notes below, they have been curiously neglected by environmental archaeologists. One aim of this conference was to bridge the gap between environmental and industrial archaeology. The effects of mining and smelting on sedimentation and vegetation in river catchments were addressed, drawing on data from sedimentology, geochemistry and palynology. Industries based on high-temperature processes, including those producing metals, ceramics, glass, lime or salt, require reliable fuel-procuring infrastructures, and the impacts of these on the wider landscape were also considered. Industrial processes are, however, also based on biological raw materials such as horn, bone, hides and shell, and these were discussed in several papers. Proxy indicators for industrial activities were also presented, employing data from diverse sources in the biological and earth sciences, and also from the application of statistical methods to interpretation of artefact distributions. In a final session, some actual and potential effects of industry on human health were evaluated. The editors are extremely grateful to the anonymous colleagues who acted as referees for the papers here published.

Those attending the conference were saddened to learn of the recent death of Professor Geoffrey Dimbleby. Besides his enormous contribution to the development of Environmental Archaeology, Professor Dimbleby was a founder member of the AEA. He will be remembered with respect and affection by many members, and it is entirely appropriate that this volume is dedicated to his memory. A short appreciation of his life and achievements by Professor Bruce Proudfoot follows.

This volume is dedicated to the memory of
Professor Geoffrey Dimbleby

1. Professor Geoffrey William Dimbleby

27.5.1917–8.4.2000

An Appreciation

Bruce Proudfoot

We are all saddened by Geoff's death and offer to the family our deepest sympathy. We share their sadness but we remember with pleasure and gratitude his distinguished career. We look back fondly on shared experiences in field and laboratory, in lecture and seminar room, and even occasionally in committee. We remember his wide knowledge, his ability to inspire others, his integrity and his helpfulness. To many of us he was a personal friend as well as a colleague or co-worker.

Geoff was a scientist. He went up to Oxford and read botany, graduating BA in 1939 and BSc in 1940, having been Departmental demonstrator in Botany from 1939 to 1940. After War service, he returned to Oxford in 1945 as Departmental Demonstrator and Research Worker in Forest Ecology. In 1947 he was appointed University Lecturer in Forestry (Ecology) and three years later was awarded his D Phil for a dissertation on *The ecology of some British podzol formations.*

At Oxford during the immediate post-war years he was one of a small number of scientists who there, and elsewhere, began research and teaching in forestry, widening the scope of both in a discipline which previously had often been narrowly production oriented. The original problems of tree production were still there, many of them indeed were highlighted by proposals from the Forestry Commission to greatly expand the areas of conifer plantation throughout Britain. Had trees ever grown on some of our moorlands with their poor soils? Why was it so difficult to establish new forests in some areas of heathland? Did some trees improve soils? Did others lead to soil deterioration? Geoff brought to such questions an inquiring mind, an openness of approach, an ability to link field and laboratory research and, perhaps above all, a remarkable knowledge of plant ecology, derived not only from his training as a botanist but from his schooldays as a field naturalist.

He himself described in an article published in 1999 how his soil research on the North York Moors led him into archaeology. It occurred to him that the prehistoric round barrows or burial mounds on the moor might be covering soils of prehistoric age so he cut a section in one barrow, from the present surface down to the old surface beneath. The present infertile moorland soil extended over the mound but the old land surface on which the barrow had been built was a more fertile soil. Pollen of deciduous trees that had grown on the site before the barrow was built had been preserved in the buried soil. In this way Geoff began, in Britain, the systematic examination of pollen in soils, elucidating the complex histories of vegetation and soil changes which had often occurred. Archaeology provided a chronological framework for some sites. Pollen analysis of soils and archaeological deposits provided new insights into early environments and into human impact on the landscape. In a series of papers in the 1950s and early 1960s the principles of soil pollen analysis were clearly enunciated and detailed analyses were reported for many archaeological and other sites. In 1962 Geoff published, as an Oxford Forestry Memoir, a major synthesis of his work – *The Development of British Heathlands and their Soils* – a classic in the field.

The principles of soil pollen analysis so clearly enunciated in the early papers were expanded in his later book *The Palynology of Archaeological Sites,* published in 1985. In this he summarised earlier work on buried soils and discussed previously unpublished data, which together could be used to interpret the structure and construction of the earthworks concerned. Geoff demonstrated in a frank and open manner the problems of interpretation of the data: a unique feature was the breadth of field experience brought to bear on the problems discussed.

Not all Geoff's work in Oxford was entirely concerned with elucidating the past. Outstanding papers were published on the role of such deciduous trees as birch in promoting soil regeneration. He was concerned not only with the understanding of the past evolution of the environment, but also with maintaining and improving our present environment.

In 1964 Geoff moved from Oxford to London on his appointment to the Chair of Human Environment at the Institute of Archaeology. He was able to carry on his own pollen work, and slowly widen the interests of the Department of Human Environment. So too his own interests expanded, and he increasingly acted as a bridge between environmental science and archaeology, and as a promoter and facilitator of interdisciplinary liaison. Expansion of teaching and research within the Institute provided the opportunity to develop distinctive courses for students with very different backgrounds in arts and sciences. The problems of training the environmental archaeologist were dealt with in a typically lucid and thoughtful manner in his Presidential Address to the Anthropology and Archaeology Section of the British Association for the Advancement of Science in 1976. With similar lucidity, he made clear in his books on *Plants and Archaeology* (1967 and 1978) and *Ecology and Archaeology* (1977), the necessity for archaeologists and ecologists to learn from each other – in his own words – 'man himself is, and has been for a long time, an ecological factor as well as a member of the ecological community'.

On a broader scale there were the quite remarkable Research Seminars in Archaeology and Related Subjects held at the Institute, with the involvement of Peter Ucko then on the staff of the UCL Department of Anthropology. These Seminars enabled researchers from different disciplines to meet in an attempt to bridge the gaps between their disciplines. The first volume resulting from these was published in 1969 on *The Domestication and Exploitation of Plants and Animals;* the second in 1972 on *Man, Settlement and Urbanism.* There was international participation of scholars old and young, and each volume stands as a benchmark of the progress made to that time in the diverse fields covered. With the limited resources available these were quite remarkable achievements, worthy successors to the notable symposium sponsored by Wenner-Gren on *Man's Role in Changing the Face of the Earth* held in the USA in 1955, the proceedings of which Geoff regarded as **the** textbook for the Department of Human Environment.

At this same time Geoff was acting as Consulting Editor for a series of Studies in Archaeological Science, published by Academic Press, with titles ranging from *Ancient Skins, Parchments and Leathers,* to *Methods of Physical Examination in Archaeology,* and *Soil Science and Archaeology.* Reflecting the growing number of archaeological scientists in the UK and abroad, the Department of Human Environment played a key role in the establishment, in 1974, of *The Journal of Archaeological Science,* of which Geoff was one of the founding editors. Similarly, in 1978 the Association for Environmental Archaeology was founded on the

initiative of Don Brothwell, then a member of the Department staff, and encouraged again by Geoff who jointly edited several of the early symposium volumes of the Association.

Fieldwork and research continued, not least in Geoff's involvement with the Experimental Earthworks on Overton Down and at Wareham. He chaired the meeting of the Committee in 1959 which began the planning of the long-term set of experiments and remained chairman until 1972, and a member of the Committee until 1978. He was responsible, with Peter Jewell, for the report on the first four years of the Earthwork on Overton Down, published in 1966, but his vision and commitment to the multidisciplinary activities embodied in the Committee have had impacts far beyond the Earthworks themselves.

At national level, outwith his work at the Institute and the research in which he was involved, Geoff played a significant role in the development of funding by the Research Councils for science-based archaeology. He was a founder member of the Science-Based Archaeology Committee of the then Science Research Council at its inception in 1977. He was also a member of the Committee for Rescue Archaeology of the Ancient Monuments Board of England, and chaired a Working Party on *The Scientific Treatment of Materials from Rescue Excavations.* The Report of the Working Party in 1978 suggested a complete restructuring and rationalisation of the haphazard arrangements then current for treating and conserving material from rescue excavations, views endorsed by the Board when the Report was transmitted to The Secretary of State for the Environment. In the Report the section on Environmental Archaeology recognised the service element which can be provided to assist in the interpretation of individual sites; and at a different level, the contribution material from individual sites can make to broader issues in human ecology – the nature of the contemporary environment, its utilisation, and the impact of human activity on it.

In recognition of his contribution to archaeology Geoff was elected a Fellow of the Society of Antiquaries in 1977, and later in the same year I had one of my happiest meetings with Geoff, when he was made an Honorary Doctor of Science of the University of St Andrews for his scientific work.

The Science- Based Archaeology *Newsletter* of Spring 2000 comments that science-based archaeology is 'now an integral component of archaeology in most universities …… and has become well- and- truly embedded'. Geoff's pioneering work as Professor of Human Environment at the Institute of Archaeology from 1964 to 1979, and his work before and since, has been an important contribution to such developments. In the wider archaeological research community his insistence on the importance of interdisciplinary approaches has also borne fruit, not only in the continuing work of the Experimental Earthworks Committee but in, for example, the interdisciplinary nature of the Avebury World Heritage Site Research Agenda.

In adding so substantially to our knowledge of early

environments, the human use of them, and the changing nature of environments, Geoff has laid a sure foundation for future developments in the study of human ecology, conceived in broad terms, as he would have wished. He has done more. He has provided us with evidence to manage our environments in a sensible fashion. Through his study of the past he has provided us with the possibility of a better future.

This appreciation is a slightly extended version of that given at the Thanksgiving Service for the life of Professor

G. W. Dimbleby held at Trinity United Reformed Church, St Albans on 17 April, 2000. Tributes to Geoff were also given by Mr Peter Williams, a close family friend and by the Rev Dr John M. Sutcliffe, President of the Partnership for Theological Education, Manchester, who was the Presiding Minister at the Service.

Obituaries appeared in *The Times* May 5, 2000; and by David Harris in *The Independent* July 28, 2000 and *Antiquity*, **74**. No 286 December 2000, 745–7.

A selection of publications is listed below

Dimbleby, G.W. 1952. Soil regeneration on the north-east Yorkshire moors *Journal of Ecology* **40**, 331–341.

Dimbleby, G.W. 1952. The historical status of moorland in north-east Yorkshire *New Phytologist* **51**, 349–354.

Dimbleby, G.W. 1952. Pleistocene ice wedges in north-east Yorkshire *Journal Soil Science* **3**, 1–19.

Dimbleby, G.W. 1952. The root sap of birch on a podzol *Plant and Soil* **4**, 141–153.

Dimbleby, G.W. 1954. A simple method for the comparative estimation of soil water *Plant and Soil* **5**, 143–154.

Dimbleby, G.W. 1954. Pollen analysis as an aid to the dating of prehistoric monuments *Proc Prehistoric Soc* **20**, 231–236.

Dimbleby, G.W. 1955. The ecological study of buried soils *Advancement of Science* **12** No 45. 11–16.

Dimbleby, G.W. 1956. The importance of historical checks in interpreting the effect of vegetation upon soil development *12 Congr. Int. Union For. Res.Org. Oxford, 1956* **1**, 181–186.

Dimbleby, G.W. 1957. Pollen analysis of terrestrial soils *New Phytologist* **50**, 12–28.

Dimbleby, G.W. 1958. *Experiments with Hardwoods on Heathland* Institute Paper **33**, Imperial Forestry Institute, University of Oxford.

Dimbleby, G.W. 1961. Soil pollen analysis *Journal Soil Science* **12**, 1–11.

Dimbleby, G.W. 1961. Transported material in the soil profile *Journal Soil Science* **12**, 12–72.

Dimbleby, G.W. 1961. The Ancient Forest of Blackamore *Antiquity* **35**, 123–128.

Dimbleby, G.W. 1962. *The Development of British Heathlands and their Soils* Oxford Forestry Memoirs **23** Oxford: The Clarendon Press.

Dimbleby, G.W. 1965. *Environmental Studies and Archaeology* Institute of Archaeology, University of London. (Inaugural Lecture, 18 May, 1965).

Dimbleby, G.W. 1965. Post-Glacial changes in soil profiles *Proc Royal Society* **B161** 355–362.

Dimbleby, G.W. 1967. *Plants and Archaeology* London: John Baker.

Dimbleby, G.W. 1975. Archaeological evidence of environmental change *Nature* **256**, No 5515, 265–7

Dimbleby, G.W. 1976. Climate, soil and man *Trans Royal Society London* **B 275** 197–208.

Dimbleby, G.W. 1977. Training the Environmental Archaeologist *Bulletin, Institute of Archaeology, University of London. No 14*, 1–12 (Presidential Address to Section H (Anthropology) British Association for the Advancement of Science, 1976).

Dimbleby, G.W. 1977. *Ecology and Archaeology* Studies in Biology **77**. London: Edward Arnold (Publishers) Ltd.

Dimbleby, G.W. 1978. *Plants and Archaeology* 2nd Edition London: Paladin, Granada Publishing .

Dimbleby, G.W. 1984. Anthropogenic changes from Neolithic through medieval times *New Phytologist* **98**, 57–72.

Dimbleby, G.W. 1985. *The Palynology of Archaeological sites* London: Academic Press.

Dimbleby, G.W. 1998/1999. Human environment at the Institute of Archaeology, 1964–1979 *Archaeology International* Institute of Archaeology, University College London **2**, 9–10.

Dimbleby, G.W. & Evans, J.G. 1974. Pollen and land-snail analysis of calcareous soils *J Archaeol. Sci* **1** 117–133.

Dimbleby, G.W. & Gill, J.M. 1955. The occurrence of podzols under deciduous woodland in the New Forest *Forestry* **28** 95–106.

Dimbleby, G.W. & Speight, M.C.D 1969. Buried soils *Advancement of Science* **26**, No 128 203–205.

Case, H.J., Dimbleby, G.W., Mitchell, G.F., Morrison, M.E.S. & Proudfoot, V.B. 1969. Land use in Goodland Townland, Co Antrim from Neolithic times until to-day *J Royal Soc Antiquaries Ireland* **99**, 39–53.

Tubbs, C.R. & Dimbleby, G.W. 1965. Early agriculture in the New Forest *Advancement of Science* **22**, No 96 88–97.

Ucko, P.J. & Dimbleby, G.W. eds 1969. *The Domestication and Exploitation of Plants and Animals* London: Gerald Duckworth

Ucko, P.J., Tringham, R.& Dimbleby, G.W. eds 1972 *Man, Settlement and Urbanism* London: Gerald Duckworth.

For the experimental earthworks see

Bell, M., Fowler, P.J. & Hillson, S.W. eds 1996. *The Experimental Earthwork Project, 1960–1992* CBA Research Report **100** York: Council for British Archaeology.

2. Setting the Scene

Frank M. Chambers

Environmental archaeology emerged in the 1970s. It was invented by enthusiastic professionals seeking greater recognition for the environmental evidence obtainable through careful analysis of the 'spoil' of archaeological excavation, and through their recognising the value of off-site studies for evaluating both the environmental setting of archaeological sites and the environmental impact of human activities, especially in prehistory. In contrast, industrial archaeology, as originally construed, was pursued by amateur enthusiasts with an interest in the buildings, plant and artefacts of the historical industrial revolution, rather than in earlier industry, and for whom the passing of the industrial age was of both nostalgic and historical interest. Environmental archaeology has become multidisciplinary, populated by a range of specialists; industrial archaeology is now multi-period and multi-faceted. It is argued here that the environmental impact of industry has long been present in the cultural landscape, that it is often difficult to distinguish from other landscape-changing pressures, and that palaeoenvironmentalists have for some decades been recording the environmental archaeology of industry, albeit without always being aware of the scale, nature or relative importance of industrial activity. Future study of the environmental archaeology of industry should embrace genuinely interdisciplinary research methodologies.

Keywords: Environmental archaeology, industrial archaeology, prehistoric mining, human impact, interdisciplinary research.

INTRODUCTION

As we (at this 1999 conference) approach the third millennium AD – which to be pedantic, does not start until January 1st 2001 (Chadwick 1999) – it is sobering to reflect that fifty years ago, Environmental Archaeology did not exist as an identifiable sub-discipline. In the UK, the pioneering site of Star Carr (Clark 1954) was yet to be excavated; pollen analysis was then principally concerned with contributing to yet more "Studies of the postglacial history of British vegetation, part XI..."; and radiocarbon dating (now the most widely used dating tool in environmental archaeology, at least in the Holocene), which had then recently been invented by Libby, remained to be applied in either palaeoecology or archaeology. Even twenty-five years ago – which only a minority of us in this room can recall with any clarity – the *Association for Environmental Archaeology* was but a gleam in the eye of a 'gang of four' researchers in the UK.

ORIGIN OF ENVIRONMENTAL ARCHAEOLOGY

Deriving in part from the pioneering work of Dimbleby (1967, 1978) – to whom this conference is dedicated – and of Butzer (1971), 'Environmental Archaeology' as a recognisable sub-discipline was introduced in Europe (UK) in the 1970s. Advocates sought to emphasise the additional information that could be obtained from linked scientific investigation of the palaeoenvironment of archaeological sites and their environmental setting, as opposed to merely the excavation of archaeological site structures or the classification of inorganic artefacts (such as flint typologies, pottery, coins, etc.). The formation of the *Association for Environmental Archaeology* (AEA) in the UK was intended to give higher profile to environmental evidence in archaeology, and to educate classical-finds- and field archaeologists in the value of integrating palaeoenvironmental research with traditional archaeological methodologies. Thus it was not until the late 1970s that Environmental Archaeology was formally distinguished as a sub-discipline, both with the formation of the AEA and with the publication in particular of an introductory student text by Evans (1978), followed shortly by another (Shackley 1981) and by research volumes on particular techniques (e.g. Dimbleby 1985).

ORIGIN OF INDUSTRIAL ARCHAEOLOGY

Twenty-five years ago, Industrial Archaeology would seem, at least at first sight, to have been slightly ahead. In the first place, it was already a recognisable term. For example, a book first published in 1972 maintained that "Industrial Archaeology has become a popular subject in the last ten years" (Buchanan 1974, 19). However, on closer inspection we find that it was described as being "Still an enthusiasm, rather than an academic discipline..." (Buchanan 1974, dust-jacket), and as if to confirm its popular rather than academic credentials, the volume itself was on the booklist of Book Club Associates, alongside the '*Shell Book of Country Crafts*' (Arnold, 1968). The topics covered by Buchanan were recent historical in age, rather than prehistoric, and were largely confined to the period of the 'Industrial Revolution'. For example, on looking up 'flint' in the index we find but one entry: for 'Flint (Wales)', which is actually concerned with coalfields! Early exploitation of copper and of other non-ferrous metals also received cursory treatment: "The nature of early techniques for extracting metal ores is largely a matter of speculation, but they seem unlikely to have been very elaborate" (Buchanan 1974, 86). There was no mention of the environmental effects of such early endeavours. However, there was acknowledgement of the pollution and waste from historical industrial production: "...it behoves the industrial archaeologist in passing to cast a discriminating eye over the scrap heaps" (Buchanan 1974, 338).

CHANGING NATURE OF ENVIRONMENTAL AND INDUSTRIAL ARCHAEOLOGY

Anyone familiar with the histories of either Environmental Archaeology or Industrial Archaeology will spot the flaws in the observations above. For example, although Environmental Archaeology might not have been widely used as a *name* for a sub-discipline before the 1970s, it did exist in practice – many had been the excavation reports that contained appendices of environmental techniques and data, albeit written by contracted specialists (palaeo-botanists; soil scientists), rather than by persons who would describe themselves as '[environmental] archaeologists'. What was different post-1970 were the attempts, particularly by palaeobotanists, (i) to develop and to apply new techniques of recovery (for example, of charred plant remains – initially in the Middle East, and later widely adopted elsewhere); (ii) to educate conventionally trained archaeologists to take greater account of palaeoenvironmental data; and (iii) to elevate environmental analytical reports to the same (or to a less subordinate) status as the account of an archaeological excavation. By contrast, the growing interest in industrial archaeology, particularly in the UK, was sparked in the 1960s by the significant transformation of the industrial landscape whereby traditional heavy industry was losing ground to light industry – characterised by the then Premier as the 'white heat of the technological revolution' – such that many of the large old factories, heavy plant and larger artefacts of the industrial revolution were very obviously redundant. It was partly out of nostalgia and partly out of the desire to document the passing of the industrial revolution that sparked this enthusiasm for a recent industrial archaeology.

So, in this rather simplistic analysis I am suggesting that environmental archaeology originated amongst enthusiastic professionals, and focused on prehistoric or early historical sites; whereas, industrial archaeology originated amongst enthusiastic amateurs and focused on late historical times. One thing both sub-disciplines had in common in the 1970s was that the first degree of their qualified practitioners was very likely not to have been in archaeology.

Although there was this preoccupation with the industrial revolution amongst enthusiasts, nevertheless twenty-five years ago, prehistoric industries *had* been investigated by mainstream archaeologists, even if the practice was not then graced with the name of 'industrial' archaeology. There had been survey (Sieveking *et al.* 1973) and further excavation in the 1970s of the flint mining site of Grime's Graves (see Mercer 1981); in Ireland, identification of putative sites of prehistoric metal mining (Jackson 1968); in continental Europe, both stone axes (Tabaczynski 1972) and copper artefacts (Novotná 1973) had received close attention; whilst in England, Cleere (1974) had written on the Roman iron industry of the Weald. What perhaps most archaeologists would contend is that the explicit use of Environmental Archaeology to investigate the *environmental impacts of industry* is a relatively recent feature in research. They would cite as evidence the relative youthfulness of the Early Mines Research Group (if not its members!); the adoption of Ph.D. topics to pursue just such avenues of research (e.g., Mighall 1992; Marshall 1994); and not least the theme of this conference, which has been marketed on this basis: "The environmental impacts of industry are obviously profound and far-reaching, yet in general they have been curiously neglected by environmental archaeologists" (editors' preface, this volume).

I would argue against this notion of newness. I contend here that whilst it may be the case that palaeoecologists have only recently been searching explicitly for the environmental effects of industry (e.g. Mighall and Chambers 1989, 1993, 1997; Rosen and Dumayne-Peaty 2001), and whilst archaeologists excavating industrial sites have only recently begun to involve environmental archaeologists in their teams, nevertheless we have, for some decades – perhaps unknowingly, or unconsciously – been looking at the environmental archaeology of industry, sometimes 'on-site', and frequently 'off-site'. This has taken place over a range of timescales, including recent historical times (e.g. Jones *et al.* 1991).

SCOPE OF ENVIRONMENTAL ARCHAEOLOGY

To examine this contention it is first necessary to define both 'Environmental Archaeology' and 'Industry'. Environmental Archaeology may be defined, broadly, as the use of biological, palaeoecological, sedimentological, geophysical and other methods to study and interpret the environment in which humans lived. It encompasses 'Bio-archaeology' (which to a degree it has as a term superseded) and 'geoarchaeology' (Chambers, in Matthews 2001). Advocates of a broader definition might include also the archaeological use of 'ancient biomolecules' (biochemical detection of biological lineage or the use of marker molecules); chemical and mineral analysis of artefacts; and the wide range of dating applications in archaeology. Some of these aspects, along with the more easily recognisable elements of Environmental Archaeology, are perhaps more appropriately regarded as part of what has become known as 'Science-based Archaeology'. However, taking a broader view, Environmental Archaeology uses a range of dating, biological and sedimentological skills to help reconstruct, provenance and date the past environments, economic base and lineage of human groups. In recent years, environmental archaeology has been regarded as being equivalent to 'human palaeoecology' (cf. Butzer 1971; Harris and Thomas 1991).

Environmental archaeology can be practised 'on-site', in which the various contexts or layers of an archaeological site excavation might be subjected to a range of field- or laboratory analyses; or 'off-site', in which the sediments of a nearby lake or the peat of a mire might be cored to produce, for example, a vegetational history for the locality or region. Although, for decades, palaeoecologists practised off-site methods such as pollen analysis, they tended to work separately from archaeologists, but there have been examples of co-operation through multi-disciplinary approaches. Current best practice would include a combination of 'on-site' and 'off-site' records, to arrive at a more complete interpretation of the archaeological site environment and its (pre-)historical context; but in cases where disturbance of the archaeological site is either not possible or not desirable, then 'off-site' methods might be used alone or in combination with non-destructive (e.g., geophysical) methods, on-site. The methods that are used by environmental archaeologists can also be used extensively to contribute to landscape archaeology through reconstruction of the cultural landscape over time, as exemplified by Berglund (1991).

SCOPE OF INDUSTRIAL ARCHAEOLOGY

Industrial archaeology as understood today is of many periods and has many facets. First there is the archaeology of the recent period of the industrial revolution (as in Buchanan 1974). Second, there is the archaeology of craft-cum-cottage- cum-factory-based industries, some of which have an ancestry of several thousand years, including textile manufacture, dyeing and weaving; pottery manufacture; basket-making and woodworking. Some highly skilled and specialised crafts, such as jewellery manufacture and glass-making, have also become industries. However, deciding when any of these activities changed from domestic 'craft' to factory 'industry' is a moot point. Third, there is the early prehistoric archaeology of stone tool manufacture (flint mines; stone axe 'factories'); fourth, there is the archaeology of prehistoric metalliferous mining and metalworking. Then there is the whole area of woodland management, of wood and timber production, the use of timber in building (not just of dwellings but also of 'ritual' sites and of means of transport, including ships), the use of both timber and wood in partitioning the landscape through fencing, and the use of wood for fuel (see paper by Gale, this volume). This simplistic division is but one of many ways of classifying the diverse elements that now comprise industrial archaeology. However, it is far from comprehensive, as it ignores brickmaking, salt mining and lime burning; it does not include some major biologically based industries, such as tanning, tawing and horn working, etc. (see papers by Albarella and by Erynck and Hillewart, this volume), and it completely ignores the 'industry' of food production. Assessing the environmental impact that each of these industries may have had is a daunting task.

THE INDUSTRIAL LANDSCAPE

During the recent industrial revolution the activity of industry locally dominated the landscape. Traditional views of such industrial landscapes include that of the smoke-bound Potteries of the 1950s (see Phillips 1993); of the heavy industry of the Ruhr; of the pithead gear of coal mining. These images are manifestly industrial. This is nature not merely conquered (*sensu* Doxiadis 1977), but vanquished and almost (if not quite) obliterated. Contrast that view with the traditional olive groves of Andalusia; of the oakwoods of south-west England; of the pastoral landscapes of rural Wales. In viewing these landscapes, we do not immediately see the imprint of industry, or the environmental effects of industrial activity.

Yet they are there. Whether it be the cork oaks (*Quercus suber* L.) of the Mediterranean – producing cork for use in the wine 'industry'; the oakwoods (*Quercus* spp.) of northern Europe, which played a major role in both the shipbuilding industry and in providing coppice underwood for charcoal production and its use in the iron industry (Rackham 1976); or the use of wood for fire-setting in the winning of some or all of copper, lead, zinc, silver and gold from the rocks of Wales, and of charcoal for smelting both these ores and of iron from the bogs, for diverse use in metalworking. Each of these activities left their mark upon the cultural landscape – however subtly and however localised. Environmental archaeology can seek out and chronicle the impacts, but differentiating the impact of industry from that of agriculture or other human activity can be problematic.

THE CULTURAL LANDSCAPE

There is another view of the landscape, which sees it as a product not merely of agricultural activity in 'cultivareas' or of industrial activity in 'industrareas' (cf. Doxiadis 1977), but as the culmination of all human endeavours and their interaction with (and, arguably, as part of) Nature. In this view, how possible is it to identify separately the imprint of industry?

Consider the uplands of South Wales in the 1960s: at first disforested, bleak, dominated by tussocky swards of purple moor grass (*Molinia caerulea* (L.) Moench); later encroached upon by serried ranks of exotic conifers, as sitka spruce (*Picea sitchensis* (Bong.) Carr) plantations were carved out on the hillsides. These coniferous plantations appear as rectilinear blots on the moorland landscape – as alien lifeforms invading a pastoral scene. Yet, the dominance of *Molinia* is itself a very recent feature: current research suggests that it post-dates the start of the industrial revolution. Very likely its dominance is a *consequence* of the industrial revolution, although the mechanisms for its spread and relative abundance, not just here, but in Mid-Wales, in parts of the Peak District, on parts of central Exmoor, are poorly understood. Was it changing moorland management practices consequent on industrialisation; was it industrial atmospheric pollution; or was it the ravages of an increased sheep population that gave it a competitive advantage over ling (*Calluna vulgaris* (L.) Hull) (Chambers *et al.* 1979)? Is it coal mining, ironworking, or the non-ferrous metal industry, or the sheep industry that is primarily responsible for the recorded vegetational shift? The economic consequences of the one (industry – in terms of changing employment patterns) may also have helped to drive the landscape impact of the other (farming – through higher stocking rates on the uplands). As for the recent forestry plantations, these derive at least in part from economic imperatives immediately after the First World War, when the UK timber resource was recognised to be inadequate; the continued (post-WW2) afforestation can be traced back to the brief given to the Forestry Commission to create a national strategic timber resource.

It may be the forestry *industry* that is transforming the landscape today; but it was the activities of prehistoric farmers, with or without the aid of metalliferous technology, that helped to create the open moorland in the first place. This upland landscape is a palimpsest of human activities, agricultural and industrial, which have interacted in complex ways.

Taking another example from upland Wales, we can read in John Leyland's 16th Century account of the uplands near Strata Florida – the great Cistercian Monastery – where he observed old tree roots, testifying to the former presence of woodland. The disappearance of woodland was explained by Leland as multi-causal:

> "The causes be these; first the wood cut doun was never copisid, and this hath bene a great cause of destruction of wood thorough Wales. Secondly after cutting doun of wooddys the gottys hath so bytten the young spring that it never grew but lyke shrubbes. Thirddely men for the nonys destroied the great woddis that thei shuld not harborow theves." (Leland 1536–9, in Toulmin-Smith 1906, 118)

The last of these – that woods should be destroyed to remove the hiding places of robbers – echoes Roman practice of laying waste on either side of (Roman) roads to prevent ambush. So, if we are to evaluate the impact of ironworking on the landscape at the ironworking hillfort of Bryn y Castell, north Wales (Mighall and Chambers 1989, 1997), how do we separate woodland decline caused by charcoal production for ironworking, from that of woodland clearance along the (Roman) road that passes the site?

Interestingly, Leland blamed former lead smelting for disappearance of woodland around Cwmystwyth, Mid-Wales (see Mighall, this volume), and he reported belief that the smelting ceased owing to shortage of fuel. This is not the impression that is gleaned from some of today's writers on early metalworking, who place emphasis (perhaps too much?) on the past practice of coppicing of renewable (and so therefore continually renewed) resources. Perhaps we are too influenced by late-20th Century notions of 'greenness', and place too altruistic motives on the part of early metalworkers. Such altruistic behaviour did not attend the goldrushes of the 19th Century, or the recent exploitative activities of some major multinational mining firms, so why should we believe that the practices of early metalliferous industry were any different?

WHITHER THE ENVIRONMENTAL ARCHAEOLOGY OF INDUSTRY?

Environmental archaeology is now a broad church. The sub-discipline has spawned a number of journals, including *Journal of Archaeological Science*, *Vegetational History and Archaeobotany*, and *Environmental Archaeology* (formerly *Circaea*), and is populated by geophysicists, sedimentological geoarchaeologists and a range of specialists, particularly from the biological sciences (for example, (palaeoethno)archaeobotanists; pollen analysts; 'bone' people; palaeoethnoparasitologists, etc.), so making the subject multidisciplinary. It embraces not just the archaeology of agricultural practices (crop growing, processing, etc.) and impact, but also urban archaeology, garden archaeology, marine archaeology and many aspects of industrial archaeology. Environmental Archaeology as practised in the future (either as human palaeoecology, or as cultural landscape history) may exhibit more of the characteristics of interdisciplinary research (*sensu* O'Riordan 1999), in which team-based researchers adopt a common methodology from the outset. There are already examples of such studies; we shall hear of some over the next two days. Perhaps more of the environmental archaeology of industry can be pursued in that enlightened way.

References

Arnold, J. 1968. *The Shell Book of Country Crafts*. London: John Baker.

Berglund, B.E. (ed.) 1991. *The Cultural Landscape During 6000 years in Southern Sweden – the Ystad Project*. Ecological Bulletins 41, Copenhagen: Munksgaard.

Buchanan, R.A. 1974. *Industrial Archaeology in Britain* (reprint of 1972 edition). London: Book Club Associates.

Butzer, K.W. 1971. *Environment and Archaeology*. London: Methuen.

Chadwick, I. 1999. Blame the madness on Dennis the Short. http://www.georgian.net/rally/madness.html (accessed 12th April 2000).

Chambers, F.M., Dresser, P.Q. and Smith, A.G. 1979. Radiocarbon dating evidence on the impact of atmospheric pollution on upland peats. *Nature* **282**, 829–831.

Clark, J.D. 1954. *Excavations at Star Carr, an Early Mesolithic Site at Seamer, Near Scarborough, Yorkshire*. Cambridge: Cambridge University Press.

Dimbleby, G.W. 1967. *Plants and Archaeology*. London: Baker.

Dimbleby, G.W. 1985. *The Palynology of Archaeological Sites*. London: Academic Press.

Doxiadis, C.A. 1977. *Ecology and Ekistics*. London: Paul Elek.

Evans, J.G. 1978. *Introduction to Environmental Archaeology*. London: Paul Elek.

Harris, D.R. and Thomas, K.D. (eds) 1991. *Modelling Ecological Change*. London: Institute of Archaeology, University of London.

Jackson, J.S. 1968. Bronze Age copper mines on Mount Gabriel, west county Cork, Ireland. *Archaeologia Austriaca* **43**, 92–103.

Jones, R., Chambers, F.M. and Benson-Evans, K. 1991. Heavy metals (Cu and Zn) in recent sediments of Llangorse Lake, Wales: non-ferrous smelting, Napoleon and the price of wheat – a palaeoecological study. *Hydrobiologia* **214**, 149–154.

Marshall, P.D. 1994. *The Environmental Impact of Mining and Metalworking Activities in Steiermark, Austria*. Unpublished Ph.D. thesis, University of Sheffield.

Matthews, J.A. (ed.) 2001. *Encyclopaedic Dictionary of Environmental Change*. London: Arnold.

Mercer, R.J. 1981. *Grimes Graves, Norfolk – Excavations 1971–72*. (DoE Archaeological Reports 11). London: HMSO.

Mighall, T.M. 1992. *Palaeoecological Aspects of Early Mining and Metalworking in Upland Wales*. Unpublished Ph.D. thesis, University of Keele.

Mighall, T.M. and Chambers, F.M. 1989. The environmental impact of ironworking at Bryn y Castell hillfort, Merioneth. *Archaeology in Wales* **29**, 17–21.

Mighall, T.M. and Chambers, F.M. 1993. Early mining and metalworking: its impact on the environment. *The Journal of the Historical Metallurgy Society* **27**, 71–84.

Mighall, T.M. and Chambers, F.M. 1997. Early ironworking and its impact on the environment: palaeoecological evidence from Bryn y Castell hillfort, Snowdonia, North Wales. *Proceedings of the Prehistoric Society* **63**, 199–219.

Novotná, M. 1973. Einige Bemerkungen zur Datierung der Kupferindustrie in der Slowakei. *Musaica* **13**, 5–21.

O'Riordan, T. (ed.) 1999. *Environmental Science for Environmental Management, 2nd edn*. London: Longman.

Phillips, A.D.M. (ed.) 1993. *The Potteries Region*. Cheltenham: Alan Sutton.

Rackham, O. 1976. *History of the Countryside*. London: Dent.

Rosen, D. and Dumayne-Peaty, L. 2001. Human impact on the vegetation of South Wales during late historical times: palynological and palaeoenvironmental results from Crymlyn Bog NNR, West Glamorgan, Wales. *The Holocene* **11**, 11–23.

Shackley, M. 1981. *Environmental Archaeology*. London: George Allen and Unwin.

Sieveking, G. de G., Longworth, I.H., Hughes, M.J., Clark, A.J. and Millett, A. 1973. A new survey of Grimes Graves, Norfolk. *Proceedings of the Prehistoric Society* **39**, 182–218.

Tabaczynski, S. 1972. Gesellschaft und Güteraustauch in Neolitkikum Europas. *Neolithische Studien* **1**, 31–95.

Toulmin-Smith, L. 1906. *Leland's Intinerary in Wales*. London.

Wiltshire, P. and Murphy, P. 1999. AEA Conference. The environmental archaeology of industry. *AEA Newsletter (supplement: pre-Conference circular)*.

Mining and smelting: environmental impacts

3. Reconstructing the environmental impact of past metallurgical activities

P. D. Marshall

Pollen, magnetic, physical and chemical data from the Neuburgsattel in the Johnsbach Valley, Steiermark, Austria has been used to reconstruct landscape history during the later Holocene, and in particular to assess the environmental impact of mining and smelting from the 12th century AD. Historical information and radiocarbon determinations indicate that small scale impacts on woodland and increases in metal pollution started during the medieval period. Historical evidence suggests that *Fagus* was preferentially used as a source of charcoal and evidence from the Neuburgsattel would seem to support this. Increases in metal deposition at the top of the profile date to the start of the industrial revolution.

Keywords: Steiermark, pollen analysis, chemical analysis, mining, smelting, human impact.

INTRODUCTION

In the past decade there has been an upsurge of interest in the investigation of early and later prehistoric mining sites in Europe, e.g. Paltental, Austria (Preßlinger and Eibner 1989), Mitterberg, Austria (Ottaway 1994) Triento, Italy (Cierny *et al.* 1995), Great Orme, Wales (Dutton and Fasham, 1994) and Mount Gabriel, Ireland (O'Brein 1994). The potential environmental effects of these activities has been postulated since the sixteenth century when Agricola described the results of mining on the landscape:

> "*the woods and groves are cut down, for there is a need of an endless amount of wood for timbers, machines and the smelting of metals. And when the woods and groves are felled, then are exterminated the beasts and birds, very many of which furnish a pleasant and agreeable food for man.*" (Agricola, 8; Hoover and Hoover 1950).

However, palaeoecological investigations have until recently been almost completely absent (for exceptions see Mighall 1992: Mighall and Chambers 1993; 1997; Wahlmüller 1992).

The study of the effects and magnitude of prehistoric and historic industrial activities must be the starting point for a thorough understanding of the present day anthropogenic changes of climate associated with global industrial activities and those predicted for the short and long term. The investigation of prehistoric and historic mining and smelting will not only answer questions regarding the exploitation of woodland for these activities (Mighall 1992) and the likelihood of widespread pollution (Hong *et al.* 1994; 1996; Nriagu 1996 Renberg *et al.* 1994; van Geel *et al.* 1989), but will also help in our understanding of the degree of pre-industrial human impacts. At present the industrial revolution is seen by the IPCC as a watershed before which human impact on the environment was virtually non-existent (IPCC 1990; Sigenthaler and Sarmiento 1993). This is due to the belief in a pristine pre-industrial environment in which people lived in harmony with nature (Rambo 1985). However, a number of recent archaeological and palaeoclimatic studies suggest that humans have played a dramatic and often destructive part in environmental management in the past (O'Hara *et al.* 1993; 1994). Important issues are raised by the possibility of major pre-industrial human impacts not only for our understanding of past human activities but also for global climate models, contemporary energy and environmental policies (Andrews, 1994; Dove, 1994).

The presence of suitable sites for palaeoenvironmental work in the vicinity of prehistoric and historic iron and copper mining and smelting sites in Steiermark, Austria, provides an opportunity for assessing the spatial and temporal impact of these activities on the landscape. Along with commonly used methods of palaeoecological reconstruction, e.g. pollen analysis, microscopic charcoal, physical sediment properties and magnetics, this study used chemical analysis of peat deposits to reconstruct trends in heavy metal deposition. The use of peat deposits for the monitoring of historical pollution is well documented (Livett 1982; 1988; MARC 1985, Stewart and Fergusson 1994). However, as Livett (1988) notes few studies extend beyond the last 200 years BP although the possibility exists to reconstruct a complete historic record of metal deposition. Two hypotheses are considered in this study: firstly that mining and smelting caused widespread destruction of woodland. This is a commonly held view (Voss 1988) although in Britain strictly 'mining' seems to have had only small scale impacts on woodland (Mighall and Chambers, 1993). Mining and smelting required large amounts of wood and in particular the smelting of copper sulphide ores, common in Austria, required the ore to be roasted and smelted up to three times before any pure copper was produced. Changes in the woodland resources used, the type of metal being produced and the magnitude of activity will have all had different effects on vegetation. The second hypothesis considered is that large amounts of anthropogenerated metals (most notably Cu, Pb and Zn) were released during past metallurgical activities. Past industrial processes were relatively inefficient and recent studies by Hong *et al.* (1994) and Renberg *et al.* (1994) show that Roman lead production caused hemispheric pollution. The impact on the local environment of increased metal deposition could have been damaging to fragile ecosystems.

ARCHAEOLOGY AND HISTORY

The Johnsbach and Radmer valleys, Steiermark, eastern Austria have a long history of human occupation and exploitation dating back to at least the Bronze Age (Preßlinger and Eibner 1989, Preßlinger and Köstler 1993; Preßlinger *et al.* 1992; Klemm pers.comm). There is also a large corpus of documentary information relating to the mining and smelting of iron and copper in the Johnsbach valley from the 12th century onwards (Köstler 1993; Redlich 1903) and copper mining and smelting in the Radmer from AD 1560 (Gröbl 1986; Sperl 1984). Between AD 1560 and 1619 the Radmer Valley produced approximately 11.8% of central Europe's copper; in AD 1596, 480.58 tonnes of copper was made (Gröbl 1986).

The production of charcoal was the most important requisite of the mining industry after a suitable ore body for exploitation had been found. In the case of the Radmer copper works the importance of charcoal can be seen in the fact that well over 75% of expenditure in producing copper was spent on obtaining charcoal (see Tables 1a and b).

The historical records are important because from them it is possible to calculate fairly accurate estimates of the charcoal and wood required by the two smelters in the Radmer valley on a yearly scale. This is based on the fact that for AD 1610 and 1622 records show the amount of charcoal used in copper production for those years (50,000 and 72,000 barrels respectively) (Pribram 1938).

The existence of an array of historical records for the area relating to mining and smelting during the later medieval period is important as it enables a direct comparison to be made between the palaeoenvironmental and historical records. The results obtained may give us some idea of what to expect in environmental reconstruction's from the prehistoric past and allow the formulation of a proxy record. The production of proxy records will potentially prove important in the study of prehistoric industrial activities when the estimates of the length and intensity of mining activity are poorly quantified, periods of activity often lack reliable dating, and the amounts of raw materials mined, metal produced, and wood needed is unknown.

METHODS

The Neuburgsattel, (G.R. 5509 2661, 1439m above sea level) is a mire located in the saddle between the Radmer and Johnsbach valleys. A 1.72m core was obtained from the from the eastern end of the site with a Russian corer (Jowsey, 1966).

Sediment analysis

In the laboratory approximately 1cm thick sub-samples were taken at 2cm intervals from the core, transferred to a glass jar and placed in cold storage. This was undertaken in an attempt to keep the possibility of contamination and decay of samples to a minimum. Down-core determinations of bulk density, organic matter content and dry matter content were carried out on known quantities of material. Samples were air dried to 105°C and then ignited to 430°C with the percentage weight loss noted at each stage, following the methods of Bengtsson and Enell (1986) and Davies (1974). The concentrations of Cu and Zn were determined by flame atomic absorption spectrometry (AAS) using a Perkin Elmer 1100B atomic absorption instrument following a 2% nitric acid digestion in a pressure digestion bomb (Marshall 1994). Analysis of samples for Pb had to be undertaken using a Perkin Elmer SP9 graphite furnace due to the very low concentrations of Pb found in some samples. During the analysis blank and spiked solutions containing a known amount of the element being analysed were run after every 10 samples to ensure that analytical errors

Table 1a. Expenditure of the smelting works in AD 1608 from Wald- und Bergamtsarifchiv, Radmer Kupferbergwerk Schuber 3363 (quoted in Gröbl, 1986).

	1st Quarter fl. ß d			2nd Quarter fl. ß d			3rd Quarter fl. ß d			4th Quarter fl. ß d			Total fl. ß d		
Salary of smelter front hut	250	3	10[1]	240	3	20[1]	236	7	–[1]	26	1	[1]	988	6	[1]
Salary of roasting hut	305	5	5[1]	270	2	25[1]	267	3	20[1]	257	3	25[1]	1100	7	15[1]
Charcoal	3433	–	8	2053	3	24	1450	3	13	1554	7	3	8491	6	18
Blacksmith	11	5	12	15	4	8	36	1	24	13	1	18	76	4	24
Clay	43	3	18	32	5	26	51	1	10	21	6	20	140	1	14
Maintenance of the path over the Neuburgsattel	13[1]			13[1]			13[1]			13[1]			52[1]		
Ore transport	191	6	17	157	5	17	119	–	9	108	7	5	577	3	19
Miscellaneous	291	5	3	375	3	10	133	2	10	**3091**	**5**	**28**	3891	–	21

Table 1b. Expenditure of the smelting works in AD 1610 from Wald- und Bergamtsarfichiv, Radmer Kupferbergwerk Schuber 3364 (quoted in Gröbl, 1986).

	1st Quarter fl. ß d			2nd Quarter fl. ß d			3rd Quarter fl. ß d			4th Quarter fl. ß d			Total fl. ß d		
Salary of smelter front hut	242	3	15[1]	215	3	25[1]	213	2	25[1]	243	1	5[1]	914	3	10[1]
Salary of roasting hut	248	4	20[1]	238	6	25[1]	220	3	20[1]	243			950	7	5
Charcoal[1]	2957	4	20[1]	1907	3	18[1]	1229	7	3[1]	1862	1	4[1]	7956	6	10[1]
Blacksmith[1]	8	–	21[1]	10	4	8[1]	16	3	29[1]	17	1	21[1]	52	2	19[1]
Clay	53	3	22	15?	2	24	32	3	2	46	5	10	147	6	28
Maintenance of the path over the Neuburgsattel	26[1]			26[1]			26[1]			26[1]			104		
Ore transport	161	4	25	119	–	17	151	2	20	163	–	25	595	–	27
Miscellaneous	302	6	11	215	1	20	224	6	29	**3066**	**2**	**15**	3809	1	15

[1] From this 2772 fl. 20 d was expenditure for wood

[2] of the 3091 fl. 5 ß 28 d, 2906 fl. 2 ß was spent on wood.

Units: fl = Gulden; ß = schilling; d = penny.

were not occurring. The elements Cu, Pb and Zn were chosen, as these are commonly associated with anthropogenic activities such as copper and iron production and 'modern industrialisation'.

The down-core elemental profiles are presented as concentration and influx curves (Figure 1). Concentration curves may not be just a reflection of metal influx trends but can be influenced by changes in sedimentation rates and peat stratigraphy (Williams 1991; Livett 1988) accordingly the "heavy metal flux rate" (Livett *et al.* 1979) was calculated using the formula from Livett (1988):

$$F = R.D.C$$

Where $F=$ flux rate µg cm-2 yr-1
         $R=$ accumulation rate
         $D=$ bulk density of the deposit
         $C=$ concentration of the element

The sub-samples used in mass specific magnetic susceptibility analyses were air dried for 48 hours at 50°C, hopefully preventing any thermal enhancement of magnetic properties, homogenised with a pestle and mortar and transferred to a 10cc polythene holder. Low frequency mass specific susceptibility was measured using a Bartington MS2 Magnetic Susceptibility Unit following the method of Gale and Hoare (1990).

Pollen analysis

1 cm³ samples for pollen analysis were prepared volumetrically using the displacement method (Bonny 1972) and treated with a standard chemical procedure following Moore *et al.* (1991) and Faegri and Iversen (1989). A pollen sum of 500 total land pollen (TLP) was employed, excluding spores and obligate aquatic taxa. The pollen

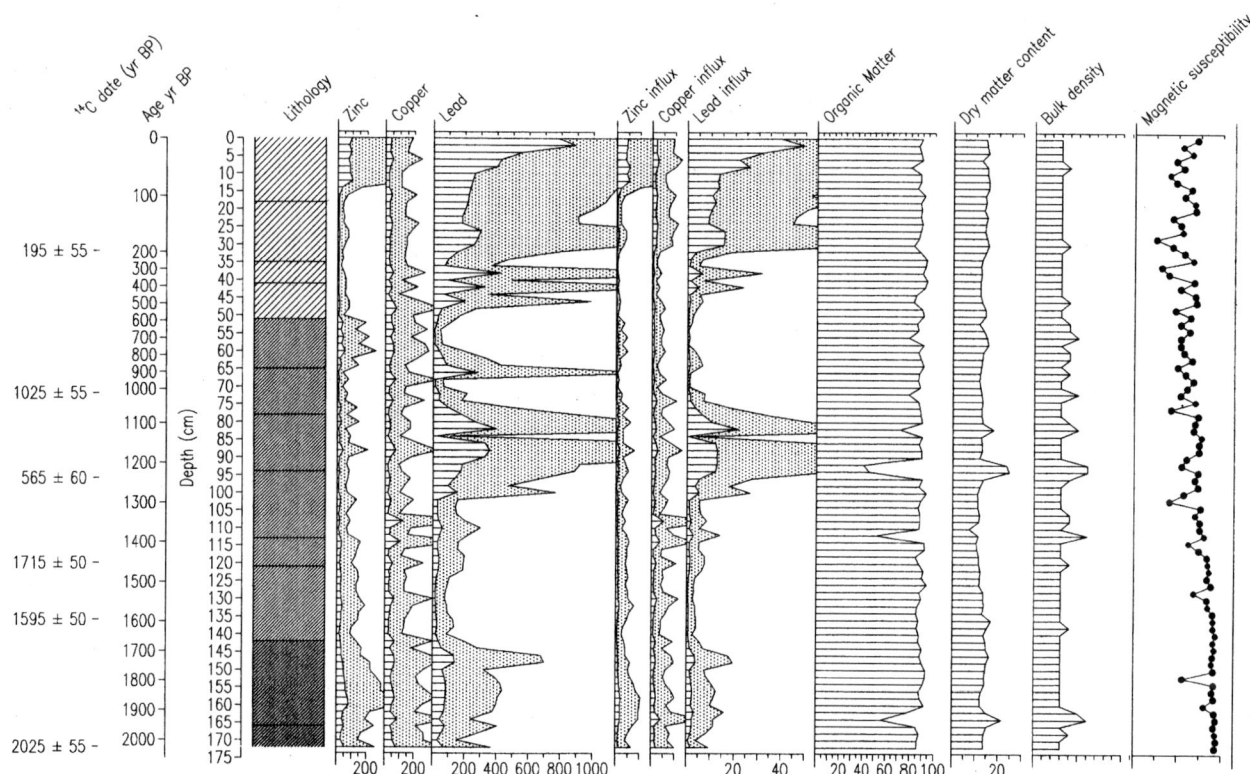

Figure 1. Neuburgsattel. Down-core elemental concentrations (μg g⁻¹), influx (μg cm⁻² yr⁻¹), bulk density (g/cm³), organic and dry matter content (% dry weight) and magnetic susceptibility (10⁻⁸ m³ kg⁻¹). Influx profiles have an exaggeration of x5.

diagram was produced using Tilia 1.08 and Tilia*Graph 1.16 (Grimm, 1991) and are shown in Figure 2. The percentage pollen diagrams were divided into "local" pollen assemblage zones (Birks 1986) and sub-zones (delimited by lower case letters a-b) with the aid of a stratigraphically constrained cluster analysis (CONISS; Grimm 1987) and the subjective identification of distinguishing changes in the fossil pollen stratigraphy. The statistical analysis was carried out on land pollen with a value of greater than 2% in at least one sample level using the Edwards and Cavalli-Sforza chord distance as the dissimilarity coefficient (Birks and Gordon 1985). Pollen nomenclature follows that of Bennett (1994).

Radiocarbon determinations

Samples from six selected levels were submitted to the University of Arizona via the NERC Radiocarbon Laboratory at East Kilbride for accelerator dating. The results are presented in Table 2.

The results are conventional radiocarbon ages (Stuiver and Polach 1977), and are quoted in accordance with the international standard known as the Trondheim convention (Stuiver and Kra 1986). The calibrated date ranges for the samples have been calculated using the maximum intercept method of Stuiver and Reimer (1986), and are quoted in the form recommended by Mook (1986) with end points rounded outwards to 10 years. The results have been calibrated using data from Stuiver *et al* (1998).

Unless stated, the determinations given are derived from the extrapolation of peat accumulation rates and therefore these dates must lie within a range and are thus not precise.

RESULTS

Radiocarbon determinations

The radiocarbon results are statistically significantly inconsistent in relation to the stratigraphic sequence (A = 0.6%, Bronk Ramsey 1995, Marshall unpublished). This is because AA-12950 and AA-12952 are too young and may have been affected by downward movement of younger material, perhaps as a result of rootlet penetration. Excluding AA-12950 and AA-12952, the four remaining determinations are consistent with the stratigraphy (A = 97.6%; Bronk Ramsey 1995, Marshall unpublished).

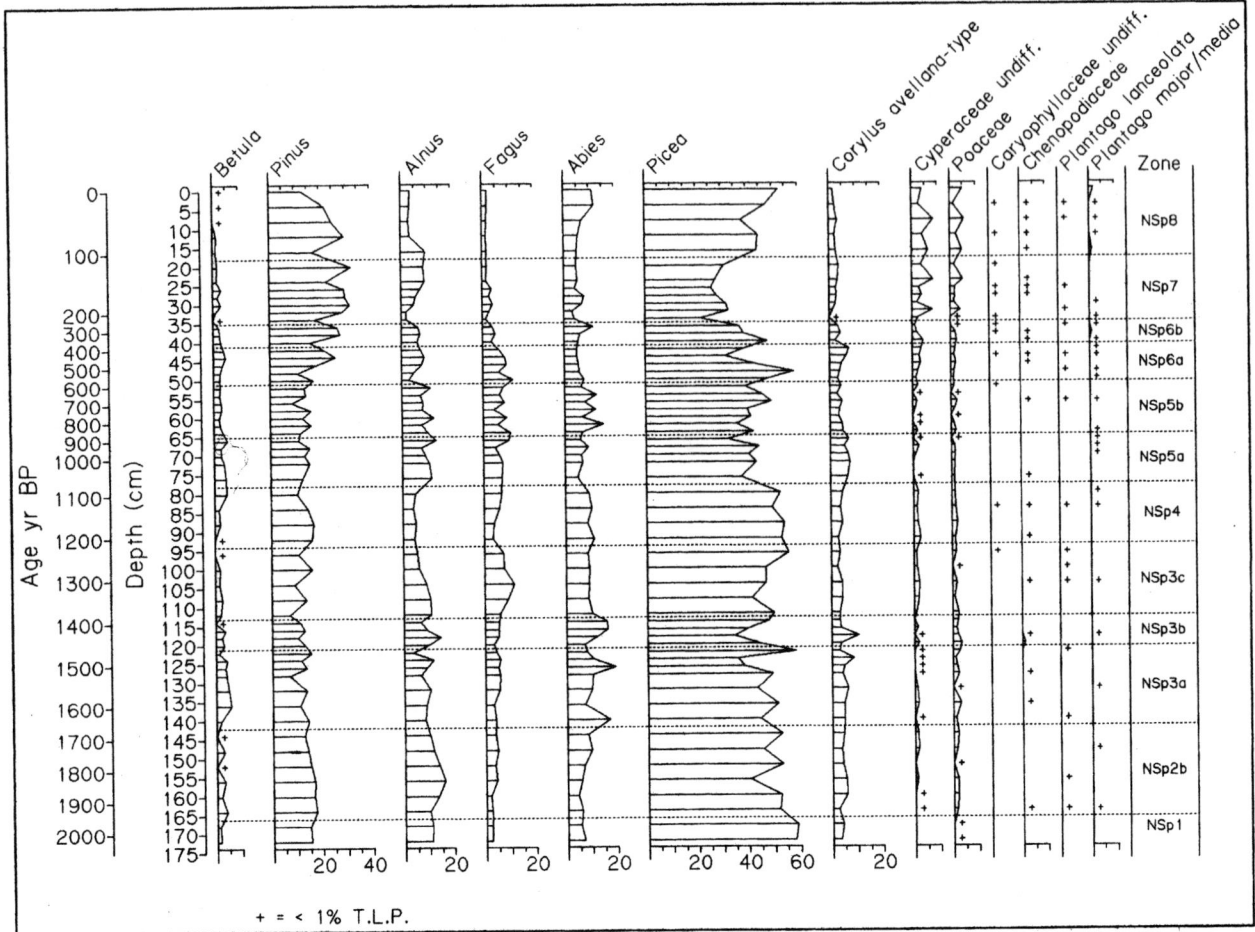

Figure 2. Neuburgsattel. Pollen percentage diagram. Values represented on the horizontal axis are expressed as a percentage of total land pollen (TLP). Crosses represent a value of less than 1%.

Sediment analysis

The sediments from the Neuburgsattel consist entirely of uniform homogenous and poorly humified brown peats. Between 136–148 cm the sediments contain some very small wood and twig fragments.

Down-core profiles of mass specific susceptibility (χ), dry and organic matter content and bulk density for the Neuburgsattel are shown in Figure 1. Values are negative throughout the profile, with the closest values to zero in the bottom part of the core between 172 and 118 cm, except for two troughs at 152 cm and 118 cm. From 118 cm to 22 cm the general trend is for χ to decrease (i.e. become more negative). The top 20 cm of the core has slightly higher χ values (closer to zero) than the middle part of the profile that increase towards the surface. The reason that is constantly below zero may be because ferrimagnetic minerals are generally rare in peat (Thompson and Oldfield 1986) and thus paramagnetic and even diamagnetic minerals may contribute significantly to susceptibility. Highly organic sediments have also been found to have low or negative susceptibility

readings at Beinn Lawers, Perthshire, Scotland (Tipping *et al.* 1993) and Loch Lang, South Uist, Scotland (Bennett *et al.* 1990). The trend for χ to increase with depth (at the Neuburgsattel to get closer to zero) mirrors the results of Lagerås and Sandgren (1994) in a study of Swedish peats, reflecting the influence of material from weathered bed rock.

The loss on ignition (LOI) profile from the Neuburgsattel shows a number of stratigraphic boundaries (Figure 1). The sediments are highly organic in nature with the majority of samples containing well over 80% organic matter.

Chemical properties

The Cu concentration profile from the Neuburgsattel shows a fairly 'noisy' record in which the general trend seems to be higher Cu levels at the base of the core which decrease upwards. The levels of Cu recorded are fairly high compared with the figures given for British peats by Livett *et al.* (1979) and do reach more than 120 μg g^{-1}.

Table 2. Radiocarbon determination from the Neuburgsattel.

Laboratory Number	Depth (cm)	Material	$\delta^{13}C \pm 0.1‰$	Radiocarbon age (BP)	Calibrated date (95% confidence)
AA-12948	32	peat	-27.4	195 ± 55	cal AD 1530–1955*
AA-12949	72	peat	-28.2	1,025 ± 55	cal AD 890–1160
AA-12950	96	peat	-27.8	565 ± 60	cal AD 1290–1450
AA-12951	120	peat	-27.7	1,715 ± 50	cal AD 220–430
AA-12952	136	peat	-27.6	1,595 ± 50	cal AD 340–540
AA-12953	172	peat	-27.7	2,025 ± 55	180 cal BC–cal AD 120

There is some similarity between the Zn and Pb profiles, with higher values at the base of the core, 172–146 cm (Zn; 52–82 µg g⁻¹, Pb: 31–87 µg g⁻¹) followed by a sharp drop in values (Zn: less than 32 µg g⁻¹; Pb less than 35 µg g⁻¹) and a further sharp increase at the top of the core from 18 cm (Zn 101 µg g⁻¹; Pb 422 µg g⁻¹). The Pb profile has a noticeable increase in values between 100 and 76 cm with concentrations of more than 300 µg g⁻¹ compared with less than 5 µg g⁻¹ in the preceding part of the core.

The Cu influx diagram shows a similar profile to the concentration data with a general reduction in values taking place over the length of the core, although there is a noticeable increase in Cu influx in the top 30 cm of the diagram (2 µg cm⁻² yr⁻¹). A similar curve to that of Cu is discernible from the Zn profile although the major rise in Zn values occurs at 15 cm. The Pb profile shows a slightly higher influx at the base of the core (0.8–3.1 µg cm⁻² yr⁻¹) compared with what would seem to be the very low "background" levels (less than 0.8 µg cm⁻² yr⁻¹). The sharp increase in values described in the Pb concentration profile between 100 and 76 cm is visible in the influx curve suggesting that this event is not a result of a change in the sediment accumulation rate. Two increases in Pb influx occur at the top of the profile the first correlates with the rise in Cu influx (15.3 µg cm⁻² yr⁻¹) and the second follows the increase in Zn influx (26 µg cm⁻² yr⁻¹).

Pollen analysis

A pollen percentage diagram, showing selected taxa from the Neuburgsattel is shown in Figure 2.

The pollen record from the Neuburgsattel shows that during the last *c.* 2000 years the area has been heavily forested throughout this period and the forest was mainly made up of *Picea*, *Abies*, *Fagus* and possibly *Pinus*. The interpretation of the *Pinus* record is difficult due to the problems of long distance transport (Huntley and Birks, 1983), although the work of Lageard *et al.* 1999) suggests that pine pollen percentages as low as 4–5% could represent a local presence. Given that pine would have probably been restricted to the lower and middle elevations of the valley (Ellenberg 1988) combined with the regionality of the pollen dispersal at higher elevations leading to a distortion of the pollen assemblage (Markgraf 1980) it is only safe to conclude that pine would have been an

important component of woodland on a regional scale. The altitudinal variations that exist in tree distribution today in the Johnsbach and Radmer valleys were probably also a major factor in the distribution of woodland in the past. At higher altitudes it is probable that *Picea* completely dominated the landscape while further down the valley sides and at lower altitudes *Abies* and deciduous trees, in particular *Fagus* began to form a more important component. However, it is likely that *Picea* still formed a major part of the woodland even at lower altitudes. For about *c* 1,600 years the woodland remained virtually unchanged with small scale changes in the percentage values of trees possibly relating to small scale human interference and natural events such as climatic change, "natural fires" or vegetation dynamics. It has only been in the last *c* 400 years that any visible changes in the pollen record due to human activity have taken place. In this period *Fagus* has become almost absent, while Cyperaceae undiff. and Poaceae have risen in importance, *Picea* values have fluctuated in tandem with these changes. Although the values of the classic "indicator species" have not increased drastically there is a definite trend for there to be a more diverse range of them in the upper parts of the core. It seems probable that the period represented by zones NSp6a-NSp8 (*c* 600 to 0 BP; *c* cal AD 1350-present) contains the most important record of human activity on the landscape.

DISCUSSION

Between 180 cal BC-cal AD 120 (AA-12953; 2,025±55 BP) and *c* 1,700 BP (*c* cal AD 350) the relatively high Pb levels compared with those in much of the core may be the result of Roman Pb smelting taking place throughout Europe or on a regional scale. Increases in recorded Pb levels interpreted as a result of Roman period mining and smelting have been found in peat deposits from Britain (Lee and Tallis 1973; Martin *et al.* 1979), Germany (Ernst *et al.* 1974) and the Netherlands (van Geel *et al.* 1989), lake deposits in Sweden (Renberg *et al.* 1994) and ice cores from Greenland (Hong *et al.* 1994). The increase in Pb deposition in these studies has been interpreted as being the result of local and hemispheric Pb pollution caused by the expansion of Pb smelting during the Roman period (Shirahata *et al.* 1980). It is difficult to assess the levels at the Neuburgsattel with any confidence because a true background level of Pb deposition could not be calculated owing to the length of core retrieved. The calculation of the background concentration of a metal in a peat requires the profile to extend back to a time when the inputs can solely be attributed to natural atmospheric inputs. In situations where this is not possible the use of enrichment factors (Shotyk 1996) can be used to normalise the concentrations of trace elements (e.g. Pb) to a conservative element (e.g. Al, Ti) known to be derived mainly from crustal weathering. It is difficult to assess the levels at the Neuburgsattell with any confidence because background levels of Pb deposition could not be calculated.

The first documentary evidence for mining in the Johnsbach valley comes from the 12th century AD when the Nunnery at Admont was given the right to mine iron. Throughout the period until the end of the 14th century AD industrial activity seems to have been sporadic and limited to mining. This would seem to correlate with the palaeoecological record that shows low levels of metal deposition and little change in the pollen record.

From *c.* 550 BP (*c.* cal AD 1400) to *c.* 250 BP (*c.* cal AD 1650) there is an increase in Pb values, while Cu and Zn both fall. There is a small decrease in the value of tree species recorded and a small increase in herb taxa. This period covers the expansion of the Radmer copper works, and the iron and copper mining industry throughout the region, including the Johnsbach valley (Sperl 1984). It seems that there is a relationship between the fortunes of the mining industry and changes identified in the palaeoecological record. However, given the position of the sampling site, in the saddle between the Johnsbach and Radmer valleys where industrial activities took place on the valley bottoms it may be that the site is too high to detect small scale clearance activity for industrial purposes. This is further compounded by the fact that records from the copper works at Radmer am Der Halsel show that beech charcoal was often transported from the Flizwald (*c* 10km west of the Neuburgsattel). The microscopic charcoal record does show a much more pronounced 'take-off' during this period than either the chemical or pollen record, perhaps reflecting its ability to pick up more regional trends in smelting activities (Marshall 1994).

From just after cal AD 1530–1955 (AA-12948; 195±55 BP) to *c.* 80 BP there was a major increase in Pb, Cu, Zn deposition at the Neuburgsattel. This event probably represents the start of the Industrial Revolution and the introduction of Blast Furnaces in Eisenerz dated to AD 1760 (Sperl 1984). The decline in *Fagus* values may to be have been the result of its preferential use as a charcoal in the smelting of copper and iron (Gröbl 1986). Evidence from other palynological work in Europe supports this hypothesis as *Fagus* is often found to decline in areas with evidence for large scale medieval mining, e.g. the Harz mountains Germany (Willutzki 1962), Ledine Valley, Serbia (Serclj 1988) and the Ariège basin, France (Galop

and Jalut 1994). After AD 1840 polluted sediments at many European and North American sites become overshadowed by regional and national trends (Williams 1991).

The only chemical profile that seems to correspond with the archaeological and historical data is Pb, and because this metal has a strong affinity for peat (Livett *et al.* 1979) it suggests that this profile has remained intact. The Zn and in particular Cu profiles do not correspond with local industrial histories and may reflect the influenced of post-depositional transformation and mobilisation. The use of Zn in peat profiles has been questioned in a number of reviews (Jones 1997, Shotyk *et al.* 1990) because of its susceptibility to changes in pH, plant bioaccumulation and changes in redox potential (Rosen and Dumayne-Peaty 2001). The difficulty in reconciling the Cu profile with the documentary records is hard to explain given the apparent integrity of the Cu record in most peat profiles (Stewart and Fergusson 1994), suggesting that some site specific physiochemical process may have been operating.

CONCLUSIONS

The results presented here suggest that Pb levels during the Roman period recorded in sediments at the Neuburgsattel may be evidence of local, regional or global pollution caused by Roman Pb smelting. At the Neuburgsattel results show that increased deposition of anthropogenerated metals and human impact on woodland took place from the medieval period onwards. After mining and smelting on a local scale stopped, regional and ultimately national trends in industrialisation can be seen in metal profiles at the sites. It does seem therefore that past metallurgical activities could cause recognisable increases in heavy metal deposition. The amount of woodland clearance was small in comparison to estimates made of the amount of wood needed by the local mining and smelting activities (Gröbl 1986; Marshall 1994). The pollen diagram, however, does show there is a large reduction in *Fagus*, which was the preferred charcoal for iron and copper smelting and even after the end of mining and smelting on a local scale *Fagus* levels fail to recover.

It is clear from the results of this study and other interdisciplinary investigations of past human interactions with their environment that the notion of a pristine environment existing until the Industrial Revolution is flawed (e.g. O'Hara *et al.* 1993; 1994). In the context of prehistoric mining the possibility exists that some of the first metal producing societies may have altered the environment not only on a local scale but regionally as well.

Acknowledgements
The work was undertaken during the tenure of a Hossien Farmy Scholarship at the Archaeology and Prehistory and Geography Departments Sheffield University, 1991–1994 under the supervision of Dr Sarah O'Hara and Dr Barbara

Ottaway. I would like to express my gratitude to Frau Dr. Susanne Klemm (Universität Wien), Dipl.-Ing. Horst Weinek (VOEST-ALPINE Erzberg), Prof. Clements Eibner (Universität Heidelberg) and Dr. Gehard Sperl (Montan Universität Leoben) for making work in Austria possible. To Berghofer- Wolf (Gasthof Kölbwirt, Johnsbach) for providing access to the site and Roger Doonan for assistance with fieldwork. Laboratory work was made less arduous by Bill Crowe (Department of Geography), Rob Cragie and Chris Grimley (Department of Archaeology). Finally I would like to thank Helen Smith for helpful comments on an earlier draft.

References

Andrews, C.J. 1994. Asynchronous regional development. *Chemosphere* **29**, 1079–86.

Bengtsson, L. and Enell, M. 1986. Chemical analysis, pp. 423–51 in Berglund, B.E. (ed.), *Handbook of Holocene Palaeoecology and Palaeohydrology*. Chichester: John Wiley and Sons.

Bennett, K.D. 1994. *Annotated catalogue of pollen and pteridophyte spores of the British Isles*. Cambridge: Dept. of Plant Sciences.

Bennett, K.D., Fossett, J.A., Sharp, M.J. and Switsur, V.R. 1990. Holocene vegetational and environmental history at Loch Lang, South Uist, Western Isles, Scotland. *New Phytologist* **114**, 281–98.

Birks, H.J.B. 1986. Numerical zonation, comparison and correlation of Quaternary pollen stratigraphical data, pp. 743–74 in Berglund, B.E. (ed.) *Handbook of Holocene Palaeoecology and Palaeohydrology*. Chichester: John Wiley and Sons.

Birks, H.J.B. and Gordon, A.D. 1985. *Numerical Methods in Quaternary Pollen Analysis*. London: Academic Press.

Bonny, A.P. 1972. A method for determining absolute pollen frequencies in lake sediments. *New Phytologist* **71**, 391–403.

Bronk Ramsey, C. 1995. Radiocarbon calibration and analysis of stratigraphy: The OxCal program. *Radiocarbon* **37**, 425–30.

Cierny, J., Hauptman, A., Hohlmann, B. and Weisgerber, G. 1995. Endbronzezeitliche Kupferproduction im Triento. *Der Anschnitt* **47**, 82–91.

Davies, B.E. 1974. Loss-on-ignition as an estimate of soil organic matter. *Soil Science Society of America-Proceedings* **38**, 150–1.

Dove, M.R. 1994. North-South differences, global warming, and the global system. *Chemosphere* **29**, 1063–77.

Dutton, A. and Fasham, P.J. 1994. Prehistoric copper mining on the Great Orme, Llandudno, Gwynedd, *Proceedings Prehistoric Society* **60**, 245–86.

Ellenberg, H. 1988. *Vegetation Ecology of Central Europe*. 4th Edition. Cambridge: Cambridge University Press.

Ernst, W., Mthys, W., Salaske, J. and Janiesch, P., 1974. Aspekte von Schwermatallbelastungen in Westfalen. *Abhandlungen aus Dem Landesmuseum Für Naturkunde zu Münster in Westfalen* **36**, 1–33.

Faegri K. and Iversen J. 1989. *Textbook of Pollen Analysis*, 4th edition by Faegri, K., Kaland, P.E. and Krzywinski., K. Chichester: John Wiley and Sons.

Gale, S.J. and Hoare, P.G. 1991. *Quaternary Sediments*. London: Belhaven.

Galop, D. and Jalut, G. 1994. Differential human impact and vegetation history in two adjacent Pyrenean valleys in the Ariège basin, southern France, from 3000 B.P. to the present. *Vegetation History and Archaeobotany* **3**, 225–44.

Grimm, E.C. 1987. CONISS: A fortran 77 program for stratigraphically constrained cluster analysis by the method of incremental sum of squares. *Computers and Geosciences* **13**, 13–35.

Grimm, E.C. 1991. *TILIA and TILIA.GRAPH*. Illinois State Museum. Illinois.

Gröbl, S. 1986. *Der Kupferbergbau in Der Radmer: von den Anfängen bis 1650*. Dissertationen der Karl-Franzens-Universität Graz, No. 69.

Hong, S., Candelone, J.P., Clair, C.C. and Boutron, C.F. 1994. Greenland ice evidence of hemispheric lead pollution two millennia ago by Greek and Roman civilizations. *Science* **265**, 1841–3.

Hong, S., Candelone, J.P., Patterson, C.C. and Boutron, C.F. 1996. History of ancient copper smelting pollution during Roman and Medieval times recorded in Greenland ice. *Science*, **272**, 246–9.

Hoover, H.C. and Hoover, L.H. 1950. *De re metallica*, translated from the Latin edition of 1556 G. Agricola. New York: Dover.

Huntley, B. and Birks, H.J.B. 1983. *An Atlas of Past and Present Pollen Maps from Europe: 0–13,000 years ago*. Cambridge: Cambridge University Press.

Intergovernmental Panel on Climate Change (IPCC) 1990. *Climate Change: The IPCC Scientific Assessment*. J.T. Houghton, G.K. Jenkins and J.J. Ephramus (eds). Cambridge: Cambridge University Press.

Jones, J.M. 1997. Pollution records in peat an appraisal, pp. 88–92 in Parkyn, L., Stoneman, R.E. and Ingram, H.A.P. (eds), *Conserving Peatlands*. Wallingford: CAB International.

Jowsey, P.C. 1966. An improved peat sampler. *New Phytologist* **65**, 245–8.

Köstler, H.J. 1993. Neuzeitliches Montanwesen im Bezirk Liezen, pp. 45–92 in Preßlinger, H. and Köstler, H.J. (eds), *Bergbau und Hüttenwesen im Bezirk Liezen, Steiermark*. Liezen: Verein Schloß Trautenfels.

Lageard, J.G.A., Chambers, F.M. and Thomas, P.A. 1999. Climatic significance of the marginalisation of Scots pine (*Pinus sylvestris* L.) c 2500 BC at White Moss, south Cheshire, UK. *The Holocene* **9**, 321–32

Lagerås, P. and Sandgren, P. 1994. The use of mineral magnetic analyses in identifying middle and late Holocene agriculture-a study of peat profiles in Småland, Southern Sweden. *Journal of Archaeological Science* **21**, 687–97.

Lee, J.A. and Tallis, J.H. 1973. Regional and historical aspects of lead pollution in Britain. *Nature* **245**, 91–7.

Livett, E.A. 1982. *The Interaction of Heavy Metals With the Peat and Vegetation of Blanket Bogs in Britain*. Unpublished Ph.D. thesis, University of Manchester.

Livett, E.A. 1988. Geochemical monitoring of atmospheric heavy metal pollution: theory and application, pp. 65–177 in Began, M., Fitter, A.H., Ford, D. and Macpadven, A. (eds), *Advances in Ecological Research Vol. 18*. London: Academic Press.

Livett, E.A., Lee, J.A. and Tallis, J.H. 1979. Lead, zinc and copper analysis of British blanket peats. *Journal of Ecology* **67**, 865–91.

MARC 1985. *Historical Monitoring*. London: Monitoring and Assessment Research Centre.

Markgraf, V. 1980. Pollen dispersal in a mountain area. *Grana* **19**, 127–46

Marshall, P.D. 1994. *The Environmental Impact of Mining and Metalworking Activities in Steiermark, Austria*. Unpublished Ph.D.thesis, University of Sheffield.

Martin, M.H., Coughtrey, P.J. and Ward, P. 1979. Historical aspects of heavy metal pollution in the Gordano Valley. *1977 Proceedings Bristol Naturalist Society* **37**, 91–7.

Mighall, T.M. 1992. *Palaeoecological aspects of early mining and metalworking in upland Wales*. Unpublished Ph.D. thesis, University of Keele.

Mighall, T.M. and Chambers, F.M. 1993. Early mining and metal-working: its impact on the environment. *Historical Metallurgy* **27**, 71–83.

Mighall, T.M. and Chambers, F.M. 1997. Early Ironworking and its Impact on the Environment: Palaeoecological Evidence from Bryn y Castell Hillfort, Snowdonia, North Wales *Proceeding Prehistoric Society* **67**, 199–220.

Mook, W.G. 1986. Business meeting: Recommendations/Resolutions adopted by the Twelfth International Radiocarbon Conference. *Radiocarbon*, **28**, 799.

Moore, P.D., Webb, J.A. and Collinson, M.E. 1991. *Pollen Analysis*. Second edition. Oxford: Blackwell Scientific Publications.

Nriagu, J.O. 1996. A history of global metal pollution, *Science* 272, 223–4.

O'Brien, W.F. 1994. *Mount Gabriel: Bronze Age Mining in Ireland*. Galway: Galway University Press.

O'Hara, S.L., Street-Perrott, F.A and Burt, T.P. 1993. Accelerated soil erosion around a Mexican highland lake caused by prehispanic agriculture. *Nature* 362, 48–51.

O'Hara, S.L., Metcalfe, S.E. and Street-Perrott, F.A. 1994. On the arid margin: The relationship between climate, humans and the environment. A review of evidence from the highlands of central Mexico. *Chemosphere* 29, 965–81

Ottaway, B.S. 1994. *Prähistorische Archäometallurgie*. Leidorf: Internationale Archäologie.

Preßlinger, H. and Eibner, C. 1989. Bronzezeitliche Kupfer-verhüttung in Paltental, Montanarchäologische und archäeo-metallurgische Untersuchungen in Ostalpenraum, pp. 235–40 in Hauptman, A., Pernicka, E. and Wagner, G.A. (eds), *Old World Archaeology*. Bochum: Svelbstverlag des Deutschen Bergbau-Museums.

Preßlinger, H. and Köstler, H.J. 1993. *Bergbau und Hüttenwesen im Bezirk Liezen (Steiermark)*. Liezen: Verein Schloß Trautenfels.

Preßlinger, H., Walach, G., Eibner, C. and Prochaska, H. 1992. Montanarchäologische Untersuchungsergebnisse eines urnen-felderzeitlichen Kupferez-Verhüttungsplatzes bei Mautern/ Steiermark. *Berg-und Hüttenmännisches Monatshef* **137**, 31–7.

Pribram, A.F. 1938. *Materialien zur Geschichte der Preise und Löhne in Österreich*. Wien.

Rambo, A.T. 1985. *Primitive Polluters: Semang Impact on the Malaysian Tropical Rainforest Ecosystem*. Anthropology Papers No. 76. University of Michigan Museum of Anthropology: Ann Arbor.

Redlich, K.A. 1903. Das Johnsbachtal, pp. 137–44 in Redlich, K.A. (ed.), *Bergbaue Steiermarks*. Separatadbruck aus dem Berg-und Hüttenmännischen Jahrbuch, Leoben.

Renberg, I., Persson, M.W. and Emteryd, O. 1994. Pre-industrial atmospheric lead contamination detected in Swedish lake sediments. *Nature* 368, 323–6.

Rosen, D. and Dumayne-Peaty, L. 2001. Human impact on the vegetation of South Wales during late historical times: palynological and palaeoenvironmental results from Crymlyn Bog NNR, West Glamorgan, Wales, UK. *The Holocene* 11, 11–23.

Shirahata, H., Elias, R.W., Patterson, C.C. and Koide, M. 1980. Chronological variations in concentrations and isotopic compositions of anthropogenic atmospheric lead in sediments of a remote subalpine pond. *Geochemica et Cosmochemica Acta* 44, 149–62.

Shotyk, W. 1996. Peat bog archives of atmospheric metal deposition: geochemical evaluation of peat profiles, natural variation in metal concentrations and metal enrichment factors. *Environmental Reviews* **41**, 149–83

Shotyk, W., Nesbitt, H.W. and Fyfe, W.S. 1990. The behaviour of major and trace elements in complete vertical peat profiles from three *Sphagnum* bogs. *International Journal of Coal Geology* **15**, 163–90.

Sercelj, A. 1988. Palynological evidence of human impact on the forests in Slovenia, pp. 47–57 in Salbitano, F. (ed.), *Human Influence on Forest Ecosystems Development in Europe*. ESF FERN-CNR. Bologna: Pitagora Editrice.

Siegenthaler, U. and Sarmiento, J.L. 1993. Atmospheric carbon dioxide and the ocean. *Nature*, **365**, 119–25.

Sperl, G. 1984. *Steierische Eisenstraße*. Leoben: Montanhistorische vereines für Österreich.

Stewart, C. and Fergusson, J.E. 1994. The use of peat in historical monitoring of trace metals in the atmosphere. *Environmental Pollution* **86**, 243–49.

Stuiver, M. and Kra, R.S. 1986. Editorial comment. *Radiocarbon* **28(2B)**, ii.

Stuiver, M. and Polach, H.A. 1977. Reporting of ^{14}C data. *Radiocarbon* **19**, 355–63.

Stuiver, M. and Reimer, P.J. 1986. A computer program for radiocarbon age calculation. *Radiocarbon*, **28**, 1022–30.

Stuiver, M., Reimer, P.J., Bard, E., Beck, J.W., Burr, G.S., Hughen K.A., Kromer, B., McCormac, G., van der Plicht, J. and Spurk, M. 1998. INTCAL98 Radiocarbon age calibration, 24,000–0 cal BP. *Radiocarbon* **40**, 1041–83.

Thompson, R. and Oldfield, F. 1986. *Environmental Magnetism*. London: Allen and Unwin.

Tipping, R., Edmonds, M. and Sheridan, A. 1993. Palaeoenvironmental investigations directly associated with a Neolithic axe "quarry" on Beinn Lawers, near Killin, Perthshire, Scotland. *New Phytologist* **123**, 585–97.

van Geel, B., Bregman, R., van der Molen, P.C., Dupont, L.M. and van Driel-Murray, C. 1989. Holocene raised bog deposits in the Netherlands as geochemical archives of prehistoric aerosols. *Acta Botanica Neerlandica* **38**, 467–76.

Voss O. 1988. The iron production in Populonia, pp. 91–100 in Sperl, G. (ed.), *The First Iron in the Meditteranean*. PACT 21. Strasbourg : Council of Europe.

Wahlmüller, N. 1992. Beitrag der Pollenanalyse zur Besiedlungs-geschichte des Haidberges bei Bischofshofen/ Salzburg, pp. 129–42 in Lippert A. (ed) *Der Götschenberg bei Bischofshofen*. Wien: Verlag der Österreichischen Ackademie der Wissenschaften.

Williams, T.M. 1991. A sedimentary record of the deposition of heavy metals and magnetic oxides in the Loch Dee basin, Galloway, Scotland, since c. AD 1500. *The Holocene* 1, 142–50.

Willutzki, H. 1962. *Zur Waldgeschichte und Vermoorung sowie über Rekurrenzflächen im Oberharz*. Nova Acta Leopold. NF 25. No. 160.

4. An environmental approach to the archaeology of tin mining on Dartmoor

V. Thorndycraft, D. Pirrie and A. G. Brown

This paper presents a summary of a recent study of the geochemistry of the Erme, Avon and Teign floodplains where elevated Sn levels and aggradation resulted from the input of tin mining waste into the headwater streams. This proxy record of mining is in general agreement with the historical record of mining and tin production, indicating that streaming increased in the 12th–14th centuries AD with a second peak in the 15th–16th centuries. However an earlier enhancement of the Erme valley may represent late Roman or early Medieval tin mining. These results are compared with the record derived from mires of both atmospheric deposition and vegetation change from pollen analysis. The ambiguity of the pollen record is discussed and it is suggested that a combination of approaches is needed to differentiate between local and regional pollen signals and in order to relate environmental change to mining activity. The historical record also illustrates that mining activity cannot be divorced from other land use changes and so the environmental record is inevitably a composite signal.

Keywords: Tin mining, Dartmoor, alluvial geochemistry, environmental change.

INTRODUCTION

The origins of tin mining on Dartmoor have long been a matter of dispute (Pearce 1979; Craddock and Craddock 1996). The principal source of archaeological information is the physical remains of both mining (the recovery of cassiterite from the parent ore-body), alluvial streaming (hydraulic mining) and tin processing (smelting etc.). The problem is that continued mining and streaming tends to destroy the record of earlier working. This paper presents a summary of the results of an investigation of the geochemistry of four Dartmoor rivers, with the aim of establishing the timing and extent of Holocene tin contamination; detailed results are published elsewhere (Thorndycraft *et al.* forthcoming). Particular attention is paid in this paper to the relationship between the fluvial record of tin mining and other proxy environmental data.

Tin mining involves the quarrying the ore-body using lode-back pits, openworks or shafts, then crushing the ore by dry or wet stamping and separation of the cassiterite by buddling. Buddles were large rectangular or triangular water-filled boxes in which the lighter sand, silts and clays were kept in suspension (and discharged to the river) whilst the cassiterite was retained (Gerrard 1997). Tin streaming of naturally reworked cassiterite involves digging a leat parallel with the river, then working a face of the floodplain floor (tin ground) between the leat and the river. Waste sand and gravel accumulates as parallel ridges and fine waste discharged directly into the river (Gerrard 1996). Streaming including the small-scale process of vanning (panning) was probably more efficient at retaining fine-grained cassiterite than the wet-stamping and buddling. The full extent of mining and streaming on Dartmoor is seldom appreciated, yet almost every alluvial basin on the granite has been worked (Gerrard pers. com.). Indeed, the only site yet discovered where streaming seems to have worked the tin ground incompletely is Taw Marsh, which is one of the largest alluvial basins on Dartmoor. A small terrace remnant at Taw Marsh provides a rare exposure of the Pleistocene alluvial fill worked by the tinners. Analysis of these deposits has allowed the measurement of natural tin levels and the grain size-distribution of tin which determines the sediment grain-size dependency of analytical results (Thorndycraft 1999). The floodplain sediments of Dartmoor rivers have rarely been investigated, the two exceptions being a natural, probably Lateglacial, tin rich gravel from the floodplain of the river Dart at Buckfastleigh (Scrivener and Walboeff-Wilson 1975) and a peat buried by clastic flood deposits in the Meavy catchment which was undated (Gomez and Sims 1981). The work described here has attempted to use the downstream deposition of tin enhanced sediment as a proxy record of tin mining in mineralised catchments (Figure 3). There is a large body of geomorphological research relating floodplain geochemistry to mining activity (see Macklin *et al.* 1994 and Pirrie *et al.* 1997 for review). Work in upland Britain has shown that mining is a major cause of channel and floodplain aggradation through increased sediment supply (Macklin 1996) although the actual timing and frequency of alluviation may be climatically controlled (Macklin and Dowsett 1989). The nearest work to Dartmoor in the South West was an early study of the alluvial record of Pb mining on the Mendips (Macklin 1985). Some preliminary results of the present study and some methodological considerations were given in Thorndycraft *et al.* (1999). In this paper the sediment derived results are compared to the palaeoecologically-based studies by Gearey *et al.* (1997) and West *et al.* (1996;1997).

METHODS

The sampling strategy concentrated as much as possible on alluvial sequences which could be independently dated. In the Erme and the Avon, palaeochannels were used and in the Taw and Teign, terrace exposures. Monolith tins were used to sample the exposures and gouge and Russian corers were used for the palaeochannel sediments. The sediment geochemistry was determined by X-Ray Fluorescence (XRF), using a Phillips PW 1400 XRF analyser. The sample was dried overnight at 40°C. The dried sample was then riffled to obtain 20g of sediment. This was then ground in a chrome steel tema mill for 90 seconds. Pressed disks of the ground sample were prepared using a boric acid jacket and a binding agent of 4% elvacite in acetone solution. Each sample was then analysed for Sn, As, Pb, Zn and W using internationally calibrated standards. The data are reported as mg/kg (equivalent to ppm). The error limit for the metal concentrations determined was ± 10 mg/kg. Particle size distribution analysis was carried out using the procedures outlined by the British Standards Institution (1975, 36). Concentrated (30–40%) hydrogen peroxide (H_2O_2) was added to air-dried samples to remove organic matter. The samples were left for several days and were occasionally warmed gently to speed up the

oxidation reaction. The remaining sample was then sieved at 2 mm and 600 μm then dried and weighed. The <600 μm fraction was centrifuged for 30 minutes, washed with methylated spirit, re-centrifuged and dried overnight at 40°C. The dried sample was weighed before addition of 0.4% sodium hexametaphosphate (mainly $(NaPO_3)_6$) and sodium carbonate (Na_2CO_3) dispersant solution. The samples were then stirred in an ultrasonic bath and analysed using a Malvern Mastersizer MS20 laser particle sizer. The Mastersizer has a measuring range of 1.2–600 μm. Selected samples were prepared for geochemical analysis of the separate particle size fractions in order to show which sediment fractions were metal-dominated. The grain size fractions examined were: <63 μm, 63–125 μm, 125–180 μm, 180–250 μm, 250–500 μm, 500–2000 μm, 2–4 mm. In order to obtain 20g of each size fraction, as required for XRF analysis, a bulk sample of 0.5–1 kg of sediment was usually required. Initial screening was carried out by dry sieving the sample on a shaker for 20–30 minutes, followed by wet sieving. Comparative studies of the particle size dependency of the natural placer deposit and the sediments downstream of streaming sites shows both a reduction in Sn concentration and a shift in peak Sn concentration from the 125–180 μm and 180–250 μm fractions to the <63 μm fraction which was unrecoverable in historical times due to the inefficiency of the mining (buddling) process (Thorndycraft 1999). This inefficiency probably reflects the speed and economics of this relatively capital intensive form of exploitation. All radiocarbon dates quoted here are given as calibrated (using the Calib 3 program, based on Stuiver and Reimer 1993) at the 1s level. More details of the grain size selectivity and mineralogy of the samples can be found in Thorndycraft (1999) and Thorndycraft *et al.* (1999).

Although Pb, Zn, Cd and Cu have all been shown to decrease downstream of a point source due to chemical weathering/speciation as well as by dispersion processes (Hudson-Edwards *et al.* 1996) tin in the form of cassiterite (SnO_2) is less susceptible to weathering reaction paragenesis especially in neutral to slightly acidic conditions. It is therefore assumed that the trends in fine sediment Sn values do represent variations in past depositional concentrations and there is little or no post-depositional movement of metal in the sediment column.

THE SEDIMENTARY AND HISTORICAL RECORD

The Erme flows north-south from Blackland Mire to Bigbury Bay. The Erme estuary is no longer navigable although, prior to AD 1000, a harbour at Oldaport could be reached (Todd 1987) suggesting that net deposition has occurred within the estuary since that date. The Sexton reach was chosen because it contained a number of river bank sections of two terraces exposed at meander bends, a buried wall suggesting significant floodplain aggradation,

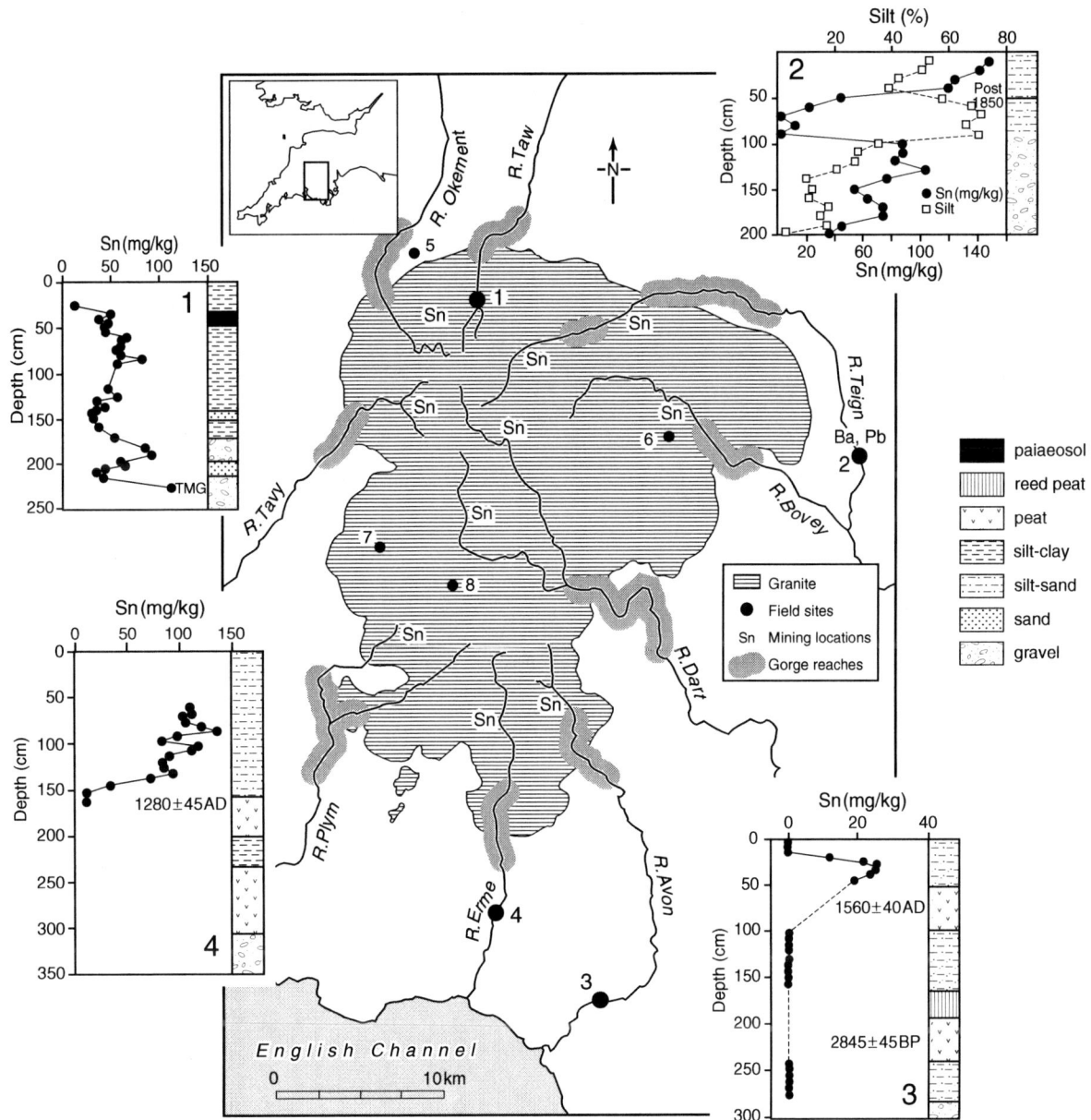

Figure 3. Map, study reaches and main Sn profiles from on and around Dartmoor. 1. Taw Marsh (R. Taw), 2. Chudleigh (R. Teign), 3. Aveton Gifford (R. Avon), 4. Ermington/Sexton (R. Erme).

and a large palaeochannel which was found to contain peat and wood *in situ* suitable for radiocarbon dating. The reach lies above the normal tidal limit. The palaeochannel of the Erme (Sexton Palaeochannel) exhibits an anomalous peak in Sn concentration just above a peat/silt contact (Fig. 4). The Sn peak is disproportionate in relation to other trace metals, especially the other elements that characterise the Dartmoor granite heavy mineral assemblage, such as Zr, Ce and Y (Thorndycraft *et al.* forthcoming). An AMS date of 245–386 cal. AD (AA-29916; 1,740±45 uncal. yr. BP) from just below the contact suggests that this peak maybe late Roman or early post-Roman in age and it certainly pre-dates 1300 cal AD and

the other floodplain records. A second rise in Sn occurs during the 12th–13th century. This increase is less disproportionate to the other metals as there is a slower increase in Cu and Pb and a later rise in As (Fig. 4). The exposures at Sexton Bridge and Ermington which post-date the Sexton palaeochannel also show elevated values of Sn, Pb and Zn, probably a response to late Medieval tin streaming and mining. It is noticeable that the sedimentary response to the earliest phase is deposition of a 0.6m fine sand bed, whilst post 1300 AD streaming is associated with 1.5m of floodplain aggradation, suggesting that streaming in the latter period was both on a larger scale and more prolonged and/or there was a change in fluvial

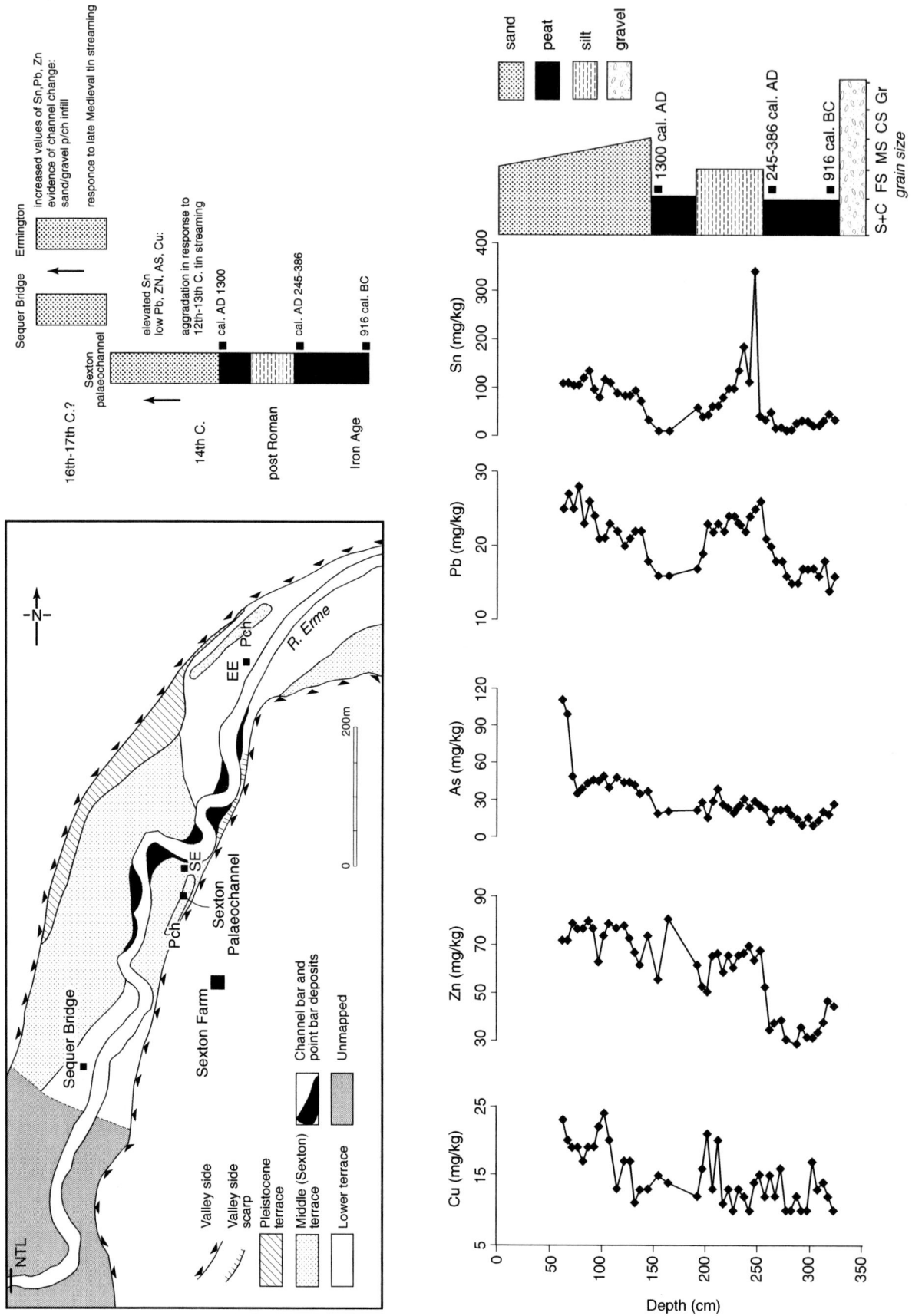

Figure 4. The Erme geochemical profile from the Sexton palaeochannel, site location map and summary diagram of the Sn sedimentology of the Erme and Ermington.

regime (see discussion). The Erme is shorter than the other rivers used in the study, with a linear basin and no significant tributaries, and so might be expected to be particularly sensitive to changes of sediment supply above the Ivybridge Gorge. A palynological study of a small flush bog adjacent to the Erme and close to the study site was undertaken by Roberts and Gilbertson (1994) in order to establish the antiquity of Piles Copse. This suggested that the low-diversity *Quercus robur* dominated wood was no older than 1700 AD. Roberts and Gilbertson (1994) suggest that this wood and a previous wood evident from the pollen record were deliberately planted, possibly to provide charcoal for smelting although there is no on-site archaeological evidence of this.

The source of the Avon is blanket bog (Avon Head) on South Dartmoor only 2km to the east of Erme Head. Like the Erme, the Avon flows through the South Hams to the South Coast with no major tributaries. The study reach was located immediately upstream of the tidal limit near Aveton Gifford. The reach was chosen because of a large palaeochannel which revealed a superficial silty sand overlying a sharp contact with peat. The palaeochannel also contained a middle and lower silt, allowing the geochemical characterisation of earlier sediments. The reach also included riverbank exposures of the superficial silty sands. The analyses show negligible Sn pre 1035–921 cal. BC (SRR-6225; 2,845±45 uncal. yr. BP) and 1035–921 cal. BC to 1448–1621 cal. AD (SRR-6224; 390±40 uncal. yr. BP). The post 1500 AD sediments show a pronounced peak in Sn which then falls to negligible levels near the top of the sequence (Fig. 3). Increases in Pb and As and to a lesser extent Zn and Cu, which occur on the declining limb of the Sn peak, may reflect local exploitation of silver-lead lodes at Loddiswell mine during the mid 19th century. The Sn peak correlates well with the boom period of tin streaming in the moorland reaches of the Avon catchment (*c.* 1460–1550 AD).

The moorland reach of the river Teign is divided between two tributaries, the North Teign and South Teign both draining Northern Dartmoor (Fig. 3). The river flows off the granite upland through Dunsford gorge. A terrace sequence (Fig. 5), located at the southern extremity of the mineralised zone of the Middle Teign valley, allowed the sampling of sediments of both pre and post-mining age. The upper terrace sequence, exposed in a 3.3m deep section, comprised boulder cobble and gravel deposits grading onto finer channel gravels, in turn overlain by 1.2m of fine grained overbank sediments (Fig. 5). The middle terrace consisted of 2m of loose, weakly bedded, coarse to medium sands and silty sands and the lower terrace consisted of 1.2m of fine silty sand. In addition to Sn mining in its headwaters the Middle Teign drains the Middle Teign Valley orefield which saw base metal (predominantly Pb and Zn) and barytes ($BaSO_4$) mining in the 19th century (Beer *et al.* 1992). This is important as a chronological marker because the sedimentary sequence produced no material suitable for radiocarbon dating. Each

of the three terrace levels has a characteristic geochemical signature based on the concentrations of Pb, Zn and Sn. The upper terrace records relatively high concentrations of Pb and especially Zn, reflecting local sulphide mineralisation within the Middle Teign Valley orefield (Thorndycraft 1999). The middle terrace is characterised by the clean waste of tin streaming, comprising granitic gangue material diluting the Pb and Zn signature. The lower terrace post-dates the onset of mining within the orefield and so the sediments are dominated by the Pb and Zn signature with a continued input of cassiterite.

The beginning of the tin industry on Dartmoor as evidenced by historical records occurred in the latter half of the 12th century (Penhallurick 1986; Greeves 1981). The coinage data from the stannery towns shows that in the latter half of the 12th century annual production increased steadily (Hatcher 1973). Up until 1243 AD the coinage includes Cornish tin but the majority of tin during this period came from Dartmoor (Hatcher 1973) This early boom was followed by a fall towards the end of the 13th century. The 15th century was characterised by a steady rise in production, with peak production occurring in 1521 AD. After this there was a steady decline to very low values in the 1600s. In the latter half of the 17th century and during the 18th century, production began to increase again reaching a peak in 1706 AD before falling again until the end of the 18th century. There was then renewed interest in Dartmoor's tin deposits with an increase in shaft and adit mining until complete closure early in the 20th century. Tin mining and ore-crushing commenced in the later Medieval period (13th century onwards) as opposed to tin streaming which declined from the late Medieval period onwards (Gerrard 2000).

PALAEOECOLOGICAL INFERENCE AND PEAT RECORDS OF ATMOSPHERIC DEPOSITION

Despite the density of pollen diagrams from Dartmoor the Medieval period is poorly represented (Caseldine and Hatton 1994; Caseldine 1999). This is due to a combination of generally low-resolution sites (i.e. shallow sites), peat cutting and a lack of radiocarbon dates, particularly towards the top of diagrams. Two radiocarbon dated Medieval diagrams from Dartmoor, Okehampton Park (Austin *et al* 1980) and Houndtor (Austin and Walker 1985) both show a fall in tree pollen, predominantly alder, in the mid 13th century AD accompanied by a rise in cereal type pollen. This supports the contention that the Medieval field systems were laid out at this time and represented an agricultural expansion and intensification with some cereal cultivation to at least 350m OD. Two new radiocarbon dated sites have added further detail for the Post-Roman period (Gearey *et al.* 1997). At Merrivale, in the Walkham Valley, there is, in the early Medieval (820–1030 cal. AD) a sudden reduction in *Alnus* which is sustained and associated with an increase in microscopic

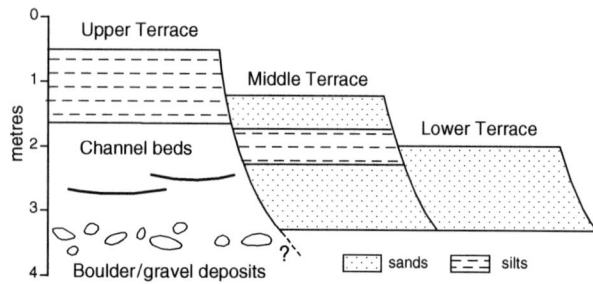

Figure 5. The low terrace sequence of the Middle Teign valley.

charcoal (Gearey *et al.* 1997). It may be pertinent that the upper Walkham Valley is one of the areas of earliest known tin processing, possibly as early as the mid-12th century (Gearey *et al.* 1997). The site recently discovered at Tor Royal by West *et al.* (1996) has offered the potential to look at this period in more detail. In the penultimate pollen zone, dated to the Medieval period (*c.* 900–1400 AD), there is a strong decline in *Corylus* and *Alnus* with a decline in micro-charcoal. This suggests woodland clearance by felling rather than by fire. Overall the record from Dartmoor (and Bodmin) are taken by Gearey *et al.* (1997) to support broadly the model of seasonal use of the uplands for grazing from the late prehistoric period until the development of settlements in the 12th to 14th centuries (Quinell 1996). However, there are significant pollen events including some early Medieval woodland removal and occasional cereal-type pollen grains. The peat core from Tor Royal has been analysed by West *et al* (1996) using EDMA (Energy Dispersive X-ray Micro Analysis on SEM samples) which gives a semi-quantitative estimate of selected elements in the peat, which can be related to atmospheric inputs to ombrotrophic sites (Livett *et al* 1979; Stewart and Fergusson 1994). At the same depth as the fall in *Corylus* and *Alnus* (*c.* 65 cm and above) Sn, As, Mn and Pb all increase above background levels. Radiocarbon dating of the peat column indicates that this occurred after AD 1100 and considering the linearity of the accumulation rate should be *c.* 1200 AD (West *et al.* 1996). In a second study West *et al.* (1997) have performed quantitative analyses of trace elements using XRF (EMMA X-ray fluorescence analysis), and although the elements analysed did not include Sn, the Pb, Zn and As profiles all show a first peak at around 2 m dated to *c.* 100 AD and a second more pronounced rise above 1 m depth dated to AD 1050–1280. West *et al.* (1997) suggest that the first peak is probably due to Roman smelting activity to the East. The later Medieval peak is also a regional phenomena. However, a component of the airborne metal deposition may have come from tin smelting on Dartmoor itself during both periods. As Gearey *et al.* (1997) point out, the interpretation of land use and its intensity from the available pollen diagrams is not straightforward, however, the clear-

ance of what are likely to have been small stream-side areas of alder and hazel from the 9th century onwards could well have been associated with tin streaming and/or tin processing, as well as increased grazing intensity. The inference of causality is complicated by variations in grazing pressure, unrelated to mining activity, and the possible substitution of peat as a smelting fuel. Another scenario, for which there is abundant historical evidence, is woodland management in order to sustain charcoal supplies. The palynological signature would have depended upon the location, scale and rotation of coppicing. Access to wood for fuel was included in the early tin miners' charters and this also included peat for charcoal production (Woolner 1967: Claughton pers. com.). The decline of alder during and after the 13th century as seen in several diagrams may well be directly related to streaming as there is little doubt that the natural vegetation of the headwater floodplains would have been dominated by alder.

A proxy record of possible impact of tin processing may be seen at Taw Marsh. Simmons (1964) produced a pollen diagram from Taw Marsh. Confident zonation of the diagram was not possible and the whole 1.20m depth was assigned to Godwin Zone VII (5,700–3,000 BP) due to the presence of *Fraxinus* and *Tilia*. The total tree percentage changed from a *Quercus* and *Betula* domination to *Alnus* domination above 0.6m depth. The location was re-sampled in this study for radiocarbon dating. The base of the herbaceous peat, overlying the fluvial gravels was dated to 8037–7972 cal. BC (SRR-6230; 8,975±45 uncal. yr. BP) and the wood peat bed to 6383–6219 cal. BC (SRR-6229; 7,490±45 uncal. yr. BP) but a sample above the base of the upper herbaceous peat dated to 80–221 cal. AD (SRR-6228; 1,885±40 uncal. yr. BP). The depth of this abrupt change in the accumulation rate (from 26 yrs cm^{-1} to 449 yrs cm^{-1} and back to 27 yrs cm^{-1}), and the stratigraphic boundary coincides with the change in pollen spectrum recorded in the pollen diagram by Simmons (1964). This clearly represents a stratigraphic hiatus. Given the location of the core (on a terrace 200m from a tributary stream), the lack of any lateral stratigraphic disturbance, and any clastic sediments mean that a fluvial explanation for the hiatus is untenable. The most likely explanation is peat cutting. Given that this is the site of probably the largest alluvial tin deposit on Dartmoor it is suggested that this could reflect Roman or even earlier tin processing, but more work in the area is required to follow this up. Also investigated at Taw Marsh was the terrace sequence. Investigations of the small remnant of the Sn bearing alluvial terrace at the edge of the valley have produced ambiguous results as dating of a palaeosol has suggested incision post 722–879 cal. AD (SRR-6227; 1,235±40 uncal. yr. BP) which could be either the direct result of direct tin mining or a change in fluvial regime (Figure 6). The palaeosol and sediments immediately overlying it also have elevated As levels (254 mg/kg whereas the underlying levels are 57 mg/kg) but there is

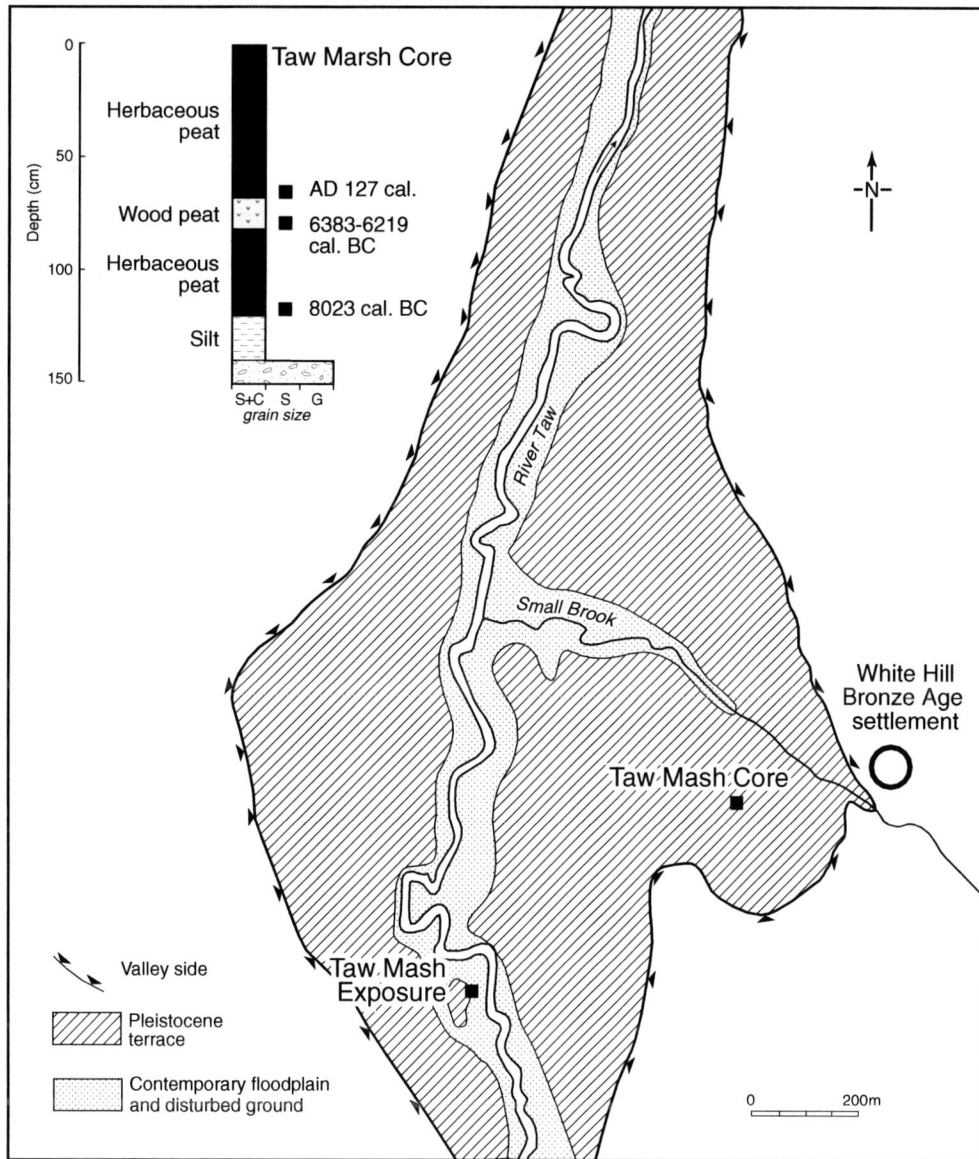

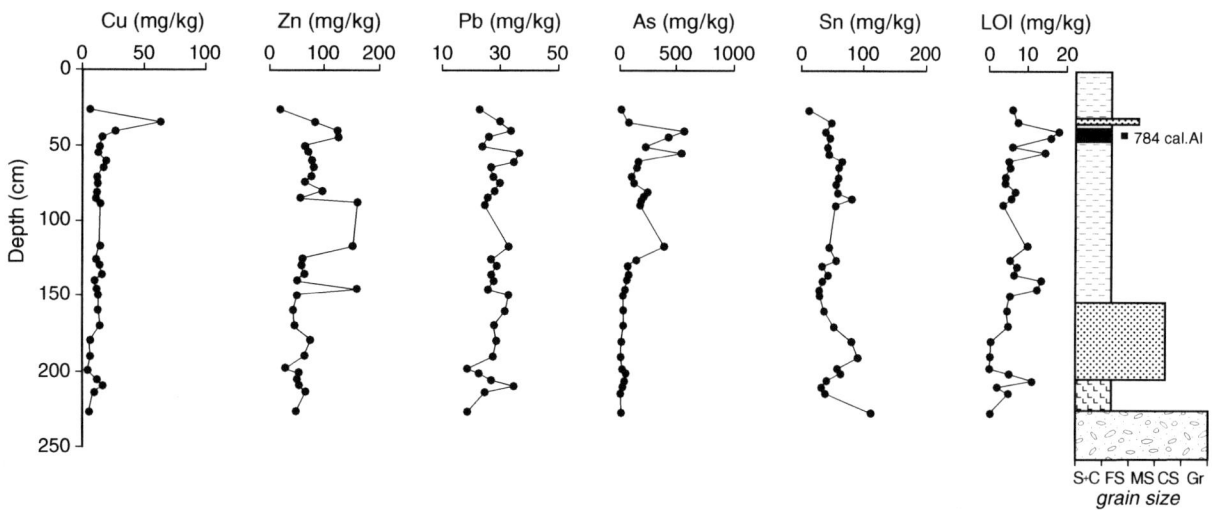

Figure 6. The terrace and peat sequence at Taw Marsh.

no enhancement of Sn. This could be the result of atmospheric input from smelting activities, but more work is required in the Taw Marsh area to evaluate this possibility. However, the area on the north face of the High Moor is particularly exposed to winds from a wide swathe of SW England including areas of early tin processing in Cornwall. It is suggested here that the two approaches, (fluvial and atmospheric), are complementary. The fluvial signal, which on chronological grounds would appear to be a record of mining (largely ore-crushing and buddling), has particular problems of a fragmentary record and difficulties in dating but does provide spatially defined data. The mire-based atmospheric record, which is a record of processing, has better chronological control but the problems of distinguishing between regional and local sources.

TIN MINING AND THE ARCHAEOLOGICAL RECORD

There is little hard archaeological evidence of prehistoric or Romano-British tin mining on Dartmoor. The current view is that in the Post-Roman period permanent settlement was rare until the 13th century AD (Allen 1994) with land use being part of a transhumance system. The evidence from account rolls indicates an expansion of settlement onto the moor between the 12th and 14th centuries with many sites continuing into the later 14th and 15th centuries, despite the Black Death (Fox 1994). Fox (1994) also mentions the possible role of tin mining in the economic prosperity and population growth of the area and gives examples of farmers who were probably also tin miners. In this light the land use activity inferred from pollen analysis can be interpreted in a less dichotomous manner. As Gearey et al. (1997) point out the pollen data do not preclude the establishment of sporadic settlements before widespread settlement. One of the most obvious causes of this would be early tin mining such as is suggested for the Erme valley. Further combined palaeoecological and geochemical studies of valley fills may be able to determine whether early tin mining was combined with grazing and perhaps small-scale cereal cultivation. The dating of the downstream alluvial tin enhancement is consistent with the view that the two periods when the technology of production (crushing and water-sorting) and socio-economic conditions favoured mining were the Roman and late Medieval periods.

DISCUSSION

The most significant finding of this research is that the major, and in most cases first, enhancement of Sn in down-valley floodplain sediment profiles broadly correlates with the documentary records of tin working in the 12th–14th and a second peak in the 14th–15th centuries AD. An exception is an earlier Sn peak in the Erme valley which may be the first evidence of Roman or early Medieval tin mining on Dartmoor. However, further chronological studies are required to validate this. In all cases the increase in Sn values is associated with aggradation of the floodplain, especially in the 15th–16th centuries. This could result directly from mining, streaming, land use change, climate change or a combination of all these factors. The pollen diagrams do show medieval intensification of land use, but this is earlier: in the 12th–13th centuries. The second possibility is that increased sediment supply was caused by the Little Ice Age which has certainly been shown to have had fluvial effects in more northern uplands (Rumsby and Macklin 1996; Brown 1996). Further dating may not resolve the problem: although it would appear that the accelerated alluviation (second Sn rise) in the Erme valley began before the generally accepted start of the Little Ice Age (1590–1850 AD) although at one s level the periods overlap (1448–1621 AD). The Little Ice Age is now regarded not as a single event but as a series of climatic anomalies with both warm and cold phases (Bradley and Jones 1995). There were particularly cold and wet phases at the end of the Little Climatic Optimum (Late Medieval Climatic Deterioration/Crusader Cold Period c. 1100–1400 AD) and the period 1750–1900 AD. These dates could be correlated with some sites (e.g. the Bovey valley, Erme second phase) but not others (Avon) but they are all correlated with the rise in Sn values. Given the land use of Dartmoor (predominantly heaths and grassland) the source for clastic sediment produced by more intense rainstorms would principally be derived from river bank erosion. There are several reasons why this seems not to be the case. Firstly the geochemistry indicates that the enhancement of Sn is greater than other gangue minerals derived from the granite. Secondly the grain-size distribution of the Sn enhanced fractions is both finer and curtailed as would be expected from the waste of wet-crushing or buddling rather than the erosion of either natural tin ground or in-situ streamed waste (which would produce sand with lower Sn values) (Thorndycraft 1999). Lastly, the plans of the streamworks suggest relatively little channel erosion during their use and subsequently. A stronger source of evidence is provided by analyses of the particle-size dependency of the Sn, which also shows a shift to finer fractions as would be expected from the pollution from tin streaming. Hybrid explanations remain possible, however. The location and pattern of streaming suggests that there is little opportunity for sediment storage and pollution would have been immediate irrespective of the fluvial regime. The reason for this is that considerable lengths of each river downstream of the mining areas are confined by bedrock (Fig. 3), often in gorges, with little or no floodplain. That tin streaming in the 14th–15th centuries caused significant pollution is illustrated by documentary evidence (Greeves 1981). The few adequately dated pollen diagrams covering the Post-Roman period do suggest woodland management and felling during the Medieval period, but higher resolution valley sites are required to investigate the effect of tin mining, streaming and processing on Dartmoor woodland. However, it is clear from the historical evidence that tin mining on Dartmoor should not be seen as a peripheral activity but one which was intimately connected with the economic prosperity of Dartmoor and its surrounds, land use and the formation of the landscape.

The data reported here broadly agree with the record of atmospheric pollution determined from an ombrogenous bog in the centre of Dartmoor (West *et al*. 1997). Although the Roman and Medieval palaeoecological records are surprisingly limited sites, such as Tor Royal, Houndtor and Okehampton Park do suggest clearance of *Corylus* and *Alnus* woodland from valleys which may have been associated with tin smelting. Along with agriculture, tin mining has been a major force for landscape change over at least the last 800 years and played the major role in creating the degraded industrial landscapes of Dartmoor's headwater valleys. The identification of mine waste signatures using an integrated geochemical, mineralogical and sedimentological framework provides great potential for tracing mining history from the Medieval period back into prehistory. In doing so it may expand our models of landscape change beyond the purely agricultural in so-called marginal areas.

SUMMARY CONCLUSIONS

In summary there are six conclusions from the studies outlined here:

1. There is significant enhancement of Sn in the alluvial floodplains downstream of mineralised and mined headwater catchments on Dartmoor.
2. In the majority of cases the dating of this enhancement can be correlated with the historical record of mining and tin production. This is an increase and peak in the 12th–13th century and again in the 14th–15th century.
3. In one basin, the Erme, there is evidence of late Roman or early post-Roman mining.
4. The fluvial record of alluviation follows the rise in tin enhancement and is diachronous suggesting that in the Late Holocene basin response to mining has predominated over climatic forcing.
5. Although there is some agreement between the alluvial results and results from the peat record of deposition and vegetation change there remain considerable problems in the identification of sources and interpretation.
6. The historical evidence of farmer-tinners suggests that palaeoecological evidence of changes in agriculture and evidence of mining may not be independent.

Acknowledgements
The research was supported by a NERC studentship (VRT) and NERC radiocarbon Scientific Services. Many archaeologists and other have assisted the authors including S. Gerrard, C Caseldine, T. Greeves, D. Griffiths and P. Claughton. The technical support of analytical laboratories of the School of Geography and Archaeology at Exeter and the Camborne School of Mines is gratefully acknowledged. The authors must thank an anonymous reviewer for improving this paper.

References

Allen, J. 1994. Medieval pottery and the dating of deserted settlements on Dartmoor. *Proceedings of the Devon Archaeological Society* 52, 141–148.

Austin, D, and Walker, M.J.C. 1985. A new landscape context for Houndtor, Devon. *Medieval Archaeology* 29, 147–151.

Austin, D., Daggett, R.H. and Walker, M.J.C. 1980. Farms and fields in Okehampton Park, Devon: the problems of studying medieval landscape. *Landscape History* 2, 39–58.

Beer, K.E., Ball, T.K., Cooper, D.C., Evans, A.D., Jones, R.C., Rollin, K.E. and Tombs, J.M.C. 1992. *Mineral Investigation of the Teign Valley, Devon. Part 2: Base Metals*. British Geological Survey Technical Report WF/92/6 70p.

Bradley, R.S. and Jones, P.D. (eds) 1995. *Climate Since AD 1500*. Routledge, London.

British Standards Institution 1975. *Methods of testing for soils for civil engineering purposes*. London, BSI, BS1377.

Brown, A.G. 1996. Human Dimensions of Palaeohydrological Change. In Branson, J. Brown, A. G. and Gregory, K.J. (eds) *Palaeohydrology and Global Changes: the Context of Palaeohydrology*, Geological Society Special Publication No. 115, Geological Society, London, 57–72.

CALIB3 *Radiocarbon calibration program Rev. 3.0*. Quaternary Isotopes Laboratory, University of Washington.

Caseldine, C.J. 1999. Archaeological and environmental change on Prehistoric Dartmoor – current understanding and future directions. *Quaternary Proceedings* 7, 575–583.

Caseldine, C.J. and Hatton, J. 1994. Into the mists? Thoughts on the prehistoric and historic environmental history of Dartmoor. *Proceedings of the Devon Archaeological Society* 52, 35–48.

Craddock, B. and Craddock, P. 1996. The beginnings of metallurgy in South-West Britain: hypotheses and evidence. In *The Archaeology of Mining and Metallurgy in South West-Britain*. P. Newman (ed.), Mining History: Bulletin Peak District Mines Historical Society and Historical Metallurgy Society Special Publication 13, 52–63.

Fox, H.S.A. 1994. Medieval Dartmoor as seen through the account rolls. *Proceedings of the Devon Archaeological Society* 52, 149–172.

Gearey, B.R., West, S. and Charman, D.J. 1997. The landscape context of Medieval settlement on the South-Western moors of England. Recent palaeoenvironmental evidence from Bodmin Moor and Dartmoor. *Medieval Archaeology* 41, 195–210.

Gerrard, S. 1996. The early South-West tin industry: an archaeological view. In *The Archaeology of Mining and Metallurgy in South West-Britain*. P. Newman (ed.), Mining History: Bulletin Peak District Mines Historical Society and Historical Metallurgy Society Special Publication 13, 67–83.

Gerrard, S. 1997. *Dartmoor*. Batsford/English Heritage, London.

Gerrard, S. 2000. The Early British Tin Industry. Tempus, Stroud.

Gomez, B. and Sims, P.C. 1981. Overbank deposits of the Narrator Brook, Dartmoor, England. *Geological Magazine* 118, 77–82.

Greeves, T.A.P. 1981. *The Devon tin industry 1450–1750: an archaeological and historical survey*. Unpub. PhD thesis, University of Exeter.

Hatcher, 1973. *English Tin Production and Trade Before 1550.* Clarendon Press, Oxford.

Hudson-Edwards, K.A., Macklin, M.G., Curtis, C.D. and Vaughan, D.J. 1996. Processes of formation and distribution of Pb-, Zn-Cd-, and Cu-bearing minerals in the Tyne basin, North-eastern England: Implications for metal-contaminated river systems. *Environmental Science and Technology* 30, 72–80.

Livett, E.A., Lee, J.A. and Tallis, J.H. 1979. Lead, zinc and copper analysis of British blanket peats. *Journal of Ecology* 67, 865–891.

Macklin, M.G. 1985. Floodplain sedimentation in the upper Axe valley, Mendip, England. *Transactions of the Institute of British Geographers* 10, 235–244.

Macklin, M.G. 1996. Fluxes and storage of sediment-associated heavy metals in floodplain systems: assessment and river basin management issues at a time of rapid environmental change. In M.G. Anderson, D.E. Walling and P.D. Bates (eds) *Floodplain Processes.* J. Wiley, Chichester, 441–460.

Macklin, M.G. and Dowsett, R.B. 1989. The chemical and physical speciation of trace metals in fine grained overbank sediments in the Tyne basin, north-eastern England. *Catena* 16, 135–151.

Macklin, M.G., Ridgeway, J., Passmore, D. and Rumsby, B.T. 1994. The use of overbank sediment for geochemical mapping and contaminant assessment: results from selected English and Welsh floodplains. *Applied Geochemistry* 9, 689–700.

Pearce, S, 1979. The distribution and production of Bronze Age metalwork. *Proceedings of the Devonshire Archaeological Society* 37, 136–145.

Penhallurick, R.D. 1986. *Tin in Antiquity.* Institute of Metals, London.

Pirrie, D., Camm, G.S., Sear, L.G. and Hughes, S.H. 1997. Mineralogical and geochemical signature of mine waste contamination, Tresillian river, Fal estuary Cornwall, UK. *Environmental Geology* 29, 58–65.

Quinell, H. 1996. Becoming marginal? Dartmoor in later prehistory. *Devon Archaeological Society Proceedings* 52, 78–55.

Roberts, C.A. and Gilbertson, D.D. 1994. The vegetational history of Pile Copse 'ancient' oak woodland, Dartmoor, and possible relationships between ancient woodland, clitter and mining. *Proceedings of the Ussher Society* 8, 298–301.

Rumsby, B.T. and Macklin, M.G. 1996. River response to the last neoglacial (the 'Little Ice Age') in northern, central and western Europe. In *Global Continental Changes: the Context of Palaeohydrology* J. Branson, A.G. Brown and K.J. Gregory (eds) Geological Society Special Publications No. 115, 217–233.

Scrivener, R.C. and Walbeoff-Wilson, J.H. 1975. Alluvial tin at Colston, Buckfastleigh. *Proceedings of the Ussher Society* 3, 237–242.

Simmons, I.G. 1964. Pollen diagrams from Dartmoor. *New Phytol.* 63, 165–80.

Stewart, C. and Ferguson, J.E. 1994. The use of peat in the monitoring of trace metals in the atmosphere. *Environmental Pollution* 86, 243–49.

Stuiver, M. and Reimer, P.J. 1993. *Radiocarbon* 35, 215–30.

Thorndycraft, V.R. 1999. *The Archaeology of Tin Mining on Dartmoor: A Sedimentary Approach.* PhD Thesis, University of Exeter.

Thorndycraft, V.R, Pirrie, D. and Brown, A.G. 1999. Tracing the record of early alluvial tin mining on Dartmoor, UK. In Pollard, A.M. (ed.). *Geoarchaeology: exploitation, environments, resources.* Geological Society, London, Special Publications, 165, 91–102.

Thorndycraft, V.R., Pirrie, D. and Brown. A.G. forthcoming. Geoarchaeology

Todd, M. 1987. *The South West to AD 1000.* Longman, London.

West, S., Charman, D. and Gratten, J. 1996. Palaeoenvironmental investigations at Tor Royal, central Dartmoor. In Charman, D., Newnham, R.M. and Croot, D.G. (eds) *Devon and East Cornwall Field Guide*, Quaternary Research Association, Cambridge, 62–0.

West, S., Charman, D.J, Grattan, J.P. and Cherbuken, A.K. 1997. Heavy metals in Holocene peats from south west England: detecting mining impacts and atmospheric pollution. *Water, Air and Soil Pollution* 100, 343–53.

Woolner, D. 1967. 'Peat charcoal' *Devon Notes and Queries* 30, 118–20.

Industrial fuels

5. Wood-based industrial fuels and their environmental impact in lowland Britain

Rowena Gale

Until the widespread use of coal in the 18th century, charcoal and wood provided the bulk of industrial fuel in lowland Britain. While archaeological finds of industrial artefacts (pot sherds, metal-working slag, kilns, briquetage etc) are usually well documented, relatively little is known of the character and source of industrial fuels. In recent years more attention has been paid to the potential of wood identification as a means of studying industrial fuels. With reference to these analyses, documentary data and knowledge of traditional techniques, this paper attempts to explore the type of fuel associated with specific industries from the Iron Age to the medieval period. Regional preferences, sources of fuel, the practicalities of fuel production and its transport to the work-place, statutes and restrictions attached to fuel production, and environmental implications are discussed.

Keywords: Wood-fuelled industries, industrial fuel, charcoal analyses, woodland management, environment.

INTRODUCTION

Until the widespread use of coal in the 18th century, most fuelled industries in lowland Britain were dependent on wood or charcoal. Current knowledge of the type and character of industrial fuels prior to the late medieval period is often sketchy or sometimes non-existent, even from the Late Saxon and earlier medieval periods, when contemporary charters, manorial accounts, legal documents and industrial licences detail industrial techniques, land use and woodland management. Consequently, for these earlier periods, data must be pieced together from archaeological evidence. Fuel residues containing well-preserved fragments of charcoal are potentially important in providing data pertaining to specific industrial processes and contemporary methods of woodmanship.

Apart from identifying the fuel woods, the anatomical examination of whole sections of roundwood (or complete radial fragments) may provide details of the season of felling, the age and approximate diameter of the round-wood when cropped and, sometimes, cropping regimes of neighbouring woodland species. The original diameter of the roundwood can never be more than an approximation since up to 40% of the wood volume is lost on charring (Gale and Cutler 2000). Regenerating stems on coppice stools characteristically produce wide annual rings during the initial years of growth, but these gradually decrease in width as the circumference of the stem enlarges and in response to increased competition from neighbouring vegetation (Huntley 1981; Morgan 1982). Coppiced stems are typically straighter and more rod-like than those of 'unmanaged' roundwood. The tendency of charred wood to fracture and fragment means that it is often difficult to ascertain the number of individual stems or rods repre-sented in a sample. When sufficient stems are available, the comparative examination of the diameter and age of coppice rods may indicate either that they were drawn (providing stems of similar diameter but different ages) or clear felled (providing a range of diameters and ages) from the stool, thereby implicating management polices (Crone 1987). In wide cordwood or trunkwood, regular bands of wide to narrowing growth rings may indicate an origin from trees grown as standards with coppice, with the rotational cycles of adjacent coppice recorded in the growth ring distribution of the standards.

Evironmental evidence from the analyses of pollen and other plant remains provide background data which can be juxtaposed with those of fuel residues to indicate preferential selection or the exploitation of certain tree species for industrial fuel. Pollen diagrams for industrial sites may also demonstrate the 'before and after' effects on the landscape of large-scale fuel procurement. In the absence of fuel residues, palynology may be the only indicator for the fuels used as, for example, at the industrial site at Sidlings Copse, north-east of Oxford, which formed the focus of a large Roman pottery industry. Here, the pollen record clearly shows a marked depletion of oak (*Quercus* sp. L.), hazel (*Corylus avellana* L.) and alder (*Alnus glutinosa* (L.) Gaertner) in the Iron Age, but total deforestation during the industrial activities of the Roman period (Young 1977; Day 1993).

Access to both raw materials and fuel were influential factors in determining the location of an industrial site. Fortuitously, these often occurred together (e.g. clay, iron and fuel), but when a resource was limited, priority was usually given to fuel. Such was the case for medieval glass-houses based in the western Weald in Sussex and Surrey, where wood fuel and sand were available locally but the refractory clays necessary for crucibles were imported (Kenyon 1967; Crossley 1994). Similarly, in the fuel-rich areas of north Devon, smithing-iron was imported from Wales (Marren 1992). Viable access to urban areas or to main routes to market goods was equally important. While some enterprises served local markets others enjoyed a surprisingly wide distribution. The 4th century Crambeck potters near Castle Howard, Yorkshire, for example, initially sold their wares in north-east England, but by the end of the century, possibly in response to a military contract, goods were also transported over the Pennines to the north-west (Wilson 1989). The importance of strategically positioned trading posts targeting the combined market forces of the Roman army and continental competition in the late 1st and 2nd centuries, is clearly reflected in the siting of large pottery factories near the coast and at the northern limit of the lowland settlement zone (Fulford 1977).

Historical accounts show that revenue from firewood and charcoal sales was not insignificant, and the increasing demand to supply industrial and domestic needs was influential in the ultimate control and development of woodland. By the early medieval period, town-based industries relied heavily on the fuel trade, which, by the 12th century and probably even earlier, operated through middlemen and dealers (Galloway *et al.* 1996).

INDUSTRIES USING WOOD FUEL OR CHARCOAL

The following survey of fuel-dependent industries includes details of firing processes and their basic fuel requirements.

It also demonstrates that some industries were regionally based. In some instances, where appropriate lowland sites have not been found, upland sites have been included to illustrate industrial practices which may also be relevant to lowland Britain.

Tin

The tin industry centred in Devon and Cornwall is probably prehistoric in origin although, at present, archaeological evidence is sparse (Newman 1998). The earliest documents date from the medieval period when mining areas were divided into administrative districts or stanneries. At this time tinners had the right to prospect for metals anywhere except in gardens, orchards, churchyards and on the highway, and, similarly, they were free to cut wood, dig peat, move rivers, and construct roads (Homer 1991). By 1314 there were complaints that the miners were destroying land (including good arable land) at the rate of 300 acres a year. Later, stannary laws applied regulations to restrict nuisance and damage (Newman 1998).

The melting point of pure tin is 232°C. (Hodges 1964). In the early days of tin extraction on Dartmoor, the ore was obtained in very pure form and would have needed little pre-smelting preparation (Newman 1998). Smelting was probably carried out in small outdoor furnaces near the tin-working sites, although the remains of both furnaces and fuels are extremely elusive. Later, and until the 14th century, it was necessary to smelt the tin twice. The first smelting was probably carried out close to the tinworks, whereas the second, to refine the metal, was performed in the stannery town. By the 14th century, tin was smelted in blowing mills which housed blast- furnaces driven by water-wheel powered bellows. The earliest known description of the smelting process was recorded in 1778 in Cornwall and refers to the use of charcoal fuel (Newman 1998).

Lead

Lead ore was worked in Somerset, South Devon, Yorkshire, Durham, the Peak District, and Flintshire. Roman lead-mining on Mendip and in north Wales probably dates from the second half of the 1st century AD (Whittick 1982).

The melting point of pure lead is 327° C (Hodges 1964). Smelting black ore galena (lead sulphide) did not require reduction with charcoal. Medieval records indicate that until the end of the 13th century, layers of brushwood and crushed ore were piled onto a log base in a hearth (Homer 1991). By the 14th century, shortages of both fuel and ore resulted in the reprocessing of bole slag using charcoal reduction in blast furnaces to recover residual lead (black-work). Charcoal reduction was also necessary to work white ore (lead carbonate) and litharge (residual lead after silver extraction) (Homer 1991).

Kiln-dried (seasoned) timber, known as whitecoal, was used in water-powered lead smelting hearths in north

Derbyshire from the end of the 16th century until the mid-eighteenth century (Crossley 1993; Jones 1993). Whitecoal was produced in characteristically q-shaped, deep depressions about 4 – 5m in diameter, spanned by timbers. Barked branches and billets from long rotation coppice (i.e. >12 years) were laid over the timbers, beneath which a hearth was fired with coppice wood or, when available, coal (Crossley 1993; Hart 1993). Evidence of hearths for whitecoal kilns has also been recorded close to ore-hearths in the Yorkshire Dales and the Lake District (Crossley 1993). Similar methods of fuel production may have been used in lowland areas.

Silver and gold

Silver was obtained from the same areas as lead, but large amounts were imported. Gold was also imported, although small quantities were obtained from Devon and Wales. As native metals, both usually required extraction from natural alloys (Hodges 1964). Silver was isolated from argentiferous lead by cupellation over an open fire (Campbell 1991), while gold was refined using charcoal in an enclosed cupel (Hodges 1964). The melting point of pure silver is 960° C, whereas gold is 1063° C, but in their pure states both are too soft for most practical purposes and they are generally alloyed with other metals (Hodges 1964). Smithing was performed over an open charcoal fire (Campbell 1991).

Copper

Copper mining in Bronze Age Britain appears to have been centred in North Wales, Cheshire and possibly the Peak District, although it is likely that the rich deposits in Devon and Cornwall, mined from at least the Roman period, were also exploited in the Bronze Age (O'Brien 1996). Bronze Age mines frequently penetrated rocks far below ground level and techniques of copper extraction employed the use of fire-setting to crack rocks containing the metal. Fuel residues from Bronze Age fire-setting were preserved in the waterlogged mine at Mount Gabriel in southwest Ireland and consisted of oak and hazel roundwood; from the size and extent of the mine, it has been estimated that thousands of tons of wood fuel would have been used for fire setting. Recent excavations on the Great Orme Head on the north coast of Wales exposed one of the largest known complexes of Bronze Age copper mines in the world (Hammond 1992). If in continuous use, the persistent quest for fire-setting fuel and timber pit-props must have made a significant impact on local woodlands.

Little is known of prehistoric smelting methods in Britain, but the low levels (<5%) of arsenic- and antimony-bearing oxides in reported finds of early Bronze-Age copper suggest that direct high-temperature smelting was not used at this time (Budd *et al.* 1992). Smelting was probably carried out in a simple bonfire type device close to the source of the ore.

To produce tools with good cutting edges, copper was hardened by alloying with tin to produce bronze (Hodges 1964). Processing the raw material depended on the character of the copper ore. Wood fuel would have been adequate for roasting the ore, while charcoal was probably the preferred fuel to obtain the melting point of about 1100° C for smelting (Hodges 1964). Compared to iron, copper smelting only requires a slightly reducing atmosphere which could probably have been achieved using wood fuel (Horne 1982).

Iron

Major centres for commercial iron-smelting were based in the Weald, the Forest of Dean, the Midlands, South Yorkshire, Cumbria, Durham and Northumberland (Geddes 1991), but, since iron-ore occurs in most counties in Britain (only 9 counties are without iron ore (Ehrenreich 1985)), small local enterprises were widespread, and processed ores were imported to fuel-rich areas which lacked iron ore (Marren 1992). Iron ores were roasted in an oxidizing atmosphere using either wood or charcoal in an open fire to attain temperatures of 400° – 500° C. For the smelting process, however, high temperatures and a reducing atmosphere were essential and could only be obtained through the use of charcoal in an enclosed kiln or furnace. Iron becomes workable at temperatures of 1100° – 1150° C, well within the range of Iron Age furnaces, which were capable of producing temperatures of 1100° – 1300° C (Ehreneich 1985). Blast furnaces (introduced into Britain from the continent by the late 15th century) allowed the manufacture of cast iron but operated at much higher temperatures, initially using vast quantities of charcoal but, later, switching to coal or coke (Hammersley 1973; Geddes 1991).

The range of kiln types has varied enormously since the first discovery of iron and working practices may have employed different types of charcoal fuel. Crew (1991), for example, suggests that prehistoric smiths used a smaller grade of charcoal, possibly from different wood species, than that used for smelting. Archaeological evidence to support this suggestion has yet to be found and may be difficult to establish, partly because fuel residues are sometimes too comminuted to assess the original character of the fuel, but also because both processes sometimes operated in the same working area and the spent fuels were probably dumped together.

Ceramics: pottery, tile and brick

Tiles and bricks were produced for Roman buildings but were not produced in Britain again until the Norman period (Clifton-Taylor 1972; Cherry 1991). Pottery, on the other hand, has been produced in Britain since the Neolithic period and was fired in various ways depending on the type of clay and the fuel available.

Pottery

For firing coarse wares with high organic and mineral content an open bonfire sufficed, but, with more refined clays, a kiln was essential to control the temperature of the firing. The design of the kiln and the type of fuel used were important factors for temperature control – a fact easily demonstrated by burning similar wood fuels in a down-draught kiln (producing temperatures up to 1100° C) and an updraught kiln (which remains significantly cooler) (Hodges 1964). Kiln-firing processes generally went through several stages during which certain temperatures were critical. Initially, a low heat using a small fire was used to dry the clay thoroughly before increasing the heat slowly. Chemical changes in the structure of the clay occur at about 400° C and 573°C. If the clay is heated too rapidly, damage may result. The progress of the firing was judged by colour changes in the smoke or gases escaping from the kiln, or in the colour of the wares (as viewed through a spy hole). The heat was finally increased to the maturing point, which varied according to the type of clay used and finish required, e.g. terracotta: 800° – 900° C; red earthenware: 900° – 1050° C; stoneware: 1200° – 1300° C (Hodges 1964).

The moisture content of the fuel and the oxygen supply (draught) also influenced the appearance of the finished product. Colour changes could be induced by firing in oxidizing (to red) or reducing atmospheres (to black); sometimes both effects occurred in the kiln, either accidently or intentionally (Hodges 1964). Glazing often required separate firings at different temperatures to that for the body fabric, depending on the chemical constituents of the glaze.

Experimental firings at 890±50° C to reproduce techniques used at the Roman pottery kilns at Alice Holt (built with long constricted flues, possibly using turves for the superstructure) proved that two- foot-long coppice poles about 1 inch in diameter worked best for the main part of the firing. Fine brushwood was used to produce the higher temperatures (Lyne and Jefferies 1979). The massive amount of charcoal remaining in the kiln flue following these firings contrasted sharply with sparse charcoal residues from the excavated kilns (mostly probably from oak (*Quercus* sp.), hazel (*Corylus* sp.) and willow (*Salix* sp.) underwood).

By the medieval period updraught kilns were in common use although the type of fuel varied with availability. In most regions wood was used, but in some parts of the Midlands and Yorkshire kilns were coal-fired, while peat was used in eastern England. In general, however, wood-fired kilns were cheaply and efficiently fuelled with bundles of brush-wood, coppice rods and loppings (Cherry 1991). The use of charcoal would have been unnecessary for firing most types of pottery, but it is worth recording Falkner's (1907) notes on local 19th century clamp kilns in which pottery was placed on the floor of the kiln with charcoal incorporated around and between the wares, with more fuel fired in the flues.

Bricks

Commercial brick-works operating in the 15th century used both kilns and clamps, which were fired with faggots, logs and greenwood (Moore 1991). Records suggest that kilns were more commonly used because they were quicker and usually fired the bricks more evenly, although clamps had the advantage of flexibility as regards siting and capacity.

Tiles

By the 13th century, floor tiles were glazed with the glaze applied to the unfired tiles. The tiles were fired in wood-fuelled kilns, to produce an initial slow-drying firing of 200° C followed by a gradual increase in temperature to about 1000° C to fuse the glaze (Cherry 1991). Firings often took about a week. Excavated kilns of the medieval period have included updraught and double-ended kilns. Unglazed roof tiles were often larger than floor tiles, but, since they could be fired at lower temperatures, kiln construction was less critical.

Glass, faience and enamel

Glass-making requires complete fluxing and melting of silica with an alkali, whereas faience is formed from a core of sintered quartz sand which holds a vitreous layer on the outer surface (Henderson 1988). Glass-making requires much higher temperatures than glass-working (see below); the latter can be carried out in a simple furnace or hearth to render glass or cullet (recycled glass) molten before moulding or blowing. Enamelling involves the attachment of glass to a metal surface through the use of high temperature bonding; the technique probably began in Britain *circa* AD 600 (Henderson and Ivens 1992).

Both glass and faience artefacts have been found at Bronze Age sites in Britain (Potterne, Wiltshire; Wallingford, Oxfordshire) and Ireland (Rathgall, Co. Wicklow). But, as yet, there is no positive evidence for home production in the Bronze Age and the items are thought to have been imported from workshops in continental Europe, possibly Frattesina, Northern Italy, where there is evidence of glass-working (and almost certainly glass-making) from the 11th – 9th centuries BC. (Henderson 1988).

Pre-medieval glass-making in Britain appears to have been rare (Winbolt 1933; Harden 1961; Kenyon 1967; Berryman 1998). Roman sites are known at Wilderspool, Cheshire and at Caistor-by-Norwich (Winbolt 1933), and, from 3rd century deposits at Coppergate, York (Cool *et al* 1999). At Dunmisk, Co. Tyrone, Ireland, monastic workers were both making and working glass from the 6th – 10th centuries, and the excavated site produced abundant remains of crucibles, charcoal and ash (Henderson and Ivens 1992). Glass-works dating from the 8th century were based at the Abbey in Barking, Essex, but left no evidence of on-site glass-making or of where or from whom the workers obtained their glass or cullet. Even in the medieval period the industry was not widespread. Major centres operated in the Weald of Surrey and Sussex, the Forest of Dean and, in the late medieval period, at Cannock Chase and Needwood Forest, Staffordshire (Kenyon 1967, Crossley 1994). Two sites in north Yorkshire have been dated to the late 16th century (see below) (Crossley and Aberg 1972). In the second decade of the 17th century, patents were issued to enforce the use of coal and, consequently, wood-fuelled glass-houses, including those in the Weald, ceased to operate (Crossley 1994).

Until about AD 1500 the main ingredients of glass were sand and plant-ash (alkali) (Charleston 1991). The preferred ash was derived from soda-rich maritime plants (particularly those from the Mediterranean) but, by the turn of the 1st millennium, supplies of soda-ash became scarce, and glass-houses in northern Europe were forced to look for alternative sources. These were obtained from various inland plants, but particularly trees. Inland plants produce ash that contains potash and, usually, lime (both useful ingredients for glassmaking), but low levels of soda. In the 12th century, Theophilus (Hawthorn and Smith 1963) recommended the use of beech (*Fagus* sp.) ash, while in the 16th – 17th centuries, Agricola (1556 *De Re Metallica,* trans. S.E Winbolt 1933) and Neri (1612, *L' Arte Vetraria* trans. C. Merrett 1662) suggested the use of ashes from oak (*Quercus* sp.), beech (*Fagus* sp.), fir, brambles and herbaceous plants, including bracken, millet, rushes, reeds, and beans.

The attraction of the Weald and the Forest of Dean for glass-making lay in the abundance of wood fuel, which was consumed in vast quantities to achieve the requisite temperatures in excess of 1200° C, and, in particular, the prevalence of beech to supply potash with a high manganese content, which allowed a wide range of colours to be produced (Charleston 1991). Fern ash was also used.

Glass furnaces in the Weald were usually working for 9 – 10 months of the year and, during this time, seasoned wood fuel was continually fed into the hearths (Kenyon 1967). Contemporary records indicate that large wood (billets) was preferred, although some refer to the use of underwood. Calculations based on 16th century records from Knole, Kent, indicate that a 4-pot glasshouse consumed 543 cords of wood in 32 weeks (Kenyon 1967), or, in other words, cleared 4 acres of 15 year old coppice per month (Crossley 1967).

Charcoal-burning

Charcoal is obtained by the controlled burning of wood with a restricted air supply (Armstrong 1978). Charcoal-burning was a specialized industry which consumed huge quantities of wood, and the process took several days to complete. Charcoal clamps constructed from roundwood were built over shallow depressions or platforms, preferably near water for dousing should the clamp accidently catch fire (an open and uncontrolled fire could reek havoc on the charring process). Wood begins to char at about 350° C and, on completion, good quality charcoal should

retain the original morphology of the wood, although much reduced in volume. The production of 1 ton of charcoal requires about 6 tons of wood depending on the methods used (Percy 1864; Armstrong 1978; Horne 1982). A standard cord of wood should produce 5 cwt of charcoal (James 1955).

Despite its tendency to fracture during transport, charcoal was lighter and easier to move around than wood, and charcoal-burners worked within the coppices camped on site alongside their clamps (Armstrong 1978). Licences issued to medieval charcoal-burners suggest that it was more often a subsidiary than a main occupation (Birrel 1969). The industry was widespread in rural districts and operated wherever there was a demand for charcoal and the means to produce it. The higher premiums paid by Wealden iron-masters for charcoal bought directly from clamps probably reflects the quality of this fuel (Crossley 1994).

The traditional methods of charcoal production in clamps (Percy 1864; Webster 1919; Edlin 1949; Armstrong 1978) is generally well known, but a different method of producing small coals was described by John Evelyn in 1662, whereby bundles of brushwood were piled up and set alight, and then added to until 500 – 600 had been burnt. These small coals were packed into sacks and sent from Surrey to London where they were used for gold-smithing and as kindling (Armstrong 1978).

The textile industry and cloth dyeing

Commercial textile producers and cloth-dyers working in large-scale enterprises required steady supplies of wood fuel for boiling-tanks and dye-vats (Walton 1991). By the late medieval period, some cloth-dying centres were experiencing difficulty in obtaining fuel and, in 1637, local shortages of firewood in the Weald were affecting dye-works in Cranbrook, Kent (Cleere and Crossley 1995).

Commercial food production

In the larger Romanized settlements and towns, ready-made food, cooked over charcoal grills or in ovens, was available in eating houses or from food vendors (Allason-Jones 1989). In Saxon settlements, local markets probably provided the main outlets for commercially prepared food, but, by 1100, permanent shops were established (e.g. in Winchester) and by 1183 a cookshop in London was selling hot and cold meals (Hagen 1995). Medieval town houses frequently had no cooking facilities and bread, pies and other foods were either cooked in commercial ovens or purchased from bakers (Hammond 1995). The popular use of reed and straw fuel by London's bakers and brewers was outlawed in 1212 and firewood was substituted (Galloway *et al.* 1996). While the requirement of 15cwt of split logs (preferably oak) to spit-roast a 120lb pig (Hagen 1995) may have been infrequent, it does give an idea of the quantities of fuel involved. By 1300, the population of London was between 80,000 and 100,000, and approximately 100,000 tons of wood were used per year for food preparation (Hammond 1995). The brewing industry also consumed fuel at a rapid rate, as demonstrated by the 13th century Lyminge customal which records that 1 large wagonload of faggots was needed to produce 8 bushels of malt (Witney 1990). In addition, wood fuel was also required for the preservation of meat, fish and cheese by smoking and, possibly, for flavouring food (Edlin 1949; Asten 1988; Hagen 1995). Thomas Tusser (1984), writing in the mid-1570's, recommended broom (*Cytisus scoparius* (L.) Link) for smoking fish. Other local uses have included birch (*Betula* sp.) for hams and herrings, oak (*Quercus* sp.) and beech (*Fagus sylvatica*) for kippers, hams and bacon, and juniper (*Juniperus* sp.) for ham (Edlin 1949; Hagen 1995). And, indirectly, fuel was required for salt production; salt was an essential ingredient in cheese-making and food preservation (see below) (Witney 1990).

Salterns

The salt industry was widespread in coastal regions, particularly around the south coast and East Anglia, namely, the Somerset Levels, north Devon, Cornwall, Isle of Purbeck, Sussex, the Kent marshes and the Fenlands (Whitelock 1955; Bradley 1992, Hagen 1994). Over 285 sites are recorded in Domesday in Sussex alone. Anglo-Saxon records indicate that from the 8th – 10th centuries grants to operate salterns usually included the provision of wood for boiling salt. In AD 732, in Kent where there was a huge demand for salt for food preservation, Ethelbert gave land to Abbot Dunn for boiling salt, and an annual fuel allowance of 120 laden wagons of wood (Whitelock 1955; Witney 1990).

The main inland salterns in Britain were in the Cheshire-Shropshire basin, Staffordshire, Worcestershire, Somerset, Teeside and Antrim (Woodiwiss 1992). At Droitwich, Worcestershire, salterns appear to have worked almost continuously from the Iron Age until the early 20th century; enormous quantities of wood were required to boil the brine, and 10th century records show that wood was carted from a wide area, even from beyond the Hwiccan frontier (Hurst 1991; Hooke1989). Local place names suggest that charcoal may also have been used at Droitwich (Hooke 1989).

Ancient salt-production processes in Britain relied mostly on evaporation by boiling brine (i.e. saline water from marine or inland sources), the ashes from halophytes (salt-tolerant plants) or salt-laden peat (Hagen1994). The ultimate size of the salt granules depended on the type of brine (i.e. saline water/ plant-based) and the rate of evaporation (or boiling). Salt was usually evaporated in shallow ceramic trays (briquetage), although by the Saxon period there is evidence of the use of lead pots (Hagen 1994). It is probable that in some areas small farmsteads set up salterns, although these may have been domestic rather than commercial. The remains of ancient coastal salterns, now located well inland in the Fens, testify to subsequent changes in sea-level and alluvial deposition (Leah 1992); examples include Iron Age deposits at Cowbit, Lincolnshire, and Roman works at Morton Fen, Lincolnshire (Lane 1993) and Blackborough End, Norfolk (Leah 1992). Boiling hearths were sometimes substantial structures with clay-lined flues, as seen at the Roman salterns at Blackborough End (Leah 1992); others were undoubtedly cruder and more makeshift.

Limeburning

Calcined lime, essential for the production of mortar for the building trade, was first used in Britain in the Roman period, although the practice fell into disuse from post-Roman times until the Norman period (Toft 1988; Williams 1989). Evidence from 12th century records referring to the use of lime to whitewash the walls of the church in York in AD 690 suggests that some limeburning continued in the interim (Williams 1989). The benefits of liming agricultural land, however, do not seem to have been realized until relatively recently; for example, in south Wales, in the mid-16th century (Toft 1988). The traditional process of limeburning involved the burning or calcining of limestone in pits, clamps or kilns and could take up to two weeks to complete, depending on the scale of the operation.

The excavation of Roman lime-kilns in Britain shows that construction usually conformed with Cato's advice for limeburning (*De Agri Cultura*, 4. XXXVIII.4, trans. W.D. Hooper, rev. H.B. Ash 1960). The Roman site at Weekley, Northamptonshire, included a wood-fuelled limestone kiln built with a 3m wide pot (Jackson 1973). Later limekilns for on-site production of mortar were recorded at several 13th century castles, fuelled with wood or coal. Contemporary documents indicate that large quantities of timber were burnt at Oxford in 1229 and Wellington Forest in Shropshire in 1255, while coal (from Newcastle) was used at the Tower of London in 1278 and Windsor Castle in 1366 (Williams 1989). Kiln design varied: one of the earliest types, a flare kiln, included a domed cavity in which wood or peat fuel was burnt. Until the more permanent structures of the mid-18th century, most kilns were temporary, serving an immediate or single purpose, after which they were dismantled or abandoned.

The type and purity of the limestone available were major factors in determining the method of limeburning (Toft 1988). Dolomite (a double carbonate of magnesium carbonate and calcium carbonate, $MgCa(CO_3)_2$) was preferred since it burnt at lower temperatures than calcium carbonate ($CaCO_3$) and was cheaper to produce. The kilns (usually built of limestone) were filled with alternate layers of fuel and stone nodules. Kiln operators were highly skilled – the limeburner had to maintain a steady temperature of about 800 – 900° C until the stone was burnt, without exceeding 1150° C when 'overburn' occurred. The critical temperatures of burn and overburn varied considerably with the composition of the limestone.

Overburn caused a glazed surface on the stone and prevented subsequent chemical reaction or 'slaking' with water. Carbon dioxide released during the firing process made it difficult to reach the burning temperature using wood fuel but, since the admission of air into the chamber could result in uncontrollably intense heat, vents to fan the fire were not used. The strict control of gases within the chamber was essential to prevent explosions and to regulate temperatures. Wood fuel was easier to useand had the advantage over coal that it allowed the limestone to burn at slightly lower temperatures (although on an extended time-scale), but coal was much cheaper.

Other fuel-based industries

Numerous other small industries also used wood fuel. These included the extraction of animal glues from the prolonged boiling of hides and bones; the production of tallow from mutton fat by repeatedly boiling the fat to purify it; the production of pigments such as sepia (from boiling cuttlefish bones) and black (from burning bone, ivory and other organic substances); the preservation of hides by smoking them over a slowly burning wood fire, and the production of lime and gypsum plasters (Hodges 1964). From the 16th century, charcoal (from coppiced wood) was used in gunpowder production (Edlin 1949).

THE PROPERTIES OF WOOD FUELS AND CHARCOAL

The thermal capacity of any given wood is influenced by its chemical composition and the ratio of lignin and cellulose to its water content (Hodges 1964; Tillman *et al.* 1981). The maximum temperature achievable on combustion will be affected by the dimensions (size and shape) of the fuel, the structure of the hearth or kiln, and the supply of oxygen. In poorly ventilated hearths, narrow gauge fuel (e.g. thin roundwood) will offer a larger surface area per unit of weight than wider logs and, weight for weight, will burn at higher temperatures but are more quickly consumed. Thus, billets and cordwood supply a long-lasting heat source, whereas narrow roundwood can be used to advantage to boost temperatures quickly. In general, denser woods (e.g. oak (*Quercus* sp.) and ash (*Fraxinus excelsior* L.) produce a longer-lasting source of heat than light-weight woods (such as willow (*Salix* sp.), alder (*Alnus glutinosa*) and poplar (*Populus* sp.) (Porter 1990). It is also worth noting that fast-grown oak is denser than slow-grown oak, and that oak heartwood is denser than sapwood.

The calorific value of charcoal depends on the percentage of carbon present. Incomplete or partial carbonization results in low grade, smokey fuel, whereas the efficient conversion of wood to charcoal (i.e. 95% carbon) provides a smokeless fuel more or less double the calorific value of the uncarbonized wood (Armstrong 1978; Horne 1982).

THE ARCHAEOLOGICAL EVIDENCE

Archaeology is often infuriatingly ambiguous and while the remains of a furnace, kiln or hearth may be obvious, its function is not always clear-cut. Sometimes features appear to have been multi-purpose or adapted from one use to another over a period of time. Also, some industries (e.g. pottery) may have employed different types of wood fuel during the firing process specifically to regulate the temperature (see above); it would be extremely difficult to detect this practice from the remains of burnt fuel left *in situ* on completion of the firing. Records of securely accredited fuel residues are scarce for most periods. When embedded in slag there can be no doubt as to the use of the charcoal, but, more frequently, industrial and domestic debris appear to have been dumped together in a common context.

The following archaeological data refer to charcoal analyses which, are to the best of my knowledge, from sites with securely designated fuel residues (see Table 3). The relatively narrow range of industries listed in Table 3 is biased towards iron-working and, although the list is not comprehensive, it does demonstrate where major gaps occur in the fuel record. Some of these gaps may be attributed to practices specific to the industry (perhaps, firing conditions allowed wood to burn to ash) or to unfavourable conditions for preservation. Charcoal was a valuable commodity and where large quantities of charcoal accumulated after firings, it may have been sold off for domestic fuel or for other uses, such as agricultural soil improvement, as suggested, for example, at the Roman pottery site at Alice Holt, Farnham (Lyne and Jefferies 1979).

The paucity of fuel residues from excavated glasshouses may be due, in part to the practice of reducing fuel residues to ash to provide this vital ingredient for the industry (see above), although at Dunmisk, Ireland (see above), charcoal was abundant around the furnace areas (if any species were identified they were not published) (Henderson and Ivens 1992). The list of known or excavated glass-houses in Britain is comparatively short and the scientific examination of organic finds from those recorded before the last war was frequently scanty or nonexistent. Kenyon (1967) knew of 42 glass-house sites in the Weald, many of which have subsequently been destroyed through land-use; only 5 new sites have been added to Kenyon's original data (Crossley 1994).

The importance of examining industrial fuel residues, especially when present in large volume, can not be overemphasized. Until a larger data-base of charcoal analyses has been established, representing a wider range of industries, the scope for comparative studies will remain limited.

Methodology

Charcoal identified by the author was examined using standard methods, as follows. Charcoal fragments measuring >2mm in radial cross-section were prepared by fracturing to expose fresh transverse, tangential and radial surfaces. These were supported in sand and examined using a Nikon Labophot incident-light microscope at magnifications of up to x400. The anatomical structures of the wood were matched to reference slides of modern wood. Where possible the maturity of the wood was assessed (i.e. sapwood or heartwood), stem diameters and ages were recorded, and evidence of wood structure or morphological features characteristic of coppice rods or managed woodland noted (see Introduction). Measurements taken from charred stems can only provide a rough guide as to the diameter of the stem when living (see Introduction). Unless stated otherwise, the measurements given below are those of charred stems.

Because archaeological charcoal readily succumbs to fragmentation, attempts to quantify taxa in a given sample, based on the frequency of fragments, is meaningless. Similarly, the collective weight of fragments per species would be equally misleading since the natural density of wood varies not only with the species, but also with edaphic and other environmental factors, and the temperature of burning; in addition, charcoal from archaeological contexts often includes extraneous mineral or organic deposits and variable amounts of moisture. The differential preservation of taxa should also be considered, although in my experience, where conditions are not conducive to preservation, degradation is usually common across the entire range of taxa present. With these restrictions in mind, there should be room for sensible flexibility of judgement, and in this paper taxa are referred to as dominant when they occurred in most or all the samples examined from a site and in consistently large volume when compared to taxa which were sporadic and/ or sparse.

In the following text the term *narrow roundwood* refers to stems with charred diameters of <20mm. *Sapwood* refers to fragments from stems, branches or trunkwood of unknown diameter, but not heartwood. *Heartwood* refers to wood with evidence of tyloses in the vessels, a feature characteristic of some ring porous woods, usually, but not exclusively, related to heartwood formation. Tyloses occur when adjacent parenchyma cells penetrate the vessel walls (via the pitting) effectively blocking the vessels.

Classification

With rare exceptions, the identification of wood from indigenous trees and shrubs is only possible to generic level. For related taxa, which share common wood features, identification to generic level can be unreliable, particularly when examining juvenile wood. In the Salicaceae, these include willow (*Salix* spp.) and (*Populus* spp.); other problematic taxa include members of the Pomoideae (a subfamily of Rosaceae) – hawthorn (*Crataegus* spp. L.), apple (*Malus sylvestris* Miller), pear (*Pyrus communis* L.), wild service tree (*Sorbus torminalis* (L.) Crantz), whitebeam (*S. aria* (L.) Crantz) and rowan (*S. aucuparia* L.); members of the Ericaceae which includes heather (*Erica* sp. L.) and ling (*Calluna vulgaris* (L.) Hull); and gorse (*Ulex sp.* L.) and broom (*Cytisus* sp.) in the Leguminosae. In the following text and tables these taxa are grouped as shown above. Where a genus is represented by a single species in the British flora this is named as the most likely origin of the wood, given the provenance and period. However, it should be noted that individual species can rarely be proven from the wood structure and that exotic species of some trees and shrubs were introduced to Britain from an early period (Mitchell 1974). The classification follows that of Tutin *et al.* (1964–80).

Industries and associated wood species *(Table 3)*

Lead-working

Evidence from a Romano-British site in an isolated cove at Duckpool, Cornwall, was probably associated with low temperature lead or pewter working. Fuel residues were sparse but indicated the use of local heath and woodland species including oak (*Quercus* sp.), alder (*Alnus glutinosa*), hazel (*Corylus avellana*), gorse/ broom (*Ulex* sp. L./ *Cytisus scoparius* (L.) Link) and possibly birch (*Betula* sp.) (Gale 1995).

Iron-working

Fuel residues from the lowland metal-working sites discussed here mostly refer to iron smelting, although smithing residues may also have been present. Charcoal analyses from 24 sites dating from the Early Iron Age to the medieval period indicate that, until the mid-medieval period, oak (*Quercus* sp.) was consistently dominant. Although 14th and 15th century iron-working sites are more sparsely represented (Castle Mall, Norwich, and London Road, Crawley, Sussex, see below), they appear to differ from earlier sites in that fuel residues from other tree species were as frequent as those from oak.

The use of oak heartwood appears to have been common practice, although it is particularly interesting that heartwood was not used at the five Roman sites in the Forest of Dean: (Woolaston (Figueiral 1992); Blakeney (Gale [a]) and three at Ariconium (Leyell 1923; Gale 2000 [e] and Gale, unpub.). Charcoal residues from these sites were unusually well preserved and abundant, and indicated the common use of relatively narrow coppiced roundwood, predominantly from oak (*Quercus* sp.) and hazel (*Corylus avellana*). The significance of this is difficult to interpret but could imply regional preferences or traditions either in woodland management or the iron-industry, or possibly (but probably less likely) local depletion of woodland resources.

Table 3. The analyses of charcoal from industrial fuel residues.

Industry	Site and reference	Period	Taxa identified
?LEAD/ TIN	Duckpool, Cornwall Gale in Ratcliffe 1995	Romano /British	alder, hazel, oak, gorse/ broom, ?birch
IRON- WORKS	Dunstan Park, Berks Gale, unpub.	Iron Age 7th C	**oak, hazel,** maple, ash, hawthorn type
	Rooksdown, Hants Gale, unpub.	Early Iron Age	**oak,** hazel
	Riseley Farm, Hants Gale 1991–3	Middle Iron Age	**oak**
	Quidney Farm, Norfolk Gale 2000 (b)	Iron Age	**oak**
	Watchfield, Oxon Gale in Birbeck, forthcoming	Iron Age	**oak,** maple, ash, blackthorn
	Creeton, Lincs Cowgill, forthcoming	Iron Age/ Rom/Brit	**oak,** maple, hazel, holly, blackthorn, elm, willow/poplar, hawthorn type
	Hatton-Silk Willoughby Rackham *et al.*1999	Late I/A– EarlyR/B	**oak,** maple, hazel, hawthorn type ?dogwood
	Blakeney, Gloucs Gale 2000 (a)	Romano /British	**oak, hazel,** maple, alder, birch, blackthorn, gorse/ broom
	Pomeroy, Devon Gale 1999	Roman 1st C	**oak,** maple, alder, birch, hazel, ash, b'thorn, willow/ poplar, elm, gorse
	Ariconium '22, Herefordshire, Leyell 1923	Roman 2nd C	oak, birch, hazel, willow/poplar, elder
	Ariconium '63, Herefordshire, Gale 2000 (e)	Roman 2nd C	**oak, hazel,** birch, spindle, ash, haw- thorn type, willow/pop, lime, gorse
	Ariconium '93, Herefordshire, Gale, unpub.	Roman 2nd C	**oak, hazel,** maple, alder, birch, ash, hawthorn type, lime, ?dogwood
	Woolaston, Gloucs Figueiral 1992	Roman 2–4th C	**oak, hazel,** maple, alder, birch, spindle, ash, holly, h'thorn, b'thorn, will/pop, elm, viburnum, ?chestnut
	Bardown, Sussex Cleere & Crossley 1995	Roman 2nd C	**oak,** birch, hornbeam, hazel, beech, elder, hawthorn type
	Lefevre Walk, Bow Rackham *et al.* 1998	Roman 2–3rd C	**oak,** alder, birch, hazel, ash, holly, hawthorn type, blackthorn, will/pop
	Parnell Road, Bow Rackham *et al.* 1998	Roman 2–3rd C	**oak,** maple, hazel, ash, holly, hawthorn type, willow/ poplar
	Welwyn Hall, Herts Gale in McDonald, forthcoming	Roman 4th C	**oak,** maple, hazel, ash, hawthorn type, ?holly
	Scole, E. Anglia Gale in Cowgill, forthcoming	Roman	oak
	Bonemills Farm, Cambs Gale, unpub.	?Roman	**oak,** willow/ poplar, elder
	Packenham, Suffolk Gale, unpub.	Roman	oak
	Coslaney Street, Norfolk Cowgill 1997	10–12th C	**oak**
	Castle Mall, Norwich Gale in Shepherd, in prep.	medieval 14–15th C	**oak, ash, maple, heather,** willow/ poplar, elm
	London Road, Crawley Gale in Cooke, forthcoming	medieval 4th C	**oak, beech, birch,** hazel, holly, hawthorn type
POTTERY/ TILE	London Road, Stanmore Gale in McKinley, in prep.	Romano /British	**oak,** maple, hazel, ash, hawthorn type, blackthorn, willow/poplar, holly,

Table 3. continued.

POTTERIES	Madresfield, Worcs Gale, unpub.	Romano /British	**oak, maple, willow/poplar,** ash
	2 Mile Bottom, Norfolk Gale in Bates, in prep.	Romano /British	**oak, heather,** alder, hazel, ash, will/ pop, hawthorn group, p. buckthorn.
	Redcliffe, Dorset Gale in Lyne, in prep.	Roman	**oak,** alder, birch, heather, willow/ poplar, gorse/ broom
	Alice Holt, Farnham Lyne and Jefferies 1979	Roman	oak, hazel and willow
	Worthing Road, Sussex Gale in Lovell, in prep.	Roman 1–2nd C	maple, ash, blackthorn, oak, elder
	Wickham Barn, Sussex Gale (m) in Butler & Lyne, forthcoming	Roman 2nd C	**oak,** maple, hazel, hawthorn type, blackthorn, willow/ poplar
	Heath Farm, Norfolk Gale (j) in Bates, in prep.	Roman 2nd C	**oak, lime, willow/ poplar, gorse,** maple, hazel, spindle, ash, holly, hawthorn group, blackthorn
	Dairy Farm, Norfolk Gale (j) in Bates, in prep.	Roman 2–3rd C	**maple, oak,** ?blackthorn, ?willow/ poplar
	Torksey Brown 1995	Late Saxon	**oak,** ash, gorse/broom
	Castle Mall, Norwich Gale in Shepherd, in prep.	Early medieval	**oak, ash,** maple, hazel, hawthorn type
	Enborne Street, Newbury Gale 2000 (c)	Medieval 12–13th C	**oak,** alder, birch
GLASS-MAKING	Hutton, Yorkshire Crossley & Aberg 1972	16th C	birch, oak, ?alder
	Rosedale, Yorkshire Crossley & Aberg 1972	16th C	**oak,** willow
SALTERNS	Middleton, Norfolk Gale unpub.	Roman	**hazel, heather,** blackthorn, oak, hawthorn type, gorse, willow/poplar
	Morton Fen, E. Anglia Gale, unpub.	Roman	**alder, willow/ poplar,** ash
LIMEBURNING	Weekley, Northants Jackson 1973	Roman	beech, poplar, oak, hazel, maple, hawthorn type

Taxa: alder (*Alnus* sp.), alder buckthorn (*Frangula alnus*), ash (*Fraxinus* sp.), beech (*Fagus* sp.), birch (*Betula* sp.), blackthorn/ cherry (*Prunus* spp.), chestnut (*Castanea* sp.), dogwood (*Cornus* sp.), elder (*Sambucus* sp.), elm (*Ulmus* sp.), gorse/ broom (*Ulex* sp. / *Cytisus* sp.), hawthorn group (Pomoideae: *Crateagus* sp., *Malus* sp., *Pyrus* sp., *Sorbus* sp.), hazel (*Corylus* sp.), heather or ling (*Erica* sp. or *Calluna* sp.), holly (*Ilex* sp.), lime (*Tilia* sp.), maple (*Acer* sp.), oak (*Quercus* sp.), purging buckthorn (*Rhamnus cathartica*), spindle (*Euonymus* sp.), viburnum (*Viburnum* sp.), willow/ poplar (*Salix* sp. / *Populus* sp.).

Taxa shown in bold type indicate those which appear to have been used most frequently (see Methodology).

Charcoal from the 10th – 12th century site at Coslany Street, Norwich, consisted of oak (*Quercus* sp.) heartwood, probably from wide billets of wood (Gale, unpub.). In contrast, at the late medieval site at Castle Mall, Norwich, ash (*Fraxinus excelsior*), maple (*Acer* sp.L.) and the heather family (Ericaceae) occurred as frequently as oak (*Quercus* sp.) (Gale, in Shepherd, in prep.). Similarly, at the late medieval site at London Road, Crawley, in the Weald, birch (*Betula* sp. L.) and, beech (*Fagus sylvatica*) were equally as common as oak (*Quercus* sp.) (Gale, in Cooke, forthcoming), although here it may have been the longstanding practice to mix these species, since a similar emphasis on birch (*Betula* sp.), beech (*Fagus sylvatica*) and oak (*Quercus* sp.) was recorded at 18 other sites in the Weald dating from the Roman period to the 18th century and identified at Kew in the 1920s (Straker 1931).

Potteries

Evidence from seven Roman and two medieval potteries indicates that, while a wide range of wood species was used, oak (*Quercus* sp.) predominated at all but one site. Oak heartwood was common and sometimes abundant. Fuel mostly consisted of roundwood of various dimensions, with clear evidence of coppiced roundwood (see above) at three of the Roman sites, although wider logs, including heartwood, were also used. Where available, the data suggests that charred roundwood was mostly within the 15 – 40mm diameter range. The three more or less contemporary Roman potteries at Heath Farm, Dairy Farm and Two Mile Bottom in Norfolk (Gale, in Bates, in prep.) serve as useful indicators of the importance of oak in the industrial economy in heathland and riverine environments.

Glass-making

The late 16th century glass-works at Rosedale and Hutton in North Riding were sited in a well-wooded valley with abundant bracken (_Pteridium aquilinum_). Identifiable charcoal from Hutton was minimal but included birch (_Betula_ sp.) and alder (_Alnus glutinosa_). Charcoal residues from Rosedale were associated with a probable ash-preparation area and consisted of branches, twigs and bark, mostly from slow-grown oak (_Quercus_ sp.) but also willow (_Salix_ sp.) (Crossley and Aberg 1972). There was no evidence of the use of bracken.

Salterns

Fuel deposits from two Roman salterns in East Anglia clearly reflect the fenland environment. At Morton Fen wood fuel appears to have been sparse, and willow (_Salix_ sp.) and alder (_Alnus glutinosa_.) were used sparingly compared to cereal residues, bracken and other herbaceous material (Gale, unpub.). At Middleton, however, fuel was predominantly from the heather family (Ericaceae) and hazel (_Corylus avellana_.) (Gale, unpub.).

Lime-burning

Fuel residues from the Roman kiln at Weekley, Northants indicated the use of twigs and branches up to about 40mm in original diameter from beech (_Fagus sylvatica_), oak (_Quercus_ sp.), hazel (_Corylus avellana_), maple (_Acer campestre_), poplar (_Populus_ sp.) and the hawthorn/_Sorbus_ group (Pomoideae) (Jackson 1973).

WOODLAND MANAGEMENT

The use of quickly renewable sources of wood from coppiced and pollarded trees would have been the most efficient method of sustaining a continuous supply for construction work and fuel; and, in addition, the practical application of the long pliable stems and poles would have been superior to non-coppiced stems for many artefactual purposes. Early evidence of the use of coppiced wood in Britain includes Neolithic trackways in the Somerset Levels (3rd millennium BC) (Rackham 1977 and 1979; Coles and Orme 1982; Morgan 1982) (although

this interpretation is challenged by Crone [1987] in favour of adventitious cropping of natural rather than managed coppice) and Bronze Age structures at Flag Fen (Peterken 1992).

Archaeology suggests that by and during the Roman occupation of England most of the great river valleys and chalklands had been deforested and ploughed (Rackham 1990). In sparsely wooded but densely populated regions woodland management must have formed a crucial element of the economy. Such was the landscape in Leicestershire and Rutland, where numerous large settlements were sited around Roman Leicester in a virtually treeless environment (a state which has persisted until the present day) (Squires and Jeeves 1994).

It seems likely, given the importance of pannage, that the system described in Anglo-Saxon chronicles of growing oak (_Quercus_ sp.) standards with coppice (Berryman 1998) was already established by this time. The significance of standard oaks and beeches (_Fagus sylvatica_) in this context is endorsed by the Saxon valuation of woodland based on its pannage potential (Witney 1990). The 7th century Laws of Ines rigidly controlled woodland resources and required the planting of replacement trees; additional by-laws were imposed by the Normans and regulated through manorial courts (Hooke, 1989; Pretty 1990). By the Late Saxon period woodland boundaries were defined by ditches and banks, and protected from grazing with hedges or fences (Rackham 1982; Hooke 1989). By the Anglo-Saxon and medieval periods woodland formed an integral part of the farm, estate or demesne system and was either managed by the estate or leased out to tenants (Hooke 1989, Pretty 1990). Tenure agreements usually carried restrictions on use (e.g. timber was to be left for the owner's use) or dictated rotational cycles for particular species and seasons of felling (Rackham 1982; Hooke 1989). Terms of sale for fuel varied and while some craftsmen bought trees or charcoal, others leased or bought woodland outright.

By the medieval period, most woodlands probably represented vestigial areas of "semi-natural" or self sown woodland, long-since managed, or areas of regeneration on derelict land – nomenclature for regenerated woodland is complex and fraught with ambiguity (Peterken 1992; 1996). The extent of coppiced areas within woodland is impossible to assess and probably fluctuated with demand. In 1608, Crown lands in England and Wales exceeded 200,000 acres of woodland, of which only about a quarter was coppiced (Hammersley 1973), but, locally, in village woodlands, the situation was probably more critical. Estimates based on extant stored coppices (uncropped trees or stands of coppice origin classified as high forest) indicate that in recent centuries the practice of coppicing in Britain was mostly confined to England (Evans 1992).

The first plantations or planted woodland in Britain may date to the Roman conquest; in Italy, Cato (_De Agri Cultura_, 1.VII.1, trans. W.D. Hooper, rev. H.B. Ash) advocated setting up different types of plantations (depending on their economic use), and Rackham (1990) suggests that some extant chestnut woods in Britain, e.g. at Stour Wood near Harwich, may derive from Roman plantations. Secure evidence of horticultural commerce dates from the reign of Edward I, when a nursery selling seeds and plants was established in London (Harvey 1981). Tree nurseries existed from at least the early 12th century, and although records of sale are rare, in 1321, a batch of 1000 hawthorn (*Crataegus* sp.) plants was sold for hedging and, in 1335, 2000 hazel (*Corylus avellana*) trees were sold for a new woodland. Woodlands were also planted using acorns and hazelnuts, as at Alton Priors, Wiltshire, in 1260, where a 12–20 acre wood was sown and enclosed with a ditch and hedge (Harvey 1981). Numerous woodland plantings were recorded during the ensuing 50 years. While the aesthetic value of woodland was appreciated at this time, especially in parks (which attracted considerable status and prestige), the combined use of oak (*Quercus* sp.) and hazel (*Corylus avellana*) suggests that these woodlands were primarily economic investments. By implication, existing woodlands were either becoming impoverished or were unable to keep up with increasing demand for woodland products, or landowners were realizing the economic potential of woodland as a cash crop.

The increasing quest for fuel in the 13th century is reflected in the enhanced value of woodland. In some areas the value of woodland products rose faster than agricultural products (Witney 1990). By the 16th century woodland production was so depleted in some parts of lowland Britain that local shortages of wood were causing hardship (Cleere and Crossley 1995). Where several industries co-existed in the same region, woodland resources were sometimes stretched beyond capacity, and small-scale or less influential ventures were squeezed out.

The fuel market

Revenue from the fuel trade was not insignificant and, although little is known about Saxon and earlier periods, contemporary documents detail fuel supplies for medieval London (Galloway *et al*.1996). By the 12th century, London's fuel consumption for both domestic and industrial purposes was beginning to outpace supply, despite the importation of sea-coal from the north (probably from Newcastle-upon-Tyne) from about 1180. By 1200 commerce in firewood, charcoal and timber was well established, with centres based on London wharves and docksides. Firewood was supplied from woodlands in the surrounding counties, particularly from the Chilterns and the Weald. Following fuel shortages in the late 13th century the price of firewood soared, and by the 14th century fuel production was specialized and regional, with a significant acreage within a 19 mile radius of the capital dedicated to the provision of fuel. The high value of firewood also encouraged the illegal felling of wood, particularly where quick access to waterways allowed easy transport to market (Birrell 1969; Witney 1990). Charcoal,

including small coals made from brushwood, was brought into the city by packhorse and cart from areas as distant as 26 miles (Armstrong 1978).

Rather surprisingly, there was also a flourishing trade in the export of fuel to the Continent during the 14th century, mainly from the Weald via the Sussex and Kentish ports (Pelham 1928). By the mid-16th century, fuel shortages throughout the country triggered legislation (1541) to conserve woodlands (Straker 1931), although the Weald, which was exempt from these restrictions, still enjoyed a thriving overseas trade from Rye, Winchelsea and Hastings mostly to Picardy for armaments production and domestic fuel (Straker 1931; Galloway *et al*. 1996). Further restrictions were introduced in 1558/9, although once again, parts of the Weald, which supplied armaments, were exempted. During the following decades more legislation was enacted (Straker 1931).

Similar data for the fuel trade are almost certainly available for other regions and an overview of fuel markets throughout the country would prove invaluable when studying local fuel-based industries.

Interestingly, the English leather industry, which during the 17th and 19th centuries was second only to the textile trade in commercial value, was almost totally dependent on the fuel and timber industry for the provision of tanbark (Clarkson 1974). 90% of all leather was tanned with oak bark and the best quality bark was stripped from 20 year-old coppice wood in the spring and early summer. Bark production could never be viable in its own right because the removal of bark killed the trees. But when carried out in conjunction with charcoal-making it proved ideal as the inclusion of bark in clamps could be problematical and bark charcoal was of little value (Percy 1869; Edlin 1949). The price of bark varied according to its quality and accessibility. Transport was relatively easy, particularly on waterways, but, in good years, could represent up to half of the total value of the bark, timber and cordwood. English bark was exported to Ireland in the late 17th century, but by the 1790s, the demand for bark in England stood at 80,000 tons per year, of which 9600 tons were imported from Europe to meet the shortfall in home production (Clarkson 1974).

ENVIRONMENTAL IMPLICATIONS

There can be no doubt that fuel-based industries had a profound effect on the woodland composition of lowland Britain, particularly from the medieval period until the 17th and 18th centuries, when rival workshops, industries and crafts competed for local fuel supplies (Straker 1931; Evans 1992; Cleere and Crossley 1995). Just how detrimental this was to woodland is open to conjecture. Trees have a natural tenacity and, unless subjected to undue stress, most have the ability to regenerate if felled before the onset of senescence (D. Patch pers comm, Forestry Commission), although not all species coppice vigorously, e.g. birch (*Betula* sp.), beech (*Fagus sylvatica*), cherry (*Prunus avium*) and some poplars (*Populus* spp.) (Evans 1992). Repeated felling by regular coppicing and pollarding can, in fact, extend the natural life of many species by several hundred years (Rackham 1990). In this respect the industrial exploitation of woodland could be regarded as beneficial through the promotion of long-term woodland maintenance – provided that local by-laws and tenancy agreements for woodland protection were observed. Woodland was essential for the socio-economic stability of a settlement (supplying domestic and industrial fuel, building materials, tanbark, fruits, ashes, wood tars and pitch, rope-bark, fodder, pannage, and employment), and formed an integral part of the Saxon and medieval manorial and estate systems (Birrell 1969; Hooke 1989; Pretty 1990; Peterken 1992). Agrarian transgression, on the other hand, was probably a more serious threat through the (often) permanent eradication of woodland, particularly between the 12th and 14th centuries when the population virtually doubled in some regions, e.g. Wiltshire (Critall 1959).

Agricultural clearance

Early settlements tended to be concentrated on the lighter soils and chalklands, and environmental evidence from sites in southern England suggests that major woodland clearance occurred in the Bronze Age in parts of Wessex (Scaife 1987), the Hampshire/Wessex region (Waton 1982), the Isle of Wight (Scaife 1984), Kent (Kerney *et al* 1964) and Sussex (Thorley 1981). In the Thames Valley, woodland was exceedingly sparse by the late Bronze Age and, by the Iron Age, some parts of the South Midlands had been disafforested (Robinson and Wilson 1987). In many areas woodlands and coppices only survived or were retained where land was unsuited to agriculture, and in lowland England this usually referred to slopes and poorly drained "upland" plateaux (Peterken 1992). Rackham (1994) estimates that by 300 BC half the land in England had ceased to be woodland, although the Romans described England as flat and densely wooded (Hanson 1978). Conflicting evidence for the regeneration of woodland after the Roman period could imply regional differences, and while woodland appears to have been re-established around Stafford, the landscape probably remained open in East Anglia and around London (Moffet 1994; Tyers *et al.* 1994; Rackham 1994; Murphy 1994). Post-Roman restoration of woodland is also indicated by the remains of Celtic field systems in mid-Anglo-Saxon woods in Hampshire and Wiltshire (Hooke 1989).

Increasingly throughout the Saxon period land was assarted, often reducing wooded areas to strips along field boundaries (Hooke 1989; Rackham 1994). While Domesday records indicate that some villages, sometimes even clusters of villages, were without woodland (Rackham 1994), it is apparent that some woodland escaped inclusion in the survey (especially that attached to distant manors or estates) (Hooke 1989). And where woodland was recorded, the size was often calculated in swine-rent (the number of pigs the wood could support), which could imply variable factors and thus acreage (Hooke 1989). Rackham (1994) estimates that, at this time, woodland made up less than 15% of the total land area, and that it was reduced to 10% by the mid 14th century. It is difficult to imagine how settlements survived without reasonable access to wood, timber or fuel. Transporting such materials was difficult and costly, but, nonetheless, medieval records show that owners of far-flung woods often went in for long-distance transport rather than buy local supplies (Rackham 1982). Overall, however, most settlements had access to some type of woodland, be it woodland proper, marginal strips along riverbanks and trackways, or hedgerows (Rackham 1982; Peterken 1992). The largest tracts of woodland were concentrated in the south east of England, although some sizeable afforested areas also survived in the south west, the Midlands and locally elsewhere (Rackham 1982; Marren 1992).

Industrial fuels

Metal-working, particularly iron smelting and smithing, was probably the greatest long-term consumer of woodland, not least through its use of charcoal. Woodlands were particularly hard-pressed in areas where iron-furnaces competed for fuels with potteries, brick-works, and glass-making. It was in the interest of both woodsmen and artisans that local woodland could sustain a supply of fuel indefinitely. With careful maintenance this usually appears to have been achieved, providing the density of industrial activity, stock grazing (in regenerating coppices) and illegal wood poaching were controlled. Medieval records indicate that this should have been common practice, although undoubtedly this was not always the case, as testified by the permanent loss of parts of Ashdown Forest and St. Leonards Forest (Sussex) by the end of the 16th century (Cleere and Crossley 1995). The latter correlates with a recent study by Smout (1999) of the western Scottish Highlands, where 18th century iron-masters converted oak woodland into managed, fenced coppice, thereby preserving the wooded areas (albeit modified in character). But after the decline of the industry in the next century, the woods were abandoned, and the fences collapsed allowing the destruction of the woods through sheep-grazing. Permanent loss also occurred in other parts of Britain where exposure and soil erosion, combined with grazing, suppressed the regeneration of coppiced or felled woodland, as seen in areas of Dartmoor. In theory, the provision of fuel should have been less detrimental to woodland than some other aspects of industrial practice, such as mining or quarrying for clay and minerals within woods, or the dumping of huge quantities of slag, which must, inevitably, have caused aerial damage and root disturbance to coppice stools and standard trees.

Recent attempts to reconstruct ancient smelting

practices and to assess the quantity of the charcoal used have produced varied results. For example, to produce 1kg of iron, Crew's (1991) experimental work to replicate fully smithed prehistoric bar iron required about 100kg of charcoal, whereas with medieval reconstructions, Wynne and Tylecote (1958) estimated that only 16kg of charcoal was used (although the latter was apparently unsmithed). Hammersley (1973) also gives estimates of charcoal consumption in the indirect making of iron.

Converting fuel consumption into acreage of woodland is difficult, since local factors affect the calculations (Crockford and Savill 1991) and, for ancient sites, these are unknown. They include the production rate of iron, the species and maturity of wood used, the regeneration and growth rates of coppiced/ pollarded trees, the density of woodland, edaphic and climatic conditions, restrictions on cutting certain types of wood or timber attached to leases or tenancies, and the demand for fuel and timber from other local industries and for domestic hearths.

Estimates by Cleere and Crossley (1995), based on the iron industry in the Weald, indicate that a blast furnace could produce about 250 tons of pig iron and required about 2500 acres of coppice, with a further 15–1600 acres for its forge. This acreage could be found within a 3-mile radius if a quarter of the land was under coppice.

In essence, fuel was the make or break ingredient for a broad range of industries. Narrow roundwood from coppice growth provided a quick means of obtaining high temperatures but, where these needed to be sustained for long periods, larger wood could be used. When charcoal fuel was employed, e.g. for iron-smelting and smithing, the fuel was probably fragmented into smaller pieces prior to use in the kiln or forge (Crewe 1991), and while these may have been relatively uniform in size, the carbon content would have varied with the species: oak (*Quercus* sp.) being considerably denser than, for example, birch (*Betula* sp.), would have produced a longer-lasting fuel. Evidence from archaeological (Table 1) and documentary sources (Galloway *et al* 1996) (the latter mostly from the medieval period and later) suggests that oak was extremely important as an industrial fuel; the frequency of oak heartwood in fuel residues suggests either the use of coppice poles or pollards from long-rotation systems of management (probably exceeding 15 years) or cordwood from timber trees.

The environment

The National Vegetation Classification project recognizes 25 tree and shrub communities that conform to type and species on a regional scale; these refer particularly to the geologically distinct regions of the warmer dryer south-east lowland and the cooler, wetter north-west upland (Rodwell 1991). For example, at a generic level, oak (*Quercus* sp.) and birch (*Betula* sp.) are common to both regions, but in the north and west of the country these are represented by *Quercus petraea* and *Betula pubescens*. In the south and east, *Q. robur* and *B. pendula* are more frequent. On a local scale, however, the type and distribution of arboreal members of woodland are determined by ecological factors. In lowland Britain, for example, oak (*Quercus* sp.) and hazel (*Corylus avellana*) tolerate a wide range of conditions and are widespread throughout, in contrast to lime *Tilia* sp. and hornbeam (*Carpinus* sp.), which tend to grow as pure stands, often contained within woodland compartments (Rackham 1990; Rodwell 1991). It could be argued that the high frequency of oak in archaeological fuel residues merely reflects its widespread distribution. This may be so, but the apparent selection of oak fuel (particularly for metal-working), in preference to faster-growing species, suggests that the calorific properties of oak (*Quercus* sp.) were recognized and exploited (as indeed, they are today for domestic firewood).

Archaeological evidence from charcoal residues and documentary evidence particularly from the bark trade (Clarkson 1974) suggest that coppiced oak was widely available. By implication, coppiced woodlands included a high proportion of oak (*Quercus* sp.). At the present time, the derelict remains of ancient coppices persist in various parts of England but are particularly noticeable in the south. Many of these were working woodlands until the mid-19th or 20th centuries and demonstrate that in recent centuries the main coppice species included hazel *(Corylus avellana)*, alder (*Alnus glutinosa*), ash (*Fraxinus excelsior*) and birch (*Betula* sp.), sycamore (*Acer pseudoplatanus*) and, sometimes, lime (*Tilia cordata*) and hornbeam (*Carpinus betulus*) depending on the region, with elm (*Ulmus glabra*) and holly (*Ilex aquifolium*) less frequent. Oak (*Quercus* sp.) occurs as coppice comparatively rarely in these old woods but almost always as the dominant standard and, frequently, as hedgerow trees and boundary markers. It is interesting to parallel this apparent decline in oak coppices with possible changes in market forces, perhaps following the more general use of coal by the iron industry from the 18th century, and the increased demand for larger oak timbers for construction. The reduced demand for charcoal presumably had severe knock-on effects for the tanbark industry. In some areas, the recent conversion of stored coppice to standard trees or its return to short-term coppice stools demonstrates the versatility of woodland. Similar policies to convert oak coppice to standards may have been undertaken in past centuries, thereby promoting faster-growing coppice species to provide faggots for domestic fuel, and rods and poles for other purposes, as well as oak hurdles, hoppoles and numerous other items.

Some industries were short-lived events initiated on-site to fulfil a particular requirement, e.g. bricks or lime or, alternatively, operated as fair-weather activities on a seasonal basis, e.g. salterns. In an area where raw materials and fuel were plentiful, industrial occupations often endured for decades or longer (Hammersley 1973). The more ephemeral industries probably left scant evidence on the landscape, while the remains or effects of long-term operations are still visible today. An outstanding example of the latter can be seen at Horner Wood on Exmoor, where the woodland supports derelict and ancient coppice and pollards which once fuelled a water-powered iron-smithing complex in the late 16th – 17th centuries. Saw pits, numerous charcoal platforms, trackways for transporting fuel and wares, and the remains of the mill are preserved as surface features at the site, which has remained undeveloped since the closure of the mill.

Many present day woodlands owe their character and diversity to past regimes of woodmanship. Woodlands were often operated commercially and tailored to accommodate specific needs, particularly those of industry, and by the Saxon and medieval periods woodland management was controlled by the terms of manorial tenancy agreements (Rackham 1982; Galloway *et al.* 1996; Berryman 1998). Fourteenth century manorial records for parts of Middlesex, Surrey, Essex, Buckinghamshire, Hertfordshire and Kent indicate widespread specialism in faggot production to supply London with fuel (Galloway *et al.* 1996) and, similarly, in the Weald, woods were compartmentalized to provide large wood (billets) for medieval glass-houses and underwood (faggots) for iron-workers (Crossley 1994).

CONCLUSION

This paper has considered the character and requirements of the major wood-fuelled industries in lowland Britain until coal became an economic and preferable alternative in the 18th century. Since Roman times (and possibly earlier) woodland frequently formed an integral element of the local community, providing vital resources for numerous aspects of daily life. From the Late Saxon period the production of fuel was a major woodland activity, particularly around industrial centres. The dynamics of wood-fuelled industries appear to have been key factors in the preservation and management of many woodland regions, thereby ensuring their long-term survival. The extent of woodland cover varied from region to region, and period to period, usually restricted to poorer soils unsuited to arable farming or within hunting forests and parks. The early realization of the value and importance of woodland assets is reflected in the enforcement of by-laws from at least the 7th century, although illegal sales of products and assarting of land continued and appear to have been common-place.

Sites of early iron-workings in areas now devoid of woodland suggest either that land was considered more valuable for arable use, or that mismanagement or grazing by domestic stock eventually destroyed woodland. Sometimes woodlands may have become uneconomic to manage and were, perhaps, abandoned to livestock.

Supplies of fuel were usually sustained through the use of coppice wood, pollards or cordwood. Evidence from archaeological contexts suggests that while industrial fuels often included a wide range of woodland taxa, oak (*Quercus* sp.) frequently appears to have been the preferred species, particularly for the iron industry. This evidence, however, is derived from a relatively narrow range of data representing almost two millennia. The potential to establish technical aspects of firing and other industrial processes through the examination of fuel residues has, to a large extent, remained unrecognized in recent years, and opportunities have undoubtedly been lost. This situation must be reversed if we are to establish a workable database and obtain a better understanding of the provision and use of industrial fuels.

Acknowledgements
I am grateful to Jon Hather for comments and helpful suggestions on the text of this paper.

References

Agricola, G. 1556. *De Re Metallica*, Basle, trans. S.E. Winbolt, 1933, in Wealden Glass, Hove.
Allason-Jones, L. 1989. *Women in Roman Britain*, British Museum Press
Armstrong, L. 1978. *Woodcolliers and Charcoal Burning.* Horsham: Coach Publishing House Ltd. and The Weald and Downland Open Air Museum.
Aston, M. 1988. *Medieval fish, fisheries and fishponds in England Part II*, BAR British Series 182 (ii).
Berryman, R. D. 1998. *Use of the woodlands in the Late Anglo-Saxon Period.* (BAR British Series 271, 1–59). Oxford: British Archaeological Reports.
Birrell, J. 1969. Peasant craftsmen in the medieval forest, *Agricultural History Review*, 17 (2), 91–107.
Bradley, R. 1992. Roman salt production in Chichester Harbour: rescue operations at Chidham, West Sussex, *Britannia*, 23, 27–44.
Brown, C.P. 1995. Castle Farm, Torksey. Archaeological Excavation Report by Preconstruct Archaeology (Lincoln). Unpublished but available from SMR.
Budd, P., Gale, D., Pollard, A.M., Thomas, R.G. and Williams, P.A. 1992. The earliest development of metallurgy in the British Isles, *Antiquity*, 66, 677–86.
Campbell, M. 1991. Gold, silver and precious stones, pp. 107–166, in Blair, J. and Ramsay, M. (eds), *English Medieval Industries.* London: The Hambledon Press.
Cato, M. *On Agriculture* (trans. Hooper, W.D., revised by Ash, H.B. 1960), Heinemann: Loeb Classical Library.
Charleston, R.J. 1991. Vessel glass, pp. 237–264, in Blair, J. and Ramsay, M. (eds), *English Medieval Industries.* London: The Hambledon Press.
Cherry, J. 1991. Pottery and tile, pp. 189–210, in Blair, J. and Ramsay, M. (eds), *English Medieval Industries.* London: The Hambledon Press.
Clarkson, L.A., 1974. The English bark trade, 1660–1830, *Agricultural History Review*, 22 (2), 136–152.
Cleere, H. and Crossley, D. 1995. *The Iron Industry of the Weald.* Merton Priory Press.
Clifton-Taylor, A. 1972. *The Pattern of English Building.* London: Faber and Faber Ltd.
Coles, J.M. and Orme, B.J. 1982. *Prehistory of the Somerset Levels.* Somerset Levels Project.

Cool, H.E.M., Jackson, C.M. and Monaghan, J. 1999. Glass-making and the Sixth Legion at York, *Britannia*, **30**, 147–161.

Cowgill, J. 1997. *The slag archive report for Coslany Street, Norwich*, Archive report in the Norfolk Museum Service Archives, SMR reference: 26435N.

Cowgill, J. (a) *An Iron Age and Romano-British smelting site at Creeton Quarry, Lincolnshire and a survey of local iron smelting sites.* In preparation.

Crew, P. 1991. The experimental production of prehistoric bar iron. *Journal of Historical Metallurgy Society*, **25** (1), 21–36.

Critall, E. (ed.) 1959. *The Victoria History of the Counties of England. History of Wiltshire*, **4**.

Crockford, K.J. and Savill, P.S. 1991 Preliminary yield tables for oak coppice, *Forestry*, 64, **1**, 29–49.

Crone, A. 1987 Tree ring studies and the reconstruction of woodland management practices in antiquity, pp. 327–336, in Jacoby. G.C. Jr. and Hornbech. J.W. (eds) *Proceedings of the International Synposium on Ecological Aspects of Tree Ring Analysis*, U.S. Department of Energy, Publication CONF-8608144.

Crossley, D. 1993. Whitecoal and charcoal in the woodlands of north Derbyshire and the Sheffield area, p. 67, in Beswick, P. and Rotherham, I.D. (eds), *Ancient woodlands, their archaeology and ecology*, Landscape Archaeology and Ecology, **1**.

Crossley, D. 1994. The Wealden glass industry re-visited, *Industrial Archaeology Review*, **17** (1), 64–74.

Crossley, D.W. 1967. *Glassmaking in Bagot's Park, Staffordshire, in the sixteenth century*, Post-Medieval Archaeology, **1**, 63.

Crossley, D.W. and Aberg, F.A. 16th century glassmaking in Yorkshire: excavations at furnaces at Hutton and Rosedale, North Riding, *Post-Medieval Archaeology*, **6**, 102–159.

Day, S.P. 1993. The origins of medieval woodland, pp. 12–25, in Beswick, P. and Rotherham, I.D. (eds), *Ancient woodlands, their archaeology and ecology*, Landscape Archaeology and Ecology, **1**.

Edlin. H.L. 1949. *Woodland crafts in Britain*. London: Batsford.

Ehrenreich, M. 1985. Trade, technology and the ironworking community in the Iron Age of Southern Britain, *(BAR No 144)*. *Oxford: British Archaeological Reports.*

Evans, J. 1992. Coppice Forestry – an overview, pp. 18–27, in Buckley, G.P. (ed) *Ecology and management of coppice woodlands*. London: Chapman and Hall.

Falkner, H. 1907. Discovery of ancient pottery near Farnham in 1906, *Surrey Archaeological Collections*, **20**, 228–32.

Figueiral, I. 1992. The fuels, pp. 159–208, in Fulford, M.G. and Allen, J.R.L. (eds), Iron-making at the Chesters Villa, Woolaston, Gloucestershire: Survey and Excavation 1987–9. *Britannia* 23.

Fulford, M. 1977. The location of Roman-British pottery kilns: institutional trade and the market, pp. 301–316, in Dore, J. and Greene, K. *Roman pottery studies in Britain and beyond*, (BAR Supplementary Series No 30). Oxford: British Archaeological Reports.

Gale, R. 1991–3. Identification of charcoal, microfiche M2: E13–F9, in Lobb, S.J. and Morris, E.L., Investigation of Bronze Age and Iron Age features at Riseley Farm, Swallowfield, *Berkshire Archaeological Journal*, **74**.

Gale, R. 1995. Charcoal, p. 158, in Ratcliffe, J., Duckpool, Morwenstow: A Romano-British and early medieval industrial site and harbour. *Cornish Archaeology*, **34**, 158 (80–171).

Gale, R. 1999. Charcoal, pp. 372–384, in Fitzpatrick A., Butterworth, C.A. and Grove, J., *Prehistoric and Roman sites in east Devon: the A30 Honiton to Exeter Improvement DBFO Scheme, 1996–9, Vol. 2: Romano-British Sites*, Wessex Archaeology Report Number 16 (2).

Gale, R. 2000. (a) The fuels, p. 51–54, in Barber, A. and Holbrook, N., *A Roman iron-smelting site at Blakeney, Gloucestershire: Excavations at Millend Lane 1997*, Transactions of the Bristol and Gloucestershire Archaeological Society, **118**, 33–60.

Gale, R. 2000. (b) Charcoal, p. 231–233, in Bates, S., *Excavations at Quidney Farm, Saham Tony, Norfolk, 1995*, Britannia, **31**, 201–238.

Gale, R. 2000. (c) Charcoal from Enborne Street, pp. 73–74, in Birbeck, V., *Archaeological investigations on the A34 Newbury Bypass, Berkshire/ Hampshire*, Wessex Archaeology on behalf of Highways Agency.

Gale, R. 2000. (d) Charcoal, pp. 30–36, in Cooke, N., *Excavations on a late medieval iron-working site at London Road, Crawley, West Sussex, 1997*. Wessex Archaeology Report Number 44200C.

Gale, R. 2000. (e) The identification of charcoal from Bridgewater 1963 excavation, p. 151–156 and 181, in Jackson, R. *The Roman settlement of Ariconium, near Western-under-Penyard, Herefordshire: an assessment and synthesis of the evidence*, Archaeological Service Worcestershire County Council Report 833.

Gale, R. Charcoal, in Bates, S., The excavation of Romano-British pottery kilns at Ellingham, Postwick and Two Mile Bottom, Norfolk, 1995–6, *East Anglian Archaeological Occasional Paper*. Forthcoming.

Gale, R. Charcoal, in Birbeck, V. Excavations at Watchfield, Shrivenham, Oxfordshire, 1998, *Oxoniensia*. Forthcoming, 2001.

Gale, R. Charcoal, in Butler, C. and Lyne, M. *A Roman pottery production site at Wickham Barn, Chiltingham, East Sussex.* London: British Archaeological Report. Forthcoming.

Gale, R. Charcoal, in Cooke, N. Excavations on the site of Crawley Leisure Park, Crawley, West Sussex, 1997, *Sussex Archaeological Collections*. Forthcoming.

Gale, R. The fuel, in Cowgill, J., McDonnell, G. and Mills, J.M., 'Iron-working Technology' in Ashwin, T., and Tester, A. *Excavations at Scole 1993–4*, East Anglian Archaeology. Forthcoming.

Gale, R. Charcoal, in Lovell, J., *Excavations at Horticultural Research International, Littlehampton, 1997*, Sussex Archaeological Collections, Forthcoming.

Gale, R. Charcoal from a Roman pottery production site, in Lyne, M.A.B. *Redcliffe Farm, Arne, near Wareham, Dorset*. In preparation.

Gale, R. Charcoal, in McDonald, T., *Excavations at Welwyn Hall, Old Welwyn, Hertfordshire*. Forthcoming.

Gale, R. Charcoal, in McKinley, J.I., *Excavations of a Romano-British road site at Brockley Hill, Stanmore, Middlesex*. London and Middlesex Archaeological Society. Forthcoming.

Gale, R. Charcoal, in Shepherd, E., *Excavations at Norwich Castle 1987–98*, E. Anglian Archaeology. In preparation.

Gale, R. and Cutler, D. 2000. *Plants in Archaeology*, Westbury Academic and Scientific Publishing in association with The Royal Botanic Gardens, Kew.

Galloway, J.A., Keene, D. and Murphy, M. 1996. Fuelling the City: production and distribution of firewood and fuel in London's region, 1290–1400, *Economic History Review*, **69** (3), 447–472.

Geddes, J. 1991. Iron, pp. 167–188, in Blair, J. and Ramsay, M. (eds), *English Medieval Industries*. London: The Hambledon Press.

Hagen, A. 1994. *A Handbook of Anglo-Saxon Food, Processing and Consumption*. Chippenham: Anglo-Saxon Books.

Hagen, A. 1995. *A Second Handbook of Anglo-Saxon Food and Drink, Production and Distribution*. Chippenham: Anglo-Saxon Books.

Hammersley, G. 1973 The charcoal iron industry and its fuel 1540–1750, *The Economic History Review*, second series, XXVI (4), 593–613.

Hammond, P.W, 1995. *Food and feast in medieval England*. Stroud: Sutton Publishing Ltd.

Hammond, T. 1992. The Great Orme Mine, *Current Archaeology,* **11** (10), 404–409.

Hanson, W.S. 1978. The organisation of Roman military timber-supply, *Britannia,* **9**, 293–305.

Harden, D.B. 1961. Domestic window glass: Roman, Saxon and medieval, pp. 39–63, in Jope, E.M. (ed.), *Studies in building history.* Oxford: University Press.

Hart, C. 1993. The ancient woodland of Eccleshall Woods, Sheffield, pp. 49–66, in Beswick, P. and Rotherham, I.D. (eds), *Ancient woodlands, their archaeology and ecology,* Landscape Archaeology and Ecology, **1.**

Harvey, J. 1981. *Medieval gardens.* London: Batsford.

Henderson, J. 1988. Glass production and Bronze Age Europe, *Antiquity,* **62 (236),** 435–51.

Henderson, J. and Ivens, R. 1992. Dunmisk and glass-making in early Christian Ireland, *Antiquity,* **66**, 52–64.

Hodges, H. 1964. *Artifacts.* London: John Baker.

Homer, R.F. 1991. Tin, lead and pewter, pp. 57–80, in Blair, J. and Ramsay, M. (eds), *English Medieval Industries.* London: The Hambledon Press.

Hooke, D. 1989. Pre-conquest woodland: its distribution and usage, *Agricultural History Review,* **37** (2), 113–129.

Horne, L. 1982. Fuel for the metal worker, *Expedition,* University of Pensylvannia Museum, **25** Fall, 6–13.

Huntley, J.P. 1981. Woodland management studies from Carlisle, *Ancient Monuments Laboratory Report* 119/87.

Hurst, D. 1991. Major Saxon discoveries at Droitwich – excavations at the Upwich brine pit, *Current Archaeology No. 126,* **11** (6), pp. 252–255.

Jackson, D.A. 1973. A Roman lime kiln at Weekley, Northants. *Britannia,* **4**, 128–140.

James, N.D.G. 1955. *The Forester's Companion,* Oxford.

Jones, M. 1993. South Yorkshire's ancient woodland: the historical evidence, pp. 26–48, in Beswick, P. and Rotherham, I.D. (eds), *Ancient woodlands, their archaeology and ecology,* Landscape Archaeology and Ecology, **1.**

Kenyon, G.H. 1967. *Glass industry of the Weald.* Leicester.

Kerney, M.P., Brown, E.H. and Chandler, T.J. 1964. The late-glacial and post-glacial history of the chalk escarpment near Brook, Kent, *Philosophical Transactions of the Royal Society London B,* **248**, 135–204.

Lane, T. 1993. The Fenland project in Lincolnshire: recent evaluations, *Fenland Research,* **8**, 40–42.

Leah, M. 1992. The Fenland Management Project, Norfolk, *Fenland Research,* **7**, 49–59.

Leyell, A.H. 1923. Charcoal identifications, p. 31, in Jack, G.H., *Excavations on the site of Ariconium, a Romano-British smelting town in the parish of Western-under-Penyard, South Herefordshire,* Woolthorpe Club 31.

Lyne, M.A.B. and Jefferies, R.S. 1979. *The Alice Holt/ Farnham Roman pottery industry,* (Research Report 30). London: Council for British Archaeology.

Marren, P. 1992. *The wild woods: a regional guide to Britain's ancient woodland.* David and Charles.

Moffett, L. 1994. Charred cereals from some oven/kilns in Late Saxon Stafford and the botanical evidence for the pre-burh economy, pp. 55–64, in Rackham, J., *Environment and economy in Anglo-Saxon England* (Research Report 89). London: Council for British Archaeology.

Mitchell, A. 1974. *A Field Guide to the Trees of Britain and Northern Europe,* London: Collins.

Moore, N.J. 1991. Brick, pp. 211–236, in Blair, J. and Ramsay, M. (eds), *English Medieval Industries.* London: The Hambledon Press.

Morgan, R.A. 1982. Tree-ring studies in the Somerset Levels; the examination of modern hazel growth in Bradfield Woods,

Suffolk, and its implications for the prehistoric data, *Ancient Monuments Laboratory Report* 3839.

Murphy, P. 1994. The Anglo-Saxon landscape and rural economy: some results from sites in East Anglia and Essex, pp. 23–39, in Rackham, J., *Environment and economy in Anglo-Saxon England* (Research Report 89). London: Council for British Archaeology.

Neri, A. 1612 *L'Arte Vetraria,* Florence (Trans. C. Merrett, 1662, The Art of Glass) Newman, P. 1998. *The Dartmoor Tin Industry: A Field Guide.* Chercombe Press.

O'Brien, W. 1996. *Bronze Age copper mining in Britain and Ireland.* Shire Publications Ltd.

Pelham, R.A. 1928. Timber exports from the Weald during the fourteenth century, *Sussex Archaeological Collections,* **69**, 171–182.

Percy, J. 1864. *Metallurgy.* London: John Murray.

Peterken, G.F. 1992. Coppices in the lowland landscape, pp. 3–17, in G.P. Buckley (ed.), *Ecology and Management of Coppice Woodlands.* London: Chapman and Hall.

Peterken, G.F. 1996. *Natural Woodland – ecology and conservation in northern temperate regions,* Cambridge University Press.

Porter, V. 1990. *Small woods and hedgerows.* Pelham Books.

Pretty, J.N. 1990. Sustainable agriculture in the Middle Ages: the English Manor, *Agricultural History Review,* **38** (1), 1–19.

Rackham, D.J., Gale, R., Holden, T., Izard, K. and Locker, A. (September 1998). Parnell Road and Lefevre Walk, Bow, London, PRB95 and LEK95, Environmental Archaeology Report. Report for Preconstruct Archeaology (London).

Rackham, D.J., Giorgi, J.A. and Gale, R. (March 1999) Hatton to Silk Willoughby Gas Pipeline, HWP98 Environmental Archaeology Report, in *Hatton to Silk Willoughby 1050 mm Gas Pipeline. Archaeological evaluation, excavation and watching brief,* **2.** Network Archaeology Ltd. Report No. 143, August 1999.

Rackham, O. 1977. Neolithic woodland management in the Somerset levels: Garvin's, Walton Heath, and Rowland's Tracks, *Somerset Levels Papers* **3**, 65–71.

Rackham, O. 1979. Neolithic woodland management in the Somerset Levels: Sweet Track 1, *Somerset Levels Papers,* **5**, 59–61.

Rackham, O. 1982. The growing and transport of timber and underwood, pp. 199–218, in McGrail, S. (ed.), *Woodworking techniques before 1500* (BAR International Series 129). Oxford: British Archaeological Reports.

Rackham, O. 1990. *Trees and Woodland in the British Landscape,* Dent.

Rackham, O. 1994. Trees and woods in Anglo-Saxon England: the documentary evidence, pp. 7–11, in Rackham, J., *Environment and economy in Anglo-Saxon England* (Research Report 89). London: Council for British Archaeology.

Robinson, M. and Wilson, B. 1987. A survey of environmental archaeology in the South Midlands, pp. 16–100, in Keeley, H.C.M., *Environmental Archaeology: a regional review,* Historic Buildings and Monuments Commission for England, Occasional Paper No.1.

Rodwell, J.S. (ed.) 1991. *British Plant Communities, Vol 1 Woodlands and Scrub,* Cambridge University Press.

Scaife, R.G. 1984 Bronze Age soil pollen data from Gallibury Down (formerly Newbarn Down), Isle of Wight, *Ancient Monument Laboratory Report,* 4240

Scaife, R.G. 1987 A review of later Quaternary plant macrofossil research in Southern England: with special reference to environmental archaeological evidence, pp. 125–203, in Keeley, H.C.M., *Environmental Archaeology: a regional review,* Historic Buildings and Monuments Commission for England, Occasional Paper No.1.

Smout, C. 1999 The myth of Caledon, *Tree News*, Autumn, 14–17.

Squires, A. and Jeeves, M. 1994 *Leicestershire and Rutland Woodlands Past and Present*. Leicestershire: Kairos Press.

Straker, E. 1931. *Wealden Iron* (1969 edition). David and Charles.

Theophilus 1963. *On divers arts. The treatise of Theophilus*, trans. J.G. Hawthorne and C.S. Smith, The University of Chicago.

Thorley, A. 1981 Pollen analytical evidence relating to the vegetation history of the chalk, *Journal of Biogeography*, **8**, 93–106

Tillman, D.A. and Rossi, J.A. and Kitto, W.D. 1981. *Wood combustion*, Academic Press.

Toft, L.A. 1988. Limeburning on the Gower Peninsular's limestone belt, *Industrial Archaeology Review*, **11** (1), 75–92.

Tusser, T. 1984. *Five hundred points of good husbandry*. Oxford: University Press.

Tutin, T.G., Heywood, V.H. *et al.* 1964–80 *Flora Europaea*, 1–5, Cambridge University Press.

Tyers, I., Hillam, J. and Groves. C. 1994. Trees and woodland in the Saxon period: the dendrochronological evidence, pp. 12–22, in Rackham, J., *Environment and economy in Anglo-Saxon England* (Research Report 89). London: Council for British Archaeology.

Walton, P. 1991. Textiles, pp. 319–354, in Blair, J. and Ramsay, M. (eds), *English Medieval Industries*. London: The Hambledon Press.

Waton, P.V. 1982. Mans's impact on the chalkland: some new pollen evidence, pp. 75–91, in Bell, M. and Limbrey, S. (eds) *Archaeological aspects of woodland ecology* (International Series 146). London: British Archaeological Reports.

Webster, A.D. 1919. *Firewoods: their production and fuel values*. London: T. Fisher Unwin Ltd.

Whitelock, D. 1955. *English Historical Documents, vol. 1, c.500–1042*. Eyre and Spottiswoode.

Whittick, G.C. 1982. The earliest Roman lead-mining on Mendip and in north Wales: a reappraisal, *Britannia*, 13, 113–126.

Williams, R. 1989 *Limekilns and limeburning*, Shire Books.

Wilson, P.R. (ed.) 1989. Crambeck Roman pottery industry, *The Roman Antiquities* Section, Yorkshire Archaeological Society.

Winbolt, S.E. 1933. *Wealden Glass*, Hove.

Witney, K.P. 1990. The woodland economy of Kent, 1066–1348, *Agricultual History Review*, **38**, (1), 20–39.

Woodiwiss, S. (ed.) 1992. Iron Age and Roman salt production and the medieval town of Droitwich. Excavations at the Old Bowling Green and Friar Street. *Council of British Archaeology Research report*, **81**.

Wynne, E.W. and Tylecote, R.F. 1958. An experimental investigation into primitive iron smelting techniques. *Journal of Iron and Steel Industry*, **190**, 339–48.

Young, C.J. 1977. *The Roman pottery industry of the Oxford region*, (BAR No 43). Oxford: British Archaeological Reports.

6. The iron production industry and its extensive demand upon woodland resources: a case study from Creeton Quarry, Lincolnshire

Jane Cowgill

This paper is primarily concerned with the main resource required by iron smelters (woodland), rather than the implications of the output. The charcoal recovered from an iron smelting site at Creeton Quarry, South Lincolnshire, forms the basis of this study The pottery and radiocarbon dates suggest that the site lasted for some duration, perhaps 100 years or more. The charcoal identifications show that oak, some from trees considerably older than 45 years, dominated the assemblage. A coppice management system is proposed after perhaps the initial felling of woodland. The quantity of iron produced at the site is estimated and from this the scale of the woodland resource exploited is suggested. This would have influenced how the industry was organised in South Lincolnshire, where a cluster of iron smelting sites is known to exist. The conclusions drawn in this paper could be tested or developed by palaeo-environmental analysis of local deposits, primarily by pollen analysis.

Keywords: Romano-British, iron, smelting, coppicing, charcoal, Lincolnshire.

INTRODUCTION

Evidence for the fuel used by the metal-production industries is not only an important part of understanding the technologies employed but it also has wider implications for understanding factors such as woodland exploitation and the impact of the industry on the local environment. As an example the iron-production site at Creeton Quarry, South Lincolnshire, will be examined. The site was exclusively an iron production site, there being no evidence for occupation associated with it and virtually no domestic rubbish (no animal bone and only 22 sherds of pottery).

The three key resources for iron production are a suitable iron ore, charcoal in considerable quantity and clay for furnace construction. Due to the amount of wood required it is thought that many Romano-British smelting sites were located in woodland. The iron ores required with a suitably high iron content are readily available in this country. Iron smelting is, to put it simply, the conversion of an iron oxide ore in a reducing atmosphere to metallic iron. This operation would have occurred in a slag-tapping shaft furnace and each furnace could have been used many times provided it was protected from the elements by some sort of shelter. The iron when it is extracted from the furnace is in the form of a bloom, a spongey mass of iron and slag. This has to be smithed down to bar iron, during which the majority of the slag component is expelled, before it can be sold onto a smith and worked into an object. The majority of the deposits on iron smelting sites are roasted ore dust and charcoal dust, trampled and wind blown when the site was functioning, intermixed with slag and furnace debris. These seldom form distinct identifiable horizons.

THE SITE

The site was excavated in 1994 by the City of Lincoln Archaeology Unit (Figure 7). A quarry extension was about to destroy the site and this allowed a period of only four days in which to excavate it, mainly by machine. The lack

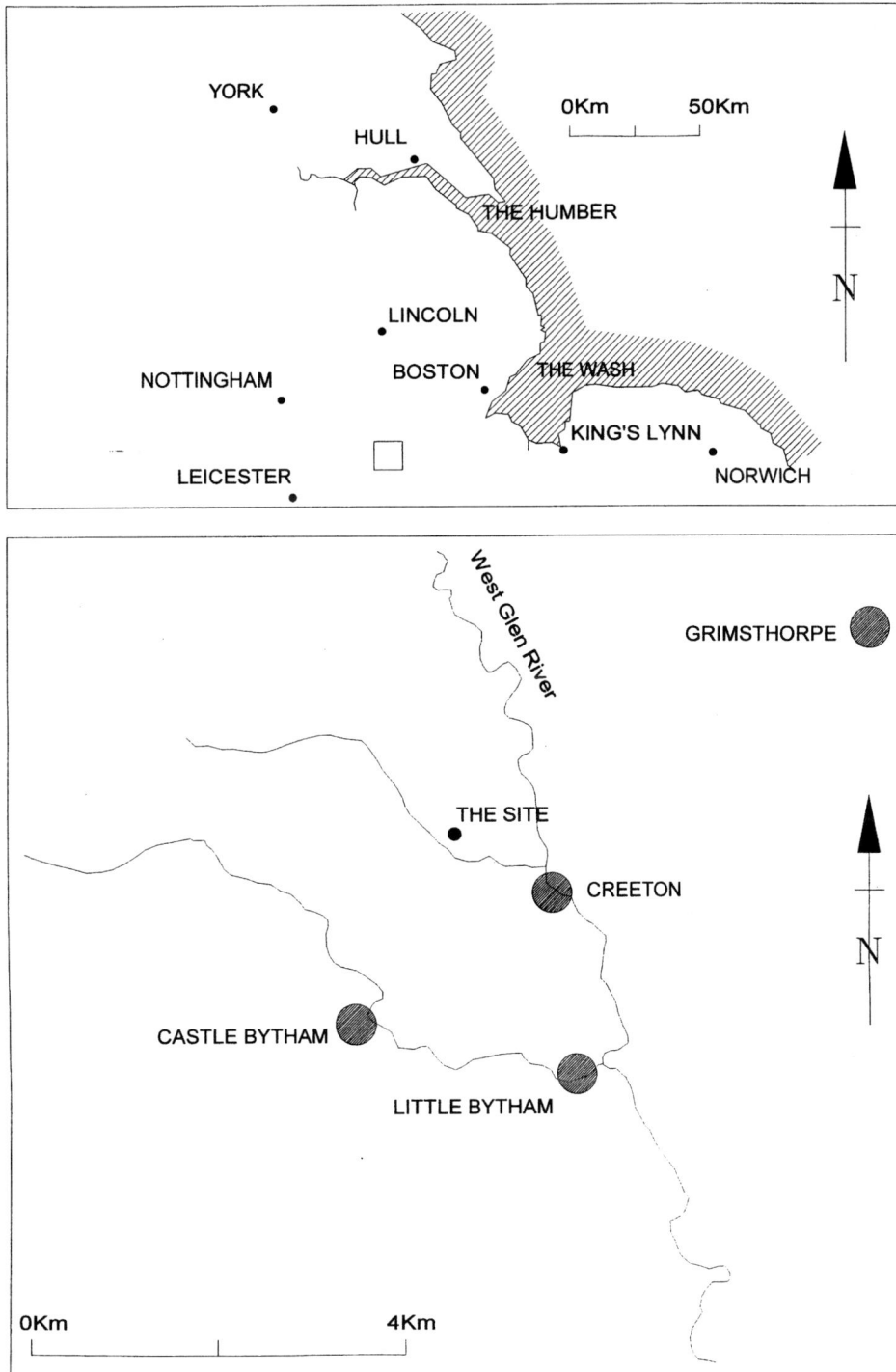

Figure 7. Site location.

of time available, the speed and method of excavation, combined with the depth of archaeology resulted in a number of problems the greatest of which was an inability to resolve the undoubtedly complex archaeological stratigraphy. Definite features were not identified until the site had been stripped down through the topsoil and *c.* 0.4m of archaeological deposits to the natural clays (Figure 8). Two areas with multiple shaft furnaces were found (161 and 156), with adjacent substantial slag heaps (171 and 127), and on the quarry edge were the remains of a charcoal heap (129, samples 2 and 10). Various other features were probably associated with ore roasting and crushing and

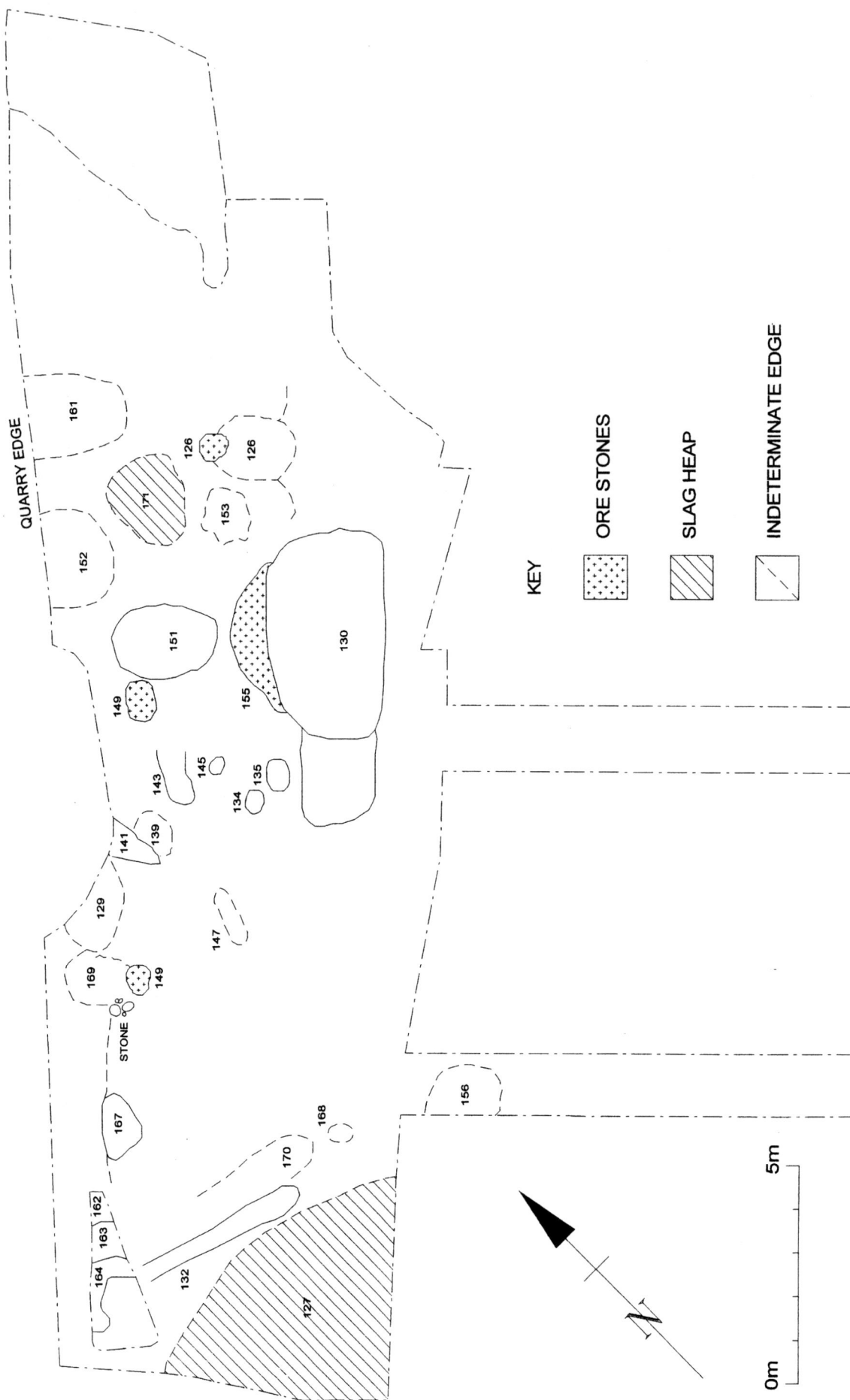

Figure 8. The main features recorded on the site.

Table 4. The Radiocarbon dates.

Context	Sample Number	Laboratory Number	Radiocarbon Age (BP)	Weighted Mean BP	Calibrated date range (95% confidence)
129	10	GU-5633	2110±50		cal BC 360–1
128	1	GU-5634	2090±70		cal BC 370–60 cal AD
151	9	UB-4092	1919±20		20–125 cal AD
165	11	UB-4093	1912±20	1921±14	30–120 cal AD
165	11	UB-4094	1930±20		

Table 5. The number of pieces of charcoal identified from each species (Gale 1995).

Context		128	129	129	151	165
Type	Samp no	1	2	10	9	11
Acer sp.	maple			21	12b	4
Corylus sp.	hazel			5b		10
Ilex sp.	holly			1		
Quercus sp.	oak	12r	62rhb	179rhb	16rhb	66rh
Pomoideae	@			11b	6b	8
Prunus sp.	*		2b	?1		
Salicaceae	#			5		
Ulmus sp.	elm		2			

Quercus: r = roundwood; h = heartwood. b = bark

@ subfamily of Rosaceae, which includes *Crataegus* sp., hawthorn; *Malus* sp., apple; *Pyrus* sp., pear; *Sorbus* spp., whitebeam, rowan and service tree. These taxa cannot be distinguished from their anatomical structure.

* blackthorn, cherry and bird cherry.

includes *Salix* sp., willow and *Populus* sp., poplar.

possibly even charcoal production (151, 130 and 126 for example, sample 9). On the western part of the site there was an area that seemed to be the focus for iron smithing (162, 163 and 164, sample 11) just to the south of which lay a ditch, 132, and adjacent clay bank with a charcoal scatter (128, sample 1) underneath. Unfortunately the smithing area was only partially excavated. (Cowgill in prep.).

Partly due to the inability to resolve the complexity of the stratigraphy there are considerable problems with dating the site (Table 4). There has been an assumption, probably incorrect, that smelting sites were likely to have functioned for a relatively short duration, determined by the availability of the ore and wood resources. A problem with dating the site was therefore not anticipated. The two initial radiocarbon dates gave dates of cal BC 360 – 60AD (95% probability) but during the excavation 22 sherds of mid – late 2nd century pottery were found well stratified within the slag heap (127). Three high precision dates were then obtained and they resulted in mid 1st to early 2nd century dates. In the 1950's a ditch had been uncovered at the quarry from which some Late Iron Age – Early Romano-British pottery sherds had been found contemporary with our later set of dates (Thompson 1955, County SMR ref. PRN 33674). The evidence from

Creeton, therefore suggests that the site was used for iron smelting for possibly 100 years or more, although not necessarily continuously.

(The calibrated date ranges for the samples have been calculated using the maximum intercept method of Stuiver and Reimer (1986). They are quoted in the form recommended by Mook (1986) with end points rounded outwards to 10 years if the error on the measurement is greater than ±25 years, and to five years when it is less than this. The probability distributions have been calculated using OxCal (v2.18) (Brook Ramsey 1995) and the usual probability method (Stuiver and Reimer 1993). The results have been calibrated using data from Stuiver and Pearson (1986)).

THE CHARCOAL ASSEMBLAGE

Large deposits of charcoal were recovered from several contexts and most of it, particularly that from contexts 129 and 165, has survived in an excellent state of preservation (Table 5). A large proportion of the charcoal samples consist of intact pieces of oak roundwood and their diameters (when charred) range from about 20mm to 60mm. Oak heartwood, which does not generally develop until trees are at least 35 years old, is present and many of the fragments examined originated from trees of considerably more than 45 years of age.

Experimental work by Crew has demonstrated that the optimal size of charcoal fuel ranges from 10mm – 50mm for smelting and smithing, with the finer charcoal being used to dampen down the smithing fire (Crew 1991, 22, 29). The charcoal analysis has shown that roundwood of >20mm (charred) diameter and ranging in age from 10 years up to, and exceeding, 45 years was selected in preference to narrower wood. Large pieces of charcoal would enable high and even temperatures to be sustained over long periods of time (Percy 1861) and would be strong enough to support the charge (the fuel and ore) within the furnace and prevent it from collapsing in on itself.

The charcoal examined indicated that wood was gathered from stems/ poles and/or branches of varying diameters and age. Some fragments were from fast growing stems including willow and/or poplar and oak. Others were from very slow growing stems (*eg* oak) or included a wide variation in growth ring width (*eg* oak, maple and hawthorn type). There was little consistency in growth patterns within or between species in any one context. The charcoal therefore represents wood from trees grown under varying conditions.

When considered weight for weight the volume of wood required to make charcoal is about 6:1 (Percy 1861; Horne 1982; pers. comm. C. Irwin). The high temperatures and reducing atmosphere necessary for successful smelting can best be achieved by the use of charcoal, which is also a very clean fuel. The quality and calorific value of charcoal is determined by the species used and the efficiency of the charcoal-making process. Partially carbonised wood, which has a low carbon content, will perform badly as charcoal fuel whereas a similar species undergoing efficient carbonisation (*ie* with a 90% carbon content) will result in high-grade charcoal and will produce excellent, smokeless fuel (pers. comm. C. Irwin). Within reason, the higher the temperature of carbonisation the greater the quantity of carbon within the charcoal. However, the more slowly, (or what is equivalent, the lower the temperature), at which the charring is effected, the greater will be the yield (Percy 1861). If carbonisation occurs at high temperatures, however, it will burn the bark away (pers. comm. C. Irwin). Many of the pieces of oak roundwood from Creeton, along with most other species, however, retained bark (Table 2).

In general, dense heavy woods emit most heat (particularly oak heartwood); to produce comparable heat from light-weight wood would incur the use of much larger volumes of fuel (pers. comm C. Irwin). The structure of the wood also affects the quality of the charcoal. Light-weight woods ignite more easily (Percy 1861); even-grained woods burn more uniformly than coarse-grained woods which require more ventilation (Hughes 1954). The species content of the samples examined contained a high ratio of oak (including heartwood), a coarse-grained wood but one

of the densest of native timbers. Other species such as holly, blackthorn, maple, members of the hawthorn group and elm are relatively dense but willow and poplar are comparatively light in weight. Charcoal making in modern kilns using mixed woods precludes the use of some thin-walled species, such as willow and poplar, since the high temperatures quickly reduce them to ash (pers. comm C. Irwin).

The evidence, therefore, suggests that high temperatures may not have been achieved during the carbonisation of the charcoal and that the fuel used may not be as efficient or clean as anticipated. The presence of large amounts of bark, and some willow and poplar suggests that the colliers were perhaps aiming for quantity over quality.

Evidence of coppicing can be difficult to establish, especially from charcoal, and could not be proven here. Species such as hazel which grows commonly in association with oak and has, traditionally, been one of the most frequently coppiced of all British trees, occurred relatively sparsely amongst the charcoal. Maple and most members of the *Pomoideae* coppice easily but the charcoal samples did not show the rapid growth usually associated with coppiced rods. Oak coppices easily but is one of the slowest-growing species (pers. comm. M. Dobson) – although some of the charcoal fragments did include fast-grown wood. Elm is not generally coppiced since it tends to sucker (Rackham 1990).

Rackham has argued convincingly (Rackham 1980, 108) that it was unlikely that the Romano-British iron smelters in the Weald continually destroyed wildwood. Any felled trees would soon grow again and this regrowth would have been much easier to use, more predictable and reliable in yield, than any remaining wildwood. It seems unlikely that in the Iron Age or Romano-British period they would have allowed such a vital resource as woodland to be cleared indiscriminately. In the historic period smelters and other industries that relied on woodland for their fuel led to conservation, rather than destruction. It is therefore probable that it was carefully managed to satisfy the wide ranging demands that were placed upon it (Rackham 1980, 153–4; Dark and Dark 1997, 38). It is therefore suggested that most, if not all of the wood, grown to convert to charcoal was from coppiced woodland. Oak was the dominant species exploited for charcoal production by the colliers at Creeton but other species may have been extracted from the woods for other purposes. Hazel, for example, may have been extracted for the production of hurdles and wattle-work, which would have been in very great demand at this date (pers. comm. D. Goodburn).

It has generally been assumed that the wood generated was produced by a 6 to 20 year rotational coppicing cycle, which has been the approximate norm since the early medieval period, although with some variations over time (Rackham 1980, 140). There is some evidence, however, that the Romano-British practised some coppicing over longer cycles. The wood used for a timber building in

Southwark was from stools that had not been cut for 30–35 years (Brigham *et al*. 1995, 37–8) and there is some evidence for even longer cycles of perhaps 45–60 years (pers. comm. D. Goodburn). This matches more closely with the evidence from Creeton, which suggests that heartwood had often developed and therefore many of the oaks were felled at a minimum age of *c*. 35 years old.

It is therefore proposed that the most likely system used for the production of wood for the iron-smelting charcoal at Creeton was that of coppicing oak woodland on a long management cycle or just possibly growing woods with closely spaced oak standards (although the heavy clays in South Lincolnshire are not really suitable for this). In the latter instance the charcoal may have been made from the top and lopped branches of trees with the timber being exported for other uses. Branch wood can look similar to slow grown trees even when taken from a fast grown tree (pers. comm. D. Goodburn).

The distance to the woodland exploited by the smelting site is considered to be important in the locating of the site. Charcoal was by far the resource required in the greatest quantity and its transportation could have generated high labour costs, which is why smelting sites are traditionally sited within woods. Potentially an area with a radius of 0.5km from the smelting site could contain up to 78.6 hectares of woodland, while a kilometre radius gives a total of 314 hectares.

SOME SUGGESTED IRON PRODUCTION RATES WITH ASSOCIATED FUEL IMPLICATIONS

Estimating the productivity of a site is fraught with difficulties but it is important in that it allows some sense of the scale of production. This can in turn be compared with other sites to give approximate regional outputs. It also enables estimates to be made concerning the quantity of raw materials exploited and the effects this may have had on the local environs.

The slag heap at Creeton was about 40m in diameter (assuming about half had been removed by quarrying based upon the circular shape visible on an aerial photograph) and approximately 0.5m deep which gives a total volume for the site of *c*.628m³. About 95% of this was slag giving a slag volume of 597m³. Taking a typical density for fayalitic iron slag the total mass present is just over 2,000 tonnes. While this should not be viewed as in any way precise it does give an order of magnitude.

The analysis of the slags and ores showed that both ores analysed were viable, given the range of slag composition (results also from analysis) at Creeton. 100kg of ore of a composition midway between the two analysed samples, producing slag of the composition of the tapped material found, would be expected to yield 61kg of slag and 25kg of iron (Table 6). Thus for an approximate estimate of the output of the site a ratio of 2.5 kg smelting slag to 1kg iron might be used (Starley 1997).

At every stage during the production process huge variables come into play. Factors such as ore type and its iron and silica content will vary significantly. The technology used and the methodology applied by the smelters and smiths is also an important factor. The socio-economic frameworks that organised the industry and the way it operated will also affect the output. Cleere's estimates for Wealden sites are for a similar technology to that used at Creeton (*ie* slag-tapping shaft furnaces) but he has suggested that it was organised on a large scale by the *Classis Britannica* and was therefore a military operation (Cleere 1974). The quality of the charcoal is also important, as has been discussed above. Apart from variables in the raw materials the skills of individual Romano-British smelters, particularly with judging and adjusting to different types or sources of raw materials, must also have played a significant role.

In experiments it has been estimated that the volume of charcoal required for a single smelting (using a slightly different technology than that used at Creeton) and smithing cycle, resulting in a single 500g bar of iron, is about 60kg with an absolute minimum of 50kg (Crew 1991, 35). A number of authors have also suggested the resources required and likely outputs and these have been converted to a standard output of 1 tonne of iron bloom (Table 7).

Cleere's estimates on wood requirements are based on both his own experiments and those of Bielinin's in Poland and Gillies (Cleere 1976, 238–41). The method of estimating the number of hectares required to produce the wood needed used by Cleere, is based upon the mean of the number of oak standards produced per hectare in wildwood (1,200 m³/ha: Walters and Christie 1958). This figure is then halved to exclude all but the branch wood with a further third deducted to exclude all but the smaller branch wood. Rackham uses Cleere's figures for iron production in the Weald but suggests that even if in the initial stages the woodland was being cleared, a woodland management system would soon be adopted (Rackham 1980, 108–9 and see above). Limited knowledge exists about the yields from native coppiced species, including oak, and the variations regarding age of tree and site. Typical rotations for various species and their end products are known but the ages of maximum annual increment in tree growth and therefore yield are not. In a study by Crockford and Savill it was found that the maximum annual increment of oaks varies between 25 years on the highest yielding sites to about 60 on the poorest (Crockford and Savill 1991, 29).

From the data in Table 7 and the estimate that there was 2000 tonnes of slag at the site the following figures can be suggested for Creeton Quarry:

Number of tonnes of iron bloom produced: 800
Number of smelts producing a 10kg bloom: 80,000
Tonnes of roasted ore required: 3,200
Tonnes of charcoal required: 11,200

Table 6. Calculation of yield of iron and slag from 100kg of the ore found at Creeton Quarry (Starley 1997).

	Ore composition		Slag composition		Slag produced	Fe within the slag	Fe as metal
	Fe (%)	SiO2 (%)	Fe (%)	SiO2 (%)	(kg)	(kg)	(kg)
Worst case:	56.9	14.3	56.1	19.4	74.0	41.5	15.4
Typical case:	57.9	13.5	53.0	22.0	61.5	32.6	25.4
Best case:	58.9	12.6	50.6	23.8	53.1	26.9	32.1
Best with ore from furnace bottom	66.8	4.1	50.6	23.8	17.2	8.7	58.1

Table 7. The ratios of raw materials required to produce 1 tonne of iron bloom. (All figures are given in tonnes except the woodland).

	Iron	Bloom	Slag	Roasted ore	Charcoal	Wood	Hectares of woodland
Cleere 1976		1[2]	3	6	12	84	0.3 felled
Rackham 1980					12	84	16.8 coppiced
Crew 1991	(0.4)[1]	1	2.6	4	16	96[4]	
Creeton estimate		1	2.5	4	14[3]	84[4]	1[5] or 0.5[6] coppiced

1   The iron yield for the Crew experimental work is given, although the fuel required to achieve this from the bloom is not included in the table.
2   Cleere describes this as a 'finished bloom' and includes a charcoal allowance for forging the bloom; it is not obvious as to which stage the iron has been taken.
3   Figure taken from midway between Cleere's estimate and the Crew experiment
4   Charcoal to wood ratio of 1:6 used as opposed to the 1:7 used by Cleere and Rackham.
5   20–25 year coppicing cycle (based on Crockford and Savill 1991)
6   50 year coppicing cycle (based on Crockford and Savill 1991)

Hectares of coppiced wood needed (on a 20–25 year cycle): 800
Hectares of coppiced wood needed (on a 50 year cycle): 400
Or hectares of woodland felled: 240

The number of smelts given above is likely to be a maximum for the tonnage of iron but undoubtedly they also would have had an occasional failure. It is likely that the site produced around 800 tonnes of iron during its period of productivity, which depending on the duration of the site maybe roughly the equivalent of eight tonnes per annum (*c.* 800 smelts).

The minimum number of people required to operate a single furnace effectively is three (Crew 1991, 35) and this is likely to be as appropriate for the tapping technology as the non-tapping. Crew also estimates that it takes 25 person days to produce a 1kg of bar iron. This includes smithing the bloom into a bar and an allowance for the time needed to extract and roast the ore and to produce the required charcoal. If, however, 10kg blooms were being produced as has been suggested by Cleere (Cleere 1976), rather than the 1.7kg bloom made in the Crew experiment (using a different technology), the amount of iron metal generated would be considerably higher. The time required can probably be further reduced if several furnaces were operating simultaneously, for example, a team of seven or eight would probably be capable of running three furnaces. We simply do not know how many may have been operating simultaneously or if indeed they were. The amount of time needed to generate the ore and charcoal required if the industry intensified, however, would be greater.

CREETON IN CONTEXT

It was thought to be unlikely that Creeton would be an isolated iron smelting site and therefore a search of the literature and Sites and Monuments record was conducted and revealed a total of 18 other probable iron-smelting sites within a ten kilometre radius of Creeton (Figure 9).

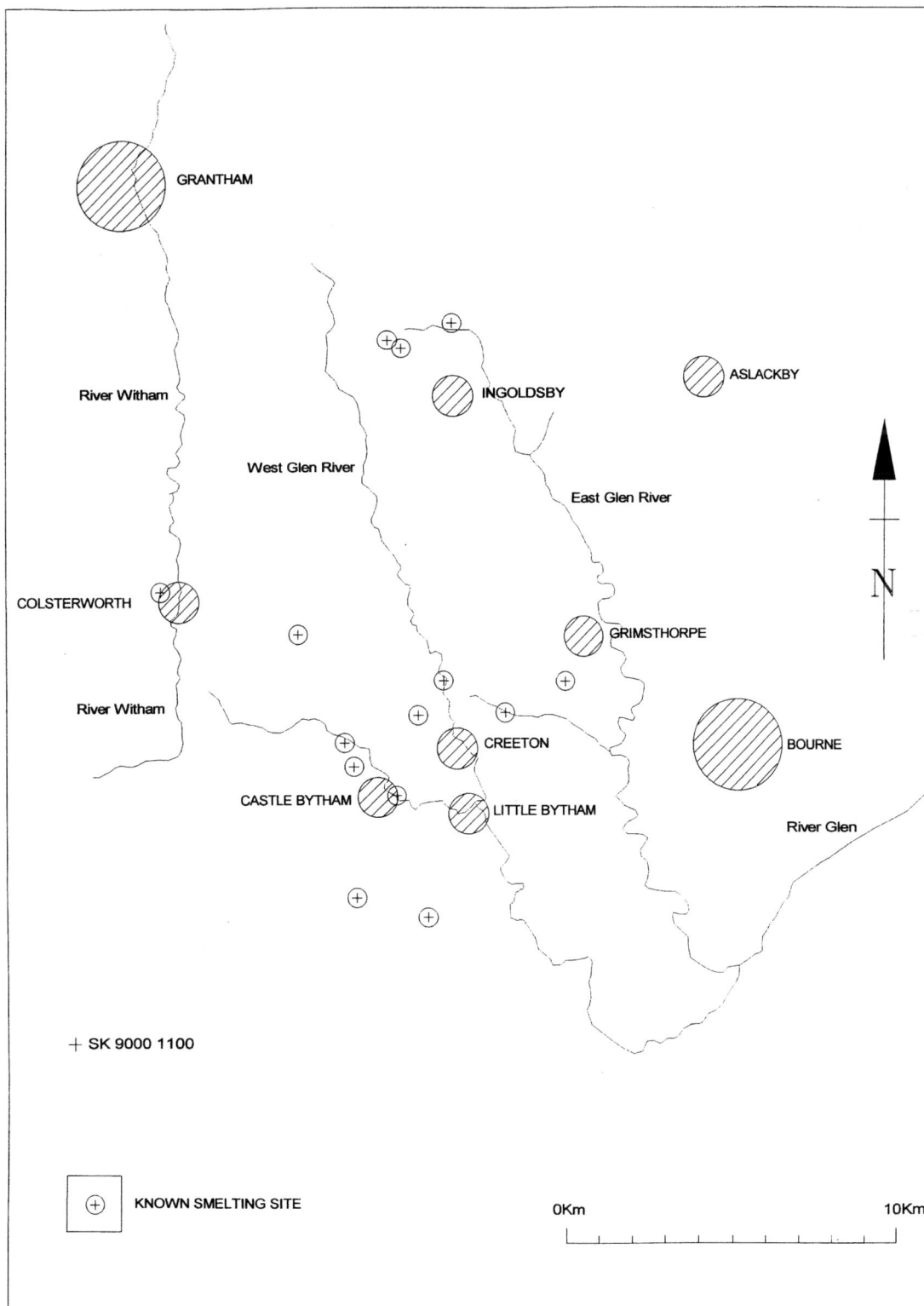

Figure 9. Smelting sites in the study area.

These represent recently extant sites but it is known that a number of additional slag heaps have been destroyed relatively recently during limestone quarrying (pers. comm. Clive Jones). These sites are typically represented by spreads of iron tap slag and sometimes furnace lining. Smelting sites in the area that are thought to be Romano-British in date are often very roughly the size of Creeton but there are a number that are much larger or smaller.

The variability in the size of the scatters and their density is partly dependent on the degree of plough damage, but it also without doubt reflects the scale, success and possibly the technology employed.

To reinforce the magnitude of the woodland required by this industry in South Lincolnshire, if all 18 sites operated on a similar scale to that proposed for Creeton (taking into account some are smaller but others are larger) between 72–144 km^2 would have been coppiced while 43.2km^2 may have been felled. The total amount of land that exists within a 10km radius of Creeton is 62.8km^2. This would have probably occurred over a lengthy period of time with the same woods being coppiced for fuel many times over, thus considerably reducing the extent of woodland suggested. Although 18 sites are known within this area, and at least four others have been destroyed in the last forty years, many others probably exist but await identification.

DISCUSSION

Although in the time estimates given above for manning the smelting site, includes time for coppicing and charcoal production, it is possible that professional woodmen or colliers were responsible for this part of the process. Wood ownership and the control of it as a resource is beyond the remit of this paper but the availability of the charcoal would have determined where and when the smelters produced iron. The charcoal from Creeton suggests that the charcoal producers were aiming for quantity over quality and this may not have been a factor the smelters could necessarily control. This may also explain the longer coppicing cycle because woodland around Creeton and the other South Lincolnshire sites would have been growing on dense heavy clays, whereas oak woodland prefers light acid sandy soils (Rackham 1980, 285). The evidence from Crockford and Saville suggests that by extending the rotational cycle it would improve the yield from these woods (Crockford and Savill 1991, 29).

Given the long duration of the site at Creeton suggested by the radiocarbon and pottery dates and the known presence of so many similar sites in the area it is a possibility that the smelters moved from site to site while the woodland regrew. When the available woodland close to one smelting site was exhausted the smelters may have moved to the next available suitable wood. By proposing a long coppicing cycle, at least for the woods around Creeton, this does not necessarily mean that the smelting sites were only used once every 40 or 50 years (no more than once in a smelters lifetime). It was common in the historic period for estates and other woodland managers to coppice a wood in a number of fells over the years, to achieve a more regular income from this resource (Rackham 1980, 135). Few of the sites in South Lincolnshire, when fieldwalked, have produced datable pottery

and therefore perhaps these should be viewed as 'satellite' work places located around the main settlement site where the smelters actually lived. This mode of working and living has been proposed by Cleere for the iron smelters in the Weald (Cleere 1976, 235).

There was an enormous demand for iron in the Romano-British period and it is quite likely that the industry functioned throughout the year run by smelters working under an iron master. It is a specialist skill, particularly if the range of irons required was to be satisfied. Although they may not have had control of the woodland or of the charcoal production, they are likely to have been responsible for ore extraction, roasting and grading, this being the key to successful production.

CONCLUSION

The number of smelting sites around Creeton suggests the presence of an important iron production industry in this area which would have had significant fuel requirements and therefore made a major impact on the woodland resources. The evidence from Creeton suggests that trees grown under a variety of conditions were exploited but most of these could have been supplied by a managed woodland system, in which case the industry need not necessarily have devastated the amount of woodland cover in the region. Rackham has indeed argued that industries usually have a protective effect on woodland and that many of the most wooded areas that survive today are there because of the density of wood using industries in the vicinity (Rackham 1980, 153–154).

Some form of oak coppicing system seems to be probable, although it could not be proven here, and the large amount of heartwood found suggests that a 35–60 year rotational system may have been employed. The figures given above assume that all the coppiced wood was converted to charcoal for the iron smelters, which is very unlikely to be the case. The good tall straight stems of oak would surely be extracted for building purposes for example. The small quantity of hazel found in the samples, a species common amongst oak coppice, may imply a hurdle or some other industry exploiting the same woodland. Although the main focus of the excavation at the Creeton Quarry site was the iron-production industry, the evidence from sites like this have much broader implications for landscape studies.

While we can consider and assess the character of the fuel product and propose methods of woodland management from industrial sites of this sort, it is extremely difficult to move from our dataset (the slag and charcoal assemblages) to statements about the state of the woods around the industrial sites and the actual impact of the industry upon them. The prodigious quantity of wood required by this industry, in particular, should have left some visible record on the landscape. By integrating archaeological and palaeoenvironmental work, a more refined interpretation of the impact of iron production should be possible than by relying on just one of the datasets (see for example Mighall and Chambers 1993). Pollen-analytical studies of suitable pollen sequences from within known areas of intensive iron production could give us some indication of the impact on woodland resources. It may further enable us to determine whether they were from managed woodland or the result of clearance and if, over time, there is any sign of the progressive reduction of the woods. It may even be possible to test the proposal here of longer than usual coppicing cycles.

The concentration of iron smelting sites in South Lincolnshire (and other counties) suggests that this part of the County must have been well wooded. Can we take this to mean that during the Iron Age and Romano-British periods, clusters of iron producing sites are an indicator of a well wooded landscape?

Acknowledgements
English Heritage funded both the excavation and post-excavation work. Much of this paper is based upon Rowena Gale's charcoal identifications and the lengthy discussions I have had with her concerning the implications for woodland management. I am therefore extremely grateful that she has allowed me to make such liberal use of her results. The following produced reports on various aspects of the site that have been drawn upon during the writing of this paper Alex Bayliss (Radiocarbon dating), Barbara Precious and Maggi Darling (Romano-British pottery), Russell Trimble (Site supervisor and site report), Dave Starley (Metallurgical analysis) and Mike Jarvis who drew the figures. Colliers have generously discussed their craft and charcoal in general, particular thanks go to M. Dodson, Bill Hogarth, C. Irwin and Walter Lloyd and Damian Goodburn discussed the evidence for coppicing from London. Andea Snelling and Dave Starley made some very constructive comments and finally I am very grateful to D.J. Rackham for his patience during the lengthy discussions involving the site and for reading and commenting upon the draft text.

It is hoped that the detailed report on the excavation will be published in the near future.

References

Brigham, Trevor, Goodburn, Damian and Tyres, Ian, 1995. A Roman Timber Building on the Southwark Waterfront, London. *Archaeology Journal* **152**, 1–72.

Brook Ramsey, C. 1995. Radiocarbon calibration and analysis of stratigraphy: the OxCal program. *Radiocarbon* **37**, 425–30.

Cleere, H. 1974. The Roman iron industry in the Weald and its connections with the *Classis Britannica. Archaeology Journal* **131** 171–99.

Cleere, H. 1976. Some operating parameters for Roman ironworks. *Bulletin of the Institute of Archaeology* **13**, 233–246, London.

Cowgill, Jane, in prep. An Iron Age and Romano-British iron-smelting site at Creeton Quarry, Lincolnshire, and a survey of local iron-smelting sites.

Crockford, K.J. and Savill, P.S. 1991. Preliminary Yield Tables for Oak Coppice. *Forestry* **64**, No1, 29–49.

Crew, P. 1991. The experimental production of prehistoric bar iron. *Historical Metallurgy* **25**, No1, 21–36.

Dark, Ken and Dark, Petra, 1997. *The Landscape of Roman Britain.* Sutton Publishing Limited.

Gale, Rowena. 1995. Creeton Quarry charcoal. Publication report produced for the City of Lincoln Archaeology Unit.

Horne, L. 1982. Fuel for the metal worker. *Expedition* **25**, 6–13.

Hughes, G.B. 1954. *Living crafts.* New York: Philosophical Library.

Mighall, T.M. and Chambers, F.M. 1993. Early mining and metal-working: its impact on the environment. *Historical Metallurgy* **27**, No2, 71–83.

Mook, W.G. 1986. Business meeting: Recommendations/Resolutions adopted by the Twelfth International Radiocarbon Conference. *Radiocarbon* **28**, 799.

Percy, J. 1861. *Metallurgy.* London: John Murray.

Rackham, O. 1980. *Ancient Woodland: its history, vegetation and uses in England.* Edward Arnold.

Rackham, O. 1990. *Trees and Woodland in the British Landscape.* Dent.

Starley, D. 1997. The analysis of slag and other metalworking debris from Creeton Quarry, Lincs, 1994. Ancient Monuments Laboratory Report 99/97.

Stuiver, M. and Pearson, G.W. 1986. High-precision calibration of the radiocarbon time scale, AD 1950–500 BC. *Radiocarbon* **28**, 805–38.

Stuiver, M. and Reimer, P.J. 1986. A computer programme for radiocarbon age calculation. *Radiocarbon* **28**, 1022–30.

Stuiver, M. and Reimer, P.J. 1993 Extended 14C data base and revised CALIB 3.0 14C ags calibration program. *Radiocarbon* **35**, 215–30.

Thompson, F.H. 1955. Archaeological notes for 1954. *Architectural and Archaeological Society Reports and Papers*, Vol 6, 5–6.

Walters, W.T. and Christie, J.M. 1958. *Provisional Yield Tables for Oak and Beech in Great Britain.* Forestry Commission Forest Record No.36.

Biological raw materials

7. Tanning and horn-working at late- and post- medieval Bruges: the organic evidence

Anton Ervynck, Bieke Hillewaert, Ann Maes and Mark Van Strydonck

During rescue excavations near the town centre of Brugge (Belgium), traces were found of two former industrial activities: horn working and tanning. The fills of more than 80 large wooden tubs were investigated, and proved to consist of lime, oak bark or cattle horncores. In one tub, parts of the (tanned) hides of at least 30 cattle were preserved. Oak bark and horncores were also found scattered over the two excavated parcels. The oldest material dates from the 13th century; the youngest is post-medieval, possibly from the 18th century.

On the basis of the excavated material, the interdependence of tanners and horn workers was clearly illustrated and some of the steps in the tanning process were illuminated. In particular, the preserved hides presented a rare source of information within the archaeology of the Low Countries. Detailed observation of a diachronic sample of 1162 horncores yielded data on the cattle breeds from which the hides had been processed, and on the age profile and sex ratio of the animals providing the raw material.

Keywords: Flanders, late- and post-medieval period, industry, urban crafts, leather working, horn working.

INTRODUCTION

The archaeological study of medieval craftsmanship or industry is not a straightforward enterprise and many activities such as textile production or woodcrafts have left almost no traces in the soil (Verhaeghe 1995). However, part of the industrial activities based on the processing of animal products are easier to illustrate archaeologically. Examples are horn, bone and antler working, and the manufacturing of leather. In some cases, structural remains have been found, locating the places of production; in other cases concentrations of waste products reveal where and how animal materials have been worked. However, it would be an exaggeration to state that, from the archaeological finds, these industries are now well known. It is in fact surprising that many medieval European cities, despite a significant number of historical indications, have yielded only a very limited archaeological record of industrial activities based on animal products.

The scarcity of the evidence for medieval industries is certainly also true for Flemish towns. The aim of the present contribution is to help fill this gap in the documentation by dealing with material from rescue excavations in the centre of Brugge, that could shed some light on leather and horn processing within town. A preliminary report on the archaeological fieldwork, but without an analysis of the finds, has been published in Dutch (Hillewaert & Ervynck 1991). A short English summary of this report was published by Shaw (1996). The present report describes the finds in more detail and focuses especially on the organic evidence. However, due to restrictions of space, the full potential of the material is not yet explored in this publication. The results of further analysis will be made available in future contributions.

THE RESCUE EXCAVATIONS

Fieldwork

During 1990, building activities in the centre of Brugge involved the removal of all archaeological layers on two parcels situated close to each other. The first site was labeled 'Garenmarkt', because it was situated at the western side of the square with that name; the second site was called 'Willemstraat', after the name of the street delimiting the southern side of the terrain (Fig. 10). On both completely built-up sites, the erection of new constructions followed immediately after the demolition of the extant houses, which gave little opportunity for archaeological research. Whilst monitoring these works, the Archaeology Department of the town of Brugge could only record the stratigraphy of the building pits, note the features present during their destruction, and try to collect evidence for the former human activities at the sites. These research conditions have of course severely hampered the interpretation of the sites. However, since the finds are in a way unique for Flanders and may be valuable on a wider geographical scale, it was decided that the excavated material merited further analysis.

Structural features

During the watching brief, about 80 large circular pits were seen: 45 at the site Willemstraat and 35 at Garenmarkt (Fig. 10). In two thirds of the cases it could still be seen that wooden tubs had been buried in the ground; in one third of the cases, however, the wood had disappeared. This was clearly not due to poor preservation conditions in the soil; the wood must have been extracted for recycling or fuel. Despite this damage, the original fills of the tubs could often still be observed. The structures varied in diameter between 0.8m and more than 2m, and consisted of planks held together by twigs or wooden hoops. The only exceptions to this pattern are three tubs found at the Willemstraat site, that were constructed using iron nails. Although the wood of the planks has not been analysed by a specialist, it was of oak.

Only the lower part of the tubs was preserved, the upper part having rotted away or having been destroyed by the bulldozers. Their location on the site Willemstraat is clearly clustered, away from the main street 'Eekhoutstraat'. In the case of the Garenmarkt site most of the finds were situated in the northern part of the site, most probably also away from the main street, although the area between the street and this part of the site could not be investigated. On both sites the remains of a ditch were unearthed. This feature was stratigraphically older than some of the tubs. Other features included circular or square brick pits, wooden wells, building remains and post holes. However, the sites could not be recorded sufficiently to allow a full reconstruction of structural features. None of the tubs themselves have been dated.

Finds

In one of the tubs at Garenmarkt two implements were found: a large iron hook and a two-handled knife. The latter represents a rare find; in a synthesis published in 1991, it was stated that no example of a medieval two-handled knife had yet been found in Northwestern Europe (Cherry 1991, 296). The filling of other tubs consisted of lime, oak bark or cattle horncores. In fact, these skeletal elements of cattle are the only bone remains present at the site. There is one exception: a structure at the Willemstraat site, containing horncores of both cattle and goat, with clear cutting and sawing traces. This structure is the oldest at both sites, and must date from the 13th century.

In one wooden tub, parts of animal hides were preserved. Oak bark and cattle horncores were also present outside the wooden structures, mostly scattered over the two investigated sites. The volume of oak bark at the Willemstraat site was estimated to be 2500 m³; the number of horncores at both sites was described as 'thousands'. Together with this refuse, scraps of hides and tufts of hair were often found. Also remarkable was a number of large cobbles. None of these items could be dated by themselves but ^{14}C-dating has been applied on four horncores (see below, Table 8). The general archaeological material (ceramics, glass, etc.) will not be discussed here but gives an indication for the dating of the sites. The oldest medieval material comes from the ditch at Willemstraat and dates from the 13th century; the youngest material is post-medieval, possibly from the 18th century, and was found on the eastern side of the same site. At the Garenmarkt, only late medieval material was found in connection with the artisanal tubs and the horncores.

An attempt was made to determine the provenance of the lime found in the tubs, on the basis of an analysis of the microfossils present (see, e.g., Robaszynski 1988). Unfortunately, preservation was too poor to allow any interpretation (Louwye 1992). A sample of oak bark has been investigated for arthropod remains but yielded no finds (J. Schelvis, pers. comm.). The oak bark itself has not been studied by a specialist but its identification posed no problems. An interesting anecdote is that the street delimiting the western side of the Willemstraat site is still called Eekhoutstraat ('Oakwood Street') today (Fig. 10, 1).

Interpretation

From the structures excavated, the material in the fills, and comparison with other, more completely excavated sites (such as The Green at Northampton, Shaw 1996), it is clear that both sites represent tanneries. The large number of horncores could further relate to horn working but this will need to be corroborated (see further below). However, before an attempt can be made to see how the excavations have added to our knowledge about leather (and possibly horn) working at Brugge, two of the find

Figure 10. Location of the excavated sites, within the town of Brugge (on the central map: 1: Willemstraat, 2: Garenmarkt) (on the inset maps: 1: wooden tubs, 2: circular brick pit, 3: wooden well, 4: square brick pit, 5: ditch, 6: canal).

Table 8. Stable isotope analysis (delta ¹³C and delta ¹⁵N) and radiocarbon dating of horncores from the Garenmarkt and Willemstraat sites, compared to similar data from another site at Brugge ('Burg'), from the medieval castrum at Ename (Belgium), the disappeared coastal fishermen's village of Raversijde (Belgium), and the moorish town of Saltés (southern Spain).

Provenance	Lab. ref.	¹⁴C date (BP)	delta ¹³C	delta ¹⁵N
Brugge – Garenmarkt	UtC-9044	360±35	-22,21	5,60
Brugge – Garenmarkt	UtC-9012	420±45	-22,11	5,26
Brugge – Willemstraat	UtC-8959	150±40	-21,92	4,22
Brugge – Willemstraat	UtC-8960	160±35	-22,32	7,55
Brugge – Burg	UtC-9011	1145±40	-22,05	5,21
Brugge – Burg	UtC-9024	1100±40	-22,03	5,85
Ename	UtC-7951	960±30	-22,57	6,76
Ename	UtC-7943	805±40	-21,71	7,25
Ename	UtC-7946	1055±30	-22,04	7,40
Raversijde	UtC-9014	455±40	-23,26	6,31
Raversijde	UtC-9054	395±30	-21,83	6,89
Raversijde	UtC-9057	330±30	-21,82	6,32
Saltés (Spain)	UtC-8955	830±35	-19,9	6,16
Saltés (Spain)	UtC-8956	870±80	-20,62	6,53

categories, (the horncores and the hides), need to be described in more detail.

ANALYSIS OF THE CATTLE HORNCORES

In the following description, the 13th-century context with sawn goat and cattle horncores will be left out. The number of cattle horncores encountered in all other contexts on both sites runs in the thousands but from both areas 581 horncores were studied into detail. The finds mostly consisted of a single horncore with parts of the frontal and the occipital bone still attached, thus representing one lateral side of a (fragmented) skull (Fig. 12). There were no skull fragments with both lateral sides of the frontal bone and both horncores attached. At some point, all skulls must have been broken along or near to the frontal suture. Taking into account the large number of finds, a fitting of left and right sides was not attempted. On the frontal bones, when present, a circular fracture could be observed. This must have been caused by the impact of the hammer or pole-axe used to sedate or kill the animals at the moment of slaughtering.

On each horncore nine measurements were taken, but only the length of the outer curvature will be used in the present report. The metrical data were gathered and interpreted within the framework of a student's project (Van Egroo 1997), but the interpretations put forward were rather contentious, and it was therefore decided to only use the raw data and to recalculate and interpret everything again.

Already during the excavations, it was clear that at the Willemstraat site, and especially in three tubs constructed

with nails, a type of horncore occurred that was not found at the Garenmarkt location. At the former site, most of the finds showed much larger dimensions and could truly represent 'longhorn' cattle. Consequently, the Garenmarkt finds were soon labeled as 'shorthorn' cattle. In fact, these terms are not in accordance with those formally introduced by Armitage (1982), who labeled 'shorthorn' all animals with the outer curvature of the horncores shorter than 220 mm, 'mediumhorns' those measuring between 220 and 360 mm, and 'longhorns' all horncores exceeding the latter dimension. In that sense, the measurements taken on the material from Brugge (Fig. 11) show that true 'longhorns' (*sensu* Armitage 1982) are hardly present, but at the same time, the biometrical data suggest that two (but presumably not more) distinct populations are represented within the collection, for which the informal terms 'shorthorn' and 'longhorn' will be used. The biometrical discrimination between the two will be fixed subjectively around 220 mm for the outer curvature. Most probably, the small proportion of shorthorns at the Willemstraat site (Fig. 11) represents no more than late medieval material that became mixed within the post-medieval longhorn collection.

The archaeological context, historical information and the radiocarbon dating of two samples of each biometrical subpopulation (Table 8) showed that the shorthorns from the Garenmarkt site most probably date from the 15th century, and that the longhorns from the Willemstraat, despite the wide intervals for the ¹⁴C dates obtained, date from the 18th century (¹⁴C calibration following Stuiver *et al.* 1998, calculated using OxCal v3.3 (c) Bronk Ramsey 1999). The late medieval shorthorn cattle type is indeed known from many other excavations in Flanders, but, since the late post-medieval period has not received too much

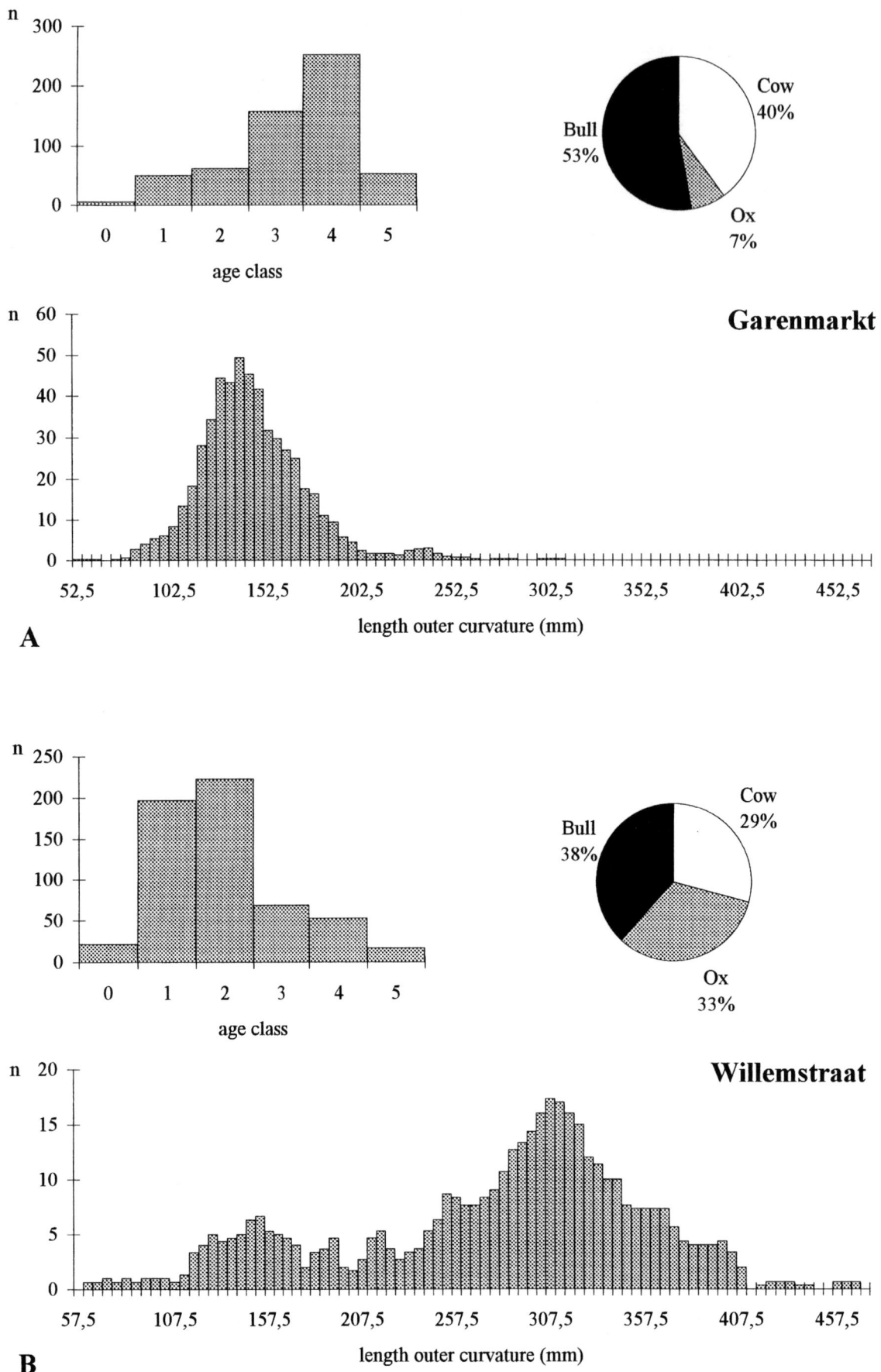

Figure 11. Primary observations on the horncore collections: age and sex distribution (following the criteria of Armitage 1982) and distribution of the length of the outer curvature (running mean) for A: the Garenmarkt site, and B: the Willemstraat site.

attention within Flemish archaeology, 18th century long-horn cattle are archaeologically unknown for the area. Iconographic material from the 19th century, however, proves the presence of cattle with rather long horns in Flanders (e.g. Van den Bergh 1998, 19). Nevertheless, the possibility was not excluded that the large horncores found at Willemstraat had been imported to Brugge, attached to hides that were meant to be tanned in town. Such import of raw materials has indeed been documented in local historical sources (Tanghe 1993) and the transport of salted hides was possible over long distances (Woodroffe 1936). Because it is known that the ratio of the ^{13}C stable isotope in an organism is influenced by the temperature of its environment (Fizet *et al.* 1995), a comparison was made between the stable isotope measurements from two samples of both Garenmarkt and Willemstraat, and data obtained from other medieval collections studied by the first author of this paper. These were from: another site at Brugge ('Burg') (see De Witte 1991), from the medieval *castrum* at Ename (Belgium) (Callebaut 1991), the lost coastal fishermen's village of Raversijde (Belgium) (Pieters 1997), and the Moorish town of Saltés (southern Spain) (Bazzana and Bedia Garcia 1993). This comparison (Table 8) showed that there is no difference between the ^{13}C-ratios of the Belgian material but that the Spanish samples showed a less negative value. The pattern can be seen as a first indication that the longhorn cattle from the Willemstraat site were also bred locally; there is at least no support for the alternative possibility. The analysis further showed important differences in the ^{15}N-ratios, even between samples from the same sites. Most probably, this must be related with differences in nutrition (see, e.g., Iacumin *et al.* 1998).

The two sets of 581 horncores were aged according to the criteria put forward by Armitage (1982). Within the shorthorn collection of the Garenmarkt site, age class 4, roughly corresponding to an age between 7 and 10 years (Luff 1994, 176, after Armitage 1982), is most frequent (Fig. 11). At Willemstraat, much younger animals dominated the collection (Fig. 11), a pattern that is even clearer when, for that site, the horncores shorter than 220 mm are excluded from the analysis (data not presented in this report). At Willemstraat, most of the longhorn horncores come from cattle that were slaughtered between the ages of 1 to 3 years (Luff 1994, 176, after Armitage 1982).

The finds were also sexed, according to morphological criteria supplied by Armitage and Clutton-Brock (1976). The observations point towards a main difference between the two sites: a low percentage of castrated males at the late medieval site, and a high percentage of this group at the 18th century site, dominated by the longhorn variety (Fig. 11). However, it must be questioned whether these primary observations, which are always subjective, are not biased, for example by the fact that the discrimination criteria could be more visible in a longhorn versus a short-horn breed. Moreover, a complicating factor is that the age distributions of the two sets are significantly different,

considering that discriminating traits could be more visible in older than in younger animals. In the future, the morphological sex observations will be evaluated against a statistical analysis of the measurements taken, but this step could not be included in the present report. It is already clear that simply measuring the length of the horncore certainly does not allow one to see sub-populations in the assemblages (Fig. 11). Nevertheless, one can be sure that male and female animals are present within the collections (see below). Finally, it must be noted that not all researchers in the field agree with the criteria put forward by Armitage and Clutton-Brock (1976) (see, e.g., Luff 1994).

A remarkable characteristic of the Willemstraat long-horn material is the frequent presence of iron nails driven into the horncore (Fig. 12), or of the traces left where a nail was formerly present.

DESCRIPTION OF THE ANIMAL HIDES

In one tub at the Willemstraat, a large number of leather pieces were found that represent parts cut away from complete, tanned animal hides (Fig. 13). The hide parts must have been tanned because they would otherwise never have been preserved. The morphology of the pieces clearly shows that only head and belly parts of the hides are present. Thirty more or less complete head parts could be recognised, but the exact number of belly parts is more difficult to count because many of these finds only represent small fragments. Generally, however, there are enough belly parts to fit the number of head parts. Species identification posed no problems; the size of the parts and the traces on the head parts, indicating where horns and ears had been removed, indicate that the remains are from cattle. The finds themselves have not been dated, and can no longer be subjected to ^{14}C-analysis because of the application of certain preserving agents. However, since they come from a tub that was constructed with wooden hoops (and not with nails), one can be certain that the hides date from the late medieval or early post-medieval period. As far as is known to the authors, these leather finds represent a rare collection. The only comparable assemblage of finds known comes from a 17th-century ship wreck, excavated off the coast of Texel (the Netherlands) (Stikker 1991).

The head parts have been cut away behind the ears and horns, and where the frontal and nasal parts of the skull meet. An incision runs from the nasal area to (and through) the eyes. On some pieces the eyelashes are still visible. Notable specimens included a piece from a hornless animal, and the head part of an individual with only one horn. All of the (completely preserved) head parts showed a mark, in the shape of a clover, impressed near the edge of the piece.

The belly parts represent a fragment of the ventral part of the hide, left or right of a line going from the genital to

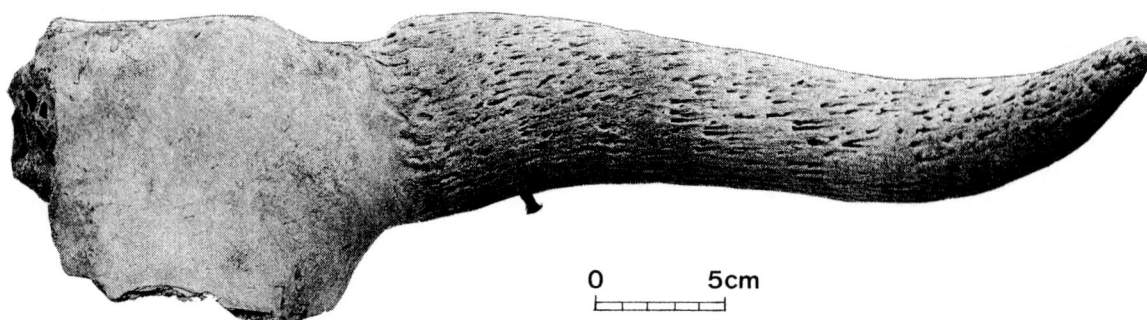

Figure 12. Post-medieval longhorn horncore from the Willemstraat site. Note the iron nail driven into the horn core.

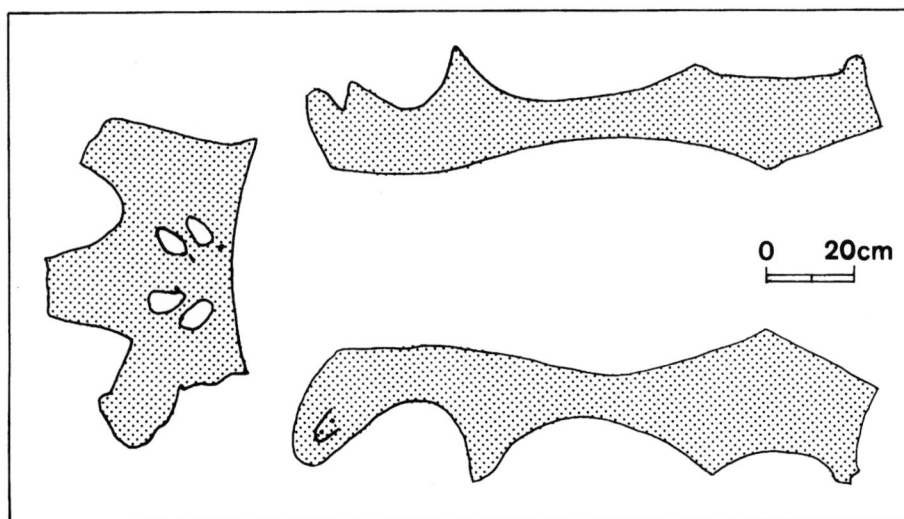

Figure 13. Head and belly parts, cut away from tanned hides. Note the C-shaped incision in the rostral zone of the belly part.

the nuchal area. Laterally, they have been separated from the dorsal part of the hide along a line connecting the places where the skin of the limbs connects with the skin of the body. In fact, the cutting line must first have been marked on the hides, because a dotted line of impressions can sometimes be observed near the lateral edges of the pieces. The latter have sometimes a jagged appearance. The belly parts also indicated the presence of both male and female animals, the former being indicated by the presence of the scrotum, the latter by the presence of the teats. The occurrence of castrated males (oxen) could not be recognised but is not to be excluded. Another characteristic of the ventral hide parts are the C-shaped incisions made in the rostral part of the fragments. In the centre of the C-shape, two additional, crossed incisions were made (Fig. 13). Finally, some of the belly parts showed a large number of cuts near their edges.

TANNERIES AT BRUGGE

When interpreting the data from Brugge in relation to the tanning industry, reference must be made to published accounts of leather processing pre-dating modern methods (Serjeantson (1989), Cherry (1991), Thomson (1998)). However, these descriptions are mostly based upon English literature and historical documents, and can therefore not simply be extrapolated to other parts of the world. Although the basic technology of tanning did not change from the Graeco-Roman world to the late 18th century (Cherry 1991, 295), it is certainly true that there were regional differences in the substances used or in the order in which processes were performed. At least, that is what is said in the introduction of a late 18th century Dutch treatise on tanning (Kasteleijn 1789). This manuscript, which claims (without reference) to be based upon an older text from the Low Countries, will be taken as the basic reference for interpreting the processes which took place at the tanning sites of Brugge.

The late and post-medieval horncores and preserved hides indicate that the tanning industry on the excavated parcels was specialising in cattle hides. However, since the oldest, (13th-century), context contained both goat and cattle horncores, the impression could arise that the craft originally combined two lines of activity: tanning, which involved the treatment of (thick) hides (typically of cattle or horse) with vegetable materials in order to produce firm, robust and dark leather; and tawing, which comprised the treatment of thinner skins (typically of sheep and goat) with alum, salt and fatty materials in order to produce a fine, white leather (Thomson 1998, 7). At some point, both processes (tanning and tawing) could have become divided as two separate crafts at Brugge, and the tawyers would have disappeared from the sites investigated. However, the oldest context from the sites only provides evidence for horn working and does not prove that tanning and/or tawing took place on the parcels investigated. It could thus well be that a local horn worker at that time used the raw materials from two different professions, and that tanning and tawing were already done at different localities within the town.

It must be stressed that the late and post-medieval finds from Brugge, which prove beyond doubt that tanning took place at the sites, do not completely exclude the possibility that tawing was also part of the profession of the local craftsmen. It is imaginable that, for example, the processing of the skin of hornless sheep (and sheep were hornless in late medieval western Flanders: Ervynck 1998) would have left no trace at the sites. However, at tawing sites, not only horncores (in the case of horned sheep) but also concentrations of other sheep bones have often been found (see Albarella, this volume), which is clearly not the case at Brugge.

A constant supply for the tanneries, coming from individual butchers or from slaughter-houses, posed no problems in a large medieval and post-medieval town. It is always assumed that the hides were delivered with the horns and the hooves still attached (Cherry 1991, 295; Thomson 1998, 4). However, the finds from Brugge, and more precisely the absence of bones from the distal part of the limbs, suggest that the hooves were already removed before arrival at the site. The preserved hide parts indicate the same, since they never show the presence of skin from distal limb parts. Kasteleijn (1789), describing that the first task of the tanner is to remove horns and tails, also makes no mention of hooves. He does suggest, however, that the tails were still present on the raw hides, a pattern that could not be corroborated by the finds from Brugge. Caudal vertebrae were completely absent from the collection, just as is generally the case in tanner's sites (Serjeantson 1989, 139).

The organic material from the tanneries, and especially the preserved hide parts, illuminate aspects of the butcher's practice, in particular flaying, that can never be investigated in archaeozoological collections consisting only of bones. It is clear that the butcher flayed the cattle carcasses in a way that was most profitable for the tanner. For example, the method used to rip the head hide (from the nasal area to and through the eyes) is the one that is now still being recommended as the most profitable way to prevent unnecessary waste of head hide (see Aten *et al.* 1955).

The preserved head parts show that the removal of the horns was performed by cutting the hide around the base of the horncore. Possibly at the same time, the ears were cut away (if they would not already have been removed during flaying). How precisely the skull and horns were detached from the hide (without damaging it), is not clear. It seems impossible to pull the horns through the circular incisions in the hide without separating left and right sides of the skull. Whether this can be done easily, remains questionable, but the action must have involved putting strong pressure on the frontal suture. The fact that this must have been done systematically (all skull parts only represent one body side) further shows that the leather made from the head hide still had some value. Otherwise, one would simply have removed the horns by making one large cut across the frontal part of the hide.

The next step in the preparation of the hides before tanning was washing, in order to remove blood and dung. Kasteleijn (1789) mentions that this was done by putting a rope through the holes in the hide where the horns had been cut away, after which the hides were spread out in (running) water. After a day, they were taken out and the water was allowed to drain out of them. Then, they were soaked in water again and this process was repeated four times. Possibly, the C-shaped incisions in the belly parts of the hide from Brugge indicate that there the hides were not held by a rope through the holes in the head part but were in some fashion held together through these incisions. Running water at the site was provided by the ditches that diverted the water from the river and canals.

For the following step, the removal of the hair, the hides were immersed in an alkaline solution, containing wood ash or slaked lime (Thomson 1998). At Brugge, only the latter product was used, since wood ash was not found during the excavations. According to Kasteleijn (1789), the hides were soaked in the lime solution for 3 to 5 weeks, after which the hair and remaining flesh were scraped off, using two-handled knifes (of which one was excavated) and curved beams. Then the hides were inspected and the good quality ones (with thick dorsal parts) were cut into pieces. The chief tanner indicated where high and low quality material could be separated on the hide, and apparently someone else performed the cutting itself. This could explain the divergence between the marking line and the actual cutting. The marking, consisting of a dotted line of impressions, must have been done with a toothed wheel, an implement depicted, for example, by Diderot and d'Alembert (1780) in their late 18th century encyclopaedia. The tool used to cut the hides at Brugge is unknown but it is striking that the edges sometimes have a jagged appearance.

After another treatment with an alkaline solution, (to make the hides receptive to the tanning agents), the actual tanning could start. Kasteleijn (1789) describes that head and belly parts were also tanned, but following a shorter process than the dorsal fragments. The latter high-quality category was covered with oak bark and put under water in a tub, staying there for 4 to 8 weeks. Then, the hides were taken out and cleaned, to be covered with bark again (but at a lower concentration), and to be put again in a soaking tub. This process was repeated 3 to 4 times, taking in total 4 to 6 months. The lower-quality parts (belly and head) were treated separately and only got two oak bark baths.

Most probably, while soaking in the tubs, the hides were kept under by the weight of large stones. The large cobbles found during the excavations must have been used for this. Taking the hides out of the tubs must have been done with the large iron hooks, one of which was also found at Brugge. It is even possible that the C-shaped incisions in the belly parts served in a way to facilitate the removal of the hides from the tubs. This hypothesis, however, does not fit with Kasteleijn's description of the separation of the high and low quality zones of the hides before tanning. Perhaps, at Brugge, this separation was performed only after the tanning process. This question also influences the interpretation of the clover-shaped mark found on the head parts. This mark must have been pressed into the hide before tanning but did not serve as a quality mark for the leather (since it was cut away from the best part of the hide). This leaves open the possibility that the mark identified the craftsman who owned the hides, where tanning tubs or workshops were shared amongst different tanners (and accepting that the hides were cut after tanning). Alternatively, the mark could identify the provenance of the raw material and was perhaps applied by the butcher.

The final steps in the leather processing involved drying and brushing of the tanned pieces, followed by the so-called currying, i.e. the application of oils, fats and dyes to make the leather supple (Thomson 1998, 8). The hides also had to be stretched, in order to prevent wrinkling. If the cut marks in the belly parts are the result of this stretching, this would mean that the action was also performed at the sites investigated at Brugge. This would perhaps also imply that the separation of ventral and dorsal parts only took place after tanning and final processing.

HORN WORKING AT BRUGGE

It is not clear what the cattle horncores found at the two sites represent: the leftovers, after the horn had been removed from the bone, or a collection of unutilised raw materials? Almost no specimen has cutting traces which would point to the removal of the horn, but it remains possible that these were removed just by pulling, after the soft tissue between bone and horn had rotted away. The latter process could be facilitated by soaking the skull parts in water, although keeping them moist is considered to be better than actually putting them under water (van Zyl 1953). Kasteleijn (1789) does not mention soaking but states that the horns were left in the open air to rot. This could indicate that the soaking was done for other purposes, such as making the material more plastic (MacGregor 1989) or rendering the horn more translucent. In any case, it is likely that the tanners indeed took the first steps in making the horns workable. Generally, the horns needed to soak for 2 to 3 months (Wenham 1964).

The most important conclusion to be drawn from the concentrations of horncores found at the tanners' sites remains that the horn workers apparently did not collect their raw materials directly at the slaughterhouse. This indicates that the presence of the horns on the hides must have been of some importance to the tanners. It has been hypothesised that the latter wanted to assess the age of the animals of which the hides were processed, as part of a quality control (Serjeantson 1989). Whether the horns were sold to the horn workers or just given away, remains obscure. A puzzling observation is the occurrence of nails driven into the horncores of the post-medieval longhorn cattle of which the hides were probably processed at the Willemstraat site. Was this done to keep the horns on the horncores while they were rotting, or during transport?

Generally, the Brugge finds suggest a close relationship between the tanners and the horn workers, but they do not prove that late or post-medieval horn working took place at the sites, nor do they illuminate aspects of this craft. It can even not be proven that horn working took place at that time at Brugge, partly because, due to the perishable nature of the material, this craft is typically an elusive aspect of the archaeological record (MacGregor 1989, 1998). Only when a concentration of horncores with cutting and sawing marks, or when structures explicable by historical evidence, are found (such as at York: Wenham 1964) will the horn workers of Brugge become part of the picture. So far, only the oldest, 13th-century context proves that horn working was practised at the Willemstraat site.

URBAN CRAFTS AND THEIR ENVIRONMENT

Although it is clear that tanneries consume a lot of water, they are not always situated close to rivers (Cherry 1991, 296). However, the sites at Brugge are examples of production centres situated at the edge of a stream. The investigated tannery sites were built along a canal that represents an artificial by-pass of the original bed of 'De Reie', the river along which Brugge was founded. The sites are situated in a part of town, south of the centre, that lies in a natural depression (Mostaert 1988), and that therefore most probably was only occupied in a secondary phase of the town's development (see Ryckaert 1995, 134). Whether the tanneries were established in that area because of the water supply or because of the location outside the main settlement, is unclear. The latter option could already point towards the nuisance caused by leather working, mainly through pollution and the production of disagreeable odours.

Considering pollution, the common-sense idea that urban tanneries were always situated downstream from the main habitation centre does not hold for the examples from Brugge. The ditches at the tanning sites flowed into the river before it passed through the main town centre. However, it could well be that other factors dictated the location of the industry, and that, for example, the prevailing wind directions were an important consideration. It could even be that the siting of the craft was determined only by practical reasons and that environmental factors were not an issue at the start. In fact, the historical record shows that the whole town quarter south of the main market square became occupied by leather workers (D'Hooghe 1991). Nevertheless, towards the end of the middle ages, the industry was pushed out of the area. This process was initiated by economic factors but furthered by wealthy people who came to live in this part of Brugge (D'Hooghe 1991). A rise in status of the neighbourhood was apparently not reconcilable with a continuation of the tanning industry. Therefore, the Garenmarkt finds represent the late medieval heyday of the industry, whilst the 18th-century finds from the Willemstraat site represent the last remains of a once thriving business.

THE ACQUISITION OF PRIMARY MATERIALS

Even closer than the relationship between tanners and horn workers must have been the connection between tanners and butchers, and between both these professions and the peasants who bred the cattle that supplied the raw materials needed for both human nutrition and leather production. In the future, when more archaeozoological data from Brugge and the surrounding countryside become available, it will be interesting to investigate the interaction (perhaps conflict) between the demands of the leather industry and the options within cattle husbandry. Such an approach could help to answer the question of whether the differences between the age and sex distributions of the late medieval shorthorn population and the post-medieval longhorns must be attributed to options taken by the meat producers or by the leather workers. Of course, it must always be remembered that the network of supply routes for the horn working craft can be very complicated (Robertson 1989).

CONCLUSION

From the excavated sites, information could be gathered concerning some aspects of late- and post-medieval craftsmanship in a Flemish town. The interdependence of tanners and horn workers could be clearly illustrated and some of the steps in the tanning process were illuminated. In particular, the preserved hides present a rare source of information within the archaeology of the Low Countries. In the future, the hides and horncores will be further studied, in order to yield information about cattle breeding in late and post-medieval western Flanders.

Acknowledgements
The authors wish to thank an anonymous referee for his or her comments, and the editors for correcting the English. The stable isotope analysis and radiocarbon dating were made possible by a grant from the Fonds voor Wetenschappelijk Onderzoek – Vlaanderen.

References

Albarella, U. (this volume). Tanners, tawyers, horn working and the mystery of the missing goat.

Aten, A., Faraday Innes, R. and Knew, E. 1955. *Flaying and curing of hides and skins as a rural industry* (FAO Agricultural Development Paper **49**). Roma: Food and Agriculture Organization of the United Nations.

Armitage, P. 1982. A system for ageing and sexing the horn cores of cattle from Britissh post-medieval sites (17th to early 18th century) with special reference to unimproved British Longhorn cattle, pp. 37–54 in Wilson, B., Grigson, C. and Payne, S. (eds), *Ageing and sexing animal bones from archaeological sites* (BAR British Series **109**). Oxford: British Archaeological Reports.

Armitage, P. and Clutton-Brock, J. 1976. A system for classification and description of the horn-cores of cattle from archaeological sites. *Journal of Archaeological Science* **3**, 329–348.

Bazzana, A. and Bedia Garcia, J. 1993. *Saltés. Una ciudad Islamica*. Madrid and Huelva: Casa de Velazquez & Museo Provincial de Huelva.

Callebaut, D. 1991. Castrum, Portus und Abtei von Ename, pp. 291–309 in Böhme, H.W. (ed.), *Burgen der Salierzeit. Teil 1. In den nördlichen Landschaften des Reiches*. Sigmaringen: Jan Thorbecke Verlag.

Cherry, J. 1991. Leather, pp. 295–318 in Blair, J. and Ramsay, N. (eds), *English medieval industries. Craftsmen, techniques, products*. London: Hambledon Press.

De Witte, H. 1991. *De Brugse Burg. Van grafelijke versterking tot moderne stadskern* (Archeo-Brugge **2**). Brugge: Archeo-Brugge.

D'Hooghe, K. 1991. Een belangrijke vestiging van leerlooiers in Brugge tussen 1300 en 1480: de gegevens uit de geschreven bronnen, pp. 124–138 in *Jaarboek 1989–1990. Brugge Stedelijke Musea*. Brugge: Vrienden van de Stedelijke Musea.

Diderot, M. and d'Alambert, M. 1780. *Encyclopédie ou dictionnaire raisonné des sciences, des arts et des métiers*. Bern and Lausanne: Sociétés Typographiques.

Ervynck, A. 1998. Wool or mutton? An archaeozoological investigation of sheep husbandry around late medieval Ypres, pp. 77–88 in Dewilde, M., Ervynck, A. & Wielemans, A. (eds), *Ypres and the medieval cloth industry in Flanders. Archaeological and historical contributions* (Archeologie in Vlaanderen Monografie **2**). Zellik: Institute for the Archaeological Heritage.

Fizet, M., Mariotti A. and Bocherens, H. 1995. Effect of diet, physiology and climate on carbon and nitrogen stable isotopes of collagen in a Late Pleistocene anthropic palaeoecosystem: Marillac, Charente, France. *Journal of Archaeological Science* **22**, 67–79

Hillewaert, B. and Ervynck, A. 1991. Leerlooierskuipen langs de Eekhoutstraat, pp. 109–123 in *Jaarboek 1989–1990. Brugge Stedelijke Musea*. Brugge: Vrienden van de Stedelijke Musea.

Iacumin, P., Bocherens, H., Chaix, L. and Marioth, A. 1998. Stable carbon and nitrogen isotopes as dietary indicators of ancient Nubian populations (Northern Sudan). *Journal of Archaeological Science* 25, 293–301

Kasteleijn, P.J. 1789. *De leerlooijer, leertouwer, wit- en zeemlooijer; of verhandeling over de bereiding der dierlijke huiden tot allerhande zoorten van leeren*. Dordrecht: Blussé & Zn.

Louwye, S. 1992. Micropaleontologisch onderzoek van kalkresten uit leerlooiersputten te Brugge (W.-Vl.). *Archaeologia Mediaevalis* 15, 14–15.

Luff, R.M. 1994. The conundrum of castration in the archaeological record: an interpretation of Roman cattle horn-cores from Chelmsford, Essex. *International Journal of Osteoarchaeology* 4, 171–192.

MacGregor, A. 1989. Bone, antler and horn industries in the urban context, pp. 107–128 in Serjeantson, D. and Waldron, T. (eds), *Diet and crafts in towns. The evidence of animal remains from the Roman to the Post-Medieval periods* (BAR British Series 199). Oxford: British Archaeological Reports.

MacGregor, A. 1998. Hides, horns and bones: animals and interdependent industries in the early urban context, pp. 11–26 in Cameron, E. (ed.), *Leather and fur. Aspects of early medieval trade and technology*. London: Archetype Publications.

Mostaert, F. 1988. De geologische en geomorfologische gesteldheid van de Brugse binnenstad, pp. 43–51 in: Dewitte, H. (ed.), *Brugge onder-zocht. Tien jaar stadsarcheologisch onderzoek* (Archeo-Brugge 1). Brugge: Archeo-Brugge.

Pieters, M. 1997. Raversijde: a late medieval fishermen's village along the Flemish coast (Belgium, province of West-Flanders, municipality of Ostend), pp. 169–177 in De Boe, G. and Verhaeghe, F. (eds), *Rural settlements in medieval Europe. Papers of the 'Medieval Europe Brugge 1997' conference. Volume 6* (I.A.P. Rapporten 6). Zellik: Institute for the Archaeological heritage of the Flemish Community.

Robaszynski, F. 1988. Nature et provenance de la craie accumulée vers le XVe siècle sous l'Ancienne Maison De Greef. *Folklore brabançon* 257, 22–29.

Robertson, J.C. 1989. Counting London's horn cores: sampling what? *Post-Medieval Archaeology* 23, 1–10.

Ryckaert, M. 1995. Les origines et l'histoire ancienne de Bruges: l'état de la question et quelques données nouvelles, pp. 117–134 in Duvosquelle, J.-M. and Thoen, E. (eds), *Peasants and townsmen in medieval Europe. Studia in honorem Adriaan Verhulst*. Gent: Snoek Ducaju & Zoon.

Serjeantson, D. 1989. Animal remains and the tanning trade, pp. 129–146 in Serjeantson, D. and Waldron, T. (eds), *Diet and crafts in towns. The evidence of animal remains from the Roman to the Post-Medieval periods* (BAR British Series 199). Oxford: British Archaeological Reports.

Shaw, M. 1996. The excavation of a late 15th- to 17th-century tanning complex at The Green, Northampton. *Post-Medieval Archaeology* 30, 63–127.

Stikker, N.G. 1991. Runderhuiden uit de zee, pp. 133–137 in Reinders, R. & Oosting, R. (eds), *Scheepsarcheologie: prioriteiten en lopend onderzoek* (Flevobericht 322). Lelystad: Nederlands Instituut voor Scheeps- en onderwaterArcheologie / ROB (NISA).

Stuiver, M. *et al.* 1998. Calibration issue. *Radiocarbon* 40 (3), 1041–1083

Tanghe, R. 1993. *De lederambachten te Brugge in de late middeleeuwen*. Unpublished Lic. thesis, University of Gent, Belgium.

Thomson, R. 1998. Leather working processes, pp. 1–9 in Cameron, E. (ed.), *Leather and fur. Aspects of early medieval trade and technology*. London: Archetypes Publications.

Van den Bergh, S. 1998. Geschiedenis van de rundveeteelt in België. *De Ark* 1998 (4), 18–31.

Van Egroo, J. 1997. *Onderzoek van runderhoornpitten uit twee laat-middeleeuwse leerlooierscontexten in Brugge*. Unpublished Lic. thesis, University of Gent, Belgium.

van Zyl, J.H.M. 1953. *A study of the removal of piths from cattle horns* (Research Bulletin 139). Grahamstown (South-Africa): Rhodes University, Leather Institute Research Institute.

Verhaeghe, F. 1995. Industry in medieval towns: the archaeological problem. An essay, pp. 271–293 in Duvosquelle, J.-M. and Thoen, E. (eds), *Peasants and townsmen in medieval Europe. Studia in honorem Adriaan Verhulst*. Gent: Snoek Ducaju & Zoon.

Wenham L.P. 1964. Hornpot lane and the horners of York. *Annual Report of the Yorkshire Philosophical Society* 1964, 25–56.

Woodroffe, D. 1936. Tanning, pp. 95–321 in Bordoli, E. (ed.), *The boot and shoe maker. A complete survey and guide*. London: The Gresham Publishing Company Ltd.

8. Tawyers, tanners, horn trade and the mystery of the missing goat

Umberto Albarella

Skin and horn are raw materials that have been used by most human societies for a very long time. The production of horn objects and leather have been activities that took place on a sufficiently large scale to deserve the definition of "industry". This paper is concerned with the interpretation of animal bones deriving from such industries, in particular in medieval and post-medieval times in England. The problems faced by the zooarchaeologist when dealing with material that may derive from industrial waste are discussed. It is argued that only rarely can animal bones alone provide an understanding of which type of craft or industry was practised in an area. The solution to the problem generally lies in the integration of different lines of evidence. A review of the animal bone data from central England raises a number of questions on how the two practices may have changed towards the end of the medieval period. The role of the goat is discussed in connection with the possibility of a long distance trade of skins and horns.

Keywords: Leather working, horn working, medieval, post-medieval England, zooarchaeology.

INTRODUCTION

To contemporary men and women living in the western world "animal" and "industry" represent opposite and incongruous concepts. They can hardly be combined in a single mental picture. Animals remind us of wilderness, zoos, farming and pets, whereas the idea of industry is likely to be associated with chimneys, fumes, chemicals and pollution. Industrial activities tend to be regarded as all but dissociated from the animal and, more generally, natural world. This is as good an indication as any of how much our world has changed in the last century or so. In fact, for most of our history, industrial activities relied heavily on the processing of animal products and were therefore closely associated with farming and husbandry (see Clarkson 1966, 26). In the present world, dominated by the production of synthetic materials, it is easy to forget that the most important industries and trades in medieval England were based on the processing of wool and woollen textiles (Clarkson 1966, 25; Farmer 1991; Dyer 1988).

The production of leather – discussed in this paper – could be regarded as "second or third only to the manufacture of woollen cloth as an industrial occupation" (Clarkson 1966, 25) in early modern England, and it was doubtless also of great importance during the Middle Ages (see Cherry 1991). Clarkson (1960–61, 245) regards it as "one of the forgotten occupations in English industrial history". The importance of leather in medieval England is also proved by a survey of animal products traded to London in the period 1290–1315 AD. This shows that "hides" were the animal products most frequently marketed (Murphy and Galloway 1992, Fig. 5), indeed they were more commonly referred to than trade in meat.

In this paper I intend to discuss the question of the identification of leather and horn working activities in the archaeological record – in particular through the use of animal remains – and to review the evidence of such activities for medieval and post-medieval central England. Although horn working must have been widespread during the Middle Ages, this was not an industrial activity that could be compared in importance to the leather trade. Whereas leather workers are frequently mentioned in medieval and early modern documents, the profession of horner seems to have been rare, and only London and York had officially registered guilds of horners (MacGregor 1991, 373). However, leather and horn working were closely associated activities (MacGregor 1998, 11), whose archaeological evidence cannot always be disentangled. At least on methodological grounds it is therefore necessary to discuss the two trades together.

The fact that this paper deals with the post-Roman period in England does not imply that leather working was not practised before. The question of how old is the use and processing of hides and skins raises the problem of defining what we mean by "leather working". The skins of animals represent a perishable material that will eventually rot if it is not cured. There is little doubt that Palaeolithic people used animal skins for clothing, making objects and possibly building tents. This means that they must have adopted some system, however primitive, to preserve the skins as leather. Blunt-edged concave tools, very similar to metal tools used until recently for scraping away the epidermis and the hairs from the skin, have been found in Palaeolithic sites (Forbes 1957, 4). Complex methods of leather preparation involving oils, mineral and vegetable agents are known to have evolved gradually since prehistoric times. Implements probably used in connection with leather working are known for Neolithic and Bronze Age Europe (Forbes 1957, 13–16). Archaeological evidence of a prehistoric (pre-dynastic) tannery was discovered in Egypt. "Goat skins ready for processing, tools, finished leather and tanning materials of acacia pods" were all found (Forbes 1957, 23). Evidence of leather working is abundant in ancient (dynastic) Egypt, in the form of leather objects and pictorial representations on reliefs and wall paintings in tombs. We also know that tanning was practised in ancient Mesopotamia and Greece. A passage in Homer mentions the preparation of a hide with oils (Waterer 1956, 148–9). Already in early Roman times leather working was a formally organised profession and tanners are mentioned amongst the first guilds (Forbes 1957, 49). This suggests that by then leather working was already regarded as an industry. This may have already been the case in Ancient Egypt and Mesopotamia, whereas it is unlikely that in pre-urban societies the trade was sufficiently centralised and organised to deserve the definition of industrial activity. Therefore, if for "leather working" we simply mean the use and basic processing of animal skins for human use, the practice possibly goes back to the Palaeolithic. If we are instead dealing with leather working as a properly organised industry this is likely to have started evolving with the beginning of urbanisation.

There is abundant archaeological evidence that horn was also a material commonly used since prehistoric times. Since this was never as important an industry as leather working, it is more difficult to track it down in the ancient

sources. Horning could even be an itinerant activity (MacGregor 1989, 117), therefore making this profession more elusive (at least archaeologically) and not necessarily connected to urban centres. However, the fact that in medieval England at least two cities had guilds of horners (see above) means that, although perhaps in a localised way, horning could also be regarded as an industrial activity.

THE LEATHER AND HORN TRADES

If we consider the importance of leather, its widespread use, and the length of its history, it is not suprising that its trade was characterised by a large variety of professions involved, materials used and systems adopted. In theory the preparation of leather may look like a simple matter. Animal skins are made of three main layers and the work of the tanner is to get rid of the internal and external (hairy) layers, and to preserve the middle portion (*derma*). In practice, there are many different ways to achieve this result.

A full account of how the leather trade was organized in medieval and early modern England is provided by several sources and it would be redundant to repeat it here. However, in order to analyse critically the archaeological evidence, the basic stages and types of leather preparation, as known from archaeological and particularly historical sources, are briefly described in Table 9.

The processes described above represent generalisations, and variations certainly occurred. Practices changed over time and differences between different areas of the country are also known. The evidence is mainly based on 16th and 17th century sources and, although it seems that the essential processes were inherited from medieval times, the possibility that in earlier times things may have been done in a slightly different way has to be considered.

The process called "tanning", strictly speaking, only applies to the use of tannin from vegetable products (in England, mainly oak bark), which is described in the left column of the table. However, tawing, which is typical of the light leather trade, is also occasionally called "mineral tanning" and the word "tanning" is sometimes loosely used to include all aspects of the leather processing. In addition to the two main processes described above, oil tanning or "chamoising" probably also deserves a mention. This was sometimes adopted to process the skins of animals such as sheep, deer, seal and calf (Waterer 1956, 155; Thomson 1981, 173).

The heavy leather trade was a much more controlled and regulated activity than the light leather trade. The separation of the various professional figures involved in the trade was quite rigid for the former, but the activities of the whittawyer, the fellmonger and the glover could from time to time be carried out by the same craftsman (Thomson 1981, 171).

Table 9. Basic stages and types of leather preparation, as known from archaeological and particularly historical sources. The information is mainly based on the evidence provided in Thomson (1981), though the works of Waterer (1956), Forbes (1957), Clarkson (1960–1 and 1966), Serjeantson (1989), Basing (1990), Cherry (1991) and Shaw (1996) have also been taken into account.

CATTLE HIDES
(HEAVY LEATHER TRADE)

Butcher: sells hide to the tanner, generally with horns and hooves still attached. Sometimes the horns are cut off and sold to the horner by the butcher himself. The hide may be treated with salt as an interim preservative.

Tanner (washing and liming): trims off bones and horns, washes the hide; immerses hides in lime pits (alkaline solution) to ease the removal of external and internal layers; extracts hide and scrapes the surface fat and hair.

Tanner (drenching): soaks hides in an acidic liquor made of rye, barley or ash bark (and/or urine) for further cleaning and removal of excess lime.

OR soaking in an alkaline solution made of dog or other animals' dung and bird droppings.

Tanner (proper tanning): immersion in tanning pits filled with a tanning liquor (oak bark) to preserve the hide and to give it a uniform colour; hides moved to other water-filled pits where they are laid with several layers of ground oak bark; after several months (at least 9) the hides are dried and sold to the currier or the shoemaker

Currier: converts the hard leather produced by the tanner into a more uniform and softer material through various operations some implying mild tanning.

Shoemaker or other leather worker: converts the leather into a finished product.

SHEEP, PIG, HORSE, DEER, DOG
AND OTHER SKINS
(LIGHT LEATHER TRADE)

Butcher: sells hide to the whittawyer (medieval) or the fellmonger (post-medieval), generally with horns and hooves still attached. Sometimes the horns are cut off and sold to the horner by the butcher himself.

Fellmonger (post-medieval): takes the skin from the farmer or butcher, removes wool (if sheepskin), preserves skin in salt and sells it to the whittawyer

Whittawyer (phase 1): acquires skin from butcher, fellmonger or (unlike the tanner) from casualty animals. Skins are limed, unhaired and washed and then usually trampled in a barrel (or tub) together with a mixture of materials including alum and oil.

Whittawyer (phase 2): the leather is then softened and dried and eventually sold (generally to the glover).

Glover or other leather worker: converts the leather into a finished product.

Horn is a keratinous material that covers the bony horncores of all bovids (i.e. animals like cattle, sheep, goat, antelopes but *not* deer). It is a plastic material very suitable for the manufacturing of objects. The first job of the horner was generally the separation of the horn from the horncore. This could be achieved by leaving the horns in the open air and waiting for the bond between the horn and the horncore to rot, so that the horn sheath could eventually simply be pulled off. Alternatively, soaking the horns in water could speed up the process. Horn removal could be facilitated by the use of a knife to loosen the horn sheath around its root (MacGregor 1991, 364). The practice of soaking the horns seems to have been predominant in England, whereas in various parts of the European mainland horns would commonly be pulled off dry (MacGregor 1989, 117). Once the horn had been separated it could be flattened, after being heated dry, and then cut and moulded to make objects. However, the finished product may not have been made by the horner, but by other craftsmen, among whom lantern-makers became predominant from the 17th century onwards (MacGregor 1991, 374). Very thin layers of horn are transparent and can therefore be used as lantern panes.

THE ARCHAEOLOGICAL EVIDENCE

Leather and horn are only preserved in the archaeological record in exceptional circumstances, waterlogging being probably the most common of these. Although occasional finds of leather and horn are well known (see for instance Ervynck *et al.* in this volume) and can provide invaluable information, more often we have to resort to indirect evidence, such as that provided by bones and horncores.

The skinning of an animal often leaves marks on the bones that can easily be detected by the zooarchaeologist. Skinning marks are normally produced by a sharp edged knife and tend to be thin, but clearly recognisable due to their very sharp edges. They are normally located at the extremities of the skeleton, since any other location would damage the pelt or hide. Cut marks located on phalanges, distal metapodials, nasal and orbital bones are almost certainly due to skinning, whereas cuts on proximal metapodials, carpals, tarsals and mandibles may also be associated with butchery, though skinning is in many cases still the more likely explanation. Cuts on frontal bones can be caused during the skinning of the animal but if located close enough to the base of the horncore may also be related to the extraction of the horn (see below). On small animals, such as cats and hares, skinning marks can be found as high on the limbs as at the level of the radius (Figure 14) and tibia and occasionally the humerus. Skinning marks on animal bones are frequently found on sites of all possible periods and areas, which confirms the universal use of hides and pelts for human purposes.

Chop, cut or saw marks at the base of horncores are also commonly found on mammal remains from archaeological

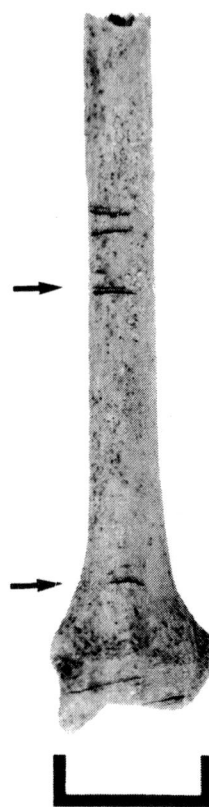

Figure 14. Cut marks on a cat radius from period 6 (late 16th–18th century) at Castle Mall, Norwich.

sites. Although less frequently, skulls with chopped off horncores are also found. Of these only sawn horncores can be taken as unquestionable evidence of the use of the horn sheath. The separation of the horncore from the skull presumably facilitated the extraction of the horn and if carried out with a saw it was unlikely to have been done by a butcher, particularly in pre-modern times. The use of saws in butchery practices is only known as a late post-medieval phenomenon. On some sites we also have evidence of cattle horncores that have been chopped close to the tip (Figure 15). This could be done to facilitate the removal of the horn sheath or because the tip in itself could be used to make objects such as handles or buttons (MacGregor 1989, 117). Horncores that have been chopped off also imply the possibility that the horn was extracted and used, but this cannot be proved, as the horncores may have been chopped off to be kept within the skin and eventually discarded by the tawyer or tanner at a later stage. Cut marks at the base of horncores may have been caused by the use of a knife to facilitate the extraction of the horn, but may alternatively be due to cutting the skin around the horns.

While evidence such as this is very useful in detecting an interest in leather and horn as working materials, if found on isolated specimens it tells us nothing about the

Figure 15. Cattle horncore sawn near the tip from period 6 (late 16th–18th century) at Castle Mall, Norwich.

existence of specialised workshops or the practice of leather and horn working as an industrial activity. To detect such features we have to turn our attention to specific deposits of animal bones, which are characterised by the fact that they derive from only one or two species, have a strong bias towards certain parts of the body – such as limb extremities and horncores – and may have evidence of cut or chop marks carried out in a regular and consistent way. When encountered these assemblages can be interpreted as industrial waste. We must then consider however the question of which craft, industry or trade may have been responsible in the accumulation of such assemblages.

THE INTERPRETATION OF ANIMAL BONE ASSEMBLAGES AS INDUSTRIAL WASTE

The interpretation of unusual assemblages of animal bones as deriving from tanning or other leather working activities relies on the assumption that once a carcass had been skinned, the extremities of the skeleton were left within the skin. We have documentary, pictorial, ethnographic

and archaeological evidence that support this assumption. Schmid (1972, 45), Thomson (1981, 162), Cherry (1991, 295) and Shaw (1996, 107) all agree that appendages of the skeleton would be left attached to the skin. Serjeantson (1989, Figs. 5 & 6) and Armitage (1990, 84) refer to pictorial evidence of this practice dating to the 16th (Germany) and 19th century (England). Shaw (1996, 117) describes skins still retaining their horns, which he observed in Moroccan present day tanneries. The best evidence of all is probably that deriving from excavated tanneries that produced deposits of animal bones. This is discussed below.

The question of which bones would have been left attached to the skin is debatable. There must have been a certain degree of variety in this, though horncores, phalanges and tail vertebrae were probably kept on a regular basis. MacGregor (1985, 42) has doubts that metapodials were ever left attached to the skin, but as we will see, the archaeological evidence is at odds with his suggestion. Nevertheless, the bones associated with an early 18th century pit at Walmgate (York) indicate that, in an assemblage interpreted as waste from sheepskin processing, phalanges were much more common than metapodials. This led O'Connor (1984, 36) to conclude that "skins arrived on site with phalanges still attached, but only a minority bore both phalanges and metapodials". "Skull" is mentioned by Shaw (1996, 107) as one of the appendages left with the skin, but this is unlikely to be the whole skull – which is heavy and bulky – and more probably refers to the frontal. The reason why this practice was adopted is discussed by Serjeantson (1989, 139–40), who quotes Schmid's (1974) suggestion that the tanner would establish the age of the animal by analysis of the horns. Serjeantson also suggests that the leather worker might have used the feet as a supply of neat's-foot oil, which would have eventually been utilised to dress the leather. It is also possible that the practice was a consequence of market practices, with the tanner being in charge of the supply of horns to the horner and metapodials to the bone worker.

It is therefore possible that concentrations of bones of the distal limb or of the top of the skull (including horncores) may be related to tanning waste. The interpretation of such assemblages is, however, far from straightforward as a number of different activities may lead to the accumulation of similar bone assemblages.

To get a better understanding of the composition of an animal bone assemblage deriving from leather working, it is worth paying attention to the type of bones found on sites that are unquestionably interpreted as tanneries, on the basis of structural and other evidence. Surprisingly this is a source of information that has been under-used by zooarchaeologists. One of the best and most revealing examples is represented by the site of The Green at Northampton (Shaw 1996). There is structural evidence – mainly in the form of circular and rectangular pits – that in the period spanning the late 15th to the 17th centuries the site was occupied by a tanning complex. Documentary, soil, chemical and zooarchaeological evidence are all consistent with this interpretation. The study of the animal bones (Harman 1996) revealed a number of bone assemblages from pits that, because of their composition, are most likely to derive from the industrial activities occurring on site. For instance, two pits dated to the 15th–16th century contained numerous sheep metapodials, whereas another pit of the same period was full of cattle horncores, cattle frontal bones (with no evidence of cut marks) and complete bones of mature horses deriving from different parts of the body (Harman 1996, 95–97). One of the pits in the 17th century phase had abundant cattle metapodials and, to a lesser extent, cattle horncores and frontal fragments. Most of the metapodials had chop and cut marks probably produced when they were cut off from the rest of the carcass (Harman 1996, 98).

An oval pit – probably dating to the 16th century – found on a site at St Albans (Hertfordshire), interpreted on the basis of archaeological and documentary information as a tannery, contained oak bark and cattle horncores (Saunders 1977, 10). Recent excavations at a tannery site in Birmingham produced accumulations of cattle horncores, leather fragments and lumps of decomposed bark in pits dated to the late 17th and 18th century (Murray 2000). Structural evidence from the York site of Skeldergate (11th–12th century) is strongly suggestive of a tannery (see Addyman 1984, 11) and accumulations of cattle and goat horncores were found at this site. O'Connor (1984, 28–9) suggests that these are more likely to derive from horn working activities, but, in view of the general archaeological evidence, his suggestion may need to be reconsidered. The deposit of sheep foot bones from probable tanning pits at Walmgate has already been mentioned (see above). Shaw (1996, 111–4) provides a useful review of known post-Roman tanneries in England. This shows that accumulations of horse bones, sheep metapodials, sheep, goat and, particularly commonly, cattle horncores can all represent tanning waste.

Among cases from overseas, remarkable are the 15th to 18th century tanneries found in Bruges (Belgium). These are described by Hillewaert and Ervynck (1991) and Ervynck *et al.* (in this volume). Huge numbers of cattle horncores with no evidence of cut marks were found, but no bones from the post-cranial skeleton. Another well known tannery (of late medieval date) is that excavated at 's-Hertogenbosch-Gertru (Netherlands). This produced bones from a greater variety of body parts, but cattle and particularly goat horncores were by far predominant (Prummel 1982, 121). Early medieval goat horncores and foot bones were found in Basel in connection with tanning liquor plants and pieces of leather clothing (Schmid 1973). A group of fifty-nine 15th century pits interpreted as tanning pits at Vác in Hungary were found in association with sheep and goat horncores, deer skull fragments and a lynx skeleton (Bartosiewicz 1995, 73). There are undoubtedly many more sites, but a full review of the European evidence is beyond the scope of this paper.

The animal bone evidence for horn workshops is much scantier. This is not surprising, considering the minor importance that this activity had in comparison with leather working. The only case I am aware of is that of Hornpot Lane in York. This remarkable site provided evidence for 14th century furnaces, a fireplace and a large shallow pit, which was lined with clay and wood and filled with large numbers of cattle and goat horncores (Wenham 1964, 26–7). This was interpreted as a soaking pit, where horns were kept in preparation for their extraction from their bony core. Cram (1982) suggests that pits from the 16th and 17th century excavated at Water Street, Stamford (Lincolnshire), which were filled with cattle horncores, might belong to a horn workshop, too. However, the lack of any other supporting evidence, such as that existing for Hornpot Lane, indicates that his assumption has to be treated with caution. The Water Street site resembles others interpreted as tanneries (see also Mahany 1982, 47 and Shaw 1996, 114).

This brief review of faunal finds from tanneries and horn workshops tries to answer the question of how animal bone assemblages that may derive from industrial activities, but for which we have no structural evidence, could be interpreted. Moreover, the evidence allows us to make a number of other considerations:

–   The archaeological findings support and complement the evidence deriving from other sources that animal skins would travel with appendages of the skeleton still attached. This may not always have been the case, but it certainly happened with some regularity.
–   Cattle horncores are the bones most commonly and most abundantly found on tannery sites. This confirms the dominant role that cattle hides had in the leather trade.
–   The presence of horncores of various animals on tannery sites suggests that horns may either not have been utilised, or that the horner would receive only the outer sheaths from the tanner. When and if the latter occurred, the horn working activity would have become zooarchaeologically invisible (except in cases of waterlogged preservation).
–   The occasional presence of cattle bones mixed with bones of other animals indicates that, as also suggested by Shaw (1996, 116–7), the division between the heavy and the light leather trade may not have been as rigid as the documentary evidence seems to imply.
–   Whereas in the case of cattle, sheep and goat only bones of either the head or the feet are generally present, elements of all parts of the horse skeleton are found on tannery sites. This means that tanneries would receive cattle hides, sheep and goatskins, but complete horse carcasses. Since horses were not generally consumed, their carcasses would not have been processed by a butcher.

There are several types of animal bone assemblages that

Table 10. Types of animal bone assemblages that we may expect from workshops related to the main professions involved in the leather and horn trades.

	Butcher	Leather worker	Horner
Skull fragments (including teeth) and feet	X		
Horncores, (frontals) and feet	(X)	X	
Feet	X	X	
Horncores	X	X	X

are usually interpreted as signifying specialised activities. Having seen what sort of animal bones are found in connection with leather and horn working, we are now in a better position to evaluate these assemblages in a critical way.

Table 10 shows what kind of assemblages we may expect from workshops related to the main professions involved in the leather and horn trades. A typical assemblage that would have been generated by a butcher is characterised by an abundance of bones of the head and feet, as these are the parts of the body that carry the least amount of meat, often regarded as being of lower quality. These are the assemblages that zooarchaeologists normally define as "primary butchery waste". However, there are parts of the head, such as brain, tongue and cheek muscles, which can be eaten. These could have been traded by the butcher, in which case only the bones of the feet ended up in the primary butchery waste. There is late medieval documentary evidence that butchers may have sold horns, either still attached to the bony core or off it, directly to the horner (Armitage 1990, 84). If the latter procedure were followed the butcher would eventually have the problem of disposing of large amounts of horncores. Accumulations of horncores may therefore have been built up by a butcher. We have seen that deposits of horncores, foot bones or a combination of the two can all represent leather working waste. On the contrary, the horner would have no need to receive any parts of the skeletons, other than the horncores. In fact, as mentioned above, even those may not always have reached the horner's workshop.

The interpretation of these assemblages of animal bones is therefore far from being straightforward, especially in the absence of structural or other archaeological evidence. The only case in which we can quite confidently attribute a deposit to one of the activities associated with the leather trade is when concentrations of foot bones and horncores – with or without the frontal part of the skull – are found in the same context. It is not impossible that such assemblages may have been formed by a butcher, but it is unlikely, as the butcher would have processed the carcasses and the horns in different moments and the rubbish generated by such activities would therefore only rarely end up together in the same context, provided that this is in a primary deposit. These bones can get mixed up as a

consequence of re-deposition, but such contexts will normally contain a variety of remains deriving from different activities and will not be possible to associate them with a particular craft in the first place.

We have seen that some pits found on tannery sites do contain combinations of horncores, metapodials and phalanges, but such deposits are otherwise rare. An accumulation of sheep phalanges, metapodials and horncores was found in a late medieval pit at the site of Castle Mall (Norwich) (Figure 16). All horncores had been chopped at the base and many of the metapodials bore skinning marks. The assemblage was interpreted as deriving from a whittawyer (Albarella *et al.* 1997). If fellmongers were already active in the 15th–early 16th century they could have also been responsible for it. Another interesting assemblage is represented by a large group of calf foot bones found in an 18th century pit at Kingston upon Thames (London) (Serjeantson *et al.* 1986). The absence of a water supply in the vicinity and of historical evidence of the presence of a tannery in the area, led the authors to suggest that a middle man, such as a fellmonger, could have "removed the feet before passing the skins on to the tanner" (Serjeantson *et al.* 1986, 232).

THE EVIDENCE FOR CENTRAL ENGLAND

In this section I will review the zooarchaeological evidence for leather and horn working activities in central England. The area under consideration includes East Anglia, the East Midlands and the West Midlands, up to the Welsh border. I have taken into consideration 275 animal bone assemblages of post-Roman date. The actual number of sites is lower than that because one site may have provided several bone assemblages of different dates, and these are included individually in the count. For this reason the expression "period/site" rather than "site" will be used. Out of the total considered a mere twenty-one period/sites have assemblages that have been interpreted as horn or leather working waste. These are listed in Appendix 1. Appendix 2 gives the characteristics of these bone assemblages. Some of the period/sites have provided evidence for the industrial use of more than one species, for instance at Midland Road (Bedford) there are accumulations of horncores of cattle, sheep *and* goat (Grant 1979a). This list is not fully comprehensive, but a substantial proportion of the sites in the region is likely to be included.

The results of this survey are presented in a diagrammatic form in Figures 18 to 22. The period under consideration has crudely been divided into "Saxon to mid medieval" and "late medieval to post-medieval". An analysis of these bar charts suggests the following:

– The actual number of sites that have provided evidence that *may* signify leather or horn working is small. Therefore, even though the total number of period/sites taken into account is quite large, any

Figure 16. Accumulation of sheep horncones, metapodials and phalanges from period 5 (mid/late 14th to mid 16th century) at Castle Mall, Norwich.

conclusions that can be drawn from the analysis of such a small sample have to be tentative.

– No sites of early or mid Saxon date have provided bone evidence that can be associated with industrial activities. However, the total number of animal bone assemblages known from this period is much lower than for any of the later periods.

– Most of the accumulations of horncores belong to the earlier period, whereas assemblages interpreted as tanning waste are mainly of late medieval or post-medieval date (Figure 18).

– The increase in the number of tanning waste sites is not matched by an equivalent increase of sites with evidence of skinning marks on the bones. On the contrary, the decline in the frequency of horn-waste assemblages goes hand in hand with a reduction in the frequency of evidence of horn working (chop and cut marks on horncores) (Figure 19).

– All sites that have provided possible evidence of industrial waste are located in towns. The few castles and industrial sites are also located in urban areas (Figure 20). Most of the evidence comes from the towns of Bedford, Warwick, Norwich, Northampton, Leicester, Lincoln and Hertford.

– Evidence of skinning is found with greater frequency on bones of non-food animals such as cats (Figure 17) and horse, than on cattle and sheep. Evidence for horn working is found with almost equal frequency in goat, sheep and cattle (Figure 21).

– Similar proportions of cattle and sheep assemblages have a predominance of bones from the extremities of the body, but no such assemblages have been

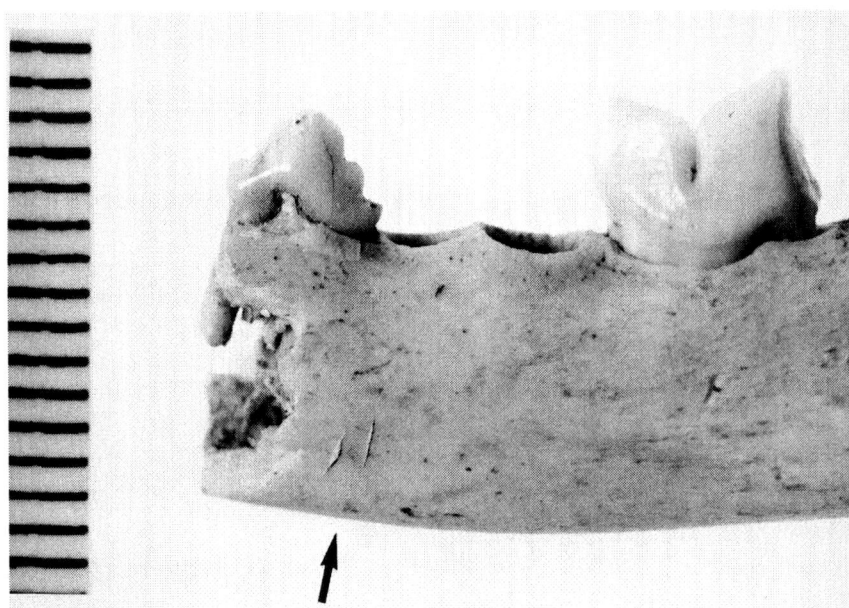

Figure 17. Cut marks on a cat mandible from period 4 (late 12th to mid 14th century) at Castle Mall, Norwich.

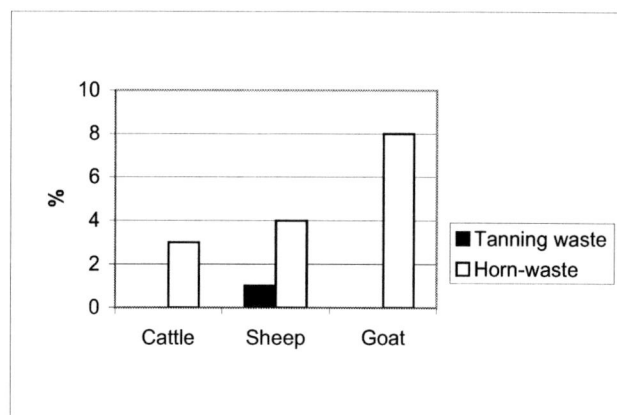

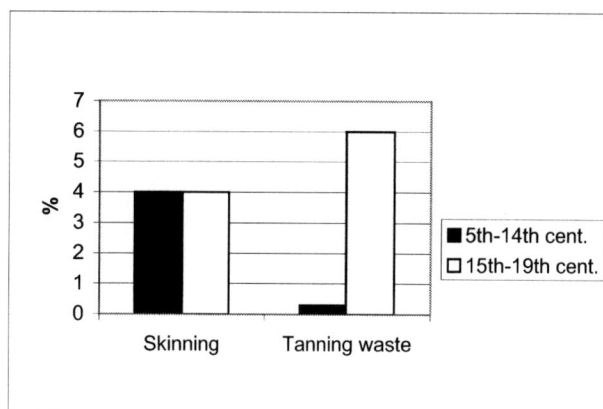

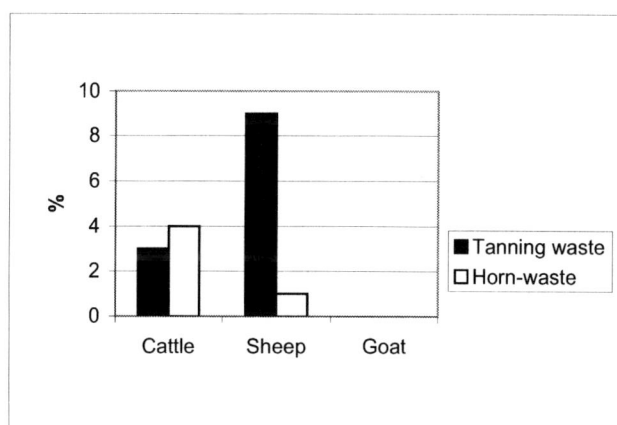

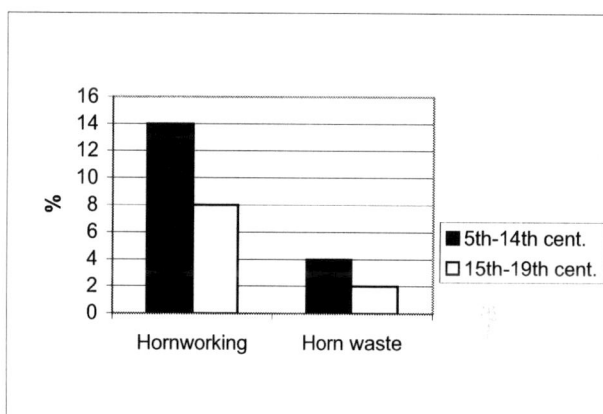

Figure 18. Frequency of tanning and horn-waste for different species in central England: 5th–14th centuries (top) and 15th–19th centuries (bottom).

Figure 19. Frequency of animal bone assemblages with evidence of skinning or tanning waste in central England (cattle and sheep); frequency of animal bone assemblages with evidence of horn-working or horn-waste in central England (cattle, sheep and goat).

recorded for the goat. On the contrary, the proportion of assemblages with goat bones in which horncores predominate is far greater than for cattle or sheep (Figure 22).

These observations may lead to a number of working hypotheses, which it is hoped will be tested against a larger sample of sites.

– The unchanged proportion of assemblages bearing skinning marks seems to suggest that the intensity of the exploitation of animal hides and skins was similar in medieval and post-medieval times in central England. However, the fact that most "tanning waste" sites are concentrated in the later period may suggest that towards the end of the Middle Ages the leather trade was becoming more and more an industrial activity organised on medium to large scale. This would have led to the formation of large accumulations of bone waste, which are more likely to be found by archaeologists. More commonly than in the later period, in medieval times unspecialised workers may have processed skins using small-scale facilities.

These would have left less substantial bone assemblages, which are more likely to have been overlooked in the archaeological record.

– The evidence points to fact that the exploitation of horn may have declined in the later period. We have seen that accumulations of horncores can also derive from tanneries. Thus their reduction in numbers may also indicate that the practice of leaving the horns in the skin may have been in decline. However, the fact that there is also a reduction in the frequency of assemblages with chopped or cut horncores suggests that the former is a more likely explanation. This phenomenon may be due to any – or more likely to a combination – of the following reasons:

1. Objects originally made in horn were replaced by others made with alternative materials. We have seen that by the 17th century horn was almost exclusively used to make lantern panes. Wenham (1964, 30) mentions a decline of the horn craft in York in the 16th century, though there was apparently a revival in

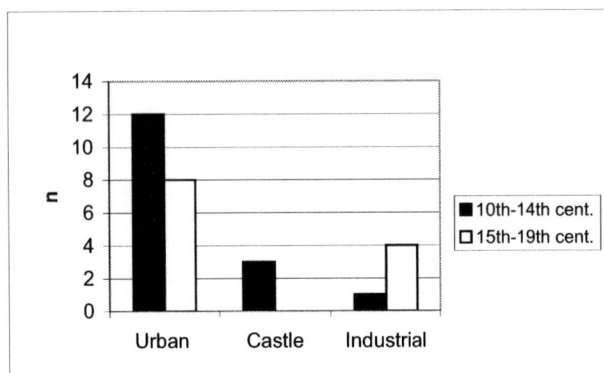

Figure 20. Types of sites with tanning or horn waste.

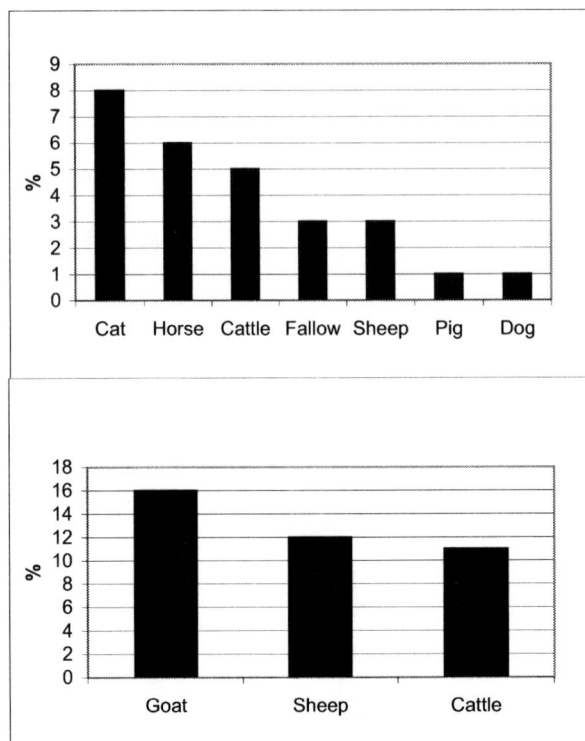

Figure 21. Medieval and post-Medieval sites in central England: frequency of sites with evidence of skinning; frequency of sites with evidence of horn-working.

the 18th century. Although late and post-medieval horn drinking vessels are known, these would be "generally reserved for special celebrations" (MacGregor 1985, 152), and ordinary vessels were presumably more commonly made in glass (see MacGregor 1991, 374).

2. The slaughtering of larger numbers of livestock in connection with the increased consumption of meat and the greater emphasis on a pastoral economy in the late/post medieval period (Albarella 1997a, 28) may have caused the creation of a *surplus* in the supply of horn. A less intensive use of the horns would therefore be expected. It is interesting in this respect to notice that in both post-medieval tanneries at Northampton and Bruges cut marks were not observed on any of the cattle horncores (see above).

3. Hornless breeds of cattle and sheep became increasingly common in the modern period.

– Leather and horn working were predominantly – if not exclusively – urban activities. This is consistent with the documentary evidence (see Cherry 1991, 301). There are some known cases of the practice of the leather craft in the countryside (Clarkson 1966, 38; Kowaleski 1995, 301–2; MacGregor 1998, 23), but these have hitherto not been found in the archaeological record. Considering the fact that tannery was a disagreeable activity that would generate water pollution and unpleasant smells it may be surprising that its practice was located in the middle of an urban centre. However, many animals would be brought to urban markets "on the hoof", and it would therefore make sense to have tanneries located in the proximity of such a large supply of hides and skins. In some respect the hide trade could be regarded as a "by-product of urban meat consumption" (Kowaleski 1995, 303).

– The high frequency of cat bones with cut marks reminds us of the fact that, although leather deriving from cattle hides was probably the most important product, the skins of smaller animals were also prized.

Some of these would be more valuable with the fur on ("pelts") and would be dealt with by the "skinner" or "furrier" (Serjeantson 1989, 129).

MISSING GOATS

The anomaly of the large predominance of horncores in goat assemblages and the simultaneous complete absence of accumulation of goat foot bones (Figures 18 and 22) represents one of the most intriguing aspects of the zoo-archaeological evidence for the English medieval period and merits some brief discussion.

Of the 275 period/sites under consideration only 27% had stated evidence of the presence of the goat, and in most cases with only a few specimens. The problem of the under-representation of the goat in the archaeological record in comparison with the data from historical documents has been discussed elsewhere (Albarella 1999, 873–4). As we have seen, the most puzzling piece of evidence regarding the goat is the fact that this under-representation applies to all anatomical elements except horncores. The latter can be found in large numbers and sometimes are even more common than sheep horncores. The fact that horncores are more easily distinguished between sheep and goat than any other bones suggests that this over-representation of goat horncores may be due to an identification bias. However, this would not explain the dearth of

Predominance of horncores

Predominance of skull and foot elements

Predominance of foot elements

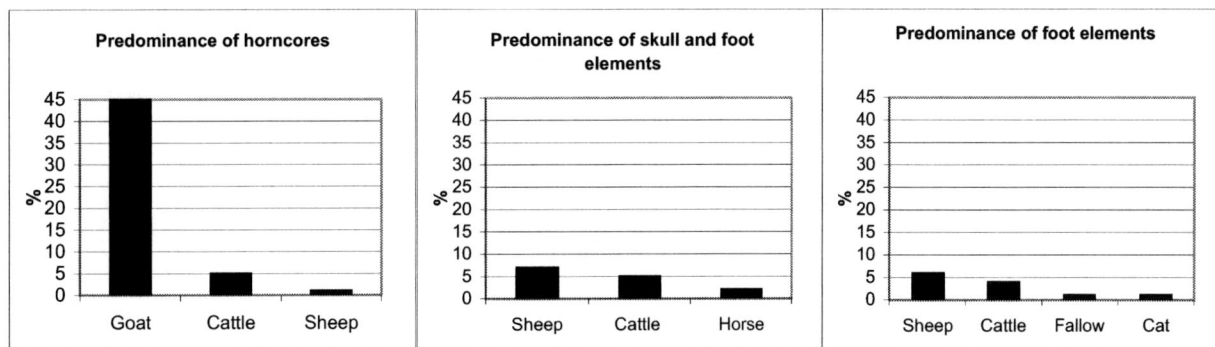

Figure 22. Medieval and post-Medieval sites in central England: predominance of horncores; predominance of skull and foot elements; predominance of foot elements.

metapodials, which are the next easier bone to identify to species. It is therefore tempting to speculate that a trade in goat horncores could have existed in medieval times. Since goat bones are rare on English sites of different sorts, this trade would have operated with overseas countries. In the Netherlands the site of Dorestad offers a situation similar to many English sites, with large numbers of goat horn-cores but hardly any post-cranial bones. Yet at the above mentioned tannery site of 's-Hertogenbosch-Gertru there are not only horncores but also many goat post-cranial bones, which in fact outnumber those of sheep (Prummel 1982, 122). This situation is unknown for English sites.

If horncores had been traded in view of the use of the horn as working material, we should wonder why a horn trade is hardly ever mentioned in the documents. The various historians I have interrogated on the subject could not come up with a single reference to such a trade. It is therefore more likely that the horncores may have been imported with their skins. The trade in hides and skins is well known for the medieval period. For instance, regions located in the west of England regularly imported skins (mainly sheep and calf) from Ireland (Clarkson 1966, 28), whereas goatskins were imported at the Norwegian site of Gamlebyen, near Olso (Lie 1988 in Noddle 1994, 120). It is possible that a similar trade took place between England and the European mainland. At the medieval site of Haithabu in northern Germany, goat bones only repre-sented 10% of the total of sheep/goat remains, but up to 40% of the identified leather remains derived from goat (Reichstein and Tiessen 1974 in Noddle 1994, 119).

The assumption that such a trade in goatskins may have existed opens the other question of why goatskins would travel with attached horncores, but no foot bones, as we have seen was commonly the case for sheep. Perhaps, this further anomaly might support the assumption of a long distance trade, in which it would have been desirable to get rid of as much weight and bulk as possible. However, the horncores – often large specimens from males – would have been a valuable source of horn and could not be left behind (see also Noddle 1994, 120). At this stage this has

to be regarded as a very tentative suggestion, but it is a question that is worth further investigation, as the solution of the mystery of the missing goat may throw additional light on our understanding of the general organisation of the leather trade.

CONCLUSIONS

The leather trade was one of the main industrial activities in medieval and early modern England. Although horn working was not of equal importance, the two trades were connected and it therefore makes sense to investigate them together. The zooarchaeological evidence for these practices can only rarely be easily interpreted. The evi-dence for the exploitation of skins and hides is normally straightforward, as cut marks located in specific parts of the skeleton are generally diagnostic of skinning. The use of the horn is more difficult to detect, as only saw marks on the horncores can provide unambiguous evidence for its occurrence. Accumulations of horncores and foot bones can be associated with specialised activities, but, in the absence of other evidence, only deposits of foot bones and horncores found together in the same context can confidently be attributed to one of the leather working activities. The existence of horners' workshops cannot be detected exclusively on the basis of the animal bone evidence, as butchers and tanners may also have accumu-lated horncores. This difficulty in the interpretation of animal bone assemblages of industrial origin emphasises the need for an analysis based on the integration of different sources of evidence. Zooarchaeologists should be wary of interpreting their evidence in isolation and should pay great attention to the general archaeological context. Hall and Kenward (in this volume), in analysing the tanning process from an archaeobotanical and archaeo-entomological point of view, stress a similar point.

A review of the evidence from central England hints at the possibility that leather working became a more central-ised activity towards the end of the Middle Ages, whereas the horn trade may have declined. The intensification of leather production may be associated with the greater emphasis on a pastoral economy and the increasing demand for meat that characterises the late medieval period and which made hides and skins easily available on the urban marketplace (Kowaleski 1990, 307). Partly as a consequence of this phenomenon, in medieval and post-medieval times the leather and horn industries were predominantly based in urban areas. Cattle hides were probably the most valuable source of leather, but we also have evidence for the intensive skinning of non-food animals such as horses and cats. The abundance of goat horncores, accompanied by the scarcity of post-cranial bones of the same species, leads to the suggestion that there may have been an international trade in goatskins and horns.

Acknowledgements
I would like to thank: Peter Murphy and Pat Wiltshire for inviting me to contribute to this volume; Ian Baxter, Allan Hall, Roel Lauwerier, Gisela Mattson, Michael McKinnon, Arturo Morales, Wietske Prummel, Jörg Schibler, Dale Serjeantson and Naomi Sykes for help with references; Marina Ciaraldi, Simon Davis, Keith Dobney, Deborah Jacques, Cluny Johnstone, Filippo Manconi, Emily Murray, Dale Serjeantson, Richard Thomas and an anonymous referee for comments on an earlier version of this paper. The evidence from central England derives from a data-set put together as part of my review of the zoo-archaeological evidence for that region; this work was commissioned and funded by English Heritage.

The photographs, Figures 14, 15 and 17 were taken by Graham Norrie (University of Birmingham), whereas Figure 16 is here reproduced courtesy of the Norfolk Archaeological Unit.

References

Addyman, P.V. 1984. The archaeology, pp. 10–11 in O'Connor, T, *Selected groups of bones from Skeldergate and Walmgate* (The Archaeology of York, The Animal Bones 15/1). York: Council for British Archaeology.

Albarella, U. 1997a. Size, power, wool and veal: zooarchaeological evidence for late medieval innovations, pp.19–30 in De Boe, G. and Verhaeghe, F. (eds), *Environment and subsistence in medieval Europe* (Papers of the 'Medieval Europe Brugge 1997' Conference Volume 9). Brugge: Institute for the Archaeological Heritage of Flanders.

Albarella, U. 1997b. *The medieval animal bones excavated in 1996 from Coslany Street, Norwich, Norfolk*. London: Ancient Monuments Laboratory Report New Series 86/97.

Albarella, U. 1999. 'The mistery of husbandry': medieval animals and the problem of integrating historical and archaeological evidence. *Antiquity* 73 (282), 867–75.

Albarella, U., Beech, M., and Mulville, J. 1997. *The Saxon, medieval and post-medieval mammal and bird bones excavated 1989-91 from Castle Mall, Norwich, Norfolk*. London: Ancient Monuments Laboratory Report New Series 72/97.

Armitage, P. 1978. Hertfordshire cattle and London meat markets in the 17th and 18th centuries. *The London Archaeologist* 3(8), 217–23.

Armitage, P.L. 1990. Post-medieval cattle horn cores from the Greyfriars site, Chichester, West Sussex, England. *Circaea* 7(2) 1990 for 1989, 81–90.

Bartosiewicz, L. 1995. *Animals in the urban landscape in the wake of the Middle Ages. A case study from Vác, Hungary* (BAR International Series 609). Oxford: British Archaeological Reports.

Basing, P. 1990. *Trades and crafts in medieval manuscripts*. London: the British Library.

Baxter, I. 1998. Late medieval tawyers' waste and pig skeletons in early post-medieval pits from Bonners Lane, Leicester, U.K. *Anthropozoologica* 28, 55–63.

Baxter, I. 1999. *Report on the animal bone from the Oxford Road Watermill (HAT 291), Aylesbury, Buckinghamsire*. Unpublished Report .

Cherry, J. 1991. Leather, pp. 295–318 in Blair, J. and Ramsay, N. *English medieval industries. Craftsmen, Techniques, Products*. London and Rio Grande: the Hambledon Press.

Clarke, C.P., Gardiner, M.F. and Huggins, P.J. 1993. Excavations at Church St. Waltham Abbey 1976–87: urban development and prehistoric evidence. *Essex Archaeology and History* 24, 69–113.

Clarkson, L.A. 1960–61. The organization of the English leather industry in the late sixteenth and seventeenth century. *The Economic History Review*, second series XIII (1,2 & 3), 245–256.

Clarkson, L.A. 1966. The leather crafts in Tudor and Stuart England. *The Agricultural History Review* XIV part I, 25–39.

Cram, L. 1982. The pits and horncores, pp. 48–51 in Mahany, C., Burchard, A. and Simpson, G. *Excavations in Stamford Lincolnshire 1963–69*. London: The Society for Medieval Archaeology monograph series.

Dobney, K., Jaques, D. and Irving, B. Undated. *Of butchers and breeds. Report on vertebrate remains from various sites in the City of Lincoln* (Lincoln Archaeological Studies 5). Lincoln: City of Lincoln Archaeology Unit.

Dyer, C. 1988. Documentary evidence: problems and enquiries, pp. 149–161 in Astill, G. and Grant, A. *The countryside of medieval England*. Oxford: Blackwell.

Farmer, D. 1991. Marketing the produce of the countryside, 1200–1500, pp. 324–430 in Miller, E. (ed.) *The Agrarian History of England and Wales. Volume III 1348–1500*. Cambridge: Cambridge University Press.

Forbes, R.J. 1957. *Studies in Ancient Technology. Volume V*. Leiden: E.J. Brill.

Grant, A. 1979a. The animal bones, pp. 94–95 in Hassall, J. Midland Road, pp. 79–95 in Baker, D., Baker, E., Hassall, J. and Simco, A. Excavations in Bedford 1967–77. *Bedfordshire Archaeological Journal* 13.

Grant, A. 1979b. The animal bones, pp. 58–62 in Baker, D and Baker, E. The excavations: Bedford Castle, pp. 7–64 in Baker, D, Baker, E, Hassall, J and Simco, A. Excavations in Bedford 1967–77. *Bedfordshire Archaeological Journal* 13.

Grant, A. 1979c. The animal bones, pp. 103–107 in Hassall, J. St John's Street, pp. 97–126 in Baker, D., Baker, E., Hassall, J. and Simco, A. Excavations in Bedford 1967–77. *Bedfordshire Archaeological Journal* 13.

Grant, A. 1983. The animal bones, pp. 51–2 in Hassall, J. Excavations in Bedford 1977–1978. *Bedfordshire Archaeology* 16, 37–64.

Hall, A.R. and Tomlinson, P. 1996. *User guide to the Environmental Archaeology Bibliography (EAB)*. London: Ancient Monuments Laboratory Report New Series 6/96.

Hamilton, J. 1992. Animal bone, pp. 30–1 and Fiche in Cracknell, S and Bishop, M.W. Excavations at 23–33 Brook Street, Warwick, 1973. *Birmingham Warwickshire Archaeological. Society* 97, 1–40 and Fiche.

Harman, M. 1979. The mammalian bones, pp. 328–32 in Williams, J.H. *St Peter's Street Northampton, excavations 1973–1976*. Northampton: Northampton Development Corporation Archaeological Monographs 2.

Harman, M. 1996. The mammal bones, pp. 89–102 in Shaw, M. The excavation of a late 15th- to 17th-century tanning complex at The Green, Northampton. *Post-Medieval Archaeology* **30**, 63–127.

Hillewaert, B. and Ervynck, A. 1991. Leerlooierskuipen Langs de Eekhoutstraat, pp. 109–23 in *Stad Brugge Stedelijke Musea Jaarboek 1989–90*. Bruges.

Kowaleski, M. 1995. *Local markets and regional trade in medieval Exeter*. Cambridge: Cambridge University Press.

MacGregor, A. 1985. *Bone, Antler, Ivory and Horn. The technology of skeletal material since the Roman period*. London: Croom Helm.

MacGregor, A. 1989. Bone, antler and horn industries in the urban context, pp. 107–128 in Serjeantson, D. and Waldron, T. (eds) *Diet and crafts in town. The evidence of animal remains from the Roman to the Post-Medieval period* (BAR British Series 199). Oxford: British Archaeological Reports.

MacGregor, A. 1991. Antler, bone and horn, pp. 355–88 in Blair, J. and Ramsay, N. *English medieval industries. Craftsmen, Techniques, Products*. London and Rio Grande: the Hambledon Press.

MacGregor, A. 1998. Hides, horns and bones: animals and inter-dependent industries in the early urban context, pp. 11–26 in Cameron E. (ed.) *Leather and fur. Aspects of early medieval trade and technology*. London: Archetype.

Mahany, C. 1982. Two urban sites and a Saxo-Norman pottery kiln, pp. 13–104 in Mahany, C., Burchard, A. and Simpson, G. *Excavations in Stamford Lincolnshire 1963–69*. London: The Society for Medieval Archaeology monograph series.

Murphy, M. and Galloway, J. 1992. Marketing animals and animal products in London's hinterland circa 1300. *Anthropozoologica* **16**, 93–100.

Murray, E. 2000. *The Custard Factory, Digbeth, Birmingham*. Assessment of the animal bone. Unpublished report.

Noddle, B. 1994. The under-rated goat, pp. 117–128 in Hall A.R. and Kenward H.K. (eds) *Urban–rural connexions: perspectives from environmental archaeology*. Oxford: Oxbow.

O'Connor, T. 1984. *Selected groups of bones from Skeldergate and Walmgate* (The Archaeology of York, The Animal Bones 15/1). York: Council for British Archaeology.

Prummel, W. 1982. The archaeozoological study of urban medieval sites in the Netherlands, pp. 117–22 in Hall, A.R. and Kenward, H.K. (eds) *Environmental archaeology in the urban context* (Research Report 43). London: Council for British Archaeology.

Saunders, C. 1977. A sixteenth century tannery in St Albans. *Hertfordshire's Past* **3**, 9–12.

Schmid, E. 1972. *Atlas of animal bones. For prehistorians, archaeologist and quaternary geologists*. Amsterdam-London-New York: Elsevier.

Schmid, E. 1973. Ziegenhörner als Gerberei-Abfall. *Schweizer Volkskunde* **63** (5/6), 65–6.

Schmid. E. 1974. Als das Gerben noch ein langwieriges Geschäft war. *Ciba-Geigy-Zeitschrift* **4**/1, 8–11

Scott, S. 1986. *A sixteenth century cattle horn assemblage from the site of St Mary's Guildhall, Lincoln*. London: Ancient Monuments Laboratory Report Old Series 4965.

Serjeantson, D. 1989. Animal remains and the tanning trade, pp. 129–46 in Serjeantson, D. and Waldron, T. (eds). *Diet and crafts in town. The evidence of animal remains from the Roman to the Post-Medieval period* (BAR British Series 199). Oxford: British Archaeological Reports.

Serjeantson, D., Waldron, T. and McCracken, S. 1986. Veal and calfskin in eighteenth century Kingston? *The London Archaeologist*, **5** (9), 227–231.

Shaw, M. with contributions by Denham, V, Harman M., and Evans J. 1996. The excavation of a late 15th- to 17th-century tanning complex at The Green, Northampton. *Post-Medieval Archaeology* **30**, 63–127.

Thomson, R. 1981. Leather manufacture in the post-medieval period with special reference to Northamptonshire. *Post-Medieval Archaeology* **15**, 161–175.

Waterer, J.W. 1956. Leather, pp. 147–90 in Singer, C. and Holmyard, E.J. *History of Technology. Volume II*. Oxford: at the Clarendon Press.

Wenham, L.P. 1965. Hornpot Lane and the horners of York. *Annual Report of The Council of the Yorkshire Philosophical Society for 1964*, 25–56.

APPENDIX 1

LIST OF PERIOD/SITES FROM CENTRAL ENGLAND THAT HAVE PROVIDED ANIMAL BONE ASSEMBLAGES INTERPRETED AS DERIVING FROM LEATHER OR HORN WORKING.

The sites are named in accordance to the terminology adopted for the Environmental Archaeology Bibliography (EAB) (Hall and Tomlinson 1996).

N	SITE	LOCALITY	REFERENCE	PERIOD	TYPE
1	Midland Rd	Bedford	Grant 1979a	10th–13th	Urban
2	Empire Cinema 78	Bedford	Grant 1983	11th–12th	Urban
3	Brook St (25-33) 73	Warwick	Hamilton 1992	11th–12th	Urban
4	Castle Mall AML 72/97	Norwich	Albarella *et al.* 1997	11th–12th	Castle
5	Empire Cinema 78	Bedford	Grant 1983	11th–12th	Urban
6	St Johns St (29–39) 74	Bedford	Grant 1979b	11th–13th	Urban
7	Bedford Castle 69–73	Bedford	Grant 1979c	12th–13th	Castle
8	Coslany St AML 86/97	Norwich	Albarella 1997b	12th–14th	Urban
9	St Peters St (Nhtn) 73–6	Northampton	Harman 1979	12th–14th	Urban
10	The Green 83	Northampton	Harman 1996	12th–14th	Industrial
11	Church St (Waltham Abbey) 76–87	Waltham Abbey (Essex)	Clarke et al. 1993	14th–16th	Urban
12	St Peters St (Nhtn) 73–6	Northampton	Harman 1979	15th-early16th	Urban
13	Bonners Ln	Leicester	Baxter 1998	15th-early16th	Urban
14	Castle Mall AML 72/97	Norwich	Albarella *et al.* 1997	15th-early16th	Urban
15	The Green 83	Northampton	Harman 1996	15th-early16th	Industrial
16	St Marys Guildhall (Linc.) AML 4965	Lincoln	Scott 1986	16th	Urban
17	Lincoln sites (bones)	Lincoln	Dobney *et al.* Undated	16th	Urban
18	The Green 83	Northampton	Harman 1996	16th–17th	Industrial
19	Oxford Rd Watermill	Aylesbury (Buckinghamshire)	Baxter 1999	17th	Urban
20	Hertford Castle	Hertford	Armitage 1978	17th–18th	Urban
21	The Green 83	Northampton	Harman 1996	18th–19th	Industrial

APPENDIX 2

DETAILS OF THE ANIMAL BONE ASSEMBLAGES FROM THE PERIOD/SITES LISTED IN APPENDIX 1 IN THE "INTEPRETATION" COLUMN THE COMMENTS IN BRACKETS ARE BY THE AUTHOR.

N	SPECIES	CHOPPING, CUTTING, SAWING	DISTRIBUTION OF BODY PARTS	INTERPRETATION
1	Cattle	Evidence of chopped and sawn horncores	Predominance of horncores	Horn working waste (due to the mix of species present horn working is probably a more likely explanation than tanning)
1	Goat	Evidence of chopped horncores	Only horncores	Horn working waste (due to the mix of species present horn working is probably a more likely explanation than tanning)
1	Sheep	Evidence of chopped and sawn horncores	Predominance of horncores	Horn working waste (due to the mix of species present horn working is probably a more likely explanation than tanning)
2	Goat	Evidence of chopped horncores	Only horncores (66 complete)	Horn working waste (tawing also possible)
3	Sheep	Horncores chopped off skulls	Predominance of skull elements with horncores chopped off (all from a single pit)	(primary butchery leading to the collection of skins for tanning and/or horns for horn working)
4	Sheep	One context has four skulls with horncores chopped off	Apart from the group of four skulls there is a variety of body parts	Horn working waste (though probably leading to horn working, this should more properly be defined as butchery waste)
5	Sheep		One group mainly represented by horncores	Horn working waste (tawing also possible)
6	Cattle	Evidence of chopped horncores	Predominance of horncores	Horn working waste (due to the mix of species present horn working is probably a more likely explanation than tanning)
6	Goat	Evidence of chopped horncores	Only horncores	Horn working waste (due to the mix of species present horn working is probably a more likely explanation than tanning)
6	Sheep	Evidence of chopped horncores	Predominance of horncores	Horn working waste (due to the mix of species present horn working is probably a more likely explanation than tanning)
7	Cattle	Evidence of chopped horncores	Horncores predominant but other bones also present	Primary butchery or horn working waste
7	Goat	Evidence of chopped horncores	Group of nine large horncores (no other goat bones)	Horn working waste (tawing also possible)
8	Cattle	Evidence of chopped horncores and skinning	Predominance of horncores	Horn working waste (tanning also possible)
8	Goat	Evidence of chopped horncores	Predominance of horncores	Horn working waste (tawing also possible)

APPENDIX 2. continued

N	SPECIES	CHOPPING, CUTTING, SAWING	DISTRIBUTION OF BODY PARTS	INTERPRETATION
9	Cattle	Evidence of chopped horncores	Accumulation of horncores at the bottom of a pit (horse bones at the top)	Horn working waste (this is much more likely to be tanning waste)
10	Sheep	Probable combination of primary butchery waste and refuse from skinning processing; most metapodials broken, either proximal or distal end present; horncores regularly chopped and skulls halved sagitally	Predominance of head and feet but head remains (mainly frontals) by far predominant (MNI is 110 for skulls and 26 for feet)	Horn and tanning waste
11	Sheep		Mainly head and foot elements (all from the same pit)	Interpreted as waste from an industrial process, likely to be sheepskin production. Cut marks are not mentioned.
12	Sheep	Cut marks on carpals and tarsals	Only foot elements (carpals, tarsals, metapodials and phalanges) of immature animals	Slaughtering waste (tanning also possible)
13	Sheep	?skinning cuts mainly on mid-shaft of metapodials, anterior on metacarpals and posterior on metatarsals	Most bones from a special deposit of metapodials, carpals, tarsals and phalanges; most carpals recovered in the sieved assemblage	Waste from a tawyer, fellmonger or glover
14	Sheep	Evidence of chopped horncores and skinning	Only horncores and foot bones	Tawing waste
15	Sheep		Mainly head and foot elements but metapodials by far predominant (75); mostly complete bones	(Tanning waste not mentioned in the text but obvious on the basis of context)
16	Cattle		Only horncores	Horn working waste (tanning also possible)
17	Sheep		Mostly metapodials	Tanning waste
18	Cattle		Concentration of horncores in three different tanning pits; most of these are still attached to the skull and there is no evidence that these were utilised	Tanning waste
18	Sheep		One tanning pit has only metapodials and phalanges, another has skull fragments and metapodials and a third has just one sheep foot	Tanning waste
19	Sheep	Most ?skinning cuts on mid-shaft of metapodials	Concentrated in a number of contexts; predominance of carpals, tarsal, metapodials and phalanges present; few horncores	Tanning waste (since no tanning pits present, primary butchery is also possible, though less likely)
20	Cattle	Evidence of chopped horncores	Only horncores	Horn working waste
21	Cattle	Most metapodials chopped, others have cuts near the proximal end; both activities probably related to the detachment of the metapodials from the carcass	Horncores with skull fragments (not chopped) and large quantities of metapodials (mainly proximal but some distal ends too), all from the same pit	Tanning waste (for this period not supported by structural evidence)

9. Choice and use of shells for artefacts at Roman sites in the Eastern Desert of Egypt

Sheila Hamilton-Dyer

In the Eastern Desert of Egypt, and along the Red Sea coast, there are several substantial Roman settlements and many smaller stations. Preservation at these sites is often extremely good and faunal remains, including marine molluscs, are frequently found in great quantity. This paper concerns the molluscan material used in artefact production at the two major inland quarry settlements of Mons Claudianus and Mons Porphyrites.

A wide variety of shell artefacts were found including small items for personal adornment, gaming pieces, dishes, cosmetic palettes and spoons. Waste material from the stages of manufacture attests to on-site production.

The taxa utilised range from small gastropods, clearly recovered from the beach, to large and heavy *Tridacna* clams collected from the reefs. Some of the raw material available for manufacture originates from the secondary use of discarded shells from food refuse. Unlike marine molluscs found at coastal sites, all the shells found at these inland sites must have been taken there deliberately. They would have been collected by the inhabitants on visits to the coast or ordered from specialist suppliers. Difficulties of transport in relation to the choice and relative value of raw materials are discussed.

Keywords: Marine molluscs, shell artefact, Roman, Egypt, Red Sea.

INTRODUCTION

In the Eastern Desert of Egypt, and along the Red Sea coast, there are several substantial Roman settlements and many smaller stations. Preservation at these sites is often extremely good and faunal remains, including those of marine molluscs, are frequently found in great quantity. This paper concerns the shell material used in artefact production at the two major inland quarry settlements of Mons Claudianus and Mons Porphyrites. These remote sites were operating mainly in the first and second centuries AD to supply prestigious monumental stone, primarily for imperial use in Rome (Peacock & Maxfield 1997).

THE MOLLUSCS FOUND

The remains of the marine molluscs are all of species found today in the Red Sea, and include several endemic species. Over 60 species have been identified at the two sites (Hamilton-Dyer 2001 a, in prep a). Both bivalves and gastropods are represented, with large bivalves the more frequent. The most common large bivalves are: pearl oyster, *Pinctada margaritifera* (Linnaeus, 1758); giant clam, *Tridacna* sp.; and the endemic oyster, *Saccostrea cucullata* (Born, 1778). The surf clam, *Atactodea glabrata* (Gmelin, 1791) is the most common of the smaller bivalves. Large gastropods include the spider conch, *Lambis truncata sebae* (Kiener, 1843); the endemic conch, *Strombus tricornis* (Humphrey, 1786); the Red Sea Arabian cowrie, *Cypraea grayana* (Schilder, 1930); and the panther cowrie, *C. pantherina* (Lightfoot 1786). The smaller gastropods cover a wide variety of species, the most frequent of which are nerites, Neritidae; the strawberry top shell, *Clanculus pharaonius* (Linnaeus, 1758) and a small whelk, *Engina mendicaria* (Linnaeus, 1758) (Nomenclature follows Sharabati 1984 and Oliver 1992).

DESCRIPTION OF THE ARTEFACTS

Numerous shells and shell pieces were used for a variety of items such as beads, gaming pieces, pendants, scoops and various types of containers. It is difficult to categorise the artefacts, for even functional items such as dishes may have had a symbolic as well as a more practical use.

Many of the shells may have been used in the raw state leaving little or no evidence of modification. Analysis of the artefacts might therefore under estimate the usage of shells, particularly in the secondary use of food species and shells used for amulets or medicine.

Small shells of many species were found at both sites. Several of these were perforated, sometimes with deliberately punched holes while others have natural holes. Occasionally they have been found with associated threading and it is assumed that these shells were used for necklaces, bracelets and pendants.

Several of the pearl oyster shells have trimmed edges, sometimes with decorative denticulation. They are likely to have been used as serving dishes and cosmetic palettes; one contained traces of a red pigment. These bivalves have large circular valves with an attractive nacreous interior, and many of the shells may have been used, but without modification.

Small or medium sized *Tridacna* clam shells of approximately 150–250mm were sometimes used for ink and paint pots, as evidenced by traces of red pigment and black ink, probably of the same type as used for the writing of the numerous *Ostraca* (documents written on pot sherds) found. These inkpots are more common at the coastal site of Quseir al-Qadim (Hamilton-Dyer 2000) where these shells are a common find. It is hoped to carry out analysis of the pigments. As in the case of the pearl oysters, these shells may also have been used for serving dishes or other containers but no direct evidence has been found.

Spoon bowls were manufactured from conch and large cowrie shells as described below.

All the above artefacts utilise, in some degree, the natural shape of the shell. There are also objects that are completely divorced from the characteristic shape and outer colour of the natural shell, merely using it as raw material. These items are made almost exclusively of *Tridacna* clam and pearl oyster, sometimes identified only by the characteristic shell structure. The *Tridacna* objects include dice, counters, stoppers and other similar small items. Gaming counters were frequent finds at both sites, apparently made of any substance to hand, such as pieces of broken glass and ceramics, and were also commonly made from pearl oyster. That these were often made on site, rather than being personal items brought in from elsewhere, is attested by the finding of waste blanks from which counters had been scribed and cut (see Hamilton-Dyer 2001 b Fig. 11.5). Pearl oyster was also cut into small flat triangles and other shapes which may have been used for inlay, a craft still much in evidence today. The most delicately worked mother of pearl objects are ear-

rings, pendants and small (possibly votive) cockerels (see Hamilton-Dyer 2001 b Fig 11.5).

MANUFACTURING TECHNIQUES

Some techniques of manufacture are similar to those employed for bone and wood artefacts found at these sites. Others are more like the techniques applied to lithic objects. This is partly in response to the natural structure of the shell: *Tridacna* for example, has a dense structure which closely resembles alabaster and other soft stones and is sufficiently robust to be sawn, chiselled, drilled and filed. There is a long tradition of carving in soft stones in Egypt: cosmetic palettes and canopic jars for example, a craft tradition still carried out today for the tourist trade. Metal finds are relatively rare from the sites but it is probable that the same tools used in manufacturing mortaria and stone bowls could have been employed in working shell, particularly the smaller saws, files and chisels.

The pearl oyster has a delicate laminated structure which can split and flake but it is still possible to mark and carve the shells. Finely executed scribe lines are frequently observed around the interior edge of several shells, indicating the use of some type of compass point to mark a smooth curve.

The small necklace shells are sometimes already conveniently drilled by predatory species such as moon snails, *Polinices* sp., also occasionally found amongst the smaller shells. Others show clear evidence of deliberate punched holes (see Hamilton-Dyer 2001 b Fig 9.44, 9.45). The surf clams with artificial holes had all been punched from the inside of the valve, at the closest convenient point to the umbone. Although specialist tools may have been employed, a simple nail would be capable of producing this type of hole. Cone shells, on the other hand, if not exploiting natural damage to the tip of the spire, had been filed or perhaps sawn to provide a suitable hole. Other small gastropods had been perforated in the main body whorl at a suitable point where it is possible to then pass a thread through the aperture.

SPOON MANUFACTURE

Among the shell artefacts are several spoon bowls, or fragments thereof. The remains clearly show the method of manufacture and further direct evidence of on-site manufacture. Apart from one spoon or scoop formed from the hinge area of a large pearl oyster, the manufacture of spoons utilised conch and, to a lesser extent, cowries. It is not certain whether it was *Strombus tricornis* or the spider conch that was used, or perhaps both. Both were usually found broken or chopped open sub-axially (Fig. 23). The use of the portion of shell for spoons may well have been fortuitous; taking advantage of the waste piece after the meat was eaten (Fig. 24).

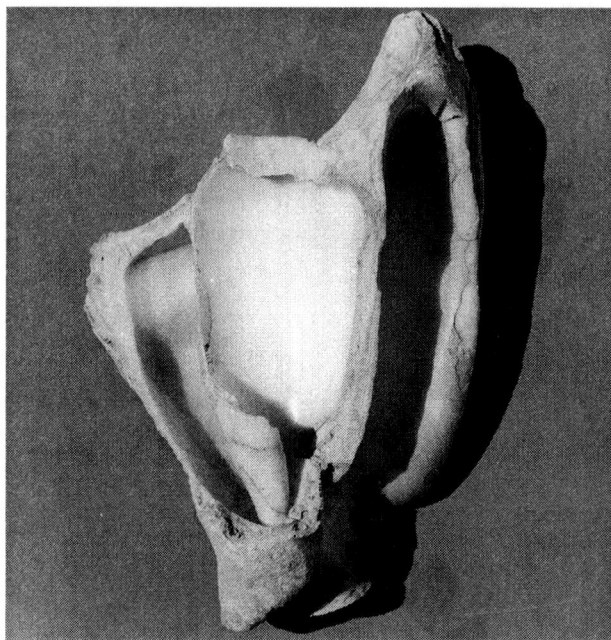

Figure 23. Strombus tricornis *conch, broken or cut open.*

Figure 25. Conch spoon bowl, front.

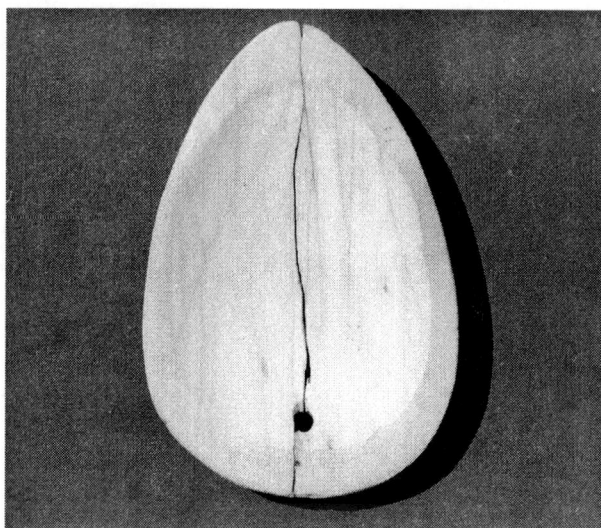

Figure 24. Conch spoon roughout.

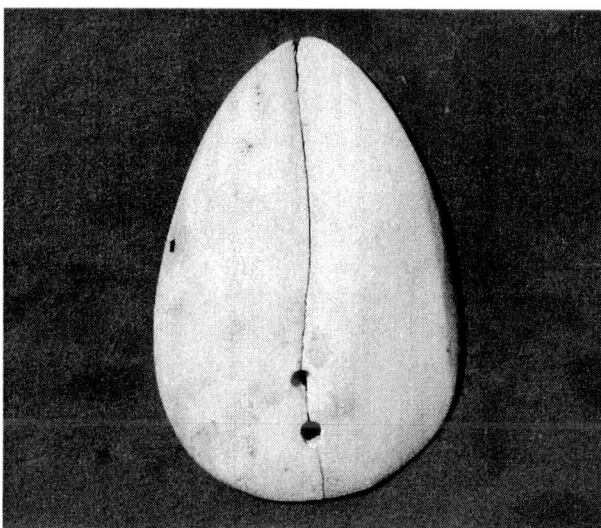

Figure 26. Conch spoon bowl, back.

Whether deliberate or not, the chosen piece of shell was then carefully shaped and smoothed to form the bowl, with a pointed apex and rounded base. From the appearance of the marks left, this process appears to have been done with files. The interior surface of the bowl was left unmodified to show the natural gloss of the shell. The next stage of manufacture was the drilling of two small holes near the base, presumably for fixing to a handle. In at least one case this drilling was done from the back, convex, side of the spoon bowl. This was probably the easiest thing to do, as the spoon blank would be more stable when drilling, and the tool less prone to skidding than on the glossy inner surface. In this artefact it can be clearly seen that although the drilling of the most basal hole was successful (Fig. 25), the operation was a failure for the second hole. The bowl split in half axially with the hole still incompletely drilled (Fig. 26). The two halves were retrieved from the sebakh, or midden, a few metres apart, and one can imagine the irritation of the worker with the piece so nearly finished.

The production method adopted for the smaller, and thinner, cowrie shell spoons was different in the initial stages but resulted in a similar spoon bowl. The cowrie species used appears to have been *Cypraea grayana* and perhaps occasionally *C. pantherina.* The glossy shell is strong but thin. The desired portion of the dorsum was

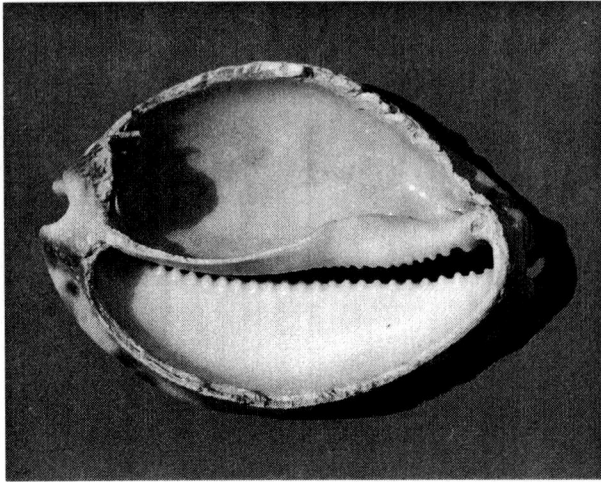

Figure 27. Cyprea grayana *cowrie, dorsum removed for spoon.*

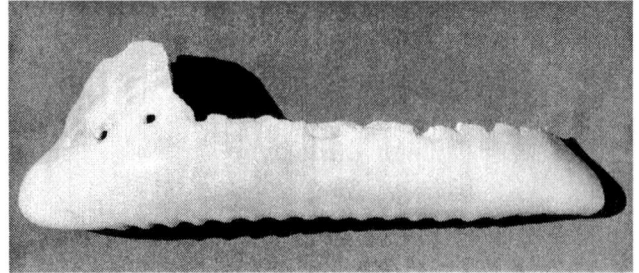

Figure 28. Cyprea grayana *cowrie, waste showing method of working.*

marked out by punching small holes along the callus margin (Fig. 27–8). How this was then removed is not clear, but in one case the offcut had smooth joins between the punch marks, carried out using a saw or file.

No handles for these spoons were found: these might have been made from wood, bone or horn which has not survived or fragments of which have not been recognised. Another possibility is that these spoons, and perhaps some of the stone bowls and other items, may have been made for trade off the site and completed elsewhere.

OTHER USES

Murex and related species, which can be used for the extraction of purple dye, have been found in small numbers at both sites, but not in the concentrations that might be expected from an industrial process. It is perhaps more likely that these would be processed on the coast to avoid unnecessary transport.

Large dumps of *Strombus tricornis* were found at Badia, the satellite station to Mons Porphyrites (Hamilton-Dyer in prep a). Most of the shells were large mature specimens and many were charred, but not calcined or crushed as might be expected from lime production. At present the purpose of these shells is unknown and unique in the area.

It should also be mentioned here that remains of other marine invertebrates were found, including corals, but few appear to have been modified.

SOURCE AND SUPPLY

As indicated above, these remains are of marine molluscs at inland sites (over 50km from the Red Sea). While some of the molluscs found at coastal sites could be incidental

remains or even modern contamination, this is clearly not the case for the quarry settlements. They were not occupied by transient workers but by a relatively large and probably sedentary workforce (Peacock and Maxfield 1997, 95). The majority of supplies of all kinds had to be brought in by pack animals. The restrictions this placed on provisioning can be seen, for example, in the replacement of beef by donkey in the diet (Hamilton-Dyer 1998, 2001 a). The relative value of different shell types may have been taken into consideration in any requests for carriage.

Some species present show no sign of use and are almost certainly discarded food refuse and nothing else. The oyster *Saccostrea cucullata* falls into this category. The valves are relatively small, crenulated and often distorted from growth on uneven substrates, they do not lend themselves to decorative use and are not large enough to be used as dishes or containers.

The pearl oysters and large conch are likely to have been taken to the sites primarily for food use, but the shells were then available for secondary uses. Although these oysters are a source of pearls, none were found in the finds and the proportion of shells with pearls is usually low, a secondary bonus rather than a primary reason for collecting.

The primary destination and use of the *Tridacna* shells is less clear. These giant clams may have been taken to the site complete for fresh meat, or already empty as a raw material for carving. The shells at the two quarry sites are not commonly of whole valves, in contrast with the contemporary deposits at Quseir al-Qadim on the coast. These large bivalve molluscs grow within the coral reef and are rarely encountered as dead shells on the beach, other than as small shells. Some of the fragments are of very large shells, comparable with complete valves of at least 4kg. There would have been a considerable amount of meat in a shell of this size but with a maximum pack load of approximately 50kg a single donkey could have carried perhaps only three or four complete shells, as each could have weighed up to 10kg or more. The meat of the clam can be dried (it is known as Sarumbak today) and the combined weight of both valves and the meat would seem to be an extravagant use of transport.

Other material is clearly not from consumption. The small gastropods with natural drill holes are obviously beach finds of dead shells, and indeed similar assemblages can still be collected. In addition to the large species dominating the assemblages, there are several other shells of large species. These were also often clearly collected from the shore as they have barnacles or worn and broken edges. These shells may have been collected, as today, for purely aesthetic reasons or for symbolic use, on visits to the coast.

The two quarry sites have slightly different compositions in their shell assemblages but are both different to the two major coastal sites, Quseir al-Qadim (Reese 1982, Hamilton-Dyer in prep b) and Berenike (Van Neer & Ervynck 1998). Quesir is the closer of these two ports and is contemporary. The major difference in the assemblage is in the number of shells of bivalves compared with those of gastropods. At the inland sites the bivalves are more common (except at the Mons Porphyrites satellite settlement at Badia where the large numbers of *Strombus tricornis* are exceptional for any site). Gastropods of all kinds are frequent at the coastal sites and large dumps of the edible turban, *Turbo* cf. *radiatus* (Gmelin 1791), and broken open spider conch are very common at Quseir-al Qadim (Hamilton-Dyer in prep b).

This difference in relative proportions is probably to do with spoilage, as those species which can remain closed for long periods out of water are more likely to be able to withstand the rigors of travel to the inland sites without going off. Large species are likely to suffer less from overheating during transport than smaller ones, which probably explains the lack of 'winkle' species inland other than the dead beach shells.

Remains of fish are also very common at all these sites and are mainly of Red Sea species. Many of these are thought to have been transported as fresh fish, especially in the colder months (Hamilton-Dyer 1994, Hamilton-Dyer 2001 a). For Mons Claudianus this has been estimated as a journey of some two days to cover the 70km to the nearest point on the coast. This would have been a little less for Mons Porphyrites, which is closer to the coast. Clams and oysters, kept cool in damp containers, would probably have arrived in better condition than most other types of mollusc. Oysters can also be preserved (and therefore transported) in jars of wine or vinegar (Flower and Rosenbaum 1958). Most molluscs could be treated in this way but the dearth of turbans and other gastropods perhaps indicates that the inhabitants of the quarry settlements preferred fresh shellfish, as indeed they did with fish.

The crenulate, *Saccostrea*, oysters were probably very difficult to open raw, and *Tridacna* clams well nigh impossible. The smaller of these giant shells could have been opened by cooking, perhaps by boiling as there are no signs of fire damage. The largest *Tridacna* might have been smashed open, as waiting for the animal to expire and open may have risked putrefaction. A few shells of *Saccostrea cucullata* were found complete and still closed, perhaps discarded as too difficult to waste time on.

It is not entirely clear how the molluscs and fish were obtained by the inhabitants of the quarry settlements. The smaller species and the dead beach shells may have been collected directly but it is likely that most were obtained from specialist suppliers. *Ostraca* and papyri sometimes mention requests for sea fish and fresh fish (Bingen *et al.* 1997, 241 & 242). It is not certain whether the supply of seafoods was centrally controlled or mainly up to individuals. The occupants of the sites were a mixture of military personnel and civilian craftsmen and probably families too. The documentary evidence shows that workmen were certainly paid in kind but also received a salary (Cuvigny 1996). Given the difficulties and constraints of the supply line the sites were supplied with not just the bare essentials but also some foods and items regarded as luxuries (van der Veen 1999). Those with sufficient income may well have been able to afford the transport costs of personal luxuries. The carriage of shelled molluscs may have been a trade off between the usefulness and desirability of particular species against the cost of transport. Secondary use of food refuse may have helped to offset these costs. The species and proportions found may therefore reflect the environmental constraints of long distance supply, the ability to pay for luxury goods, and the suitability of the species for artefacts.

At present it cannot be ascertained whether shell craft was a sideline for stonemasons or other workers, nor whether the items were made for trade, personal use or more probably both.

Although shell artefacts have been made for millennia, little attention has been paid to typology and the physical properties of the material (Claassen 1998, 196, 218). Continuing research may offer further information on the species chosen and the objects produced.

References

Apicius *The Roman cookery book*. A critical translation of 'The art of cooking' by Apicius. Translation B. Flower and E. Rosenbaum (1958), London

Bingen, J., Bulow-Jacobsen, A., Cockle, W.E.H., Cuvigny, H., Kayser, F., Van Ringen, W. 1997 *Mons Claudianus Ostraca Graeca et Latina II, O.Claud. 191 à 416* (Institut Français d'Archéologie Orientale Documents de Fouilles, XXXII). Cairo: Institut Français d'Archéologie Orientale

Claassen, C. 1998 *Shells* (Cambridge manuals in archaeology). Cambridge: University Press

Cuvigny, H. 1996 The amount of wages paid to the quarry workers at Mons Claudianus pp. 139–145 *Journal of Roman Studies* 86

Hamilton-Dyer, S. 1994 Preliminary report on the fish remains from Mons Claudianus, Egypt. Pp. 275–278 in Heinrich, D. *Archaeo-Ichthyological Studies* (Papers presented at the 6th Meeting of the I.C.A.Z. Fish Remains Working Group). Offa, Sonderdruck 51. Neümunster: Watchholtz Verlag

Hamilton-Dyer, S. (2000) Faunal Remains, in Peacock, D.P.S. *et al.* (eds) *Myos Hormos - Quseir al-Qadim: A Roman and Islamic Port Site on the Red Sea Coast of Egypt*, Interim Report 2000, University of Southampton

Hamilton-Dyer, S. (2001 a) The Faunal Remains, pp 251–301 in Peacock, D.P.S. and Maxfield, V.A. (eds) *Mons Claudianus, Survey and Excavation: Vol. II Excavations Part 1* (Institut Français d'Archéologie Orientale Documents de Fouilles, 43). Cairo: Institut Français d'Archéologie Orientale

Hamilton-Dyer, S. (2001 b) Objects of Bone, Horn and Shell, pp. 357–364 in Peacock, D.P.S. and Maxfield, V.A. (eds) *Mons Claudianus, Survey and Excavation: Vol. II Excavations Part 1* (Institut Français d'Archéologie Orientale Documents de Fouilles, 43). Cairo: Institut Français d'Archéologie Orientale

Hamilton-Dyer, S. (in prep a) Faunal Remains, in Peacock, D.P.S. and Maxfield, V.A. (eds) *Mons Porphyrites, Survey and Excavation: Vol. 2 Finds.* Exeter University

Hamilton-Dyer, S. (in prep b) Faunal Remains, in Peacock, D.P.S. *et al.* (eds) *Myos Hormos – Quseir al-Qadim: A Roman and Islamic Port Site on the Red Sea Coast of Egypt*, University of Southampton

Oliver, P.G. 1992 *Bivalved Seashells of the Red Sea.* Weisbaden: Verlag Christa Hemmen, and Cardiff: National Museum of Wales

Peacock, D.P.S. and Maxfield, V.A. 1997 *Mons Claudianus, Survey and Excavation: Vol. 1 Topography and Quarries*, (Institut Français d'Archéologie Orientale Documents de Fouilles, XXXVII). Cairo: Institut Français d'Archéologie Orientale

Reese, D.S. 1982 marine invertebrates, pp 347–353 in, Whitcomb, D.S. and Johnson, J.H. (eds) *Quseir al-Qadim 1980 Preliminary Report.* (ARCE Reports 7). Malibu: ARCE

Sharabati, D. 1984 *Red Sea Shells.* London: Routledge & Kegan Paul

Van Neer, W. & Ervynck, A. 1998 The faunal remains, pp 349–388 in Sidebotham, S. and Wendrich, W. (eds) *Berenike 1996 Report of the 1996 Excavations at Berenike (Egyptian Red Sea Coast) and the Survey of the Eastern Desert.* Leiden: Research School of Asian, African and Amerindian Studies (CNWS) Publications. Special Series 2

van der Veen, M. 1999 The food and fodder supply to Roman quarry settlements in the Eastern Desert of Egypt, pp 171–183 in van der Veen (ed.) *The Exploitation of Plant Resources in Ancient Africa.* New York: Kluwer Academic/Plenum Publishers

Proxy indicators for industry

10. Industrial activities –
some suggested microstratigraphic signatures:
ochre, building materials and iron working

Richard Macphail

A suggested role for geoarchaeology in the study of industrial activities, with specific reference to microstratigraphic (e.g. soil micromorphology, chemistry) analyses, is discussed. The paper gives examples of ochre, earth-based and lime-based constructional materials and some iron-working residues. Although the investigation of most industrial activities is the realm of specialists (e.g. conservators, archaeo-metallurgists), soil micromorphology and allied geoarchaeological methods can play a crucial role in the understanding of overall site formation processes, including post-depositional effects. This approach can therefore greatly contribute to the placing industrial activities in their archaeological context.

Keywords: Archaeology, construction, industry, soil micromorphology.

INTRODUCTION

Field indicators of industrial activity are easily recognisable and iron slag, for example, can be picked out of soil samples by employing a magnet. Macrofossil analysis will also contribute to the identification of past straw-thatched and turf roofs, and malting and cereal processing can also be distinguished when malted barley and fused cereal ash are collected from bulk samples. Field archaeologists recognise the remains of ovens and kilns because of the rubified nature of the walls, and traces of these could also have been found by various geophysical methods, such as by a magnetic susceptibility survey. The geoarchaeology/soil micromorphology can nevertheless play an important role in the study of industrial environmental archaeology, albeit often ancillary and supportive. Crucially this discipline often provides unique insights into site formation processes. It is also important that traces of industrial activity are recognised, and soil micromorphology is a key method here.

First and perhaps foremost, the geoarchaeologist needs to be aware of the possibility of industrial activities, and be trained in how to recognise traces of industrial processes when field features are not obvious, or before the archaeo-metallurgist and/or the archaeo-botanist has reported their evidence of such findings. Then he/she can report independently. Normally, the geoarchaeologist has been taught to recognise materials of different industrial origin, through the study of reference and analogue materials.

Secondly, it is commonly the main task of the geoarchaeologist to improve the understanding of site formation processes, which now more often deal with anthropogenic sediments rather than natural soils (Roskams 2000). In the context of studying industrial activity, the site formation processes often involve:

- dismantling processes,
- secondary deposition, and
- a range of post-depositional effects.

This present paper takes an eclectic approach to the study of past industry, because in prehistoric and protohistoric sites the difference between domestic and industrial activities is blurred. It also examines some building methods and materials, because when decayed, constructional debris may form the bulk of some archaeological deposits. It is also important that soil micromorphology is able to differentiate between constructed floors, for example, and the effects of use upon them. This would include the differentiation of constructed floor layers, possible floor coverings and deposits developed by trampling/use and ultimately formed by re-use or decay of the structure in which the floor is located. The technical approach can therefore be termed microstratigraphic, in that soil micromorphology is commonly combined with the basic measurement of organic matter, phosphate and magnetic susceptibility.

After a brief methods section, the following case studies are presented:

– red ochre
– Romano-British, Roman and Medieval building materials
– Iron working
– Residues of industrial and constructional activities

METHODS

Soil micromorphological analyses are based upon description, numerical, semi-numerical, SEM and microprobe studies (spot and grid analysis and mapping of elements), and the use of reference and experimental materials (Bullock *et al.* 1985, Courty *et al.* 1989, Crowther *et al.* 1996; Macphail and Cruise 2001). It can be noted that anthropogenic materials are not included in the standard textbook of Bullock *et al.* (1985), although a number are described, many for the first time, in Courty *et al.* (1989). Many more have been analysed internationally since that time (e.g. Stoops 1984, Rentzel 1998, Canti 1998, Goldberg and Macphail, in preparation).

In addition to standard physical (e.g. grain size) and chemical (e.g. LOI and P) assays, magnetic susceptibility (χ x 10^{-8} SI kg^{-1}) has also been applied in this field (Clark 1996).

AN EXAMPLE OF PREHISTORIC INDUSTRIAL ACTIVITY – OCHRE AT ARENE CANDIDE, FINALE, LIGURIA, ITALY

This paper presents a broad-brush approach to the study of past industrial activities. For example, XRD and petrological analyses of red (2.5YR4/8) "ochre cakes" show that these were 'manufactured' during the Neolithic at Arene Candide, by the gathering of local iron oxide- (e.g. haematite) rich weathered limestone ("Terra Rosa") (Ferraris 1997). This material was then formed into hand-size 'cakes'. These contain sand-size clasts of limestone that have been cemented by secondary calcite within the cave. Soil micromorphological studies were employed to differentiate this 'manufactured' material from other red coloured cave deposits noted in the cave sediments at the macro-scale. Some of the latter are purely natural, and comprise reddish cave earth of clay and aeolian sand, while thin (1 mm) red lamellae of localised hydromorphic origin actually reflect past floor surfaces, possibly covered in poorly permeable skins (Macphail *et al.* 1997).

SOME ROMANO-BRITISH, ROMAN AND MEDIEVAL BUILDING MATERIALS

Turf

Romano-British and Roman populations in Europe employed local, imported and processed-soil and -geological materials for constructional purposes (Blake 1947). Turf used for construction at the Romano-British site of Folly Lane, St. Albans, was recognised on the basis of its soil micromorphology and microchemical (microprobe) characteristics that demonstrated use of topsoils (Ah horizon) from natural 'woodland soils' (acidic argillic brown earths) and topsoils that had been likely associated with animal management (Macphail *et al.* 1998). This finding was consistent with pollen analysis of the same samples and macrofossil remains at the site (Wiltshire 1999, Murphy and Fryer 1999).

Pollen analysis and soil micromorphology, were also combined in order to characterise the experimental turf roof used on a wooden structure built by Roger Engelmark on the experimental 'ancient farm' of Bagböle in northern Sweden (University of Umeå). Results showed, for example, that local grassland turf (L/F, Ah and Ah2 soil horizons), with an active rooting system had been employed, and that this living system had maintained itself (Cruise and Macphail 2000). It can be noted that the 140 mm thick turf roof comprised two turves over a birch bark roof liner, with the bottom turf being face down and top turf facing upwards and displaying a living grass sward. This profile was consistent with the microstratigraphic analysis (*n*=12), as investigated through pollen counts, %LOI (organic matter) and counts of the soil micromorphology (e.g., mineral grains, roots, various excrement types of soil fauna; Cruise and Macphail 2000; Figures 22.1 and 22.2).

Ancient turf has been identified through pollen analysis, macrofossil analysis, but even when strongly transformed by the effects of burial, the biological traits of the turf employed should still be recogniseable through soil micromorphology (e.g., turf mounds, turf roofs, turf ramparts; Scaife and Macphail 1983, Dimbleby 1985, Babel 1975, Bal 1982, Crowther *et al.* 1996, Wiltshire 1997; Dickson 1999, Macphail *et al.*, in press). Certainly, as demonstrated below, turf can be differentiated from other earth-based building materials, such as brickearth (see Figure 29b).

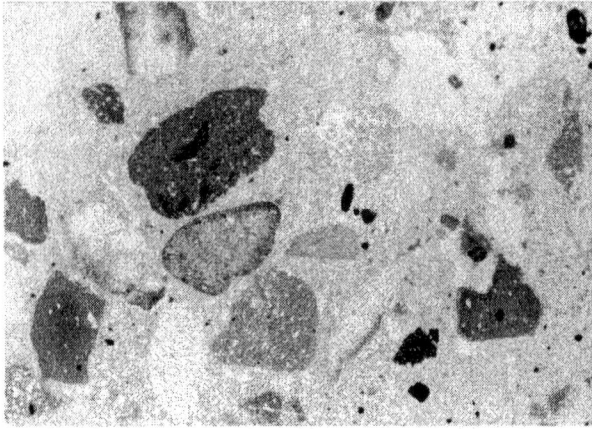

Figure 29a. 28, Park St., Southwark, London (Courage Brewery site); macro-photograph Roman Opus signinum (mortar) containing angular stone size clasts of pottery, brick and flint, set in a calcareous (micritic) greyish brown matrix, itself including medium-size river sand. Plane polarised light (PPL), frame length is 9 mm (see Figure 31).

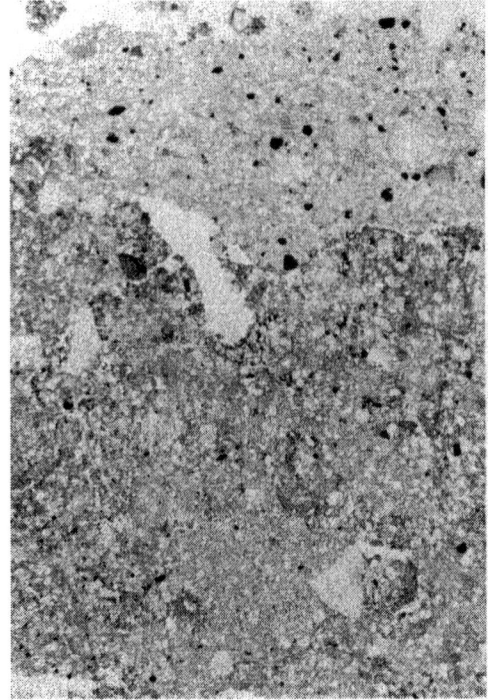

Figure 29b. Courage Brewery site, Southwark, London: macro-photograph of thin section of plaster coated brickearth clay wall (top of photo). Sample was taken from a plaster-coated upstanding 1st–2nd century Roman brickearth clay wall. The plaster is composed of well-sorted medium sized river sand, set in a dense grey to brownish grey calcareous cement containing many fine humic inclusions (see Table 1). The dark burrow fills are evidence of the activity of earthworms mixing humic dark earth soil with the grey, clean, fine sandy silt loam mineral-dominated brickearth – a soil material quarried and used to construct 'clay' walls. Plane polarised light (PPL), frame length is 9 mm. (see Figure 31).

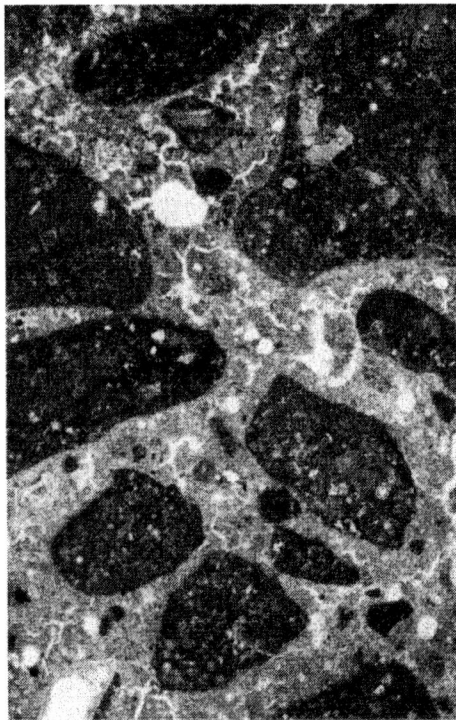

Figure 29c. Fishbourne Roman Palace, West Sussex: Roman mortar-cemented flint wall constructed of a dark greyish fine micritic mortar mainly tempered with coarse sand-size to fine gravel-size sub-rounded chalk clasts. PPL, frame length is 5.5 mm.

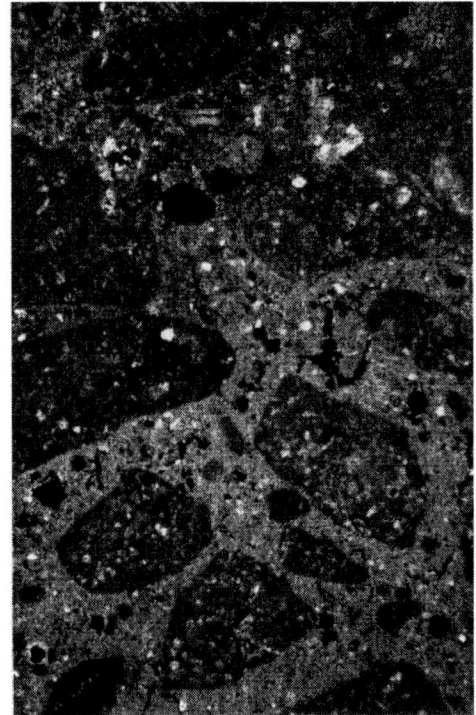

Figure 29d. Fishbourne Roman Palace, West Sussex: Roman mortar-cemented flint wall, the mortar comprising micritic calcite with moderate interference colours, chalk with low interference colours, and a scatter of silt-size quartz. Crossed polarised light, XPL, frame length is 5.5 mm.

Constructional materials

There are numerous types of lime-based constructional materials. For convenience and as a very broad generalisation, coarse-tempered materials are termed *'mortar'* *(e.g.* arriccio: a coarse layer applied directly to the face of a wall) and generally finer-tempered coatings are called 'plaster' (e.g. intonoco: fine surface layer applied on top of arriccio (Mora *et al.* 1984, 10; Sue Wright and MoLAS staff, pers. comm.). A painted, fine 'plaster' over a coarse-tempered ('mortar') wall covering is well illustrated in Pye (2001, Fig. 1).

Mortar

At the Courage Brewery site, Southwark, London (Dillon *et al.* 1991), a reference fragment of 1st century AD *opus signinum* was found to be composed of a rather pure microcrystalline (micritic) calcite cement with dominant gravel-size (>2 mm) clasts (temper) that include flint, burned brickearth, limestone, chalk and pot (Figure 29a) (Macphail 1996). It also has a fine and medium sand-size temper of a likely local river sand (Thames alluvium) origin (Table 11, samples 12 and 24). Chalk fragments may be relic of incompletely burned lime, whereas limestone and pounded pottery were typical tempers added for strength and to produce a strong water-resistant 'hydraulic' mortar (Blake 1947, 322–323; Stoops 1984; Rentzel 1998). The low amount of organic matter present in the cement may originate from accidental contamination of material from the mixing trough, although a small addition (10%) of impurities was said to add to the mortar's hardness (Blake 1947). The ratio of coarse (gravel and sand) to fine (cement) material at 60:40 is comparable to the soil micromorphological findings of Stoops (1984) from 15 examples of mortar from Roman Pessinus, Turkey. It also appears similar to an example of wall cement from Pompeii, mortar found in dark earth at Bath, mortar cementing a flint wall at Fishbourne Roman Palace, West Sussex (Figures 29c and 29d) and in mortar floors at Colchester House, London (Macphail and Cruise 1997, unpublished report to MoLAS). Whilst at the Courage Brewery site burned brickearth is included as a coarse temper, oolitic limestone and chalk are the major coarse components at Bath and at Fishbourne, respectively (Goldberg and Macphail in prep.). Similarly, local building materials are found in mortars used at Roman Augst, Switzerland (Rentzell 1998). It is important that these lime-based building materials are defined in terms of their soil micromorphology, because in deposits such as 'dark earth', limestone building stone, chalk and other natural geological materials need to be differentiated from manufactured materials – and this is not always easy.

Mortar floor

At the Norman site of Dragons Hall, Norwich, a well-made mortar floor composed of flint gravel temper and a calcium carbonate cement matrix was investigated (Figure 30a and 30b)(Shelley 1998). Here, the mortar floor had a fine plaster screed surface (see below). Microprobe mapping picked out the siliceous (Si) nature of the flint gravel and quartz sands present in the mortar and plaster screed surface, and the dominance of calcium (Ca) in the fine matrix of micritic calcium carbonate, as identified petrologically. More siliceous sands are present in the floor and post-abandonment deposits, which are more phosphate-rich then the floor make-up (Table 12).

Plaster

Plaster was examined from the *opus signinum* sample and from an *in situ* standing brickearth clay wall at the Roman Courage Brewery site (Dillon *et al.* 1991)(Table 11). Both plaster samples differ from mortar by containing a temper dominated by sand rather than gravel (Courty *et al.* 1989, 121). In the case of the *opus signinum* sample the sand-size material is poorly sorted and the cement is very similar to the cement of the attached mortar (Table 11). On the other hand, the plaster coating the brickearth clay wall is finely (3–5 mm) layered (Figure 29b) reflecting several applications of plaster to the wall. It has a well sorted fine and medium sand-size temper set in a weakly organic micritic cement producing a coarse:fine ratio of 60:40 (cf. Stoops 1984). Some of the sand-size material could be from 'clean' local alluvial sand whereas other sandy material has clay coatings associated with it, the last suggesting the use of local argillic brown sandy subsoil B(t) horizon material (a pedologically clay-enriched 'forest' soil horizon; Duchaufour 1970; Avery 1990; cf. Table 13). The higher amount of organic matter present, in comparison to the mortar cement, could again relate to contamination from the mixing trough, the addition of weakly humic soil and/or the possible addition of oil lees or equivalent material (Blake 1947, 318). Stoops (1984), suggests the use of sieved 'river sand' for plaster, although at Southwark the local sandy subsoil is already sufficiently well-sorted to produce the kind of plaster temper studied (Figure 31).

Brickearth

This is a naturally occurring superficial deposit commonly dates to the Devensian (Pleistocene), and is formed from loess and reworked loess, with fluvial activity for example often adding a fine and medium sand content to the silt-dominated loess (Avery 1990, 13; see below). It can be noted that during the Roman and Saxon periods people used local silt-dominated loessic brickearth at Canterbury while in London the locally-employed brickearth has a marked sand-size component (see below). Findings from London so far, suggest that during the Roman period the more clay-rich subsoils and natural (Bt and C[t]) horizons were utilised whilst later (Saxon and Medieval) the compact and clay depleted upper subsoil horizon material (Eb or A2) seems to have been employed with equal frequency (Table 12).

Table 11. Courage Brewery Site: Characteristics of natural and anthropogenic constructional components (Figure 31).

Material	Sample No.	Soil Micromorphology (SM) and Bulk Data (BD)	Interpretation
Natural components Sand	12	SM: dominant well sorted subrounded to subangular fine (100-200 μm) and medium (200–500 μm) sand-size quartz, flint and iron minerals (e.g. limonite); occasional glauconite; simple packing voids.	Typical well sorted alluvial sand.
	* Fig. 31	BD: clay (5%) and silt (8%) – poor medium loamy sand (87%); poorly humic and non-calcareous.	
Flood clay	23	BD: clay (24%) and medium (6–20 μm) silt (total silt 51%) – rich clay loam; highly humic and moderately calcareous.	Typical fine alluvium.
Anthropogenic components			
Opus signinum: 'mortar'	24	SM: clasts – dominant well sorted rounded to subangular gravel-size (generally 5–10 mm) common flint and frequent pot, burned brickearth, quartzite and limestone; frequent fine to medium-size sand; matrix – dense grey (PPL; OIL) micritic cement with moderate interference colours (XPL) and contains many fine organic fragments; few fine vesicular pores (coarse:fine 60:40).	Manufactured material: gravel in a dense sand-rich rather pure calcitic cement.
Opus signinum: 'plaster' (10 mm thick)	24	SM: clasts – poorly sorted very fine (50–100 μm) to coarse (500–1000 μm) sand; matrix – patchy grey (PPL, OIL) micritic cement with moderate interference colours (XPL) (coarse:fine 55:45).	Manufactured material: sand in a rather pure calcitic cement.
'Plaster' (6-17 mm thick) plaster coated brickearth clay wall (horizontal section)	1	SM: clasts - dominantly well sorted fine and medium sand; matrix - moderately dense grey to brownish grey (PPL), yellowish grey (OIL) and moderately birefringent micritic cement containing many fine organic inclusions (coarse:fine 60:40). Plaster comprises two to three 3-5 mm thick layers, which may be separated by narrow (50 μm) fissures.	Manufactured plaster applied in layers, composed of sand in a layered, rather impure and weakly organic calcitic cement.
Brickearth wall (earthworm burrowed)	1	SM: unworked brickearth (55%) – massive; common angular to subangular coarse silt (20–50 μm) and very fine sand (50–100 μm) with subrounded fine and medium sand set in a darkish brown (PPL), yellowish (OIL) and speckled matrix with low interference colours (XPL) (coarse:fine 80:20). Brickearth may contain calcareous material and pedofeatures such as iron and manganese impregnations and textural features such as thin coatings and intercalations.	Natural brickearth subsoil (Bt horizon), quarried and used as a building material.
		Biologically mixed brickearth (45%) – finely fragmented "pure" brickearth within dark brown and blackish brown, dotted (PPL), brown (OIL), poorly to non-birefringent humic soil; burrows (e.g. 4 mm wide) in the form of passage features and bow-shaped infills; occasional many thin organo-mineral probable Enchytraeid excrements.	Biologically worked brickearth (soil) building material.

Table 11. continued.

Material	Sample No.	Soil Micromorphology (SM) and Bulk Data (BD)	Interpretation
Brickearth wall and its disturbed edge (vertical section)	2	SM: brickearth – massive with few medium channels; very dominant coarse silt and very fine sand, with frequent fine and medium sand, set in a pale brown (PPL), yellow (OIL) and calcitic matrix with moderately high interference colours (coarse:fine 65:35); frequent fine shell. Pedofeatures include many calcitic void hypocoatings and occasional biopore infills of both humic and mammilated (earthworm) working of the brickearth.	Natural brickearth deep unweathered subsoil (B/C horizon), quarried and used as a building material.
(Disturbed edge)		SM: disturbed edge (10–20 mm thick)- coarsely mixed generally non-calcitic brickearth fragments and humic medium sandy soil containing charcoal. Pedofeatures include occasional calcitic root pseudomorphs and rare dusty clay void coatings and ferruginised root fragments.	Biologically worked and partially decalcified brickearth (soil) building material.
Brickearth wall	3	BD: moderately clayey (14%), with conspicuous coarse silt and very fine sand (total 44%) and fine and medium sand elements (total sand 46%); fine sandy silt loam. Non-humic and weakly calcareous.	Natural little weathered brickearth with fluvially mixed loessic elements; quarried and used as a building material.
Brickearth wall (burrowed)	8	SM: brickearth (70%) – as sample 4, with few calcitic patches as sample 5. Burrowed brickearth (30%) – as sample 4, with rare biogenic (earthworm) granules and fine pores infilled with likely phosphatic (BL autofluorescent) soil.	Burrowed natural brickearth subsoil (Bt horizon) building material.
Brickearth floor (burrowed)	7	SM: massive and compact with weakly layered brickearth (see samples 4 and 5) with some fine (400 μm) layers of coarse, fine and calcareous material; patches of clay-rich material (Bt horizon); narrow (0.5–1mm) remains of BL autofluorescent phosphatised floor surface, with thin (200–280 μm) phosphatised layer within floor; rare dusty clay void infills; common humic soil-infilled biopores.	Manufactured and compacted weakly calcareous brickearth, weakly contaminated by phosphate; 'floor surface' was possibly protected.

NB: PPL – plane polarised light; OIL – oblique incident light; interference colours – degree of "light" under crossed polarised light (XPL); BL – Blue light.

Brickearth walls

Three thin sections from 1st century Roman contexts at the Courage Brewery site, London (Table 11), including vertical and horizontal sections, and a bulk sample of walls made of brickearth, were investigated. Both undisturbed brickearth wall and wall material that underwent burrowing by earthworms, were examined (Figure 29b). The brickearth building material is a coarse silt and very fine sand-dominated fine sandy silt loam (Figures 29b and 31; Table 11, sample 3). Its grain size and micromorphological character is typical of *in situ* brickearth argillic brown earth soils present in Roman London, as found for example, in the Leadenhall Street area of the City. The Eb upper subsoil and upper Bt horizons tend to be sandy silt loams, whereas the more clay enriched lower subsoil Bt horizons are clay loams (Macphail 1980; Macphail and

Cruise 2000; Table 12). The brickearth is also typical of brickearth used elsewhere in London for constructional purposes, for example, at Whittington Ave. (Macphail 1994; Brown and Macphail submitted). The part of the natural soil profile typically used for brickearth walls is either decalcified Bt horizon subsoil material (e.g. Table 11, samples 1 and 7) or the more deeply quarried and still calcareous B/C horizon material (i.e. little-weathered geology; e.g. Table 11, sample 3). It is probable that brickearth was imported from the nearby City because brickearth is not present in Southwark, and south of the Thames the nearest brickearth apparently occurs some 3–4 km to the south east (Armitage *et al.* 1987). The digging of Roman "silt pits" can also be cited from 1st/2nd century Paris, France (Ciezar *et al.* 1994).

Table 12. Argillic brown earth 'forest' soil formed in brickearth and examples of its use in constructions in Roman-Medieval London.

Soil Horizon	Typical soil depth (mm)	General character	Use in domestic constructions and stables
Ah ('turf')	0–300	Humic and biologically active; many roots and fauna, with an open void structure. (Decalcified)	Use of such turf not yet recorded in London. ('Woodland' turf not suitable for wall or roof construction; possibly 'grassland turf' used once soils had been cleared; see above). Humic topsoils used in manufacture of daub.
Eb (A2)	300–500(700)	Poorly humic; clay-depleted and compact. (Decalcified)	Saxon and Medieval floors.
Bt	500(700)–1200	Poorly humic; clay-enriched and moderately porous and compact. (Decalcified)	Dominant Roman building material for ground-raising, walls and floors.
B/C	1200–1500(2000)	Very poorly humic; moderately clay-enriched and compact. (Junction of decalcified 'soil' and calcareous brickearth and river gravel 'geology')	Dominant Roman building material for ground-raising, walls and floors.

Floors

Examples of floors made from brickearth can be noted from the Courage Brewery site (Table 11, sample 7), as well as from Norman contexts at No. 1, Poultry, London (Macphail 1996; Macphail and Cruise 2000). At the latter, the 'floors' comprise a) 20–40 mm thick brickearth slab layers, with b) dark, charcoal-rich 10–20 mm thick trampled occupation soils between them. These two different contexts (a and b) differ chemically too (Table 13), with the brickearth clay being pure or only a little contaminated by occupation (mixing and solutions). Thus they are poorly humic, only moderately contaminated with phosphate and have maintained their naturally low magnetic susceptibility. On the other hand, the trampled floors contain much charred organic material, including burned bone and wood charcoal and iron slag, the last indicative of local iron working, a suggestion confirmed archaeologically (see below). The chemical signature of this trampled soil reflects the presence of the anthropogenic inclusions identified in thin section, and the deposit is humic, phosphate-rich and displays a strongly enhanced magnetic susceptibility.

IRON WORKING

Jane Cowgill presented a paper at this conference on the Roman iron-working site at Creeton Quarry, Lincolnshire

(Cowgill, this vol.). This present author was kindly given a sample of poorly-preserved Roman iron-working debris from Creeton Quarry by Jane Cowgill. A better-preserved piece of iron slag from Roman Oakley, Suffolk, was also supplied. These samples were impregnated with crystic resin and manufactured into thin sections. Even when ground down to the standard thin section thickness of 20–30 μm, the 7.5 x 5 cm size thin section of iron slag from Oakley (Figure 30c) registered a higher magnetic susceptibility when passed through a standard Bartington coil (mean 6.8 units, *n*=10), compared to weathered material from Creeton Quarry (mean 0.5 units, *n*=10). Although only a qualitative exercise, this records the likely effects on soil magnetic susceptibility when iron-working debris becomes weathered.

Under the petrological microscope iron slag from Oakley is grey under plane polarised light (PPL), with a component of orthorhombic crystals of neoformed olivine, that show very high relief (cf. fayalite [Fe,Mg]$_2$SiO$_4$; Kerr 1959; Kresten and Hjärthner-Holdar 2001)(Figure 30c). Under crossed polarised light (XPL), the crystals show high interference colours, with second order birefringence reds and blues. Under oblique incident light (OIL), a metallic lustre is apparent. Weathered iron-working debris, on the other hand, is generally opaque (PPL), non-birefringent and strongly reddish/rust coloured under OIL. Fayalite olivine is a common birefringent crystal in slag (Figure 30c), with dark dendritic patterns (see Figure 30d)

Figure 30a. Dragon Hall, Norwich: macro-scan of thin section through a Norman (11th–12th century) mortar floor (context 11347), and the overlying occupation (context 11317) and post-abandonment (contexts 12424) levels. Plane light, frame length is 70 mm.

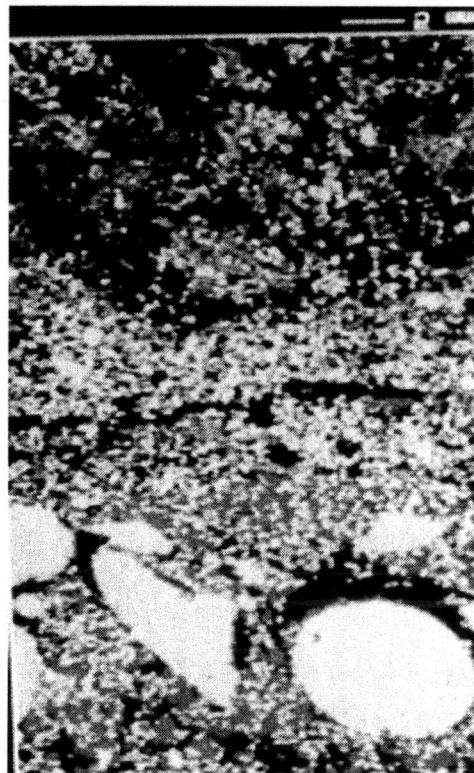

Figure 30b. Dragon Hall, Norwich: combined elemental map of Si, P and Ca, across a Norman (11th–12th century) mortar floor (context 11347) and the overlying occupation (context 11317) and post-abandonment (context 12424) levels. The mortar floor is tempered with flint gravel (Si), set in a calcitic matrix (Ca) containing sand-size quartz (Si). The occupation and post-abandonment levels are also sandy but increasingly phosphate-rich (P). 5 mm bar (Table 12).

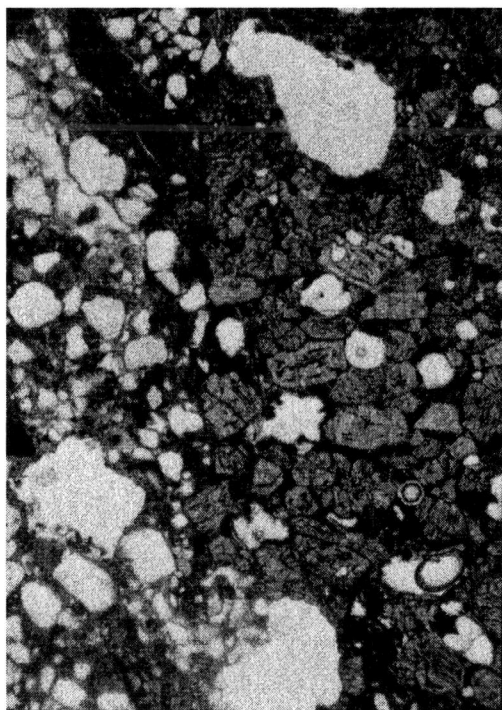

Figure 30c. Oakley, Suffolk: Roman iron slag (courtesy of Jane Cowgill); grey coloured orthorhombic neoformed crystals of olivine (possible fayalite); note typical high relief of the material and the presence of vesicles (voids). PPL, frame length is 5.5 mm.

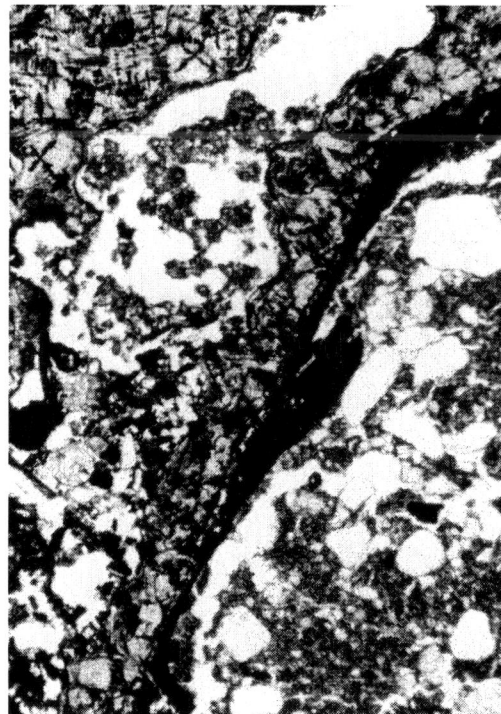

Figure 30d. Deansway, Worcester: Roman iron slag as residual material in dark earth soil that pre-dates the late 9th century Saxon burh. Crystals of olivine (possible fayalite) are present, with dendritic patterns possibly formed of wüstite (FeO). Edge of slag has become 'blackened' with iron oxides through weathering and small soil fauna have left organo-mineral excrements in coarse vesicular voids. PPL, frame length is 5.5 mm.

Table 13. Norman Manufactured Floors and occupation layers; brickearth floor at No. 1, Poultry, London and 'plaster' coated 'mortar' floor at Dragon's Hall, Norwich Figures 30a and 30b) – microstratigraphy.

Site/sample	%LOI	MS x 10⁻⁸ SI Kg⁻¹	P₂O₅ (2% citric acid ext.) (ppm)	Other data (microprobe data)
No. 1, Poultry Trampled layers	8.1–9.6	779–785	3400–3860 (0.15–0.17 % P)	Contains burned bone, burned brickearth, charcoal, slag, organic fragments and secondary phosphate features
No. 1, Poultry Brickearth slabs	2.3–2.4	37–38	720–1540 (0.03–0.07% P)	Sandy silt loam with secondary iron and phosphate features.
Dragon Hall Destruction debris	6.9	2081		Sand-rich orange-coloured burned guano, with charcoal and oblate fused silica from burned thatch. (12.1% Si, 0.49% Ca, 0.49% P; n=21)
Dragon Hall occupation layers	10.3	405		Sand-rich, with laminated plant remains and charred shell, bone, eggshell, charcoal and oblate fused silica from burned thatch. (12.9% Si, 3.2% Ca, 0.3% P; n=40)
Dragon Hall plaster-coated mortar floor	5.1	403		Gravel-size 'porous' flint showing trace contamination (32.7% Si, 0.28% Ca, 0.07% P; n=4) set in sand-rich mortar (9.68% Si, 5.38% Ca, 0.86% P; n=4)

NB: Microprobe Data supplied by Kevin Reeves, UCL.

LOI, phosphate and MS data supplied by Jöhan Linderholm, University of Umeå, Sweden.

occurring as likely wüstite (FeO); but detailed archaeo-metallurgical analyses are needed to confirm such identifications (e.g. Kerr 1959; Geoarchaeological Laboratory 1998, 19; Peter Kresten and Lena Grandin, pers. comm.). Hammerscale is opaque under the petrological microscope, but a layered edge can be perceived under OIL. This shows up as various grey zones in a back-scattered electron image, resulting from an outer haematite, and inner magnetite and wüstite layers (Geoarchaeological Laboratory 1998, 14; Peter Kresten and Lena Grandin, pers. comm.).

In dark earth at Roman Deansway, Worcester iron slag is strongly residual compared, for example, to many organic materials of anthropogenic origin. It is present in many of the dark earth (see below) contexts studied through soil micromorphology (Figure 30c)(Dalwood 1992; Macphail. forthcoming). It is also likely that the presence of this magnetic material contributes to the general enhancement of magnetic susceptibility here. The magnetic susceptibility of some soil samples at Deansway (MS: mean 259 x 10⁻⁸ SI kg⁻¹; range 212–302 x 10⁻⁸ SI kg⁻¹; n=4) can be compared with MS values for dark earth from three London sites (Colchester House, Courage Brewery and 7–11, Bishopsgate)(MS: mean 142 x 10⁻⁸ SI kg⁻¹; range 75–215 x 10⁻⁸ SI kg⁻¹; n=13)(Macphail; Macphail and Cruise, unpublished reports to MoLAS) (Figure 32). Although, the dark earth at these three London sites contains burned material and traces of industrial waste, overall the importance of iron slag at the Roman iron-working site of Deansway is reflected in the higher MS values of the dark earth, demonstrating the high residuality of iron slag at this site (Figure 32d).

It is well known that burning raises magnetic susceptibility in soils (Clark, 1996), but at the Saxon site of West Heslerton, North Yorkshire extremely high MS values were recorded (Haughton and Powlesland 1999; Macphail *et al*. submitted 2000). Here, natural soils have average MS values between 30 and 40 units (x 10⁻⁸ SI kg⁻¹). Saxon occupation soils in general, however, have mean values of 500-800 units (x 10⁻⁸ SI kg⁻¹), some contexts attaining many thousands of units, for example some Middle Saxon 'red' ditch (3330 x 10⁻⁸ SI kg⁻¹), pit (3424–7479 x 10⁻⁸ SI kg⁻¹) and Grubenhäuser (5507 x 10⁻⁸ SI kg⁻¹) fills. These high values were sometimes reflected in the presence of rare iron slag and common burned ferruginous soil observed in thin section; but these extremely high values remain enigmatic because deposits are insufficiently iron-rich (Jane Cowgill, Gerry MacDonnell, pers comm.) to be iron-working deposits (Macphail *et al*., submitted 2000). Colleagues then suggested that MS values could be raised progressively by being successive burning. This was briefly tested by Johan Linderholm (a collaborator in the study of the soils West Heslerton) at the Centre for Environmental Archaeology, University of Umeå, Sweden.

An experimental oven was constructed of "red chalk" (work carried out by excavation team), a local parent material at West Heslerton, used both during the Roman and Saxon periods. A red chalk daub and straw tempered roof was sampled after a single firing. The poorly charred uppermost part of the roof attained an MS of 59 units (x 10⁻⁸ SI kg⁻¹), while the inner rubified layer recorded an MS of 140–177 units (x 10⁻⁸ SI kg⁻¹). This material and some red Grubenhaus fill were successively heated to 550° C,

Table 14. Examples of West Heslerton soils that underwent 1 and/or 4 ignitions at 550° C.

Sample	Initial MS (x 10^{-8} SI kg^{-1})	550° C x1 (x 10^{-8} SI kg^{-1})	550° C x4 (x 10^{-8} SI kg^{-1})
iii/ Orange subsoil sands	54	76	77
v/Yellow subsoil sands	18	33	33
10/Late burned dung (011BA00NCS)	685	679	n.d.
117/Experimental oven rubified "Red Chalk"	270	274	272
128a 128b 127 Late rubified *Grubenhaus* fills (012AD08007)	1580 4659 1779	1763 4672 1770	n.d. n.d. n.d.
140/Late rubified *Grubenhaus* fill (012AD08069)	5290 5507	4960 5581	4940 n.d.
141/Late humic *Grubenhaus* fill (012AD08030)	988	1228	n.d.

NB: Sample 140 - Microprobe analysis: mean values; 11.7% Fe, 0.10% Mg, 0.97% Si, 0.36% Al, 0.23% P, 0.62% Ca, 0.04% S, 0.84% Mn, 0.00% K, 0.12% Na)(n=258); XRD analysis: quartz, calcite, haematite and magnetite present (Data supplied by Kevin Reeves, UCL). MS data supplied by Jöhan Linderholm, University of Umeå, Sweden.

but exhibited no further rise in MS (Table 14). The use of 550°C is standard for measurements of LOI (loss on ignition) in geoarchaeology. Moreover, this moderate temperature is appropriate to test the MS of burned soil at West Heslerton, which has been rubified by heating, but where organic matter has not been fully combusted. In addition, phytoliths have not been transformed by melting (temperature <800°C) and calcite ash can still be pseudo-morphic of organic materials (temperature <650–700°C)(Courty *et al.* 1989, 109).

The high to extremely high MS values at West Heslerton therefore could not be explained by soils being successively burned with MS values being incrementally raised and the use of higher temperature burning was not appropriate here. High MS values at Saxon West Heslerton therefore remain enigmatic, but perhaps can be partly explained by a background of industrial/iron working activity and ferruginous soils (Table 14, XRD and micro-probe data) being burned, albeit commonly at moderately low temperatures (Macphail *et al.* submitted 2000). En-hanced values for MS that are not easily accounted for, are a common trait of Saxon settlements, and this phenom-enon has yet to be fully investigated (Powlesland, pers. comm, 2001).

RESIDUES OF INDUSTRIAL AND CONSTRUCTIONAL ACTIVITIES

Weathering products of mortar and plaster

Essentially, cements are formed through the heating of limestone ($CaCO_3$) to produce quicklime (CaO), from which slaked lime ($Ca(OH)_2$) is formed through the addition of water; the hydrated lime then reacts with carbon dioxide (CO_2) in the atmosphere to produce $CaCO_3 + H_2O$ (Blake 1947; Stoops 1984). Weathering in the form of decarbonation occurs under moist conditions when calcium bicarbonate ($Ca(HCO_3)_2$) is removed in solution by rain water containing more or less dissolved CO_2 – carbonic acid (Duchaufour 1982, 74). At Courage Brewery weathered cement becomes 'thinned', more porous and the temper becomes less and less well retained. Dissolution leads to the liberation of sand and gravel-size material into the soil. At the same time unweathered carbonate is mixed into the fine fabric by biological activity and a calcareous dark earth soil is formed (Macphail and Cruise, 2000). In dry years, a loss of water from soil containing calcium bicarbonate can lead to the deposition of secondary calcium carbonate, as found at the Courage Brewery site. It can also be noted that if the mortar floor at Dragon Hall, Norwich was demolished and became weathered, sands and gravels would be released into the resulting anthropogenic soil.

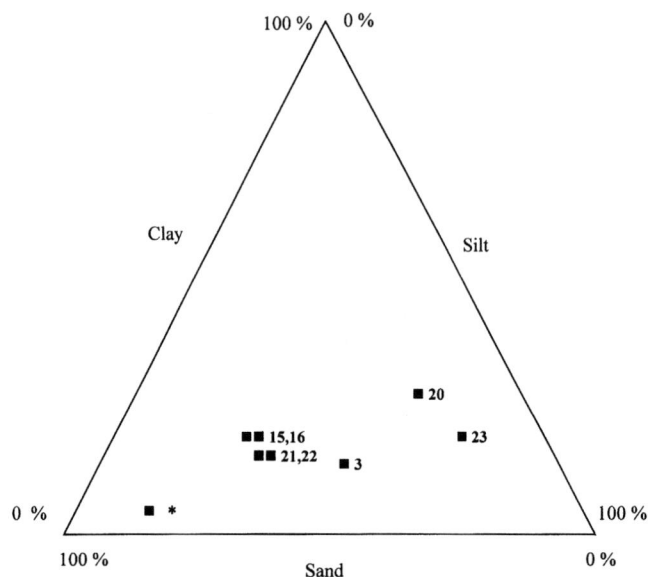

Figure 31. Courage Brewery site: particle size classes for local sand (*), alluvium (23), brickearth building clay (3), 'silty' dumps (20) and dark earth (15, 16, 21, and 22).

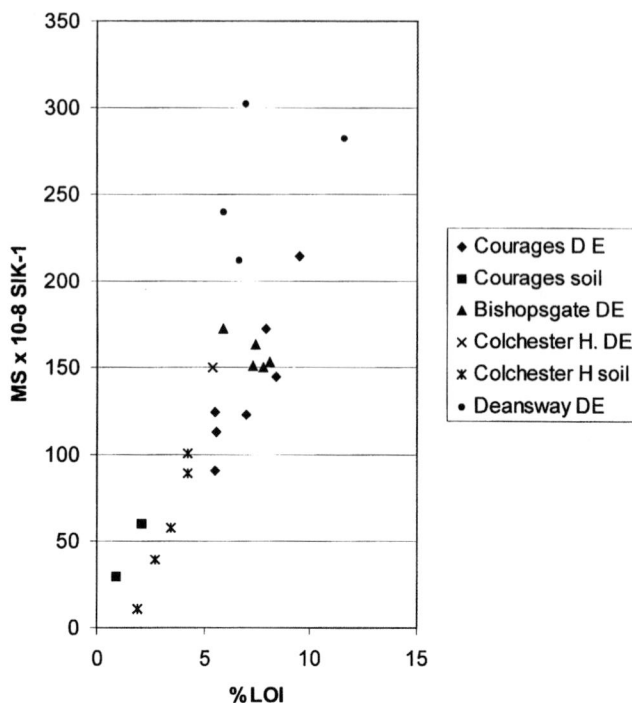

Figure 32. Magnetic susceptibility (MS) and % LOI for Roman soils and Dark Earth.

Daub and Turf

Brickearth fragments and burned brickearth are ubiquitous in dark earth and leveling deposits in London. As noted above, most originate from clay-rich Bt and B/C subsoil material. Also present, however, are fragments of pale clay-poor Eb upper subsoil brickearth soil material (see Table 12). Where fragments of soil from Eb, Bt and B/C soil horizons contain planar voids, pseudomorphic of plant temper, and inclusions such as charcoal, these can be regarded as fragments of daub (cf. Blake 1947, 49; Courty *et al.* 1989, 120; Butser Ancient Farm reference material). Both unburned and rubified (reddened) and blackened burned daub occur in the dark earth. Unburned daub weathers rapidly into soil, and disappears. Equally, turf when reworked may be difficult to identify, although when as coarse soil fragments these can be preserved in fills and identified in thin section. On the other hand, turf has been used as a fuel, and charred turf as a residue of hearth rake-out has been recognised as a major component in farm mound deposits in northern Scotland (Carter 1998a, Carter 1998b).

Dark earth

The formation of dark earth through the weathering of Roman building material, and the pedological formation of pararendzinas, rendzinas and calcareous brown earths, has been dealt with at length (Macphail 1994, 1996; Macphail and Cruise 2000). It is therefore sufficient here to draw the readers attention to Figure 31 and Table 11, and the contention that weathered silty clay loam brick-

earth and river sands released from decarbonated mortar and plaster can produce dark earth in London that has a sandy loam texture. Figure 31 and Table 11, also show that Roman flood clay loams probably contributed little to the formation of dark earth in Southwark.

Iron working

As shown at Deansway, identifiable sand-size pieces of iron slag in well-drained and aerated dark earth soils, is strongly residual. This is in comparison, for instance, to the rarity of fragments of dung produced by Late Roman animal pounds that can occur in the same dark earth soils. When affected by intense post-depositional weathering iron working debris becomes difficult to recognise, and also seems to lose most of its magnetic properties (Jane Cowgill, pers. comm.; see above). The microscopic presence of iron slag along with wood charcoal and ashes in trampled occupation layers formed over constructed brickearth floors at No. 1, Poultry, also permitted some inferred interpretations concerning an industrial use of space around a Norman structure consistent with archaeological hypotheses concerning this period and area of the site (Table 13).

CONCLUSIONS

Although geoarchaeology is perhaps not commonly a primary technique for the identification of industrial activity, the microstratigraphical approach as demonstrated above, can be a useful tool in augmenting information from field analysis, geophysical surveys, and metallurgical and macro-fossil studies. Certainly, petrological techniques are the mainstay for the analysis of materials like red ochre and building materials, while iron working debris is commonly studied through SEM/X-ray and microprobe techniques. The present chapter reveals the importance of a microstratigraphic approach to the study of the use and disuse of earth-based building materials, and has allowed the recognition of how the breakdown of mortars and plasters, through weathering, has created calcareous dark earth soils in places like London. Fine resolution studies of the microstratigraphy of brickearth and mortar constructed floors reveals much about building practices and the formation of occupation and post-abandonment deposits, microscopic inclusions giving clues to local industrial activities. Iron working can produce iron slag, often a highly residual material that affects the soil's magnetic properties, but post-depositional weathering can also effect this material. Finally, soil micromorphology and allied geoarchaeological methods appear to play a crucial role in the understanding of site formation processes, including post-depositional effects, and can greatly contribute to the placing of industrial activities into their archaeological context.

Acknowledgements
The author wishes to gratefully acknowledge long term funding from English Heritage and the collaboration of numerous archaeological units (Museum of London Archaeological Service, Norfolk Archaeological Unit, Suffolk Archaeological Unit and Sussex Archaeological Trust). He wishes to thank the following for their collaboration and comments on the various aspects of this work: Justine Bayley, Jane Cowgill (reference iron working debris), G.M. Cruise (Figure 31), Hal Dalwood (Deansway), Neil Linford (English Heritage), John Manley (Fishbourne Roman Palace), Peter Murphy, Dominic Powlesland (West Heslerton), James Rackham, Kevin Reeves (microprobe data), Pete Rowsome (No. 1, Poultry), Andy Shelley (Dragon Hall), G. Stoops and P.E.J. Wiltshire; Liz Pye (UCL) and Sue Wright (and other MoLAS staff), who gathered opinions on terms used to describe plaster and mortar, are thanked for discussion of lime-based building materials. Discussion of iron slag was greatly aided by comments from Peter Kresten and Lena Grandin (Geoarchaeology Laboratory, Department of Excavations, National Heritage Board Uppsala, Sweden). The reviewer is greatly thanked for their comments.

References

Armitage, P.L., Locker, A. and Straker, V. 1987. Environmental archaeology in London: a review, pp. 252–331 in Keeley, H.C.M. (ed.), *Environmental Archaeology: a regional review Vol II* (English Heritage Occasional paper No. 1). London: English Heritage.

Avery, B.W. 1990. *Soils of the British Isles.* Wallingford: CAB International.

Babel, U. 1975. Micromorphology of soil organic matter, pp. 369–473 in Giesking, J.E. (ed.), *Soil Components: Organic Components* (Vol. 1). New York: Springer-Verlag.

Bal, L. 1982. *Zoological ripening of soils.* Wageningen: Centre for Agricultural Publishing and Documentation.

Blake, M.E. 1947. *Ancient Roman Construction in Italy from the Prehistoric period to Augustus.* Washington: Carnegie Institution of Washington.

Brown, G. and Macphail, R.I. (submitted) First century horticultural activities close to the municipal boundaries of Londinium: archaeological and soil micromorphological evidence. *Britania.*

Bullock, P., Fedoroff, N., Jongerius, A., Stoops, G. and Tursina, T. 1985. *Handbook for Soil Thin Section Description.* Wolverhampton: Waine Research Publications.

Canti, M.G. 1998. The micromorphological identification of feacal spherulites from archaeological and modern materials. *Journal of Archaeological Science,* **25**, 435–444.

Carter, S. 1998a. Soil micromorphology, pp. 172–186 in Lowe, C. (ed.), *St. Boniface Church, Orkney: coastal erosion and archaeological assessment.* Stroud: Sutton Publishing/Historic Scotland.

Carter, S. 1998b. The use of peat and other organic sediments as fuel in northern Scotland : identifications derived from soil thin sections, pp. 99–104 in Coles, G. (ed.), *Life on the Edge: Human Settlement and Marginality* (Oxbow Monograph 100). Oxford: Oxford.

Ciezar, P., Gonzalez, V., Pieters, M., Rodet-Belarbi, I. and Van-Ossel, P. 1994. In suburbano – new data on the immediate surroundings of Roman and early medieval Paris, pp. 137–146 in Hall, A.R. and Kenward, H.K. (eds), *Urban-Rural Connexions: Perspectives from Environmental Archaeology.* Oxford: Oxbow Books.

Clark, A. 1996. *Seeing Beneath the Soil: prospecting methods in archaeology.* London: Batsford.

Courty, M.A., Goldberg, P. and Macphail, R.I. 1989. *Soils and Micromorphology in Archaeology.* Cambridge: Cambridge University Press.

Crowther, J., Macphail, R.I. and Cruise, G.M. 1996. Short-term burial change in a humic rendzina, Overton Down Experimental Earthwork, Wiltshire, England. *Geoarchaeology,* **11(2)**, 95–117.

Cruise, G.M. and Macphail, R.I. 2000. Microstratigraphical Signatures of Experimental Rural Occupation Deposits and Archaeological Sites, pp. 183–191, in Roskams, S. (ed.), *Interpreting Stratigraphy* (Vol. 9). York: University of York.

Dalwood, H. 1992. The use of soil micromorphology for investigating site formation processes, pp. 3–6 in K. Steane (ed.), *Interpretation of Stratigraphy: a review of the art* (City of Lincoln Archaeological report No 31). Lincoln: City of Lincoln Archaeological Unit.

Dickson, C. 1999. Past uses of turf in the Northern Isles, pp. 106–109 in Mills, C.M. and Coles, G (eds), *Life on the Edge: Human Settlement and Marginality.* Oxford: Oxbow.

Dillon, J., Jackson, S. and Jones, H. 1991. Excavations at the Courage Brewery and Park Street 1984–90. *London Archaeologist,* **6**, 255–62.

Dimbleby, G.W. 1985. *The Palynology of Archaeological Sites.* London: Academic Press.

Duchaufour, P. 1982. *Pedology*. London: Allen and Unwin.

Ferraris, M. 1997. Ochre remains, pp. 593–598 in Maggi, R. (ed.), *Arene Candide: a Functional and Environmental Assessment of the Holocene Sequence (Excavations Bernarbo' Brea-Cardini 1940–50)*. Roma: Istituto Italiano di Paleontologia Umana.

Geoarchaeological Laboratory, G. 1998. *Activity Report 1998*. Uppsala: Department of Excavations, National Heritage Board, UV GAL.

Goldberg, P. and Macphail, R.I. (In preparation). *Color Guide to Geoarchaeological Microstratigraphy* (CD-ROM). New York: Kluwer Academic/Plenum Publishers.

Haughton, C. and Powlesland, D. 1999. *West Heslerton. The Anglian Cemetery*. London: English Heritage.

Kerr, P.F. 1959. *Optical Mineralogy*. New York: McGraw-Hill Book Company.

Kresten, P. and Hjärthner-Holdar, E. 2001. Analyses of the Swedish ancient iron reference slag W-25:R. *Historical Metallurgy*, **35(1)**, 48–51.

Macphail, R.I. 1980. Report on a soil in a Romano-British context at Lloyds Merchant Bank, London (LLO78) London. Unpublished Ancient Monument Report 3045.

Macphail, R.I. 1994. The reworking of urban stratigraphy by human and natural processes, pp. 13–43 in Hall, A.R. and Kenward, H.K. (eds), *Urban-Rural Connexions: Perspectives from environmental Archaeology* (Oxbow Monograph 47). Oxford: Oxbow.

Macphail, R.I. 1996. North-West Roman Southwark – Courages: Soil Microstratigraphy: a soil micromorphological and chemical approach. Unpublished report to Museum of London Archaeological Service.

Macphail, R.I., Acott, T.G., Bell, M., Crowther, J. and Cruise, G.M. (in press 2002) The Experimental Earthwork at Wareham, Dorset after 33 years: changes to the buried soil. *Journal of Archaeological Science*.

Macphail, R.I., Courty, M.A., Hather, J. and Wattez, J. 1997. The soil micromorphological evidence of domestic occupation and stabling activities, pp. 53–88 in Maggi, R. (ed.), *Arene Candide: a Functional and Environmental Assessment of the Holocene Sequence*. Roma: Istituto Italiano di Paleontologia Umana.

Macphail, R.I. and Cruise, G.M. 1997. 7–11, Bishopsgate and Colchester House (PEP89), London: preliminary report on soil microstratigraphy and chemistry. Unpublished Report. Unpublished report to Museum of London Archaeological Service.

Macphail, R.I. and Cruise, G.M. 2000. Rescuing our urban archaeological soil heritage: a multidisciplinary microstratigraphical approach, pp. 9–14 in Burghardt, W. and Dornauf (eds), *Proceedings of the First International Conference on Soils of Urban, Industrial, Traffic and Mining Areas* (Vol. 1). Essen: IUSS/IBU.

Macphail, R.I. and Cruise, G.M. 2001. The soil micromorphologist as team player: a multianalytical approach to the study of European microstratigraphy, pp. 241–267 in Goldberg, P.,

Holliday, V. and Ferring, R. (eds), *Earth Science and Archaeology*. New York: Kluwer Academic/Plenum Publishers.

Macphail, R.I., Cruise, G.M., Gebhardt, A. and Linderholm, J. (Submitted 2000). West Heslerton: soil micromorphology and chemistry of the Roman and Saxon deposits. Unpublished report to English Heritage, London.

Macphail, R.I., Cruise, G.M., Mellalieu, S.J. and Niblett, R. 1998. Micromorphological interpretation of a "Turf-filled" funerary shaft at St. Albans, United Kingdom. *Geoarchaeology*, **13**, 617–644.

Macphail, R.I. (Forthcoming) Soil micromorphology, in Mundy, C.F. and Dalwood, C.H. (eds), *Excavations in Deansway, Worcester, 1988–89* (CBA Research Report). York: Council for British Archaeology.

Mora, P, Mora, L, and Philipott, P, 1984. *Conservation of wall paintings*. London: Butterworths.

Murphy, P. and Fryer, V. 1999. The plant macrofossils, pp. 384–388 in Niblett, R. (ed.), *The Excavation of a Ceremonial site at Folly Lane, Verulamium* (Britannia Monograph No. 14). London: Society for the Promotion of Roman Studies.

Pye, E. 2000/2001. Wall painting in the Roman empire: colour, design and technology. *Archaeology International*, 24–27.

Rentzel, P. 1998. Ausgewähite Grubenstrukturen aus spätlatènezeitlichen Fundstelle Basel-Gasfabrik: Geoarchäologische interpretation der Grubenfüllungen, pp. 35–79, in *Jahresbericht der archäologischen Bodenforschung des Kantons Basel-Stadt 1995*. Basel: Verlag und Bestelladresse.

Roskams, S. (ed.) 2000. *Interpreting Stratigraphy. Site evaluation, recording procedures and stratigraphic analysis (Paper presented to Interpreting Stratigraphy Conferences 1993–1997)*. Oxford: British Archaeological Reports.

Scaife, R.G. and Macphail, R.I. 1983. The post-Devensian development of heathland soils and vegetation, pp. 70–99 in Burnham, P. (ed.), *Soils of the Heathlands and Chalklands* (SEESOIL Vol. 1). Wye: South-East Soils Discussion Group.

Shelley, A. 1998. Dragon Hall Archaeological project. Norwich: Norfolk Archaeological Unit.

Stoops, G. 1984. The environmental physiography of Pessinus in function of the study of the archaeological stratigraphy and natural building materials, pp. 38–50 in Devreker, J. and Waelkens, M. (eds), Les Fouilles de la Rijksuniversiteit te Gent a Pessiononte 1967–73. *Dissertationes Archaeologicae Gardenses*, **XXII**.

Wiltshire, P.E.J. 1997. The pre-Roman Environment, pp. 25–40 in Wilmott, T. (ed.), Birdoswald: Excavations of a Roman fort on Hadrian's Wall and its successor settlements: 1987–92 (English Heritage Archaeological Report 14). London: English Heritage.

Wiltshire, P.E.J. 1999. Palynological analysis of filling in the funerary shaft, pp. 347–365 in Niblett, R. (ed.), *The Excavation of a Ceremonial site at Folly Lane, Verulamium* (Britannia Monograph No. 14). London: Society for the Promotion of Roman Studies.

11. Deriving information efficiently from surveys of artefact distribution

R. S. Shiel and S. B. Mohamed

Artefact distribution, like that of most materials in soil, varies greatly over short distances and, in order to derive useful conclusion about any underlying trends, a method of map realisation is required which can both deal with the extent of variability and with abrupt changes over short distances. Some map realisation methods tend to smooth excessively, resulting in underestimation of the density at 'hotspots' while overestimating the surrounding background. Bilinear and Fault algorithms in Unimap are shown to be more effective at avoiding this problem than is Kriging. Fault produces maps that model the data slightly more accurately than Bilinear. Fault uses precise location for data points whereas Bilinear uses a cell centre value, but for large datasets Bilinear requires less computing resources. For all three methods, the correlation between measured and predicted values decreases as both the sample number and density decrease. With less than about 0.7 samples per hectare the correlation coefficient decreases very rapidly. There is shown to be little advantage from a sample density >1 ha^{-1}. It seems from this and other data that there is a relationship between the geostatistical range and the density of samples needed to give an accurate map, but it is unusual to know the range before the samples are collected. However, based on previous data investigations it appears that for inherent properties of soils, which typically have a range of about 200 m, then 4 samples must be taken per hectare, whereas for pottery from village settlements the range is much large (here it was 750 m) allowing the lower sample density suggested earlier. Smaller features would not be detected with such wide sample spacing. Unless there is either a preliminary survey or a clear view of the size and distribution of features sought, then the sample density may be such that either no pattern is detected or many of the points are redundant and a larger area could have been surveyed with the same resource.

Keywords: Geostatistics, map precision, mapping algorithms, sample number, sample spacing, feature dimensions.

INTRODUCTION

Whereas a map of land use may be correct at every point, one showing elevation will only be precise at the survey points, and even along a contour joining these points there are likely to be substantial deviations. In general, as more points are surveyed then there will be less inaccuracy along the intermediate parts of the contour. If the scale of the map is changed, then either detail will be lost or the contour line may be excessively smooth and ignore substantial fluctuations (Gillings & Wise 1990). Off the contour line, the elevation is likely to be intermediate between the height of successive contours, but once again there will be considerable deviations and small areas may exceed the range of inter-contour values. The value at any point between contours cannot be assumed to be anything other than an intermediate at best, as there can be no assumption that the slope is uniform between adjoining contours.

The above example describes the situation where the property being mapped is visible. Where properties, such as the pH of a soil, are based on a small number of widely spaced samples, whose value was not known when the sample point was selected, then any map that is produced is likely to have isolines which model reality rather inefficiently. This is the common situation when soil type or soil properties are mapped, and soil surveyors accept that their maps contain substantial areas of other soil types than those shown (Avery 1987). The soil surveyor has at least a set of rules available relating the outward appearance of the earth to the natural properties of the immediately underlying material, but when properties such as soil elemental composition or content of abandoned material, such as pottery, are concerned, then there may be no clear rule to assist the surveyor, other than the values obtained from samples taken at specific positions. Where these are based on counting material visible at the surface, there are still problems because visibility affects the efficiency of collection, as does the colour and soil adhesiveness. There is also only a small fraction of the material exposed at any time.

The problem of estimating real variation in soil properties has long concerned agronomists who wish to assess the fertility of the soil. They originally developed systems of sampling management units (fields) and taking the average for that area (MAFF 1994). It was accepted that there was frequently a considerable variation of properties within that area; the the first map demonstrating this was produced as long ago as 1910 (Mercer and Hall, 1911). At that time, it was concluded that practical considerations made any approach that attempted to allow for within-field variation unworkable, but recently the development of GPS and improvements in data analysis and handling have allowed the production of 'maps' of such variation of soil properties, based on a number of samples taken from precisely known locations. Because of the economic benefits that can be obtained by producing an accurate prediction of fertiliser requirement at every point in the field, this opportunity is very attractive (Hammond, 1993). The accuracy of the prediction will be affected by the number of sample points, but the cost also will depend directly on this number (Mohamed et al. 1997). There is therefore an optimum number and density of samples, which provides a sufficiently accurate predictive map without excessively increasing the cost of producing the map. It has been shown that for agronomically important soil properties this seems to occur at about 4 samples ha⁻¹ (Shiel & Mohamed 1997; Franzen & Peck 1995). At large sample densities there is little increase in map precision, while at lower densities the map accuracy decreases rapidly.

These principles may be transferred to studies of the distribution of materials in the soil resulting from non-agronomic activities, in particular for studies of the impact of past societies on the soil and on the density of artefacts or other remains of their industry left behind by them. The geographic distribution of artefacts may, however, vary over shorter and longer distances and have a greater or lesser intensity of variation. Once again, there is the problem of having an incomplete sample with much of the material hidden from view. Also, analytical resources, which can be equated with time and effort, must be allocated most efficiently in order to obtain the most accurate possible view of the properties in question. These problems have exercised those carrying out surveys such as those reported in Macready & Thompson (1985) and Haselgrove et al. (1985).

The variation in intensity of finds from 'sites' to 'background' is important because it will determine the magnitude of the change in semivariance with distance between samples. Samples which are close together (small lag distance) will be expected to be more similar to one another than those at a greater separation (large lag distance) and the distance at which the maximum difference (semivariance) occurs is said to be the range. The semivariance at this distance (the sill) should be substantially larger than at the shortest lag spacing (the nugget). Whereas soil properties vary as a result of changes such as the underlying geology or topography, and tend to result in a pattern that repeats across the landscape, features such as knapping floors, kilns or mills may be of small geographic extent but have a great local density of material and do not occur in a regular repeating pattern.

It has also been found from agronomic studies that the method of map realisation can substantially affect the precision of the map that results from a particular set of data (Mohamed et al. 1997). Many of the mapping techniques use a smoothing routine, which tends to underestimate 'hotspots' and give excess values to points where data is absent. Furthermore, in soils there are abrupt changes in property over short distances and, to allow for this, some of the mapping methods within Unimap permit properties to change suddenly (UNIRAS 1989). The Fault algorithm has been found to be the most effective in creating accurate maps of variation in soil nutrient content (Mohamed et al. 1997). In order to validate the procedure, data on some of the sampled points is used for the map realisation, and the algorithm's ability to predict the value of the intermediate points is then tested using the remaining points, which were excluded earlier. This procedure has been used not only to test which of the algorithms is most effective, but also to examine how well they model the variation in nutrient content at different sample spacing.

Robinson & Zubrow (1999) found that the algorithm used had major impacts on the efficiency of interpolation but only tested this with a pattern of computer generated data. This paper therefore uses a set of real archaeological data, collected as part of the Boeotia survey in Greece (Bintliff 1997), to examine whether the procedures developed in agronomy to minimise the density of sampling, while retaining accuracy of site interpretation, can provide the same benefits when they are applied to a comparable archaeological situation.

MATERIALS AND METHODS

Data on ceramic density in the area immediately to the south of the city of Thespiai, corrected for visibility, was obtained from the Boeotia project (Bintliff 1991). The

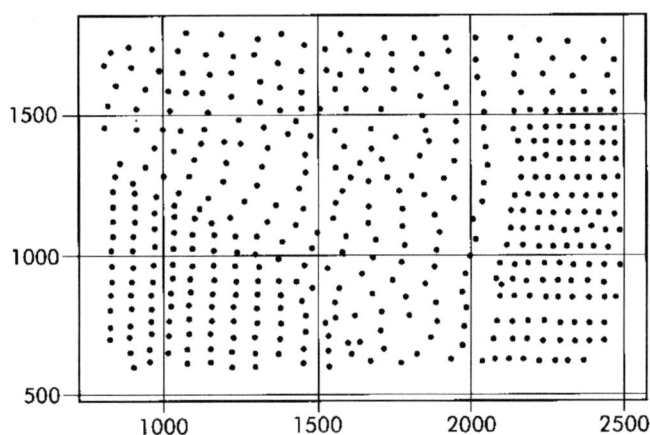

Figure 33. Plan of the original 434 sample points. Note the uneven distribution of the points. The figures on the axes are metres.

Figure 34. Semi-variogram of the semi-variance (γ) (x10⁻⁵) of the pottery data from Thespiai against lag distance (h).

data had been collected in 1989 and 1990 by fieldwalkers on transects of various widths determined largely by field and natural boundaries. The number of sherds found was recorded, as was the type of ground surface. Each of the values was then attributed to a grid co-ordinate at the centre of a rectangle separating the sample area from those around. A total of over 1800 samples were available but, as these did not form a rectangular area and problems can occur with mapping procedures when they are presented with a narrow region of sampling, a large rectangle was selected from within the area (Figure 33) containing 434 samples. The map algorithms calculate values at points based on a distance weighting rule (UNIRAS 1989). In narrow regions there is an uneven distribution of information for many of the points. This problem always occurs at edges and corners of a mapped area, where it is unavoidable.

These samples had not been collected at a uniform spacing. As Unimap requires a grid cell size to be defined, a grid of 50 m side was superimposed on the data. This grid size resulted in only two of the cells containing more than one sample point, while minimising the number of empty cells. This formed the 'full' dataset. The sample locations were then printed out as a map and a number were deleted so as to result in a grid with more even sample spacing. After this had been achieved, five more reductions in sample number were made. At each reduction the person making the reduction knew only the location of the points within the map and nothing of the ceramic density at that or any other point. The only objective at this stage was to create a series of grids with reasonably even sample spacing. The data for all 7 (original full data set and six progressive reductions) was then mapped using Fault, Bilinear and Kriging routines in Unimap (UNIRAS 1989). Bilinear approximates points into a grid and inter-

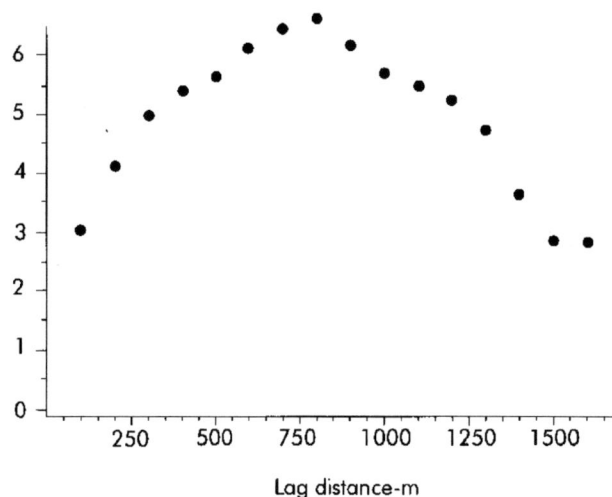

polates using a quadratic function; it recognises discontinuities in the data. Fault is a variation of bilinear but uses the exact position of irregular data points. Kriging requires that search radius and angle are defined by the user. This normally involves a process of selecting values and adjusting them on the basis of results to obtain the best relationship. A semi-variogram was created (McBratney & Webster 1986) as the first step in the procedure to create the Kriged map. The maps were printed as smooth contours and also an Excel spreadsheet of the predicted values for each grid square was created in Unimap. This procedure does not result in any loss of accuracy (Shiel *et al.* 1997). The cells for which no measured field data was available were deleted. For the other cells, the predicted value could then be compared with the measured value. In the case of the full data set, this comparison relates only the accuracy with which the algorithms represented the measured data, but in the reduced data sets there is both this type of information (included data) and also the accuracy with which the algorithm predicted the intermediate values at the points at which the measured data values had been 'excluded'. The extent to which the map realisation methods modelled the field data accurately was measured by the correlation coefficient between the two sets of values. Also, the difference between the measured and predicted values was found and the mean and standard deviation of this used to indicate the nature of the differences propagated by the algorithm. A map of the deviations was also produced at each sample spacing to detect any remaining pattern in the difference data. An efficient mapping algorithm should leave relatively little pattern in these residual values.

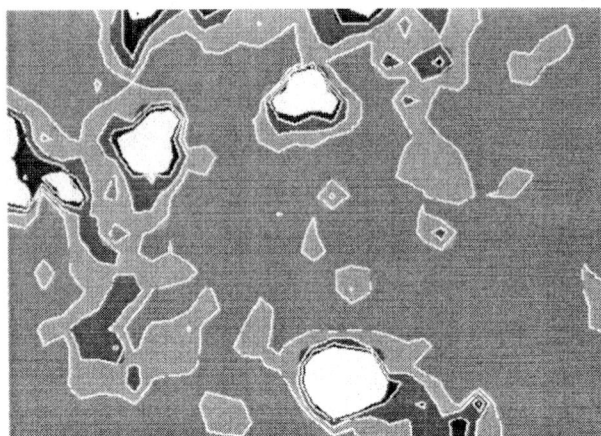

a.

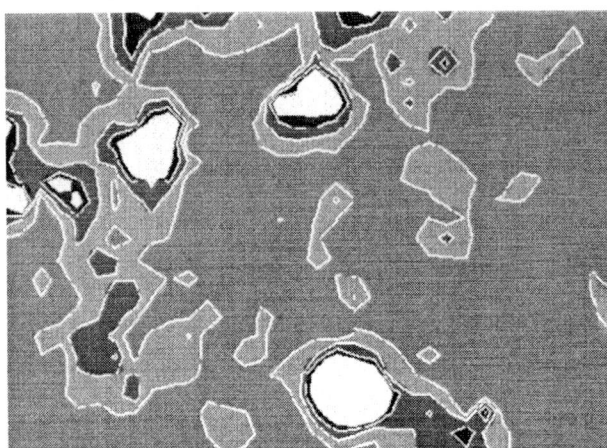

b.

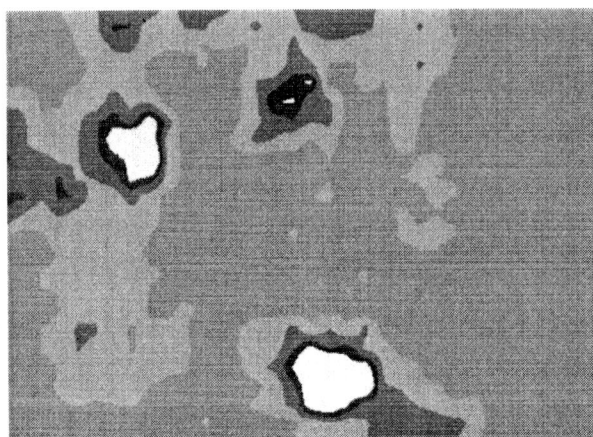

c.

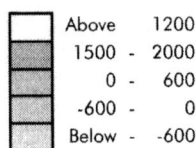

	Above	1200
	1500 -	2000
	0 -	600
	-600 -	0
	Below -	-600

Figure 35. Greyscale maps of interpolated pottery density at Thespiai produced using the Fault, Bilinear and Kriging algorithms in Unimap.

RESULTS

The semi-variogram has a very marked sill, at about 750 m (the range), at which the semi-variance was twice the nugget, but thereafter the semi-variance decreased to a value similar to the nugget at 1300 m (Figure 34). The maps of the full data set produced by all three algorithms were similar in their general outlines and all showed a number of concentrations of sherds (Figure 35). The correlation between the measured and predicted values (Table 15) decreased as the number of sample points decreased and was consistently largest for Fault. The variance accounted for (R^2), which measures how well the modelled values are relate to the measured values with decreasing sample number. It fell below 50% when there were fewer than 0.5 samples ha[-1]. The standard deviation of the difference between real and predicted values also increased with decreasing sample number, and again was larger for Bilinear than Fault. The correlation between predicted and measured values was much smaller for Kriging than for the other mapping methods. In all three methods there was a very rapid decrease in correlation coefficient between 0.49 and 0.33 samples ha[-1]. The introduction of a seventh sample density at 0.40 ha[-1] (data not shown) resulted in a correlation coefficient much more like that at 0.49 ha[-1] except for Kriging, which was more like that at 0.33 ha[-1].

The values predicted for grid squares that contained measured values which were available to the mapping algorithm (included) were similar to the measured values ($r>0.90$) except for Kriging, where the relationship was much poorer (Table 16). Values predicted for grid squares that contained known data but which had not been available to the mapping algorithm when the maps were being created (excluded) were less well correlated to the measured data and the correlation coefficients decreased with the number of sample points used. There was little difference between the correlations for Fault and Bilinear, but those for Kriging were again much smaller.

In maps of the difference between measured and predicted values (Figure 36), several of the original 'hotspots' remained locations of high density. This suggests that none of the mapping methods were adequately mapping the density of material at sites where it was most common. There were also a number of sites with large negative differences; these correspond to areas where the algorithms overestimate the density. The differences between predicted and measured values for points which were excluded (Table 17) showed very similar values for Bilinear and Fault. The means tended to be near zero but the standard deviations increased consistently as the number of points used to create the map decreased. These large standard deviations correspond to the increasing areas on the maps with extreme differences from the measured data and are greatest at low intensity of sample inclusion.

Table 15. Effect of sample density and map realisation method on map accuracy.

Dataset	Sample points	Spacing ha⁻¹	Correlation (r) between measured data and that predicted by			Variance loss %/point for Fault	SD of difference between measured data and that predicted by		
			Kriging	Fault	Bilinear		Kriging	Fault	Bilinear
Full	434	2.78	0.818	0.901	0.871	–	440	317	358
First	302	1.94	0.795	0.904	0.877	0.004	463	314	351
Second	192	1.23	0.655	0.832	0.826	0.049	560	406	412
Third	129	0.83	0.532	0.756	0.740	0.079	621	483	496
Fourth	76	0.49	0.587	0.655	0.641	0.107	617	556	563
Fifth	52	0.33	0.258	0.342	0.326	0.182	713	712	719
Sixth	35	0.22	–	0.279	0.268	0.184	–	774	781

Table 16. Correlation coefficients (r) between predicted and measured values discriminating between those measured values that were used to create the maps (included) and those that were excluded.

Grid points		Bilinear		Fault		Kriging	
included	excluded	included	excluded	included	excluded	included	excluded
35	399	0.998	0.179	0.999	0.191	–	–
52	382	0.990	0.215	0.997	0.234	0.341	0.087
76	358	0.968	0.535	0.995	0.538	0.496	0.186
129	305	0.955	0.587	0.990	0.587	0.691	0.444
192	242	0.932	0.673	0.953	0.664	0.741	0.553
302	132	0.900	0.678	0.931	0.676	0.830	0.495

Table 17. Mean and SD of differences between predicted and measured values for excluded values.

Points used	Fault		Bilinear		Kriged	
	Mean	SD	Mean	SD	Mean	SD
35	-70.0	807	-74.7	814	–	–
52	20.9	765	19.9	759	-22.8	856
76	-27.7	612	-27.6	611	-11.2	716
129	-29.9	571	-37.2	568	-38.9	383
192	-49.0	488	-55.0	474	-72.5	517
302	20.6	345	3.7	343	-16.5	405

DISCUSSION

The humped back pattern in the semi-variance is due to the small size of the centres of pottery concentration. Thus, at large and small lag distances, there is a tendency for the pair of samples being compared to be located in the 'background'. This occurs initially at short lags when both are on one side of a 'hotspot' or, at large lag distances, when they are on opposite sides of the 'hotspots' of pottery concentration and, as these values tend to be similar to one another then the semivariance is small. However, when the lag distance is such that one sample is in the 'background' and one on the 'site' then they will be very different and result in a large semivariance. Such semi-variograms occur where there is a periodic variation in properties (McBratney & Webster 1981) but in natural soils rarely have such a marked humpback form as this one. Fault once again produced the best relationship between measured and predicted values, though the im-

provement over Bilinear was generally smaller than was found for variation in soil nutrient content, pH or texture (Mohamed 1997). Kriging tended to produce much poorer relationships than had been found formerly and required a much more skilled operator to adjust the angle and lag distance so as to optimise the relationship. Examination of the maps and of the distribution of differences between measured and predicted values also suggested that Kriging tended to produce a considerable smoothing out of the topography, a feature that was produced to the smallest extent by Fault. Oliver (1987) has suggested that to avoid the smoothing problem, Kriging should only be carried out within regions that have no abrupt boundaries. This places considerable extra effort on the operator to distinguish such boundaries, and indicates that Kriging may not be the most appropriate technique where such boundaries are likely to occur. Robinson & Zubrow (1999) also suggest that Kriging is not the best method 'unless you

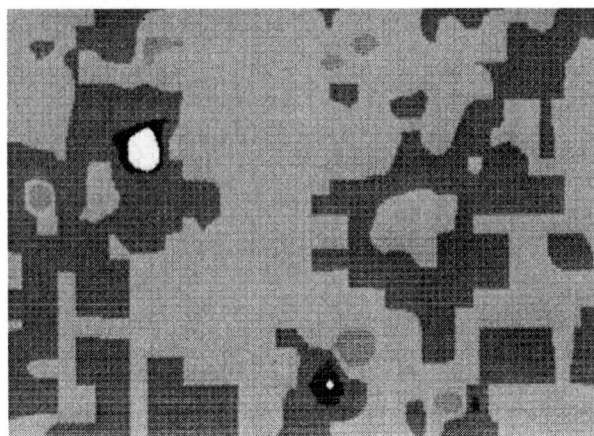

a.

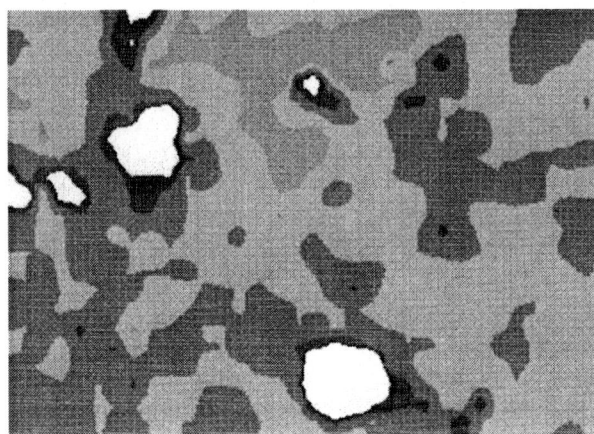

b.

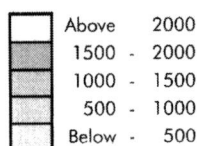

	Above	2000
	1500 -	2000
	1000 -	1500
	500 -	1000
	Below -	500

Figure 36. Greyscale maps of difference between predicted and measured pottery density produced by Fault algorithm in Unimap using 434 and 52 data points.

have special need and special justification'. Although Fault was marginally the best technique, Bilinear is faster to use, especially when there are many (>1000) points (UNIRAS 1989); the advantage of using the precise location of the data points appears in this case to be marginal. Nevertheless, even at close sample spacing where R^2 had ceased to increase with decreasing inter-sample distance, none of the methods were able adequately to model the peaks of pottery density. Where such abrupt features do occur there is a risk that their magnitude may therefore be underestimated from the resulting map, and, in the Mediterranean region, the famous 'background noise' (Cherry 1983) may be enhanced where the intermediate density is overestimated.

As the number of sample points used to create the maps

was reduced, the ability to predict the values of known intermediate points that had not been included, decreased. This decrease was most marked at about 0.5 ha^{-1} for all three algorithms At the highest density of sampling there was no advantage from the additional density; a larger area could have been mapped using the same number of points without compromising the accuracy of the map produced. Even when the distance between samples increased to about one third of the range (at 0.22 ha^{-1}) the maps did give a general indication of the distribution, though substantial areas of pottery concentration were missed and some areas of low pottery concentration were overestimated. Even at this very small sample number the map did provide some useful information, though it was not possible to create maps with Kriging if there were less than 50 datapoints. It would appear that in order to produce an accurate map then the density of samples in this case would need to be no less than 0.5 ha^{-1}. This is substantially less than the 4 ha^{-1} suggested by Shiel & Mohamed (1997). However, Shiel & Mohamed wereexamining soil nutrients that had a range of about 250 m; a much smaller value than that found here. In fact the differences between the ranges (750:250 m) is not substantially different to the difference in the inter-sample spacing at 0.5 and 4 ha^{-1} (141:50 m). Although it would be rash from this to suggest a general relationship between minimum inter-sample distance, range and precision of the map produced, in the absence of other information this relationship may be helpful. The relationship between range and inter-sample spacing, in the case of the unusual semi-variogram, has a logical foundation. The three main areas of large pottery density in this example (Figure 35) all have mean diameters of about 250 m. Thus, with an inter-sample spacing of >140 m, there may be only one point within the zone which has the largest concentration of pottery. Hence the mapping algorithm has scant data with which to produce an appropriately sized hotspot, and the resulting correlation of predicted values with the excluded, but measured, values is poor. There remains considerable uncertainly as to the range over which materials in soil change. Trangmar et al. (1985) suggest that natural variation occurs over greater distances than does that induced by human activity. The type of human activity must, however, be considered with care. Whereas fertilising materials, which may include those containing pottery, may be spread reasonably evenly over the surface of a particular uniformly managed area, there are likely to be large changes between adjoining areas managed in different ways or by different people. Also, settlement debris will vary in scale from that associated with a field hut to that of a city the size of Thespiai, with its surrounding 'village' hotspots, noted here. If the feature is, for example, 50 m across, a sample spacing of >25 m (<16 ha^{-1}) can not result in both an accurate estimate of the maximum density, and the size or central location of the 'hotspot'. An accurate estimate of size will be obtained if the samples are from close to the edge, where the density is likely to be smaller. If the sample is central to the 'hotspot', the maximum density will be estimated accurately but, as the surrounding samples will be in the 'background', the estimate of size will be poor. An intermediate situation of a sample distant from both the true edge and centre of a 'hotspot' will result in neither the density nor central location being accurate. Thus, the surveyor must have a very clear view of the size of the feature being investigated. McBratney *et al.* (1981) have suggested a multistage approach in which the nature of the semi-variogram is investigated before the main survey is carried out, and Oliver (1987) gives an example of where the pattern of variation is completely missed because of an excessively wide sampling distance. As knowledge of variation within the soil improves, it will become easier to predict the likely size of areas of high and low intensity and therefore to plan the sampling strategy in advance.

References

Avery, B.W. 1987 *Soil survey methods: a review*. Technical Monograph No. 18. Silsoe: Soil Survey and Land research Centre.

Bintliff, J.L. 1991 The Boeotia Project: Field survey 1990. *University of Newcastle and University of Durham Archaeological Reports* **14**, 13–16.

Bintliff, J.L. 1997 The Boeotia Project 1997 Field Season. *University of Newcastle and University of Durham Archaeological Reports* **21**, 89–95.

Cherry, J.F. 1983 Frogs around the pond: perspectives on current archaeological survey projects in the Mediterranean region, pp. 375–416 in Keller, D.R. & Rupp, D.W. (eds) *Archaeological survey in the Mediterranean area*. BAR S155 Oxford.

Franzen, D.W. & Peck, T.R. (1995) Sampling for site-specific management, pp. 535–551 in Robert, P.C., Rust, R.H. & Larson, W.E. (eds) *Site Specific management for Agricultural systems* Proceedings of the Second International Conference of the ASA-CSSA-SSSA, 1994 Minneapolis, Minnesota.

Gillings, M. & Wise, A. 1990 *GIS guide to good practice*. Oxford: Oxbow Books.

Hammond, M.W. 1993 Cost analysis of variable fertility management of phosphorus and potassium for potato production in central Washington, pp. 213–228 in Robert, P.C., Rust, R.H. & Larson, W.E. (eds) *Soil specific crop management* Proceedings of the First Workshop of the ASA-CSSA-SSSA 1992. Madison, Wisconsin.

Haselgrove, C., Millett, M. & Smith, I. (eds) 1985 *Archaeology from the ploughsoil: studies in the collection and interpretation of field survey data*. Sheffield: University of Sheffield.

MAFF 1994 *Fertiliser recommendations for agricultural and horticultural crops*. RB209 London: The Stationery Office.

McBratney, A.B. & Webster, R. 1981 Spatial dependence and classification of the soil along a transect in Northeast Scotland. *Geoderma* **26**, 63–82.

McBratney, A.B. & Webster, R. 1986 Choosing functions for semi-variograms of soil properties and fitting them to sampling estimates. *Journal of Soil Science* **37**, 617–639.

McBratney, A.B., Webster, R. & Burgess, T.M. 1981 The design of optimal sampling schemes for local estimation and mapping of regionalized variables. I. Theory and method. *Computers and Geosciences* **7**, 331–334.

Macready, S. & Thompson, F.H. (eds) 1985 *Archaeological field survey in Britain and abroad*. London: Society of Antiquaries.

Mercer, W.B. & Hall, A.D. 1911 The experimental error of field trials. *Journal of Agricultural Science* **4**, 107–127.

Mohamed, S.B. 1997 *Management of spatial patterns in soil acidity and in P and K fertility using geostatistics and mapping techniques to improve crop performance*. Unpublished PhD thesis. University of Newcastle upon Tyne.

Mohamed, S.B., Evans, E.J. & Shiel, R.S. 1997 Mapping techniques and intensity of soil sampling for precision farming pp. 217–226 in Robert, P.C., Rust, R.H. & Larson, W.E. (eds) *Precision Agriculture: Proceedings of the 3rd International Conference*. Madison: ASA.

Oliver, M.A. 1987 Geostatistics and its application to soil science. *Soil Use and Management* **3**, 8–20.

Robinson, J.M. & Zubrow, E. 1999 Between spaces: interpolation in archaeology, pp. 50–58 in Gillings, M., Mattingly, D. & van Dalen, J. (eds) *Geographical information systems and landscape archaeology* The archaeology of the Mediterranean landscape 3. Oxford: Oxbow.

Shiel, R.S. & Mohamed, S.B. 1997 Reducing cost of soil fertility maps for precision farming without a proportionate loss of accuracy, p. 44 in Shiel, R.S. (ed.) *Current progress in soil research. Abstracts of posters at the Golden Jubilee meeting of the British Society of Soil Science*. Newcastle upon Tyne.

Shiel, R.S., Mohamed, S.B. & Evans, E.J. 1997 Planning phosphorus and potassium fertilisation of fields with varying nutrient contents and potential, pp. 171–178 in Stafford, J.V. (ed.) *Precision Agriculture '97 Volume 1: Spatial Variability in Soil and Crop*, Bios Scientific; Oxford.

Trangmar, B.B., Yost, R.S. & Uehara, G. 1985 Application of geostatistics to spatial studies of soil properties. *Advances in Agronomy* **38**, 45–94.

UNIRAS 1989 *Unimap 2000 Users Manual*. Soborg, Denmark.

12. Can we identify biological indicator groups for craft, industry and other activities?

Allan Hall and Harry Kenward

It has been suggested that a range of biological remains diagnostic for stable manure in archaeological deposits can be recognised. This led to the concept of 'indicator groups', valuable both as a means of obtaining information about the past more rapidly and as a way of focusing on the pathways by which characteristic assemblages of plant and animal remains came together in the ground. The extent to which indicator groups can be identified for a range of other materials, activity areas, and craft and industrial processes, is considered here, with an emphasis on sites where there is good preservation of organic materials by anoxic waterlogging. For some activities, suites of indicator remains can readily be recognised, but the evidence for some others may be more ambiguous, and there is inevitably a general danger of over-interpretation of slender evidence.

Keywords: Indicator groups, plant remains, invertebrate remains, insects, craft, industry.

INTRODUCTION

In a previous paper (Kenward and Hall 1997), we identified a range of biological remains which we suggested were diagnostic for stable manure in archaeological deposits. The value of the concept of 'indicator groups' was argued, both as a means of obtaining information about the past more rapidly and as a way of focusing on the pathways by which characteristic groups of plant and animal remains came together in the ground. The pathways to stable manure were considered further by Hall and Kenward (1998). Subsequently, Smith *et al.* (1999) have discussed possible components of the indicator group and package for thatch.

Here, we explore the extent to which indicator groups can be identified for a range of other materials, activity areas, or for craft and industrial processes, and we are very much drawing on our own experience rather than attempting a comprehensive survey. A good proportion of what we say may appear obvious to some readers, but we hope that most will find at least a few new ideas. We are considering, particularly, sites where there is good preservation of organic materials by anoxic waterlogging. Evidence concerning the construction and domestic occupation of buildings (as opposed to the winning of building materials) has largely been ignored here; Table 18 summarises the areas of human endeavour which we do consider.

The definition of 'craft and industry', as opposed to 'domestic activity' is debatable and it is probably not profitable to make a rigid distinction. Textile working in a 10th century urban tenement may have been an essentially domestic activity or have been meshed into a complex commercial system, but it may have left much the same evidence in the ground, whatever the socio-economic context. Is grain cleaning an industry in a producer settlement, but domestic activity if it is carried out by the consumer? Within the terms of this paper, we can see no value in distinguishing the economic nature of processes. What matters in the first place to the archaeologist is that reliable ways of recognising the processes themselves should be explored.

WHAT IS AN INDICATOR GROUP?

In our 1997 paper, we failed to offer an explicit definition of indicator groups. We suggest the following: *an indicator group is a collection of organisms which, when occurring together in ancient deposits, reliably carry the implication of the occurrence of some event, activity, or ecological condition in the past.* The concept was illustrated using stable manure, which we now realise is probably one of the commonest sources of biological remains in richly organic deposits formed in and around intensive occupation sites of the Roman and later medieval periods. Stable manure demonstrates particularly well the way an indicator group may form, the ease with which it may often be recognised, its potential variability, and thus the problems of identifying atypical variations.

WHAT OTHER INDICATOR GROUPS MIGHT WE HOPE TO RECOGNISE?

We think that it is very likely that a large number of characteristic death associations of plant and animal remains will eventually be seen to be the product of particular past activities or ecologies. In the rest of this paper we will explore a few which we think may prove useful in detecting past craft, industry and some other activities. It must be emphasised that many of these are only very tentative and that it would be most unwise to regard them, and especially their individual components, as established indicators. In general we would echo Smith's (1996) warning against over-literal use of indicator groups (he was discussing insect indicators of thatch, in particular).

Textile working

For some activities, suites of indicator remains can readily be recognised, and this is particularly true for a range of processes related to the pre-industrial textile industry: fibre processing (especially retting), wool cleaning, and dyeing. There is a good reason for this. Some of the processes employed plant materials whose remains are unlikely ever to occur in the fossil record in more than traces, except as a result of textile processing. Other processes will have led to the deposition of insect remains which, although not raw materials, and only accidentally or incidentally introduced, are also most unlikely to have been abundant in the ground unless as a result of human activity. In other cases, where plants were processed, they may have left little durable (or at least identifiable) evidence, but the remains of insects shed from them may have survived.

Anglo-Scandinavian deposits in York illustrate all of this very well. Remains of plants with a known history of use in dyeing and mordanting were consistently very abundant at the 16–22 Coppergate site (Kenward and Hall 1995, fig. 196), many deposits containing at least some of two if not three taxa, sometimes even four, together. With these plants there were frequently remains of the weevil *Apion difficile* Herbst, whose host in Britain is dyer's greenweed (*Genista tinctoria* L.) – one of the more abundant of the dyeplants at the site. There were also numerous sheep keds (*Melophagus ovinus* Linnaeus) and sheep lice (*Damalinia ovis* (Schrank)), undoubtedly deposited during wool cleaning. While some of the dyeplants may have grown as weeds or have arrived with other materials, and small numbers of the insects could conceivably have found their way into the deposits through other pathways, the observed frequency and abundance of this characteristic assemblage of taxa can only reasonably be accounted for by wool cleaning and dyeing. The indicator group can be extended to an indicator package, *sensu* Kenward and Hall (1997), by including artefactual evidence, a review of which for Coppergate is given by Walton Rogers (1997). (An indicator package is defined by Kenward and Hall (p. 665) as ...'a collection of recordable data of any kind which, when occurring together, can be accepted as evidence of some past state or activity.')

However, it is extremely common for there to be no more than traces of evidence, and it is then that the indicator group of 'dyeplants plus sheep parasites' becomes particularly valuable. Traces of remains of plants which might have been used in dyeing can occur in many assemblages, and certain of them may be abundant even though dyeing was not carried out – but both groups of remains are unlikely to occur together in a series of samples as a result of anything other than wool-cleaning and dyeing.

Analyses of the association of insect species in the Coppergate deposits has produced some interesting results relevant here. Firstly, the sheep parasites are statistically very closely tied to a group of insects which undoubtedly represent the fauna of buildings (Carrott and Kenward 2001), placing the activity indoors. Secondly, *Melophagus ovinus* and *Damalinia ovis* have strong positive correlations with *Apion* species (probably including numerous unrecognised *A. difficile*) and, perhaps more surprisingly, with three scarabaeid dung beetle taxa (*Geotrupes* spp., *Aphodius prodromus* Brahm and *A. granarius* (Linnaeus)). A reasonable explanation for this observation is that wool cleanings, including sheep 'dags' (wool matted with dung), were deposited on surfaces and invaded by the scarabaeids, although at least some of them may have arrived with the wool, since dung beetles may be found in fleeces according to D.N. Smith (pers. comm.). The survival of these kinds of remains in floors will depend very much on local conditions for preservation and levels of cleanliness, but the same suites of organisms may be found in pits and other cuts, having been ejected from buildings. This has been inferred to have taken place repeatedly at 16–22 Coppergate, York, and at other sites.

To turn to some other aspects of textile working, evidence for water-retting of fibre plants such as hemp (*Cannabis sativa* L.) and flax (*Linum usitatissimum* L.) may be almost irrefutable where large quantities of fibres, propagules or, in the case of flax, also seed capsules, are

Table 18. Craft, industry and other activities: prospects for their detection using bioarchaeological remains. Note that this table deals with indicator groups of biological remains and not with the excavational and artefactual evidence which would complement them to form indicator packages. Although prospects for finding some indicator groups seem likely to be poor, they may nevertheless be discovered by chance and should not be ignored. In general, the end products of craft or industrial processes (e.g. building stone, worked wooden artefacts, leather shoes, and so on) have not been included.

Material/Activity	Characteristic biological remains expected in:		Notes	Potential for developing indicator groups
	Producer areas	Consumer areas		
1. Geological resources				
A. Building stone	colonisers of disturbed or contaminated ground (whose remains may also provide a date for extraction)	ancient fossils from biogenic rocks	but also easily dispersed in drift deposits	generally not relevant
		for chalk and other limestones: snails imported with rocks	but may colonise occupation areas with building stone and stone debris	
B. Coal	ancient fossils, especially pre-Quaternary megaspores and microspores		but also easily dispersed in drift deposits	barely relevant in this context
C. Drift (other than peat), including gravel, sand, clay, etc.	fossils from rocks older than the drift, remains contemporaneous with the drift, and remains of organisms which became incorporated into it after formation (e.g. in soils)			good where depositional location is clearly inappropriate to the sediment or contained organisms
D. Peat	regrowth of peat (with characteristic flora) on cut surfaces	characteristic range of plants and invertebrates	but may be *in situ* and pre-date occupation	very good
E. Turf/sods	remains of plants and invertebrates able to colonise de-turfed soil profiles	characteristic range of plants and invertebrates	but may be *in situ* and pre-date occupation	very good
F. Ores and their processing, lime burning	large concentrations of charcoal and/or ash	none	but charcoal/ash may have been produced by various activities	some prospects where end product is highly modified, for example in lime burning (may be indicated by evidence for deforestation, charcoal mixed with part-burned limestone, etc.)
G. Clay for pottery, tile and brick	natural biota in infill of abandoned pits; large concentrations of charcoal and/or ash	evidence of imported plants used for packing	but charcoal/ash may have been produced by various activities	poor
H. Sand and other materials for glassmaking	large concentrations of charcoal and/or ash; remains of marine and coastal organisms including seaweed; ?bracken	none	but charcoal/ash may have been produced by various activities; bracken also used as litter; marine organisms imported with shellfish; coastal plants brought with hay	some

Table 18. continued.

2. Leather and parchment production				
A. Coralling and slaughter, skinning	surface-laid concentrations of dung in non-agricultural contexts gut contents insects attracted to offal	n/a	but may be carried out far from leather manufacturing area; gut contents may be difficult to distinguish from dung	some
B. Skin-cleaning and primary preparation	horns and hooves cut from hides; concentrations of hair or wool, ectoparasites; flesh scrapings and insects attracted to carrion and damp hides	insect invaders of stored skins and fleeces		probably good
C. Hide washing	remains from bird droppings, dog dung, fermented barley or rye; insects attracted to these materials; organisms brought with water	n/a		probably good
D. Tanning	some hair? concentrations of bark, especially oak; insects attracted to tanning liquor and wet leather; organisms brought with water	n/a		probably good (see text)
E. Tawing	?some hair; attracted insects	n/a		small
F. Parchment making (steeping and liming stages)	?some hair; attracted insects	n/a		small
G. Leather working	leather offcuts and insects attracted to them (if any)	n/a		small
3. Furriery				
A. Preparation and processing of skins	ecto- and endoparasites of squirrel, mole, cat, dog and other small to medium-sized mammals; bones of these animals, especially from paws left on furs; waste and offcuts	n/a		some
4. Textile manufacture and working				
A. Shearing	waste wool, with dung and both ecto- and endoparasites; insects attracted to dung; plant remains caught in wool (burs)	see wool-cleaning		good
B. Retting	remains of plants being retted, especially mature seeds and fruits and fibres; aquatic organisms, especially pollution-tolerant forms, from water body if crop water-retted	see fibre extraction		good
C. Fibre extraction/carding	scutching waste and seeds/fruits from fibre plants; ectoparasites and burs from sheep's wool; traces of dung and endoparasites	see later processes		good

Table 18. continued.

D. Dyeing (includes dyeing of leather)	remains of organisms used in dyeing and mordanting; remains of organisms incidentally brought with dyestuffs; aquatic organisms brought with water; organisms from material used in certain dyeing processes, such as bran and dung; invaders of dyebath waste	n/a	danger of misinterpreting many plants as having been used in dyeing	good
E. Fulling, cleaning, spinning, weaving, finishing	aquatic organisms brought in water used for washing	n/a		poor
5. Antler, bone and horn working				
A. Antler and bone working	offcuts from antlers and bone	n/a		poor
B. Horn working	horncores and offcuts; aquatic organisms brought in water used for soaking; insects attracted to carrion and species tolerant of polluted water	n/a		some
6. Woodworking and basketry				
	wood chips and shavings; strips of bark; stems and leaves of various herbaceous plants; scale insects and perhaps some wood-associated beetles	beetles infesting basketwork, furniture and other wooden objects		some
7. Medicine				
	wide range of plants employed in herbal medicine; insects used medicinally; insects brought accidentally with plants or infesting stored materials; exotics	remains of medicines spilled or voided in faeces	danger of misinterpreting many plants as medicinal	good
8. Grain processing				
	chaff and weed seeds from threshing and winnowing	weed seeds not extracted during earlier processing; pests of stored grain		good
9. Butchery and other meat, fish and shellfish processing				
A. Coralling, slaughter and primary preparation	see **2***A* and *B*	n/a		probably good
B. Butchery	bones, feathers, hair from processed animals; gut contents; ecto- and endoparasites; insects attracted to flesh, fresh and rotting, and waste materials; remains of smoking materials	characteristic suites of bones		good

Table 18. continued.

C. Fish processing	fish rejected as not suitable for consumption; gut contents; scales and bones from rejected parts; insects attracted to offal; remains of smoking materials	characteristic suites of bones		good
D. Shellfish processing	small shells and taxa unsuitable for food; shells; epibionts; remains of smoking materials	characteristic suites of shells and epibionts		good
10. Salt-making				
A. Sea salt	concentrations of marine and salt-marsh organisms in pits	marine and salt-marsh organisms brought with unrefined sea salt		poor
B. Halites	?Permo-Trias fossils brought up in brine from depth and remaining in evaporating tanks; remains of salt-marsh plants colonising salt-contaminated ground	traces of remains incorporated at producer site		very poor
11. Wax, resins, pitch, tar	waste, including bee remains, from rendering down comb wax; lumps of resin and plant and animal remains contaminated with resin, having been extracted during purification	n/a		poor

recognised in waterlain deposits. Two examples from the authors' immediate experience are from Layerthorpe Bridge, York (concentrations of flax stems with seeds and capsule fragments in a waterlain sediment formed close to the medieval city walls; Carrott *et al.* 1997a; Hall *et al.* 2000a) and Askham Bog (concentrations of hemp achenes in detrital peat; Bradshaw *et al.* 1981).

A few insects are associated with hemp or flax and, if found in large enough numbers, might conceivably be recognised as 'proxy' evidence for the vegetative parts of hosts in archaeological deposits. Two groups of beetles include numerous plant-feeders: Chrysomelidae (leaf beetles) and Curculionidae (*sensu lato*, weevils). Among the leaf beetles, Hansen (1927) gives flax as a host of *Aphthona euphorbiae* (Schrank) and *Longitarsus parvulus* (Paykull) and hemp as a host of *Psylliodes attenuata* (Koch); however, Hoffmann (1958) lists no weevils as feeding on these plants.

In the case of plants, some characteristic flax-field weeds such as gold-of-pleasure (*Camelina sativa* (L.) Crantz) and the parasite flax dodder (*Cuscuta epilinum* Weihe) have been described by continental workers, and the former was recently recorded in the form of pod fragments from samples rich in flax from Layerthorpe Bridge, York (Hall *et al.* 2000a). These plants themselves may have hosted insects: Hoffmann (1958) mentions the weevils *Ceutorhynchus syrites* Germar and (the non-British) *Baris coerulescens* Scopoli as occurring on *Camelina* (as well as various other crucifers and weld, *Reseda luteola* L.) and *Smicronyx jungermanniae* (Reich) and (again non-British) *S. brevicornis* Solari on *Cuscuta*, including *C. epilinum*. The pollution caused by retting might give rise to a characteristic invertebrate fauna, although not inevitably (Robinson, this volume).

A third plant often regarded as a likely source of textile fibres in the past is stinging nettle, *Urtica dioica* L., which has numerous species of insect associated with it (Davis 1983). Nettles almost certainly grew wherever humans settled (as well as in a variety of 'natural' habitats of which fen woodland is probably the most characteristic), and would have been accompanied by at least some of its insects, which occur at most archaeological occupation sites with suitable preservation. However, the occurrence of abundant nettle insects together with pollution indicators and large quantities of the fibre (and, if most had not already been shed when the plants were collected, abundant achenes) would give rise to a strong suspicion of retting of this plant.

Another stage in textile production, fulling – which will essentially have involved the pounding of cloth in water, perhaps with an agent such as stale urine or fuller's earth to assist in cleaning – seems unlikely to leave bioarchaeological traces other than some aquatic organisms (which would certainly not be diagnostic of this process). The identification of the clay mineral mont-morillonite (or perhaps some suitable substitute) is one *geoarchaeological* route to an indicator package.

The teasing of cloth with the dried flower heads of fullers' teasel (*Dipsacus sativus* (L.) Honckeny) is a case where one taxon may make a plausible indicator group when sufficiently abundant and in an appropriate context (i.e. where, with evidence from stratigraphy, structures and artefacts, an indicator package can be constructed). An example of this comes from 12th century Eastgate, Beverley, where remains of teasel heads were found in deposits with a wide range of evidence for textile manufacture, including some dyeplants (McKenna 1992). However, small quantities of remains of teasel in isolation cannot stand as good evidence for teasing, especially as the plant is well able to become a ruderal in the vicinity of occupation. Records of the common teasel, unfortunately named *D. fullonum* L., are no evidence for teasing; the heads of this plant cannot have been used for the purpose since the spines on the receptacular bracts are not stiff and recurved like those of *D. sativus* (cf. Hall 1992).

Grain cleaning

The process of grain cleaning and the evidence by which it may be recognised archaeologically have been investigated as part of the general study of charred plant assemblages and of modern ethnographic parallels, particularly in the Eastern Mediterranean and Asia Minor (e.g. Hillman 1981; Jones 1984), but also with reference to some British sites (van der Veen 1992). Suites of cornfield weed seeds which resemble those one imagines were produced by cleaning are often extremely common in assemblages of plant remains on occupation sites of various kinds, including urban ones. Such suites have often been interpreted as indicating grain cleaning, but we would argue that this would rarely be correct and that they do not necessarily constitute an indicator group for this process – at least in towns. We consider that seeds of cornfield weeds commonly became incorporated into urban deposits via stable manure, either with poorly cleaned grain (of which no evidence for the cereal component may remain) or with straw used for thatch or for litter on floors in human dwellings. The negative evidence of 'purity' – lack of contaminant weed seeds (especially the smaller ones) – is conventionally used to indicate that grain has been cleaned (e.g. Hall and Kenward 1990, 411). Where the remains of the grain itself are rare, the relative proportions of the grain pests which infested it may offer evidence of cleaning. Of the three commonest pests of stored grain, the grain weevil *Sitophilus granarius* (Linnaeus) seems to become steadily more dominant as the medieval period progresses. This is probably because it is harder to remove by sieving than other species, since it passes much of its life within grains.

Woodworking and basketry

Woodworking is traditionally recognised through tools, offcuts and turning pieces, and chippings and shavings. We can offer no evidence which might be usefully regarded as an indicator group (other than the fragments of wood themselves). Unconverted timber (i.e. bearing bark) might bring with it corticolous mosses and insects (but so might firewood), and the bark with which they are associated seems very likely to be found. Insects emerging from stacked timber would be virtually impossible to distinguish from those originating in converted timber in use.

The making of basketry might be predicted to produce large quantities of fine bark strips, particularly from certain willow species, and this might be accompanied by scale insects such as *Lepidosaphes ulmi* (Linnaeus) and *Chionaspis salicis* (Linnaeus). We know of no records of abundant twig bark such as might have been pulled from green twigs – although it is probably preservationally especially delicate at this stage. The scale insects are very common in archaeological deposits (e.g. at 16–22 Coppergate, York: Kenward and Hall 1995), but they were perhaps brought with twigs and stems used for a wide range of purposes. Thus the largest concentrations of scale insects at Coppergate were in some brushwood layers which seem as likely to have been structural as to represent the raw material or waste from basketry. One point to make here is that, although some longhorn beetles (e.g. *Gracilia minuta* (Fabricius), and members of some other families also) are described in the literature as infesting basketry, archaeological records of them are certainly not evidence of basket-making at a particular site. The beetles take at least a year to develop, and populations of adults would only have occurred in basketry articles in use, or, of course, in structural materials.

Butchery and other meat and fish processing

The evidence for butchery is traditionally drawn from studies of vertebrate remains, but may be open to misinterpretation, and plant and invertebrate indicators of slaughtering and gutting, should they be found, may be as clear, or more so. We have not recognised such assemblages yet, but the following should be looked for: (a) evidence for penning of stock awaiting slaughter in situations where they are unlikely to have been kept in the long term: surface-laid deposits with concentrations of dung; (b) evidence of layers consisting entirely of gut contents, i.e. comminuted dung-like plant material, perhaps (if left exposed) with an invertebrate fauna of exposed dung or stable manure, or perhaps with flies and fly-predating beetles tolerant of extreme foulness; (c) evidence of hairs and ectoparasites (and, in the case of sheep, also of dags) shed during skinning or scraping of skins; (d) characteristic groups of insects which might invade piles of freshly butchered bone; such bones are likely to have been removed from the site of butchery fairly quickly, restricting the size and diversity of the insect communities they supported at that stage.

An example which seems to fall in the first of these categories – evidence for penning of stock – comes from an excavation at Low Fisher Gate (also known as North Bridge), Doncaster (Carrott *et al.* 1997b; Hall *et al.* 2000b). At some stage, probably in the late 15th century, a massive circular cut, 8.5m in diameter, was excavated in the centre of the site. On the basis of the entomological evidence, it appears to have been a pond in the middle of an area used to pen large herbivores. There were huge numbers of dung beetles in at least one of the fills, the insect assemblage being dominated by *Aphodius prodromus*, with numerous *Geotrupes spiniger* (Marsham), and few other true dung beetles. The rarity of other insects associated with dung and soil indicated that the insects arrived in flight rather than in dung or turf cut from grazing land. It thus appears that there were large quantities of herbivore dung on nearby surfaces (had dung been removed from surfaces and dumped in the pit, much larger numbers of taxa such as various Sphaeridiidae (*Cercyon, Sphaeridium*) and Staphylinidae would have been predicted, and a substantially different component would inevitably have been introduced with turf). The plant remains gave rather sparse evidence for grassland habitats, reinforcing the impression that dung and grazing land turf were not substantial components of the deposit. Some *Aphodius* species, including *A. prodromus*, have been observed to migrate in large numbers, but mass migration seems unlikely to lead to such high concentrations, unless from very nearby – a few metres. Both *Aphodius* and *Geotrupes* species are unable to escape and soon drown if they land on water. Horses might seem the most likely beasts to have been kept in a built-up area, but the absence of any evidence for horse manure (including the rarity of grain pests) at Low Fisher Gate was notable. It is possible that other livestock were held in this area awaiting sale or slaughter; cow manure, for example, may have supported the beetles by contributed little or nothing to the preserved plant assemblage.

Examples of evidence for ectoparasites from processes involving skins are considered below.

Finbar McCormick (pers. comm.) has pointed out that huge quantities of vegetable matter may be produced by slaughtering large herbivores, especially ruminants, and this material should be recognisable both through plant and insect remains from the fields or byres where the animals last fed, and through the foul decomposer insects which would be attracted to it unless it was immediately buried. McCormick observed material of this kind in a sample from Viking Age Dublin, Ireland, the identification being made through comparison of the archaeological material with fresh gut contents at an abattoir.

Another aspect of the utilisation of flesh is smoking. Bones cannot safely be used as evidence for fish and meat smoking at a particular location (since they would often have been transported in meat or fish), and the remains of fuel and structures associated with smoking need to be sought. Evidence may be found for the use of materials for smoke generation. Oak chips, traditionally used for this purpose, might have resulted from various processes but, if found in large quantities with evidence of burning would be rather more convincing. Other plants used to impart flavours in smoking might be found, such as juniper (used in the 20th century for smoking freshwater fish in Sweden).

It may prove possible to detect organisms introduced as a result of salting. The preparation of sea salt could have led to the inclusion of at least some marine or littoral organisms and these may occasionally have passed through the pathway of transport and consumption into waste pits. Saltmarsh plants occur quite frequently on occupation sites, sometimes at great distances from suitable habitats, but these are usually thought of as arriving in herbivore dung (Hall and Kenward 1990; Kenward and Hall 1997).

Tanning, tawing, parchment making and horn-working

Perhaps the first thing to emphasise is that offcuts of tanned leather do not constitute evidence for tanning as an activity in the place where such offcuts are found. Indeed, the converse is probably true, for all the indications are that leather working usually took place within densely built-up areas in towns, in places where tan pits seem rarely to have been tolerated. Thus we need to make positive identification of the pits themselves, or of suites of organisms (and other evidence) unlikely to have come together except as a result of tanning. Bark, as a source of tannins, is the obvious biological indicator for vegetable tanning (as opposed to tawing, see below). While bark in archaeological deposits may represent waste from conversion or have survived after the decay of the timber to which it was attached, it is also an important raw material in its own right. There is ample documentation of the use of bark in tanning, with a strong preference for oak for routine leather production from cow hides. The bark of other trees, such as pine and spruce and sometimes birch, willow or alder was used for used for tanning in N. Europe (Howes 1953), birch being used specifically for 'Russian leather' (Henslow 1905). Table 20 lists the tannin content of a range of plants, together with some of their other uses.

Some sites have yielded pits which are reasonably safely interpreted as tanning pits, typically being clay- or wood-lined and associated with bones likely to have been imported with skins (e.g. O'Connor 1984; Albarella, this vol; Ervynck *et al.* this vol.). However, it seems very likely that much tanning was carried out in pits of less characteristic form, particularly where the soil was not freely draining, so that no lining was required. Unfortunately, bark might occur in pits – or, indeed, in other deposits – for many reasons, so it, alone, cannot be taken as evidence of tanning except where it is present in high concentrations, perhaps making up the bulk of the organic content of a layer and especially if found in a pit large enough to have held soaking hides. This was the case in a 16th/17th century wooden vat in Chartres, France (Hall 1997), in an 18th century pit (considered on documentary evidence to have been used for tanning) in Derry, N. Ireland (Hall, unpublished) and in pits probably of 18th or 19th century date from an excavation in the aptly-named street Gerbergässlein (lit. Little Tanner Lane) in Basel, Switzerland (Matt and Reicke 1990; Hall, unpublished). The conditions in a tanning pit are hardly likely to have been favourable for the development of a characteristic insect fauna, although a few species with exceptional resistance to anoxia may have survived, the rat-tailed maggot (*Eristalis tenax* (Linnaeus)) perhaps being a case in point. Again, such insects do not provide specific evidence for the function of a pit.

Recent evidence from York seems to indicate that the prospects for recognising tanning from plant and insect remains are not entirely gloomy. Anglo-Scandinavian to early post-Conquest layers apparently formed at the margins of the River Foss at the Layerthorpe Bridge site have produced concentrations of very decayed bark with the characteristic sclereids (stone cell clusters) which seem to be present in the bark of many trees. Accompanying these were unusually large numbers of the unmistakable scarabaeid beetle *Trox scaber* (it was present in 30 of the samples from this site, at a mean frequency of 3.6 per sample when present, and at concentrations of 10 or more per kilogramme of sediment in some cases). The records of bark, sclereids and *Trox* were strongly positively correlated (Table 19), in contrast with records from the largest data-set available for a single site, that for 16–22 Coppergate, York. There, although *T. scaber* was present in a large proportion of the samples, there were only three cases where three individuals were noted and five where four were found, the rest being ones or twos and the mean number of individuals per sample where the beetle was present being 1.2. At Coppergate, there was no significant correlation between records of bark and *Trox*, though it should be borne in mind that records for bark from those samples are not so complete as for the Layerthorpe material (and sclereids were not recognised when the Coppergate material was examined).

Trox scaber is a scavenger generally found in dry animal remains or in wood mould, but perhaps most typically associated with birds' nests (Leatherdale 1955; Britton 1956, 6; Palm 1959; Jessop 1986). It is sometimes found in habitats created by human activity, and occurs very frequently in archaeological deposits, Hall *et al.* (1983, 183) suggesting that it exploited a wide range of habitats. On the basis of records from a very large number of occupation sites, we can say that *T. scaber* usually occurs in small numbers, typically only one per kilogramme of sediment, as at Coppergate, so that when it is more abundant it is reasonable to look for some characteristic cause. We suggest that at the Layerthorpe Bridge site it was attracted either to skins awaiting tanning or to

Table 19. Spearman's rank-order correlation coefficients (and probability estimates) for semi-quantitative scores for bark fragments, bark sclereids and Trox *remains from Anglo-Scandinavian and medieval deposits at Layerthorpe Bridge, York. For comparison: for a group of 301 samples from Anglo-Scandinavian deposits at 16-22 Coppergate, York, there was a correlation between semi-quantitative scores for bark fragments and* Trox *of 0.0287 (p = 0.62).*

bark sclereids	0.445, p = 0.026	–
Trox counts	0.516, p = 0.008	0.589, p = 0.002
n = 25	bark	bark sclereids

the tanning pits themselves, and that the archaeological deposits contained material discarded from tanning carried out in the immediate vicinity. That this was an area in which foul-smelling activities were tolerated is indicated by evidence of flax retting in somewhat later deposits from the same site. The area excavated might well have been far enough away from centres of (politically powerful) population to be an acceptable location for such vile-smelling activities. Tanneries in this part of the city would certainly have been downwind of most of York's medieval inhabitants, and though the effluent they caused would have polluted a river (the Foss), a large area of marsh into which it subsequently flowed may have acted as a filter.

We may therefore suggest that comminuted bark, bark sclereids, and *T. scaber* constitute the bones of an indicator group for tanning. Whether additional biological raw materials or insects (or other invertebrates) can be added to this group remains to be seen; beetles such as *Hister* and its relatives might come to such environments, as perhaps might burying beetles (various Silphidae) and a few specialist flies.

The longhorn beetle *Phymatodes testaceus* might appear in deposits associated with bark tanning. It lays its eggs under bark of recently dead wood, including newly cut timber from which the bark has not been removed. It has been recorded to be a pest of the tanning industry, destroying oak bark in store, although not important in damaging timber (Duffy 1953). However, it may have been brought in firewood, from stacks of which it is reported to emerge not infrequently in central Europe (Harde 1984); such may be the origin of specimens found in Anglo-Scandinavian York (Kenward and Hall 2000).

The tanning process seems amenable to the construction of an indicator package (as defined by Kenward and Hall 1997), including – in addition to biological remains – site location (close to water supplies and away from high-class habitation), form of pits, and probably certain artefacts like the knives used for scraping and defleshing skins and hides.

Table 20. Tannin content of some plant materials and literature references to their use in the past for tanning. Data concerning tannin content taken from tables in Wilson and Thomas (1927); their table dealing with the source and content of vegetable tannin materials gives these figures for taxa likely to have been available in the British Isles in the past (though it should be emphasised that these figures are drawn from a wide range of sources without the certainty of similar measurement of tannin content and making the assumption that all relate to percentage dry weight of air-dried material).

			Used for tanning skins according to			
Taxon	material	tannin content (% dry wt?)	Henslow (1905)	Howes (1953)	Polunin (1976)	Other uses of material (excluding artefacts, fuel, structural)
Acer campestre	bark	4	–	–	–	
Alnus glutinosa	bark	16–20	–	–	+	dyeing, medicine, also for tanning *nets*
Betula spp.	bark	–	–	+	–	
Betula alba [*pendula*]	bark	2–18	–	+	–	roofing; oil for torches; bulking flour in famine food
Calluna vulgaris	?plant	–	+	–	–	dyeing, bedding
Frangula alnus	bark	–	–	–	–	medicinal; dyeing
Fraxinus spp.	bark	–	–	–	[+]	[for tanning nets]
Ilex aquifolium	inner bark	–	–	–	–	bird-lime; medicinal
Myrica gale	?twigs	–	+	–	–	dyeing, medicinal, brewing
Pinus sylvestris	bark	4–5	–	–	–	
Populus tremula	bark	3	–	–	+	
Populus (poplars)	bark		–	–	+	
[*Potentilla erecta*]	roots	20–46	+	–	–	'1 lb equalling 7 lb of oak bark' in respect of tanning; also dyeing, medicinal
Prunus spinosa	bark		–	–	–	medicinal
Prunus spp.	bark		–	–	–	dyeing
Pyrus communis	bark		–	–	–	dyeing
Quercus robur	bark	9–12	–	+	+	dyeing
	wood	2–4	–	–	–	
Salix spp.	bark	–	+	–	+	
Salix alba	bark	9	–	–	–	
S. caprea	bark	8–12	–	–	–	
S. fragilis	bark	9–12	–	–	–	
S. viminalis	bark	7–10	–	–	–	
Sambucus nigra	middle bark	–	–	–	–	medicinal; dyeing
Sorbus aucuparia	do	–	–	–	+	
Succisa pratensis	rhizome	–	+	–	–	dyeing
Ulmus spp.	do	–	–	–	–	astringent and demulcent (?medicinal)

We would strongly warn against using abundance of *Trox scaber* alone as an indicator of tanning, however. It occasionally is abundant in general occupation deposits, for example in a late 14th century 'organic dump' from High Street, Kingston upon Hull (Carrott *et al.* 1994a), but no association with tanning is suspected. Some other cases are less clear: *T. scaber* was abundant in a dump of material containing much leather in a late- or post-medieval deposit at Palmer Lane, York (Carrott *et al.* 1992), and another dump of similar date at the nearby Adams Hydraulics II site also produced unusually large numbers of *T. scaber* (Allison *et al.* 1991). In this latter case, too, there was much leather and it was uncertain whether the beetle may have lived in it or have been in some way associated with its production. There is also a record of several tens of individuals from a sample of unknown size from a pit fill of post-medieval date from the Chaucer House site, Southwark, London (Kenward 1990). A record of abundant *Trox*, together with beetles which may have been imported with bark, was given for the same site by Girling (1979), who suggested that these beetles might indicate tanning; it is not known whether Girling's and Kenward's records were for the same or a related feature.

Various materials are recorded in the literature as

having been employed in the past for processes in leather making other than vegetable tanning. They include (*fide* Cherry 1991) bird droppings, dog dung, fermenting barley or rye, as well as lime or wood ash. All of these might be expected to leave a recognisable signature which might contribute to an indicator group. From bird droppings we might recover comminuted seeds or insect remains. The former have been recorded by Körber-Grohne (1991) from an Iron Age well fill in Fellbach-Schmiden, Germany, and the latter by Hall and Kenward (1990), although in neither case was there a suggestion that the remains had anything to do with tanning. Dog faeces might contribute highly eroded fragments of bone, and eggs of intestinal parasites (of which *Trichuris vulpis* (Fröhlich) and *Toxocara canis* (Werner) might be recognised). The remains of fermenting cereals (and perhaps associated stored products insects) might survive where there was excellent waterlogged preservation. Lime will often be recognisable from the partly-burned fragments of the source rock or from concentrations of slaked material stabilised by conversion to carbonate or sulphate (cf. Ervynck *et al.* this volume), and ash is certainly recognisable in the ground unless too thinly dispersed amongst other materials.

A suite of biological remains including fine charcoal, together with ash, from Anglo-Scandinavian deposits with abundant leather offcuts at 6–8 Pavement (Lloyds Bank site), York, was tentatively identified as related to leather making by Buckland *et al.* (1974); however, most or all of the materials are quite likely to have had some other origin, and were frequent in contemporaneous deposits at Coppergate for which there is no absolutely no reason to suppose an association with tanning. Indeed, the remarks made above concerning the improbability of tanning being carried out in the centre of the town apply to the Lloyds Bank site, even though it was fairly close to the River Foss. The abundant leather offcuts at Lloyds Bank (Addyman and Hall 1991) indicate a later stage in the utilisation of leather, either its working into articles or the use of offcuts as litter on house or stable floors, and this seems to be a reasonable interpretation to be placed on leather offcuts generally (Hall and Kenward 1998). *Trox scaber* was present in 24 of the 56 samples examined at Lloyds Bank, but mostly as single individuals and in a few cases as two, suggesting that there was no particular association of this beetles with tanned leather.

The processes of tawing (tanning leather by means of oils and salts such as alum) seem much less likely to be detectable via plant and animal remains other than those durable parts of the vertebrates whose skins are contributing to the desired product, and the ectoparasites mentioned above.

For the manufacture of horn, the horn sheath must be removed from the bony core, and this usually involves the soaking of whole horns in pits containing water. As in the case of leather tanning, some structural evidence might be expected to indicate the process, but it is the concentrated remains of the cores which on the face of it seem likely to

be best evidence for the industry and such concentrations have fairly often been reported. At sites adjacent to St Peter's Church and at St Peter's Street, Northampton (Shaw 1984; Harman 1979), assemblages of horn-cores were associated with shallow water-tight pits and layers of ash and lime and might be taken to indicate horn working. However, these features were actually interpreted as evidence for tanning, the horn-cores evidently having been delivered to the tanner attached to the hides. At Stamford, Lincolnshire, a series of shallow pits was found, some of which had been lined with clay (Cram 1982) – features which were interpreted as 'soaking pits' in which the horns were placed for some weeks. Horn-cores were found apparently *in situ* at the bottom of eight of these clay-lined pits. At Hornpot Lane, York, in addition to a large shallow clay- and wood-lined pit containing approximately 200 horn-cores, there were hearths and furnaces (Wenham 1964; Ryder 1970). This evidence for heating was thought to represent the next stage of hornworking – softening the sheath prior to cutting, shaping and moulding.

Thus it can be argued that while large numbers of horn-cores may be evidence of hornery, they may give little idea as to where the craft was practised, for the cores were a useful building material (as described by Armitage 1982, 102–3). Where pits used for soaking have waterlogged preservation there might be a thin basal deposit exceptionally rich in flesh-feeding insects and maggot predators, imported aquatics, and pollution-tolerant species such as rat-tailed maggots, representing the use phase. Such evidence would show more convincingly that a pit was used for soaking (though it might not indicate what animal material was being soaked), since a fill consisting of abundant bones may simply represent material which was dumped into a convenient pit previously used for some other purpose.

A last industry involving the bones and skins of vertebrates is furriery. Finds of phalanges of small mammals are sometimes interpreted as originating in pelts or furs, e.g. the large concentration of 'paw' bones of red squirrel, *Sciurus vulgaris* L. from The Bedern, York (Bond and O'Connor 1999, 365) and also some from 16–22 Coppergate, O'Connor (1989, 190). One of the 267 squirrel fragments from The Bedern bore a knife mark.

Extraction of raw materials

The extraction of raw materials from drift or solid rock will have had an appreciable and sometimes profound impact on the surroundings, by modifying vegetation and in its effects on water-courses and the quality of the water within them (see various papers in this volume and, for example, Küster 1988; Macklin *et al.* 2000) or even in creating aquatic habitats (extraction pits, among which 'clay' and 'marl' pits are most frequently interpreted from the archaeological record). For 'hard rock' geological raw materials there may be evidence from quarries for extraction, but they are likely to be virtually undatable and it will be hard to determine which settlement was exploiting them except where localised rock or mineral types are involved. This kind of industrial activity is not really amenable to identification at its producer sites through indicator groups; at consumer sites, the materials themselves typically suffice unless the material is too thinly dispersed to be recognisable as having been utilised or, in the case of hard rock, can be shown not to have been introduced naturally in drift.

The recognition of redeposited sediments employed in levelling, for example in making floors, may be equally straightforward on lithological or stratigraphic grounds, but where the material has become admixed with occupation site debris identification through biological remains may be more worthwhile. An example is perhaps provided by medieval (late 14th-early 15th century) floor deposits at Coffee Yard, York (Robertson *et al.* 1989) where various aquatic organisms occurred – notable were records of water flea (*Daphnia*) ephippia and statoblasts of the bryozoan *Lophopus crystallinus* (Pallas) which had no immediately obvious origin but seem likely to have been imported either in water or in waterlain deposits used as floor make-up. It is worth noting here that there is increasing evidence that delicate plant and invertebrate remains have frequently been redeposited (Dobney *et al.* 1998). A particularly striking example is provided by deposits at the Magistrates' Courts site, Kingston-upon-Hull (Hall *et al.* 2000c).

Peat winning leaves recognisable discontinuities in the litho- and biostratigraphic records at the site of extraction and the date of the onset of regrowth offers at least a guide to the date of extraction. The removal of turves or sods (see definition below) may be recognised by truncated soil profiles but dating will be difficult unless settlement layers or other datable deposits immediately covered them.

Recognition of peat in archaeological occupation deposits is generally straightforward, especially if clasts of peat have survived, whilst a characteristic suite of peatland organisms usually indicates the presence of dispersed peat. Both categories were recorded from Roman deposits at Skeldergate and at Tanner Row and Rougier Street, in the 'Colonia' of York, for example (Hall *et al.* 1980; Hall and Kenward 1990). Plants may include major components of acid peat, such as *Sphagnum* species or *Eriophorum vaginatum*, or species typical of intermediate or base-rich mires, such as the 'brown mosses', including *Calliergon* spp., and maybe species which have become rare or extinct in Britain, such as *Homalothecium nitens*, *Paludella squarrosa* or *Meesia longiseta*. Insects from acid peats tend to be distinctive but there may be a substantial overlap with those found in certain kinds of acid turf. There is little doubt that the 'peatland' insects from the Roman well in Skeldergate arrived in peat, but more often such species appear to have been imported in turf, e.g. at Low Fisher Gate, Doncaster (Hall *et al.* 2000b) and various sites in Carlisle.

Fen peat may be impoverished from an entomological point of view, but may include characteristic species. Small quantities of fen peat reworked into an archaeological deposit may leave their greatest signature through plant remains such as bogbean (*Menyanthes trifoliata* L.) seeds and sedge (*Carex*) nutlets rather than through vegetative remains or insects (which may have been imported with cut fen vegetation) or fragments of the peat itself; some examples include medieval deposits in Beverley and Hull, especially in many deposits at the Magistrates' Courts site in Kingston-upon-Hull (Hall *et al.* 2000c).

It is also likely that some diatoms and rhizopods could be added to the peat indicator group, as well as that component of a peat pollen assemblage which reflects local vegetation rather than woodland at some distance from the mire. Thus we can define a clear indicator group for peat-winning, whose components have been recognised frequently in archaeological deposits.

Turves (in the sense of 'sods' from grassland, rather than blocks of peat) are frequently identified in archaeological excavations on the basis of lithostratigraphy or a reasonable supposition as to the nature of material used to make earthen banks, but there are rather few cases where good bioarchaeological evidence has been obtained in confirmation. In theory, a wide range of organisms found in turf should be discernible in the fossil record but there is clearly a gradation into mire, heathland and waterside communities which might indicate some other material than turves. Remains such as the cleistogenes (basal cleistogamous – non-opening – flowers) of the grass *Danthonia decumbens* (L.) DC. in Lam. & DC. seem unlikely to have arrived at an occupation site other than in turves, unless in some kinds of herbivore dung (if the plants are ripped rather than snipped). Larvae of soil-dwelling elaterid beetles seem likely to have been imported in turf, although an overlapping range of species may have been brought in peat. For turves cut from calcareous or neutral grassland, the importation of characteristic land-snail assemblages might be detected. Overall, there is a reasonable prospect of defining an indicator group for some kinds of turf, but this will vary from place to place because of regional, and especially altitudinal, variations in the nature of turf.

Determining the origin of peat and turves found in settlements may be difficult. The type of mire can be determined but peat is usually very much older than its exploitation date and so probably will not reflect the contemporaneous state of the landscape from which it was won. Vegetation regime can be determined from well-preserved turves, and some guesses made as to the nearest landscape likely to have supported such vegetation, but such deductions need to be made with the greatest caution since we do not necessarily know the date of, for example, the development of heathland.

Medicine

Herbal medicine has, perhaps more than any other 'craft', been over-interpreted by archaeobotanists. Numerous plants with medicinal properties ascribed to them somewhere in the literature can be found in almost any archaeological deposits with waterlogged preservation, but these cannot reasonably be seen as components of an indicator group – it is dangerous to leap from a list of, say, ten taxa from an occupation deposit which have some recorded herbal properties (amongst many other possible uses) and which are widespread plants, to an interpretation that the local apothecary lived in the house! Other evidence, such as quantities of more specialised medicines, insects, jars, instruments, is required.

Another aspect of the problem of recognising evidence for medicinal uses of plants revolves around the parts of the plants normally identified from archaeological deposits: seeds, which are rather rarely the part actually used in medicine (though they might be brought if mature plants were required). The remains of concentrations of vegetative parts such as might result from 'boiling up' plants for extraction of active principles would be far more convincing evidence.

Invertebrates have doubtless found various uses in medicine over the millennia, whether simply superstitious or based on the doctrine of signatures. Bristowe (1958, 193–4) mentions that eating a house spider (*Tegenaria*) was once believed to be a cure for malaria, and also the swallowing of spiders to overcome arachnophobia – a medical use of a sort! One insect which has been extensively used, with identifiable effect, is 'Spanish fly', the blister beetle *Lytta vesicatoria* (Linnaeus), which produces a fiercely irritating substance. Hakbjil (1987) reported a container of ground up *L. vesicatoria* from a wrecked Dutch East Indies ship; the drug had been adulterated with the chafer *Cetonia aurata* (Linnaeus), although according to Kirby and Spence (1859, 179), *C. aurata* has also been employed medicinally. There is a further archaeological record of *Lytta vesicatoria* from Novaya Zemlya (Hakbijl and de Groot 1997). The recovery of finely ground insects intended for medicinal use, like the detection of grain pests derived from flour, will demand a modification of extraction techniques and cannot be done routinely. Fragments may be detected in 'squashes' for microfossils (as described by Dainton 1992), however.

The use of the 'eyes' of crayfish as a cure-all medicine in western Europe in the past is described by Schmitt (1965). These 'eyes', in fact discoidal nodules of limey material laid down in the stomach, probably as a reserve of calcium which can be mobilised after moulting, may well preserve and may be added to the list of invertebrate curiosities which should not be overlooked.

Hopkin (1991) says that 'Woodlice ... have featured prominently throughout history in recipes' and also states that they were used as a cure for stomach aches and other minor ailments. Earthworms have also found use as medicine (Sabine 1983, quoted by Sims and Gerard 1985).

The latter authors list uses ranging from 'hair restorer to an aphrodisiac and even as treatment for haemorrhoids'. We might conceivably recover at least circumstantial evidence for such uses.

An example where we feel there is probably such an indicator package for medicines are Knörzer's records for charred remains of a range of medicinal plants from a room deduced, on artefactual evidence, to be an *valetudinarium* (hospital or infirmary) at the Roman fort at Neuss, Germany (Knörzer 1967). Buurman's (1988) Roman ampulla full of radish seed (with some celery, marjoram and mallow seed) from Uitgeest, the Netherlands, considered by her to be raw materials for medicine, might also fall in this category (the vessel itself being critical to interpretation). There is, however, very little doubt that the records of Spanish fly mentioned above relate to medicinal preparation.

Water as a raw material

An aspect of many crafts and industries which is easily overlooked from the bioarchaeological point of view is the utilisation of large quantities of water. Aquatic organisms, particularly the seeds of aquatic and aquatic-marginal plants, the resting stages of water fleas (especially *Daphnia*, but also various other as yet unidentified cladocerans, and statoblasts of the bryozoans *Cristatella mucedo* Cuvier and *Lophopus crystallinus*), and aquatic beetles and bugs, occur very regularly in occupation deposits. Many of these remains may have entered as a result of the importation of moss, cut wetland vegetation, or peat, or naturally through flooding or natural dispersal (water beetles, especially, are very mobile and occur in death assemblages formed where no suitable habitat was available: Kenward 1976; 1978). However, there is frequently a suspicion that aquatics were imported in water, in some cases indirectly in the guts of domestic animals (Kenward and Hall 1997) or even humans, but often directly as the water itself.

The act of collecting water in buckets or other containers, whether from rivers, ponds or wells, would inevitably have caught up small swimming animals and sometimes the larger ones such as beetles and bugs. Where water was shallow or disturbed (e.g. by frequent extraction), live organisms and the remains of plants and animals would have been swirled up from the bottom mud. The final resting place of most of these aquatic organisms would be wherever water was thrown after use: in sumps, pits and drains, and on surfaces. Only rarely will it be possible to be sure of the means of entry of these organisms and remains to the fossil record, the numbers generally being small and thus indistinguishable from groups of 'background' origin. A gully within one of the Anglo-Scandinavian plank-built structures at 16–22 Coppergate provides one example where the resting eggs of cladocerans almost certainly came from waste water from a craft process, in this case probably either the washing of wool or dyeing (Kenward and Hall 1995, 596). It seems possible that water flea remains at Swinegate and Coffee Yard, also in York, were brought with water (Carrott *et al.* 1994b; Robertson *et al.* 1989), but perhaps for watering stock at the former site and for domestic use at the latter. Importation in mud used for flooring or daub is also a possibility. Where there is structural evidence, or the remains of associated raw materials, an origin of aquatic organisms in water used for processes may be established, so that the use to which it was put may be speculated upon. Microfossils represent an untapped source of information about imported water and its quality.

DISCUSSION

Although we believe that indicator groups are a useful tool for understanding and recognising the evidence for various activities, it would be unreasonable to expect all, or even most, industrial or craft processes to produce characteristic sets of biological remains. Some will yield little or nothing which one might hope to recognise, or the associated biological evidence may be too non-specific or ambiguous to be of value. Nevertheless, we feel that for some processes there is considerable potential in exploration of biological remains likely to have accreted along the route to final deposition, as we showed for stable manure (Hall and Kenward 1998).

We would re-emphasise here the dangers of looking for 'easy' single indicator taxa. The facile association of a particular insect species with particular materials or processes is especially dangerous. Concentrations of the beetle *Trox scaber*, mentioned in the context of tanning, above, for example, are quite definitely *not* in themselves *necessarily* indicative of this activity, any more than is bark. Both may be present for entirely different reasons – the beetles may have lived in a bird's nest, the bark be the discarded waste from preparing timber for woodworking. A few honeybees (*Apis mellifera*) are not evidence of bee-keeping on a site, bearing in mind their enormous foraging range (bee-keeping is an activity for which an indicator group or package might usefully be defined).

This *caveat* extends even to more specific raw materials as dyeplants. Scraps of dyeplants, even of several taxa together, are very likely to results from reworking, trampling or even wind-blow. Thus at the Lloyds Bank (6–8 Pavement) site in York remains of some of the dyeplant taxa recorded at nearby 16–22 Coppergate (Kenward and Hall 1995) were found to be present in small amounts in many of the samples (Hall 1999), but never in the concentrations recorded at Coppergate; these seem very likely to be fragments transported by wind or feet along the Anglo-Scandinavian street from one set of tenements to another (in this case the two sites were barely 75 m apart). Clearly they indicate dyeing, but not at the site in question. (As an aside, the importance of wind transport on occupation sites may be greater than would

generally be thought likely. Kenward and Large (1998), for example, suspected that remains of the woodworm beetle *Anobium punctatum* may have occurred in more deposits than would be expected in view of its short flight season as a result of processes which included wind-blow.)

Single taxa or low concentrations of a range of taxa take on much more interpretative significance if other components of an indicator package are present – remains of a woven 'skep' in a deposit containing modest numbers of remains of honeybees, or cow metapodials associated with contemporaneous bark-rich layers, for example. Archaeologists cannot always deal with evidence which gives the sort of confidence in deductions that are demanded in most other areas of science, but we can at least aspire to the balance of evidence which might sway a jury in court. In particular, what we need to do is evaluate whether the observed evidence could have been generated by other plausible means; we always need to adopt multiple working hypotheses rather than draping the evidence onto preconceptions or onto the story most likely to attract academic or popular attention.

A further reason to be wary of deducing too much from the presence of remains of individual taxa (especially in small quantities) which seem strongly indicative of a process or activity is the range of uses to which some organisms were put in the past. Even such plants as woad and madder, seemingly definitively interpretable as dye-plants, have had other uses if one cares to examine the literature – both have been used in medicine, and the tinctorial properties of both have been used in painting as well as textile dyeing. Woad, too, may become a weed, surviving locally after it was last used as a dyeplant.

Clearly, for many activities and processes the evidence will be very localised and rare, even where preservation is suitable. Some crafts will have produced only small amounts of recognisable material, in any case. Evidence for such activities as herbal medicine is unlikely to be discovered except through rare chance while we continue to carry out most investigations of plant and invertebrate remains on a rather small scale. The authors have frequently emphasised their belief in the need for large-scale surveys of occupation deposits where there is good water-logged preservation (cf. Kenward and Hall 1995) or even where preservation is localised or sparse (Hall *et al.* 2000b), in order to provide sufficient data for valid comparison of phases, feature types and areas. The search for what will usually be localised evidence of crafts and industries represents another cogent reason for examining large numbers of samples.

Having said all this, the biological evidence must never stand in isolation from its archaeological context, difficult though it is sometimes to bridge the gap as a result of the way projects have to be organised. Time and money rarely allow for the various members of a post-excavation team to come together at intervals throughout the project under the relaxed circumstances necessary for exchange of ideas as well as of data. Perhaps – and making a realistic allowance for the current chronic under-resourcing of developer-funded projects – we all need to be far more assertive in insisting that such meetings take place.

Acknowledgments
The authors are grateful to the Centre for Archaeology of English Heritage for support and encouragement. Prof. Dr. Steffi Jacomet, University of Basel, has been especially helpful in providing information, references and samples in connection with excavations in Switzerland, whilst Paul Logue of the Archaeological Survey of Environment and Heritage Services in N. Ireland, kindly provided samples from and information concerning excavations in Derry. Dr Finbar McCormick, Queens University of Belfast, helpfully reminded us of his observations on a sample of presumed herbivore gut contents from Viking Dublin and Debs Jaques, Environmental Archaeology Unit, and Dr Keith Dobney, University of Durham, provided information concerning horn-cores.

References

Addyman, P.V. and Hall, R.A. 1991. *Urban structures and defences. Lloyds Bank, Pavement and other sites, with a survey of defences north-east of the Ouse* (The Archaeology of York 8, 3). London: Council for British Archaeology.

Allison, E.P., Carrott, J.B., Hall, A.R. and Kenward, H.K. 1991. *Environmental evidence from Adams Hydraulics III (YAT/Yorkshire Museum sitecode 1991.13).* Prepared for York Archaeological Trust.

Armitage, P.L. 1982. Studies on the remains of domestic livestock from Roman, medieval and early modern London: objectives and methods, pp. 94–106 in Hall, A.R. and Kenward, H.K. (eds), Environmental archaeology in the urban context. *CBA Research Report* **43**. London.

Bond, J.M. and O'Connor, T.P. 1999. *Bones from medieval deposits at 16–22 Coppergate and other sites in York* (The Archaeology of York 15, 5). York: Council for British Archaeology.

Bradshaw, R.H.W., Coxon, P. Greig, J.R.A. and Hall, A.R. 1981. New fossil evidence for the past cultivation and processing of hemp (*Cannabis sativa* L.) in eastern England. *New Phytologist* **89**, 503–10.

Bristowe, W.S. 1958. *The world of spiders.* London: Collins.

Britton, E B. 1956. Coleoptera Scarabaeoidea (Lucanidae, Trigidae, Geotrupidae, Scarabaeidae). *Handbooks for the identification of British insects* **5** (11). London: Royal Entomological Society.

Buckland, P.C., Greig, J.R.A. and Kenward, H.K. 1974. York: an early medieval site. *Antiquity* **48**, 25–33.

Buurman, J. 1998. Roman medicine from Uitgeest, pp. 341–51 in Küster, H.-J. (ed.) *Der Prähistorische Mensch und seine Umwelt. Festschrift für U. Körber-Grohne* (Forschungen und Berichte zur Vor- und Frühgeschichte in Baden-Württemberg 31). Stuttgart: Theiss.

Carrott, J., Dobney, K., Hall, A., Issitt, M., Jaques, D., Johnstone, C., Kenward, H., Large, F. and Skidmore, P. 1997b. Technical Report: Environment, land use and activity at a medieval and post-medieval site at North Bridge, Doncaster, South Yorkshire. *Reports from the Environmental Archaeology Unit, York* **97/16**, 64 pp. + 103 pp. appendix.

Carrott, J., Dobney, K., Hall, A., Issitt, M., Jaques, D., Kenward, H., Large, F. and McKenna, B. 1997a. Archaeological excavations at Layerthorpe Bridge and in Peasholme Green, York (site code: 1996–7.345): assessment of the interpretative potential of biological remains. *Reports from the Environmental Archaeology Unit, York* **97/25**, 66 pp.

Carrott, J., Dobney, K., Hall, A., Issitt, M., Jaques, D., Kenward, H., Large, F. and Milles, A. 1994a. An evaluation of biological remains from excavations at 34A-40 High Street, Hull (site code HHS93). *Reports from the Environmental Archaeology Unit, York* **94/1**, 6 pp.

Carrott, J.B., Dobney, K.M., Hall, A.R., Kenward, H.K., Milles, A. and Nicholson, R. 1992. *Evaluation of biological remains from boreholes at Palmer Lane, York (YAT/Yorkshire Museum code 1992.3).* Prepared for York Archaeological Trust.

Carrott, J., Dobney, K., Hall, A., Jaques, D., Kenward, H., Lancaster, S. and Milles, A. 1994b. Assessment of biological remains from excavations at 12–18 Swinegate, 8 Grape Lane, and 14, 18, 20 and 22 Back Swinegate/Little Stonegate, York (YAT/Yorkshire Museum sitecodes 1989–90.28 and 1990.1). *Reports from the Environmental Archaeology Unit, York* **94/13**, 16 pp. + 53 pp. appendix.

Carrott, J. and Kenward, H. 2001. species associations among insect remains from urban archaeological deposits and their significance in reconstructing the past human environment. *Journal of Archaeological Science* **28**, 887–905.

Cherry, J. 1991. Leather, Ch. 12, pp. 295–318 in Blair, J. and Ramsay, N. (eds), *English medieval industries.* London: Hambledon.

Cram, L. 1982. The pits and horncores, pp. 48–51 in Mahany, C., Burchard, A. and Simpson, G., Excavations in Stamford, Lincolnshire 1963–69. *Society for Medieval Archaeology, Monograph Series* **9**.

Dainton, M. 1992. A quick, semi-quantitative method for recording nematode gut parasite eggs from archaeological deposits. *Circaea, the Journal of the Association for Environmental Archaeology* **9**, 58–63.

Davis, B.N.K. 1983. *Insects on nettles.* Cambridge: University Press.

Dobney, K., Kenward, H., Ottaway, P. and Donel, L. 1998. Down, but not out: biological evidence for complex economic organisation in Lincoln in the late fourth century. *Antiquity* **72**, 417–24.

Duffy, E.A.J. 1953. *A monograph of the immature stages of British and imported timber beetles (Cerambycidae).* London: British Museum (Natural History).

Girling M. 1979. Entomological evidence for tanning from a post-medieval pit at Southwark. *Ancient Monuments Laboratory Report* **2735**.

Hakbijl, T. 1987. Insect remains: Unadulterated cantharidium and tobacco from the West Indies, pp. 93–4 in Gawronski, J.H.G. (ed.), *Annual report of the VOC-ship "Amsterdam" Foundation 1986.* Amsterdam.

Hakbijl, T. and de Groot, M. 1997. Insect remains from Willem Barents' 1596 arctic exploration preserved in "Het Behouden Huys", Novaya Zemlya – with notes on the medicinal use of cantharides, pp. 129–34 in Ashworth, A.C., Buckland, P.C. and Sadler, J.P. (eds), Studies in Quaternary entomology – and inordinate fondness for insects. *Quaternary Proceedings* **5**. Chichester, UK: Wiley.

Hall, A.R. 1992. The last teasel factory in Britain, and some observations on teasel (*Dipsacus fullonum* L. and *D. sativus* (L.) Honckeny) remains from archaeological deposits. *Circaea, the Journal of the Association for Environmental Archaeology* **9**, 9–15.

Hall, A. 1997. Rapport sir un échantillon de matière végétale trouvé dans une cuve en bois du 16e/17e siècle à Chartres (Eure-et-Loire), France. *Reports from the Environmental Archaeology Unit, York* **97/6**, 2 pp.

Hall, A. 1999. Adding colour to the story: recognising remains of dyeplants in medieval archaeological deposits, pp. 101–7 in Dewilde, M., Ervynck, A. and Wielemans, A. (eds), Ypres and the medieval cloth industry in Flanders. *Archeologie in*

Vlaanderen, *Monografie* **2**. Asse-Zellik: Instituut voor het Archeologisch Patrimonium.

Hall, A., Carrott, J., Jaques, D., Johnstone, C., Kenward, H., Large, F. and Usai, R. 2000c. Technical report: Studies on biological remains and sediments from medieval deposits at the Magistrates' Courts site, Kingston-upon-Hull (site codes HMC 94 and MCH99). Part 1: Text. *Reports from the Environmental Archaeology Unit, York* **2000/25**, 78 pp.

Hall, A.R., Dobney, K.M., Jaques, S.D., Kenward, H.K., Large, F.D. and McComish, J.M. 2000b. Low Fisher Gate (North Bridge), Doncaster, U.K. – bioarchaeological aspects of a 11th-18th century urban site. *Reports from the Environmental Archaeology Unit, York* **2000/40**, 61 pp. + 8 figures.

Hall, A.R. and Kenward, H.K. 1990. *Environmental evidence from the Colonia: General Accident and Rougier Street* (The Archaeology of York 14, 6). London: Council for British Archaeology.

Hall, A. and Kenward, H. 1998. Disentangling dung: pathways to stable manure. *Environmental Archaeology* **1**, 123–6.

Hall, A., Kenward, H., Jaques, D. and Carrott, J. (2000a). Technical Report: Environment and industry at Layerthorpe Bridge, York (site code YORYM 1996.345). *Reports from the Environmental Archaeology Unit, York* **2000/64**, 117 pp.

Hall, A.R., Kenward, H.K. and Williams, D. 1980. *Environmental evidence from Roman deposits in Skeldergate* (The Archaeology of York 14, 3). London: Council for British Archaeology.

Hall, A.R., Kenward, H.K., Williams, D. and Greig, J.R.A. 1983. *Environment and living conditions at two Anglo-Scandinavian sites* (The Archaeology of York 14, 4). London: Council for British Archaeology.

Hansen, V. 1927. *Biller. 7. Bladbiller og bønnebiller (Chrysomelidae og Lariidae)*. Danmarks Fauna 31 København: Gads.

Harde, K.W. (edited and with additional introductory material by P.M. Hammond, illustrated by F. Severa) 1984. *A field-guide in colour to beetles*. London: Octopus Books.

Harman, M. 1979. The mammalian bones, pp. 328–32 in Williams, J.H. and Shaw, M., *St Peter's Street, Northampton, Excavations 1973–1976*. Northampton: Northampton Development Corporation.

Henslow, G. 1905. *The uses of British plants...* London: Lovell Reeve & Co.

Hillman, G.C. 1981. Reconstructing crop husbandry practices from charred remains of crops, pp. 123–62 in Mercer, R. (ed.), *Farming practice in British prehistory*. Edinburgh: University Press.

Hoffmann, A. 1958. Coléoptères curculionides. *Faune de France* **62**. Paris: Librairie de la Faculté des Sciences.

Hopkin, S. 1991. A key to the woodlice of Britain and Ireland. *Field Studies* **7**, 599–650. (also published as AIDGAP publication 204.)

Howes, F.N. 1953. *Vegetable tanning agents*. London: Butterworth.

Jessop, L. 1986. Dung beetles and chafers. Coleoptera: Scarabaeoidea. *Handbooks for the identification of British insects* **5** (11), 53 pp. London: Royal Entomological Society.

Jones, G.E.M. 1984. Interpretation of archaeological plant remains: ethnographic models from Greece. pp. 43–61 in van Zeist, W. and Casparie, W. A. (eds) *Plants and ancient man*. Rotterdam: Balkema (Proceedings of 6th Symposium, International Work Group for Palaeoethnobotany).

Kenward, H.K. 1976. Reconstructing ancient ecological conditions from insect remains: some problems and an experimental approach. *Ecological Entomology* **1**, 7–17.

Kenward, H.K. 1978. *The analysis of archaeological insect assemblages: a new approach* (The Archaeology of York 19, 1). London: Council for British Archaeology.

Kenward, H.K. 1990. Insect remains from various sites in Southwark. Prepared for D.J. Rackham. [*Reports from the EAU, York* **90/10**]

Kenward, H.K. and Hall, A.R. 1995. *Biological evidence from Anglo-Scandinavian deposits at 16–22 Coppergate* (The Archaeology of York 14, 7). York: Council for British Archaeology.

Kenward, H. and Hall, A. 1997. Enhancing bioarchaeological interpretation using indicator groups: stable manure as a paradigm. *Journal of Archaeological Science* **24**, 663–73.

Kenward, H. and Hall, A. 2000. Technical Report: Plant and invertebrate remains from Anglo-Scandinavian deposits at the Queen's Hotel site, 1–9 Micklegate, York (site code 88–9.17). *Reports from the Environmental Archaeology Unit, York* **2000/14**, 80 pp.

Kenward, H. and Large, F. 1998. Insects in urban waste pits in Viking York: another kind of seasonality, in Pals, J.P. and van Wijngaarden-Bakker, L. (eds), Proceedings of the Association for Environmental Archaeology conference 1994, held in Zwartsluis, Netherlands. Oxbow. *Environmental Archaeology* **3**, 35–53.

Kirby, W., and Spence, W. 1859. *An introduction to entomology or elements of the natural history of insects, etc.* London: Longman, Green, Longman and Roberts.

Knörzer, K.-H. 1967. Die römerzeitliche Heilkräuterfund aus Neuss/Rh. *Archaeo-Physika* **2**, 65–75.

Körber-Grohne, U. 1991. Identification methods, pp. 3–24 in van Zeist, W., Wasylikowa, K. and Behre, K.-E (eds), *Progress in Old World Palaeoethnobotany*. Rotterdam: Balkema.

Küster, H. 1988. Beziehungen zwischen der Landnutzung und der Deposition von Blei und Cadmium in Torfen am Nordrand der Alpen. *Naturwissenschaften* **75**, 611–13.

Leatherdale, D. 1955. House infestation by *Trox scaber* (L.) (Col., Trogidae) from a jackdaws' nest. *Entomologist's Monthly Magazine* **91**, 266.

Macklin, M.G., Taylor, M.P., Hudson-Edward, K.A. and Howard, A.J. 2000. Holocene environmental change in the Yorkshire Ouse basin and its influence on river dynamics sediment fluxes to the coastal zone, pp. 87–96 in Shennan, I. and Andrews, J.E. (eds) Holocene land-ocean interaction and environmental change around the North Sea. *Geological Society Special Publication* **166**. London: Geological Society.

Matt, C.P. and Reicke, D. 1990. Gerbergässlein 2 (1989/6). Zur Baugeschichte der Häuser "zum Schwarzen Turm" und "zum Grünen Stern" sowie Reste einer Gerberei aus dem 18./19. Jh. *Jahresbericht der Archäologischen Bodenforschung des Kantons Basel-Stadt 1990*. Basel.

McKenna, W.J.B. 1992. The environmental evidence, pp. 227–33 in Evans, D.H. and Tomlinson, D.G. (eds), Excavations at 33–5 Eastgate, Beverley, 1983–86. *Sheffield Excavation Reports* **3**. Sheffield.

O'Connor, T.P. 1984. *Selected groups of bones from Skeldergate and Walmgate* (The Archaeology of York 15, 1). London: Council for British Archaeology.

O'Connor, T.P. 1989. *Bones from Anglo-Scandinavian levels at 16–22 Coppergate* (The Archaeology of York 15, 3). London: Council for British Archaeology.

Palm, T. 1959. Die Holz- und Rinden-Käfer der süd- und mittelschwedischen Laubbäume. *Opuscula Entomologica Supplementum* **16**.

Polunin, O. 1976. *Trees and bushes of Britain and Europe*. St Albans: Granada.

Robertson, A., Tomlinson, P. and Kenward, H.K. 1989. Plant and insect remains from Coffee Yard, York. Prepared for York Archaeological Trust. [*Reports from the Environmental Archaeology Unit, York* **89/12**]

Ryder, M.L. 1970. The animal remains from Petergate, York. *Yorkshire Archaeological Journal* **42**, 418–28.

Sabine, J.R. 1983. Earthworms as a source of food and drugs, pp. 285–96 in Satchell, J.E. (ed.), *Earthworm ecology from Darwin to vermiculture*. London: Chapman and Hall.

Schmitt, W.L. 1965. *Crustaceans*. Ann Arbor: University of Michigan.

Shaw, M. 1984. Northampton: excavating a 16th century tannery. *Current Archaeology* **91**, 241–4.

Sims, R.W. and Gerard, B.M. 1985. Earthworms: keys and notes for the identification and study of the species. *Synopses of the British fauna* (new series) **31**. London, etc.: Brill.

Smith, D.N. 1996. Thatch, turves and floor deposits: a survey of Coleoptera in materials from abandoned Hebridean Blackhouses and the implications for their visibility in the archaeological record. *Journal of Archaeological Science* **23**, 161–74.

Smith, D., Letts, J. and Cox, A. 1999. Coleoptera from late medieval smoke-blackened thatch (SBT): their archaeological implications. *Environmental Archaeology* **4**, 9–17.

van der Veen, M. 1992. Crop husbandry regimes: an archaeo-botanical study of farming in northern England 1000 BC – AD 500. *Sheffield Archaeology Monograph* **3**. Sheffield.

Walton Rogers, P. 1997. *Textile production at 16–22 Coppergate* (Archaeology of York 17, 11). York: Council for British Archaeology.

Wenham, L.P. 1964. Hornpot Lane and the horners of York. *Annual Report of the Yorkshire Philosophical Society, York, for the year 1964*, 25–56.

Wilson, J.A. and Thomas, A.W. 1927. Tannins and vegetable tanning materials, pp. 239–50 in Washburn, E.W. (ed.) *International Critical Tables...* **2**. New York and London: McGraw-Hill.

13. Archaeological arthropod faunas as indicators of past industrial activities. Species composition, appearance and body-part representation

Jaap Schelvis

Various arthropods are considered reliable indicators of the palaeoecology of a site or the activities which took place at a particular site. Apart from the species composition of these archaeological arthropod death assemblages, the appearance and body-part representation of the species found should also be studied. Examples are given in which the appearance of remains is found to be an essential step in the interpretation of oribatid faunas. Another example deals with the interpretation of finds of ectoparasites of sheep.

Keywords: Bioarchaeology, arthropod remains, interpretation, body-part representation, combs, ectoparasites, wool processing.

INTRODUCTION

Unlike animal bones, arthropod remains found during archaeological excavations are only rarely the result of deliberate processes. Whereas animal bones can often be allotted to taphonomical categories such as kitchen refuse, artefacts or corpses, the remains of insects and mites are generally not the obvious result of a particular process or event. The only exceptions are those instances where attempts have been made to get rid of certain species because they were, for instance, detrimental to stored food products. Large numbers of remains of stored food product pests such as grain pests may be found when spoiled stocks are dumped or alternatively covered up as suggested by Hall and Kenward (1976). Another way in which arthropod remains can accumulate in an archaeological context as a result of a deliberate effort is between the teeth of combs. It is most likely that in these cases the persons using the combs were actually trying to gather as many lice, nits and fleas as possible (Schelvis 1994). In fact, the analysis of arthropod remains from Dutch medieval combs was my first attempt in the environmental archaeology of industry.

Although generally not the result of deliberate processes, arthropod faunas may still be useful in identifying certain industrial or craft activities or in establishing the location where these activities took place.

SPECIES COMPOSITION

The most obvious characteristic of any given arthropod death assemblage is of course its species composition. This is usually also the basis of the bioarchaeological interpretation. On the basis of the species list one can then proceed, for instance, by computing the mutual climatic range of the beetle species (Atkinson *et al* 1986) or by allocating the oribatid mite species found to ecological groups (Schelvis 1990). However, when the amount of time to be spent on the bioarchaeological interpretation of a given site is limited (which is practically always the case and without exception as a result of financial restrictions) it is suggested that indicator groups of biological remains rather than full species lists provide a cost-effective way to achieve this goal (Kenward and Hall 1997). The potential of this promising approach in identifying certain craft and industry activities is discussed by Hall and Kenward (this volume).

Figure 37. Long comb dated to the 12th century which was found to contain the remains of headlouse Pedicularis humanus *(L.). Length of comb 139 mm.*

In the case of the medieval combs from The Netherlands it was also the species composition of the faunal remains which led to the interpretation of the combs. Figure 37 shows a type of comb made from a cattle metapodial which is regularly found during excavations in the Netherlands. This type of comb, which was produced from the ninth to the fifteenth centuries, is usually refered to as a wool comb or carding comb in Dutch archaeological literature. However, analysis of the arthropod remains found between the bases of the teeth (Schelvis 1994) invariably produces the remains of human ectoparasites such as the headlouse *Pediculus humanus* (L.) or our own 'human' flea *Pulex irritans* (L). What we would expect to find if these combs were really used for wool processing would be the remains of specific ectoparasites of wool-producing domestic animals such as the sheep biting louse *Damalinia ovis* (Schrank) or the goat biting louse *Damalinia caprae* (Gurlt).

However, apart from their species composition archaeological arthropod faunas sometimes show other characteristics which may also be useful in their interpretation. In this paper I would like to discuss two of these characteristics: the appearance of the remains and the body part representation of the species found.

APPEARANCE OF THE REMAINS

Erickson (1988) was the first to describe various classes of preservation of oribatid mites in quaternary paleoecology in order to analyse the taphonomy of these remains. Even though his method did not prove to be of much use in interpreting archaeological deposits it did prompt me to look a bit further than my species lists. In some cases this led to the somewhat negative result that certain mite faunas were not suitable for reconstructing the local environment (Sanz Bretón and Schelvis 1994).

Especially in (semi) arid regions oribatid mites have developed various ways to avoid dehydration, usually by morphological adaptations allowing the mites to penetrate deeper into the soil. These so-called euedaphic mites can be recognised by their slender cylindrical body shape and the presence of very short hairs and appendages. As a result of their burrowing life- style remains of these species may end up in much older archaeological deposits thereby complicating the paleoecological interpretation of the site.

Another example of the use of the appearance of arthropod remains in archaeological deposits is the distinction between mossmites from 'living' *Sphagnum* and those from cut peat or other sources of fossil *Sphagnum*. Various oribatid species are characteristically found in soaking wet *Sphagnum* mosses in bogs and marshes. Some of these species, such as the representatives of the family Limnozetidae, are regularly found in paleontological as well as archaeological deposits. [Indeed, *Limnozetes ciliatus* (Schrank) is one of the seven species of oribatids which for unknown reasons can be found in more than two thirds of all archaeological samples.] However, the interpretation of such finds depends partly on the appearance of these remains. When the remains are completely dorsoventrally flattened it is most likely that they originate from "fossil" *Sphagnum*. On the other hand when the oribatids found are almost spherical, as they were when they were still alive, we can safely assume that they came from living mosses. Therefore, when a medieval cesspit yields hundreds of flattened individuals of *L. ciliatus* this may lead to the conclusion that the house to which the cesspit belonged was heated by burning peat. When the same oribatids are found in their "normal" state of preservation the conclusion could be that the occupants of the house used *Sphagnum* mosses for sanitary purposes.

BODY-PART REPRESENTATION

The study of samples from Iron age farms near Middendelfland (Schelvis & Koot 1995) was the first to produce large numbers of remains of ectoparasitic insects in Dutch archaeology.

Initially this study focused on the remains of specific predatory mites to identify the producer of dung deposits. These acarine remains indeed gave clear indications for cattle as the producers of the excrement. This result was confirmed by the unexpected find of dozens of biting lice (Mallophaga) in the same samples. The most numerous species by far was the cattle biting louse *Damalinia bovis* (L.), but two other bovine ectoparasites were also recorded: the little blue louse *Solenopotes capillatus* Enderlein and the long-nosed cattle louse *Linognathus vituli* (L.), both representatives of the sucking lice (Anoplura). In the light of these results an attempt was made at the same site to identify the producer of large quantities of ungulate droppings produced by either sheep or goats. The find of dozens of remains of the sheep biting louse *D. ovis* left little doubt about which domestic animal produced these droppings. The closely related, but anatomically different, goat biting louse *D. caprae* was not found. *D. caprae* was at that moment the only representative of the Mallophaga identified tentatively at a Dutch archeological site (Hakbijl 1989).

The first record of remains of ectoparasitic insects in Belgian archaeology was in Ypres (Schelvis 1999). Samples from 13th/14th century urban deposits yielded large numbers of remains of sheep parasites (Figure 38). One sample for instance, from a ditch alongside the Koomenstraat, had a volume of less than one litre but produced 140 remains of *D. ovis*, including 80 isolated heads and 60 abdomens. Furthermore, this sample was found to contain at least 75 remains of the sheep ked *Melophagus ovinus* (L.), both fragments of puparia and body-parts of adult flies.

When we compare the two parasite faunas from Ypres and Middendelfland we find two striking differences, one related to the species composition and another related to the body-part representation of the species found. First of all, why is *M. ovinus* absent in the Dutch deposits? The differences in biology of the two species may provide the answer: *Damalinia* lice die within hours when separated from their host (Lancaster and Meisch, 1986), for instance when the sheep rub against each other or against structures. The minute lice (adults of *D. ovis* are less than 2 mm long) get trampled into the floor deposits and may be preserved there under favourable conditions. Sheep keds, although wingless, are relatively large (up to 10 mm), mobile creatures which are able to survive without their host for several days. Once separated from their hosts they simply climb back onto them or when the fleece is removed from the sheep they pass (temporarily) over to any other warm-blooded creature nearby.

Another major difference between the two sites was

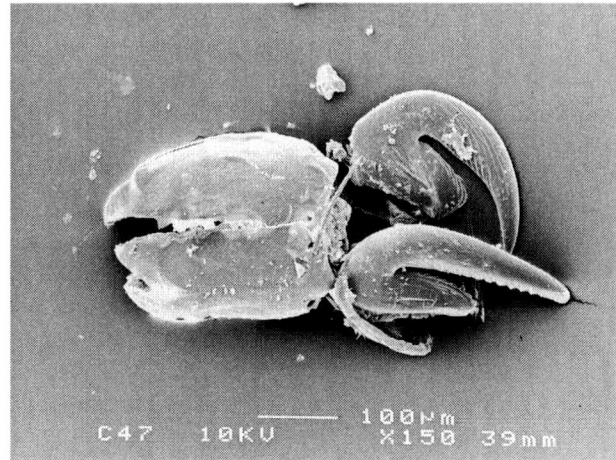

Figure 38. Last tarsal segment with claws of the sheep ked Melophagus ovinus *found in 13th/14th century Ypres, Belgium.*

the level of isolation of the various body-parts of the parasites, even though the quality of preservation was similar at both sites. At Middendelfland some "complete" lice were found, with the head, thorax and abdomen in anatomical position. Although the number of lice remains was even higher in Ypres not a single complete louse was found at this site, only isolated heads and abdomens. The same is true for the remains of the sheep keds; apart from a handful of more or less complete puparia only isolated heads, claws and hypostomes of adult flies were found. It seems plausible that this mechanical damage was caused by some form of processing of the wool (washing, shearing, fulling) or even at an earlier stage when the fleece is separated from the skin. It may be noteworthy that the relatively strong and large thorax of the sheep ked was not found, whereas minute body-parts used to pierce the skin (hypostome) or to cling to the skin (claws) were found in large numbers. Could it be that the thorax and abdomen, which are clearly visible, were removed when combing or cleaning the wool? Another sample from Ypres, taken from a pit fill, produced a similarly high density of *Damalinia* lice remains but only very few (and even further fragmented) remains of sheep ked *Melophagus*. Could this then indicate that this fauna is the result of one of the more advanced stages of the processing of the wool? *Damalinia* lice belong to the group of biting lice and do not possess mouthparts or claws with which they can hold on to the skin of their hosts like sheep keds. Therefore, the differences between the two samples from Ypres could also reflect the difference between the processing of fleece still attached to the skin and the handling of wool which had already been separated from the skin.

More research will be necessary to differentiate the various steps in the processing of wool on the basis of arthropod remains. However, it seems justified at this stage to conclude that deposits yielding high densities of isolated body-parts of both sheep biting louse (*D. ovis*) and sheep ked (*M. ovinus*) are likely to be the result of some sort of wool processing.

CONCLUSION

The overall conclusion is that when we try to reconstruct paleoecological conditions, whether they are related to industrial activities or not, we should always look further than the species list. Both the appearance of the remains and the body-part representation of the species found can give additional information which may prove vital for the interpretation.

Acknowledgements

I would like to thank Anton Ervynck (Institute for the Archaeological Heritage, Asse – Zellik) for his assistance in the preparation of the SEM figure.

References

Atkinson, T.C., Briffa, K.R., Coope, G.R., Joachim, J.M. and Perry, D.W. 1986. Climatic calibration of coleopteran data, pp. 851–8 in Berglund, B.E. (ed.) *Handbook of Holocene Palaeoecology and Palaeohydrology*. Chichester: J. Wiley & Son.

Erickson, J.M. 1988. Fossil oribatid mites as tools for quaternary paleoecologists: preservation quality, quantities and taphonomy, pp. 207–26 in Laub, R.S., Miller, N.G. and Steadman, D.W. (eds) *Late Pleistocene and Early Holocene Paleoecology and Archeology of the Eastern Great Lakes Region*. Bulletin of the Buffalo Society of Natural Sciences 33.

Hakbijl, T. 1989. Insect Remains from site Q, an early Iron Age Farmstead of the Assendelver Polders Project. *Helinium* **28**, 77–102.

Hall, A.R. and Kenward, H.K. in press. Can we identify biological indicator groups for craft and industry? This volume.

Hall, R.A. and Kenward, H.K. 1976. Biological Evidence for the usage of Roman riverside warehouses at York. *Britannia* 7, 274–276.

Kenward, H. and Hall, A. 1997. Enhancing bioarchaeological interpretation using indicator groups: stable manure as a paradigm. *Journal of Archaeological Science* **24**, 663–73.

Lancaster, J.L. and Meisch, M.V., 1986. *Arthropods in livestock and poultry production*. (Ellis Horwood series in acarology) Chichester: J. Wiley & Son.

Sanz Bretón, J.L. and Schelvis, J. 1994. De mijten (Acari) uit Peñalosa en Cerro de la Cruz (Spanje) en Halos (Griekenland). De mogelijkheden van acaro-archeologisch onderzoek in het Mediterrane gebied. *Paleoaktueel* **5**, 47–49.

Schelvis, J. 1990. The reconstruction of local environments on the basis of remains of oribatid mites (Acari;Oribatida). *Journal of Archaeological Science* **17**, 559–71.

Schelvis, J. 1994. Caught between the teeth. A review of Dutch finds of archeological remains of ectoparasites in combs. *Experimental and Applied Entomology. Proceedings of the Netherlands Entomological Society* **5**, 131–132.

Schelvis, J. and Koot C., 1995. Sheep or goat? *Damalinia* deals with the dilemma. *Experimental and Applied Entomology. Proceedings of the Netherlands Entomological Society* **6**, 161–162.

Schelvis, J. 1999. Remains of sheep ectoparasites as indicators of wool processing in the past, pp. 89–100 in Dewilde, M., Ervynck A. and Wielemans A. (eds) *Ypres and the Medieval Cloth industry in Flanders. Archaeological and historical contributions. Ieper en de middeleeuwse lakennijverheid in Vlaanderen. Archeologische en historische bijdragen*. (Archeologie in Vlaanderen IAP-Monografie 2).

14. Charred mollusc shells as indicators of industrial activities

Peter Murphy

Shells of land, fresh- and brackish-water molluscs have generally been employed by environmental archaeologists as palaeoecological indicators. However, charred shells also provide data on the importation and heat-treatment of raw materials for industrial and other purposes. These include clays, peat, hay and other plant materials. The need to separate charred shells from normally preserved ones in archaeological assemblages is emphasised, for the taphonomy of these two categories differs. The possibility of AMS dating is considered.

Keywords: Molluscs, sub-fossil, charred, environmental archaeology.

INTRODUCTION

Shells of land and freshwater molluscs have been widely used to provide palaeoecological data from archaeological sites. The larger marine species have generally been considered in terms of their economic significance as a food resource since at least the Mesolithic, in Britain (Simmons and Tooley 1981; Bell and Walker 1992, 24). More recently, brackish-water and marine species have become important in Eastern England, and in other areas, as palaeoecological indicators, due to the increased emphasis on the excavation of coastal/intertidal sites (*e.g.* Murphy 1992, 1994; Wilkinson and Murphy 1995).

Evans (1972) and Sparks (1961, 1969) remain the basis for the palaeoecological interpretation of the non-marine species, though more recent studies examining modern populations, shell taphonomy, preservation and residence times have resulted in the development of new interpretive frameworks (*e.g.* Bell and Johnson 1996; Carter 1990; Evans 1990; Rouse 1996; Rouse and Evans 1994). Palaeoecological interpretation has commonly been based on uniformitarian principles, comparing modern mollusc faunas from known habitats with sub-fossil assemblages, but it is now widely appreciated that communities of organisms do not respond to environmental change *as* communities: each individual species responds separately. This may lead to new groupings of species which were not formerly associated. Partly in response to this perception, a different interpretational approach involving characterisation of taxocenes has been developed (Evans 1991; Evans *et al.* 1992; Davies 1996). Interpretation of mollusc shell assemblages has therefore been developed in several directions in recent years.

The purpose of this short paper is to draw attention to another feature of shell preservation and taphonomy, which appears not to have been discussed before: the significance of 'burnt' or charred shells. Charred and normally preserved shells commonly occur in the same sample, and it is important to differentiate them, for their taphonomy differs. Charring occurs wherever raw materials with associated molluscs (*e.g.* plant materials, clays) are burnt, and it can provide a useful indication of the importation of 'exotic' materials to a site. It may also occur where molluscs forming part of the resident site population are accidentally trapped within or under fires.

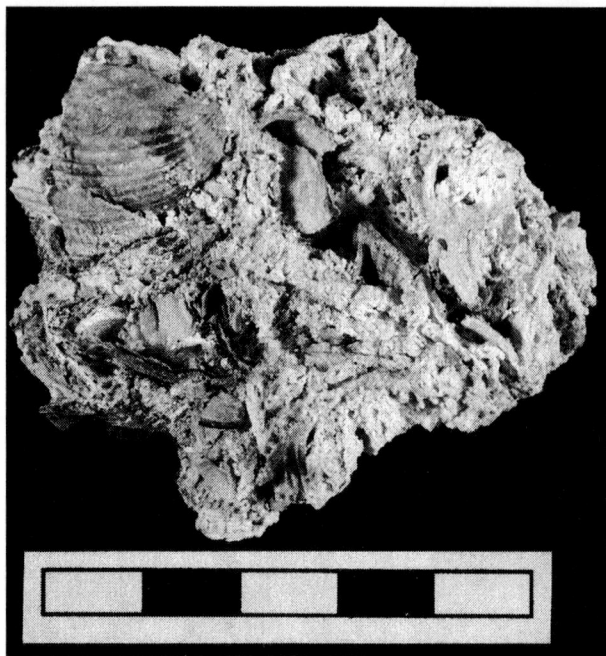

Figure 39. Gilberd School, Colchester, Essex. Fused mass of calcite with Cerastoderma and other mollusc shell fragments from medieval lime-kiln. Scale 50 mm.

CHARRED MOLLUSC SHELLS

The mineral component of mollusc shell is crystalline calcium carbonate. In terrestrial snails this is usually aragonite, but in the limacid slugs and *Arion* internal shells are of calcite, a more stable form (Evans 1972, 23). Marine gastropod shells are similarly mainly of vertically-arranged aragonite crystals often with an inner layer of calcite sheets ('mother of pearl'), whilst bivalve shells may be of calcite or aragonite, or partly of both (Yonge and Thompson 1976).

Exposure of shell to temperatures of 800–1000°C results in conversion of $CaCO_3$ to CaO (Hicks 1963, 335). Indeed, this was done intentionally at the Gilberd School, Colchester, Essex in the medieval period, where shells of cockle (*Cerastoderma edule* (L)) were used as the raw material in a lime-kiln (Murphy 1992a). The valves from this feature were generally small (18–30mm; mean 23mm), and some were abraded and perforated by boring organisms, which suggests that they were dredged from offshore shell-banks specifically for lime production, rather than being re-used food waste (Figure 39).

At lower temperatures of combustion, and in poorly oxygenated conditions, the protein component of shell, including the periostracum, becomes charred. This results in the shell becoming discoloured, through shades of bluish-grey to black and sometimes developing a very glossy surface. The effects of high temperatures are not to be confused with the superficially similar grey coloration of shells from anoxic sediments containing reduced iron compounds.

There are also indications that charring makes shell more resistant to leaching and soil acids. This might perhaps involve a modification of crystal structure, although Mark Robinson (pers. comm.) suggests that the surface layer of carbon coating the shell might be implicated. For example, at a site at North Shoebury, Essex, on decalcified terrace brickearth, mollusc shells were not preserved in prehistoric features, apart from a single charred shell of *Clausilia* sp from a Middle Bronze Age pit, possibly representing a snail which reached the site attached to firewood (Murphy 1995). The survival of 'burnt' bone in acidic soils and sediments where 'unburnt' bone is not preserved has commonly been noted (*e.g.* Gilchrist and Mytum 1986). Despite the different chemical composition of mollusc shell and bone, (the mineral component of which is composed of crystalline calcium phosphate in a form resembling apatite: Davis 1987, 48), analogous processes appear to be involved.

Nomenclature in this paper follows Kerney (1976), Kerney and Cameron (1979) and Smith and Heppell (1991).

SOME SITE STUDIES

Local habitat change

Even where uncharred shells are preserved at a given site, charred shells may consist of a range of species differing from that associated with the main phase of activity. In some cases, they may relate to the vegetation of an earlier phase of the site. For example, at the Bronze Age settlement site of West Row Fen, Mildenhall, Suffolk charred shells of woodland taxa, including *Carychium tridentatum* (Risso), *Clausilia bidentata* (Ström), *Discus rotundatus* (Mueller) and *Vertigo pusilla* (Mueller) were recovered at low densities from a range of features. They probably related to a phase of pre-occupation woodland fire clearance: a charred *in situ* oak root system at the site was dated to 3650 ± 100 BP (HAR-5637). Subsequently, it is suggested, some shells charred at that time remained in the palaeosol, whilst others were re-worked into later cut features. The main settlement phase, on a fen-edge sand ridge, was characterised by assemblages mostly of uncharred shells, in which 'open country' taxa predominated: especially *Pupilla muscorum* (L.) and *Helicella itala* (L.), snails characteristic of bare ground and sand dunes. (Martin and Murphy 1988).

Alternatively, shells may become charred in a late phase of site activity. At Deeping St Nicholas, Lincolnshire, a pit sealed by a Bronze Age barrow produced a sparse uncharred shell assemblage dominated by *Carychium* spp with other woodland taxa, but a Bronze Age cremation from the site included a charred shell assemblage, in which *Vallonia* spp and *Pupilla muscorum* predominated. The former appeared to relate to pre-barrow woodland or scrub; the latter to an open habitat in which a pyre had been

Table 21. Selected charred mollusc shell assemblages from the East of England.

Site	Period and context	Taxa	Interpretation	Reference
West Row, Mildenhall, Suffolk	Early-Middle Bronze Age. Various features.	*Carychium tridentatum, Clausilia bidentata, Discus rotundatus, Vertigo pusilla, Hydrobia ulvae.*	Woodland taxa thought to represent site clearance by burning. Some importation of material (clay and/or plant material) from intertidal zone.	Martin and Murphy 1988
North Shoebury, Essex	Middle Bronze Age. Pit.	*Clausilia* sp.	No other molluscs preserved in de-calcified feature fills. This shell perhaps reached site attached to firewood.	Murphy 1995
Deeping St Nicholas, Lincolnshire	Bronze Age. Cremation.	Mostly *Pupilla muscorum* and *Vallonia* spp	Represents shells from an open-country fauna, accidentally buried beneath cremation pyre.	Murphy 1994
Hoe Hills, Dowsby, Lincolnshire.	Late Bronze Age. Ditch.	*Hydrobia ulvae*	Imported to site in intertidal clay, or attached to salt-marsh plant material or seaweed etc., subsequently charred during firing or burning.	Murphy, unpublished
Culver Street, Colchester, Essex.	Roman. Urban deposits, various features.	*Lymnaea truncatula, Anisus leucostoma, Carychium minimum, Vertigo* spp.	Associated with part-charred herbivore coprolites and charred macrofossils of grassland plants. Thought to represent byre-sweepings including hay.	Murphy 1992a
Morton Fen, Lincolnshire	Roman. Saltern features.	*Hydrobia ulvae, H. ventrosa*	Either imported to site attached to plant material (e.g. *Scirpus maritimus*) intended for use as fuel, or in intertidal clay fired during brine evaporation.	Murphy 2001
Middleton, Norfolk.	Roman. Saltern features.	*Hydrobia ulvae, H. ventrosa*	No evidence for burning of halophytic vegetation; probably just accidental charring of shells in intertidal clay during brine evaporation.	Murphy 2001
St Martin-at-Palace, Norwich, Norfolk.	Late 14th century. Fired clay of oven wall.	Poorly preserved freshwater assemblage, mostly *Bithynia* opercula.	Alluvial clay including shells was used to construct the oven walls.	Murphy 1987
Barton Bendish, Norfolk	14th- 16th century. Rural settlement. Various features.	Wide range of freshwater molluscs, notably *Valvata cristata* and *Lymnaea* spp with marsh and terrestrial taxa (*Succinea* spp and *Vertigo* spp etc).	Imported to site either in fen peat, or associated with plant material from fen vegetation, imported as litter or fuel.	Murphy 1997b
Castle Mall, Norwich, Norfolk	Medieval fills of Barbican well and late medieval industrial pits.	Similar range of freshwater species (*Bithynia tentaculata* common) with marsh and terrestrial species.	Imported to site either in fen peat, or associated with plant material from fen vegetation, imported as litter or fuel.	Murphy, unpublished

burnt. This latter assemblage could have been produced because shells of molluscs trapped underneath the pyre became charred, or else could reflect the use of turves in the pyre structure (Murphy 1994). No matter exactly how charring occurred, the shell assemblage is indicative of the local Bronze Age habitat.

Importation of materials

Clays

Clays commonly include sub-fossil molluscs, and when they are fired for industrial or other purposes, shells may become charred. An example of this was clay used to construct a 14th century oven at St Martin-at-Palace Plain, Norwich (Murphy 1987). Temperatures had been sufficiently high to result in conversion of $CaCO_3$ to CaO, so that most shells had been destroyed: only robust components such as opercula of *Bithynia* sp survived charred in an identifiable form. These were, however, sufficient to indicate an alluvial clay source.

Similarly, shells in intertidal clay became charred at saltern sites, where brine was evaporated in hearths. Examples include Roman sites investigated as part of the Fenland Management Project. At a saltern on Morton Fen, Lincolnshire mollusc assemblages from ditch fills comprised principally *Hydrobia ulvae* (Pennant) and *H. ventrosa* (Montagu), with uncharred shells of terrestrial and freshwater species and occasional scraps of mussel and winkle shell (Murphy 2001, 151). Assemblages from settling tanks and ditches at the saltern at Middleton, Norfolk were similarly dominated by hydrobiids, with the intertidal species *Leucophytia bidentata* (Montagu), *Macoma balthica* (L.) and *Mytilus edulis* (L.) including charred shells related to the nearby evaporating hearths (*ibid*, 222). Deposits of burnt saltern debris under the Roman road, the Fen Causeway at Nordelph, Norfolk and from a ditch adjacent to the Bourne-Morton canal, Lincolnshire produced hydrobiids and terrestrial snails (ibid, 321). An isolated charred shell of *H. ulvae* from a Bronze Age ditch at Hoe Hills, Dowsby, Lincolnshire could relate to importation of intertidal clay to the site (Murphy, unpublished).

Peat

Some sites have produced shell assemblages which could relate to the use of base-rich peat as a fuel. Medieval features at Barton Bendish, Norfolk and Castle Mall, Norwich contained charred shells of freshwater and marsh species (mainly *Valvata cristata* (Mueller), *Lymnaea* spp, *Bithynia tentaculata* (L.), *Succinea* spp and *Vertigo* spp) which must either have reached the site in peat fuel, or associated with sedge or 'marsh hay' (Figure 40). Peat is known to have been used extensively as fuel in medieval Norfolk: Rackham (1986, 359) estimates total extraction at 900×10^6 cubic feet and considers that at this time Norwich was "a peat-burning city". It is likely that the only palaeoecological evidence from archaeological sites

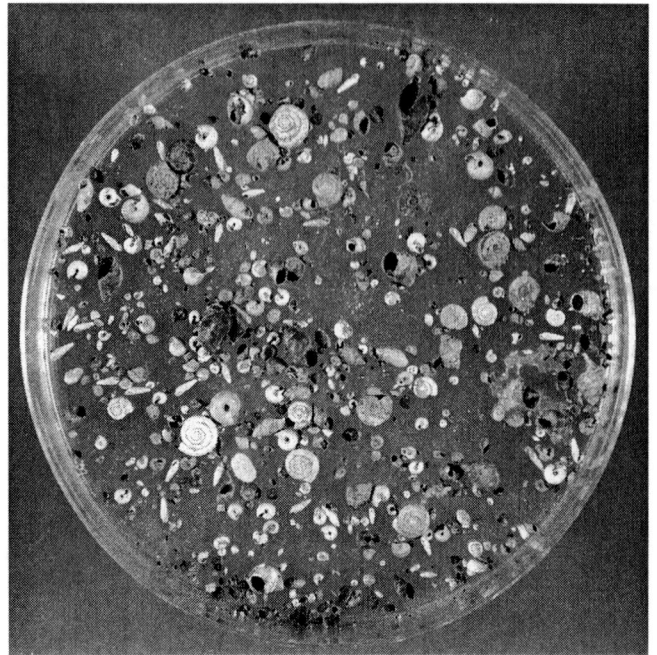

Figure 40. Barton Bendish, Norfolk. Mixed assemblage of charred shells (including Valvata cristata, Bithynia tentaculata, Lymnaea spp, Succineidae, Vertigo spp) with normally preserved specimens (mostly terrestrial taxa including Trichia hispida and Vallonia spp). Late Medieval. 90mm petri dish.

for this very large-scale industry will be charred plant macrofossil residues and molluscs. However, to demonstrate undoubted peat-burning, radiocarbon dates on charred fuel residues will be required, to show that they were, already subfossil when burnt (see below).

Hay and other plant materials

A charred shell assemblage including *Lymnaea truncatula* (Mueller), *Anisus leucostoma* (Millet), *Carychium minimum* (Mueller), *Vertigo antivertigo* (Draparnaud), *Vertigo pygmaea* (Draparnaud) and *Vertigo angustior* (Jeffreys) was associated with partly burnt herbivore coprolites and charred remains of grassland plants in Roman deposits at Culver Street, Colchester (Murphy 1992a, 276). This was interpreted as charred debris from a bonfire on which sweepings from a byre (including spoilt hay) had been burnt.

FUTURE WORK

It is hoped that the above examples support the contention that it is necessary to separate charred shells from 'normally preserved' ones, and to consider the taphonomy of the two separately. In this way, charred shells may yield information on ecological change and on the use of raw materials for industrial and other processes. Possible future applications could focus on sourcing materials. Studies of the mollusc shells in medieval and later bricks might help to help locate clay sources and production sites; and charred shells could help in establishing when peat extraction began in specific areas. Charred shells could also indicate ecological changes at sites, otherwise unrepresented by macrofossils. However, for many applications, dating is critical.

Consideration should therefore be given to the possibility of AMS dating of charred shell. *If* this proves possible, the economic and ecological interpretation of mixed assemblages of charred and uncharred shells would be on firmer ground. For example, it has been suggested above that the charred shells of woodland molluscs from the Bronze Age site of West Row Fen, Suffolk relate to pre-settlement clearance of woodland by fire. If AMS dates on charred shells proved to be significantly earlier than radiocarbon dates from the settlement features, then this interpretation would be supported and a direct date for site clearance would be obtained. Another application would be for detecting the use of calcareous peat as a fuel. Charred shells of freshwater and marsh molluscs from sites such as Barton Bendish could be used here. AMS dates markedly earlier than the deposits from which the shells came could confirm that they reached the site in calcareous fen peat.

This general approach has already been applied with charred nutlets of sedge (*Cladium mariscus* (L.)) from Roman saltern deposits at Nordelph, Norfolk. AMS dates of 2225 ± 50 BP (Cal BC 390–200: OxA-5437) and 2540 ± 55 BP (Cal BC 820–510: OxA-5438) were obtained, plainly indicating that the nutlets were sub-fossil when burnt, *i.e.* that they came from sedge peat which had formed in the Iron Age (Murphy 2001, 320).

Dating charred shells could be more problematic than using charred plant macrofossils. Pre-treatment with acid would be required to remove the carbon in shell calcite and aragonite ($CaCO_3$), leaving a carbon residue derived from the charred protein component of the shell. Whether this would be sufficient for dating remains to be determined. Furthermore, understanding the metabolic pathways leading to shell formation would be necessary: does the carbon in shell proteins come from groundwater, food or a mixture of both? Further work is plainly needed.

References

Bell, M. and Johnson, S. 1996. Land molluscs, pp. 140–142 in Bell, M., Fowler, P.J. and Hillson, S.W. (eds) *The Experimental Earthwork Project 1960 – 1992*. Council for British Archaeology Research Report **100**. London: CBA.

Bell, M. and Walker, M.J.C, 1992. *Late Quaternary Environmental change. Physical and human perspectives*. Harlow: Longman.

Carter, S.P. 1990. The stratification and taphonomy of shells in calcareous soils; implications for land snail analysis in archaeology. *Journal of Archaeological Science* **17**, 495–507.

Davies, P. 1996. Sub-fossil Mollusca: improving environmental interpretation. *Circaea* **12 (2)**, 251–2.

Davis, S.J.M. 1987. The archaeology of animals. London: Batsford.

Evans, J.G. 1972. *Land snails in archaeology*. London: Seminar Press.

Evans, J.G. 1990. Notes on some Late Neolithic and Bronze Age events in Long Barrow ditches in southern and eastern England. *Procceddings of the Prehistoric Society* **56**, 111–116.

Evans, J.G. 1991. An approach to the interpretation of dry-ground and wet-ground molluscan taxocenes from central-southern England, pp. 75–89 in Harris, D.R. and Thomas, K.D. (eds) *Modelling ecological change*. London: Institute of Archaeology.

Evans, J.G., Davies, P., Mount, R. and Williams, D. 1992. Molluscan taxocenes from Holocene overbank alluvium in central southern England, pp. 65–74 in Needham, S. and Macklin, M.G. (eds) *Alluvial archaeology in Britain*. Oxford: Oxbow Monograph **27**.

Gilchrist, R. and Mytum, H.C. 1986. Experimental archaeology and burnt animal bone from archaeological sites. *Circaea* 4 (1), 29–38.

Hicks, J. 1963. *Comprehensive Chemistry*. London: Cleaver-Hume Press.

Kerney, M.P. 1976. A list of the fresh and brackish-water Mollusca of the British Isles. *Journal of Conchology* **29**, 26–8.

Kerney, M.P. and Cameron, A. 1979. *A field guide to the land snails of Britain and North-west Europe*. London: Collins.

Murphy, P. 1987. Mollusca, pp. 117–8 in Ayers, B.S. Excavations at St Martin-at-Palace Plain, 1981, *East Anglian Archaeology* 37.

Martin, E. and Murphy, P. 1988. West Row Fen, Suffolk: A Bronze Age fen-edge settlement site. *Antiquity* **62**, 353–8.

Murphy, P. 1992. Stonea Camp, Cambridgeshire: plant macrofossils and molluscs from Iron Age fort ditch fills. *Ancient Monuments Laboratory Report* **58/92**. London: English Heritage.

Murphy, P. 1992a. Land and freshwater molluscs; marine invertebrates; sample from the medieval lime-kiln, pp. 276–8 and 288–9 in Crummy, P. *Colchester Archaeological Report 6: Excavations at Culver Street, the Gilberd School and other sites in Colchester 1971–85*. Colchester: Colchester Archaeological Trust.

Murphy, P. 1994. The molluscs, pp. 79–80 in French, C.A.I (1994) Excavation of the Deeping St. Nicholas barrow complex, South Lincolnshire, *Lincolnshire Archaeology and Heritage Reports Series* No. **1**.

Murphy, P. 1995. Mollusca, in Wymer, J.J. and Brown, N.R. Excavations at North Shoebury: settlement and economy in south-east Essex 1500BC–AD1500, *East Anglian Archaeology* **75**, 142–145.

Murphy, P. 1997b. Plant and animal macrofossils, in Rogerson, A, Davison, A, Pritchard, D. and Silvester, R, Barton Bendish and Caldecote: field work in south-west Norfolk, *East Anglian Archaeology* **80**, 66–70.

Murphy, P. 2001. Various reports, in Lane, T. and Morris, E. (eds) A millennium of salt-making: prehistoric and Romano-British salt production in the Fenland. *Lincolnshire Archaeology and Heritage Reports Series* No. **4**. Heritage Trust of Lincolnshire: Heckington.

Rackham, O. 1986. The History of the Countryside. London: Dent.

Rouse, A.G. 1996. Modern molluscs, pp. 143–6 in Bell, M., Fowler, P.J. and Hillson, S. (eds) *The Experimental Earthwork Project 1960–1992*. Council for British Archaeology Research Report **100**. London: Council for British Archaeology.

Rouse, A.G. and Evans, J.G. 1994. Modern land Mollusca from Maiden Castle, Dorset, and their relevance to the interpretation of subfossil archaeological assemblages. *Journal of Molluscan Studies* **60**, 315–329.

Simmons, I.G. and Tooley, M.J. 1981. *The environment in British prehistory*. London: Duckworth.

Smith, S.M. and Heppell, D. 1991. *Checklist of British marine*

Mollusca, National Museums of Scotland Information Series No. **11**. Edinburgh: National Museums of Scotland.

Sparks, B.W. 1961. The ecological interpretation of Quaternary non-marine Mollusca. *Proceedings of the Linnaean Society of London* **172**, 71–80.

Sparks, B.W. 1969. Non-marine Mollusca and archaeology, pp. 395–406 in Brothwell, D. and Higgs, E. (eds) *Science in*

archaeology. A survey of progress and research (2nd edn.). London: Thames and Hudson.

Wilkinson, T.J. and Murphy, P.L. 1995 Archaeology of the Essex Coast, Volume I: the Hullbridge Survey. *East Anglian Archaeology* **71**.

Yonge, C.M. and Thompson, T.E. 1976. *Living marine molluscs*. London; Collins.

15. Saxon flax retting in river channels and the apparent lack of water pollution

Mark Robinson

Flax (*Linum usitatissimum* L.) was a significant crop in Saxon England. Numerous finds have been made of flax processing remains from waterlogged deposits in circumstances that would suggest flax was being retted in water (Robinson 1992, 60). Retting is the process by which the stems of flax are subjected to bacterial action in order to facilitate the separation of the fibres when they are subsequently beaten. The soaking of flax has the reputation for being a particularly foul process, which is malodorous and results in the production of noxious effluent. Some Saxon retting was undertaken in tanks or small gullies and doubtless an oxygen deficit developed in the water in which this was occurring. For example, abundant flax seeds, capsules and stem fragments were identified from a Middle Saxon wattle-lined gully at 79–80 St Aldates, Oxford (Brown 1977), from which aquatic insects were absent (Robinson, unpublished).

However, some discoveries have been made of flax retting remains in company with insects suggestive of clean, well-oxygenated water including beetles from the family Elmidae which are extremely fastidious in their requirements (Table 22). High concentrations of flax capsules and flax seeds were discovered in palaeochannel sediments of the River Nene at West Cotton, Northants (Campbell 1994). Although no flax stems were found, oak pegs had been inserted into the channel bed, possibly to peg down bundles of flax. A radiocarbon date of AD620–890 (cal 2 sigma) was obtained on flax capsules, and dates of AD660–880 (UB-3323 cal 2 sigma) and AD640–860 (UB-3328 cal 2 sigma) were obtained on the pegs. A rich fauna of elmid beetles was present, with at least five species represented (Robinson, unpublished).

These beetles, which cling to stones or aquatic plants, are so fastidious in their requirements for unpolluted, well-oxygenated water that in most of the major English lowland river systems, if they occur at all, they are restricted to weir outflows and fast-flowing tributary streams.

Of particular interest was the occurrence of *Stenelmis canaliculata*, which was only added to the British list about 40 years ago when it was discovered to live in Lake Windermere (Claridge and Staddon 1960). It has subsequently been discovered in several other drainage systems in Britain (Ormerod 1985) including some recent captures further downstream in the Nene at Water Newton (G. Foster, pers. comm). In Europe, *S. canaliculata* lives in clean, well-oxygenated water in weirs, rapids and on submerged plants in flowing water (Freude *et al.* 1979, 277). A few flax capsule fragments were found in a Saxon palaeochannel of the Thames at 42 St Aldates, again in the company of *Stenelmis canaliculata*, which no longer occurs in the Thames (Robinson unpublished).

Further upstream on the Thames a beet (twisted bundle) of flax plants, numerous flax capsule fragments and flax seeds were discovered in a palaeochannel at Oxey Mead, Yarnton (Robinson, unpublished). A radiocarbon date of AD660–1010 (OxA-3643 cal 2 sigma) was given by the flax beet while the overlying sediments were dated to AD 630–890 (OxA-7359 cal 2 sigma). Although there was probably little flow to the channel in the Saxon period, the beetle *Oulimnius* sp. was present.

The entomological results suggest the waters of the Rivers Nene and Thames were clean in Saxon times even when they were flowing over flax that was being retted. It might be argued that the insect remains at West Cotton

Table 22. Flax and Elmid Beetles from Saxon Palaeochannels.

		West Cotton				42 St Aldates		Oxey Mead	
Sample		3	5	6	7	11	10	3/6	3/5
FLAX REMAINS									
Linum usitatissimum L.	– seeds	+	+	+	+	–	–	+	+
L. usitatissimum L.	– capsules	+	+	+	+	+	–	+	+
ELMID BEETLES									
Elmis aenea (Müll.)		+	–	+	–	–	–	–	–
Normandia nitens (Müll.)		–	+	–	–	–	–	–	–
Oulimnius sp.		+	+	+	+	–	+	+	–
Riolus subviolaceus (Müll.)		–	–	+	+	–	–	–	–
Stenelmis canaliculata (Gyll.)		–	+	–	–	+	–	–	–

and Yarnton had been derived from further upstream and the water where the flax retting was occurring was polluted. Dead insects are certainly carried along by the current of rivers and could have been introduced from tributaries. However, numerous excavations in the St Aldates area of Oxford have shown flax remains are present in Saxon deposits in palaeochannels at many locations (Robinson 1992, 60; Robinson, unpublished). The water in the channel at 42 St Aldates would almost certainly have flowed over sites of flax retting upstream. It is thought probable that the scale of flax retting was small enough that the flow of water was able to maintain sufficiently well-oxygenated conditions for the survival of elmid beetles. Thus, although the flax retting industry has the potential to cause serious water pollution, it does not seem to have caused grave problems in the Rivers Nene or Thames in Saxon times.

Acknowledgement
I am grateful to Professor G Foster for details of recent records of *Stenelmis canaliculata*.

References

Brown, A. 1977. Plant remains, in Durham, B., Archaeological investigations in St Aldates, Oxford, *Oxoniensia*.

Campbell, G.V. 1994. The preliminary archaeobotanical results from Anglo-Saxon West Cotton and Raunds, in Rackham, J. ed. Environment and economy in Anglo-Saxon England, 65–82. York: Council for British Archaeology Research Report 89.

Claridge, M.F. and Staddon, B.W. 1960. (*Stenelmis canaliculata* Gyll. (Col. Elmidae): a species new to the British list, *Entomologists' Monthly Magazine*. 96, 141–4.

Freude, H., Harde, K.W. and Lohse, G.A. 1979. Die Käfer Mitteleuropas 6. Krefeld: Goecke and Evers.

Omerod, S.J. 1985. Stenelmis canaliculata (Gyllenhall 1908) Col, Elmenthidae new to Wales, *Entymologists' Monthly Magazine*. 121, 54.

Robinson, M.A. 1992. Environmental archaeology of the river gravels: past achievements and future directions, in Fulford, M. and Nichols, E. eds. Developing landscapes of lowland Britain: a review, 47–62. London: Society of Antiquaries Research paper 14.

Industry and human health

16. The rise and fall of rickets in England

S. A. Mays

Rickets first began to be noted as a significant problem in England during the early part of the 17th century, and its frequency rose thereafter, so that by the later years of the 19th century it had reached epidemic proportions. Its rapid rise to prominence was matched by its equally precipitate decline during the early 20th century. The prevalence of rickets is intimately associated with a population's way of life, so its rise and fall during the post-Mediaeval period presents an interesting illustration of the effects of the great social, environmental, technological and scientific changes which took place over this time on the human populations who lived through them.

Keywords: Medical history, palaeopathology, bone, vitamin D, metabolic disease.

INTRODUCTION: THE NATURE OF RICKETS

Rickets is a systemic disease of infancy and childhood. It is characterised by inadequate mineralisation of bone and epiphysial cartilage during growth, and manifests clinically by skeletal deformity. Rickets is caused by a deficiency of effective vitamin D. It is a disease of the growing years; vitamin D deficiency syndrome in adults, where endochondral bone growth has ceased, is termed osteomalacia, and the skeletal and other manifestations are generally much less marked than for rickets (Mankin 1974a).

Vitamin D is naturally present only in minor quantities in most foodstuffs (although oily fish and egg-yolk do contain significant amounts). In man, most vitamin D is synthesised by the action of ultra-violet rays in sunlight upon a chemical pre-cursor, 7-dehydroxycholesterol, in the skin. This then undergoes successive hydroxylation in the liver and the kidney to produce the biologically active form, 1,25-dihydroxyvitamin D, which acts upon target tissues such as gut, kidneys and bone (Henry & Norman 1992). 1,25-dihydroxyvitamin D plays a role in absorption of calcium in the gut, the transport of calcium from bone to the extra-cellular fluid, and resorption of calcium in the kidney (Mankin 1974a).

Rickets may be caused by a variety of factors affecting vitamin D metabolism, including absorptive disorders of the gut, liver disease and renal disorders (Mankin 1974b; Resnick & Niwayama 1988, 2089–2126), but the most important causes relate to inadequate acquisition of vitamin D. Given that the main natural source of vitamin D is not dietary but synthesis in the skin in the presence of ultra-violet light, insufficient exposure to sunlight is the main cause of vitamin D deficiency (Stuart-Macadam 1988).

In the absence of adequate vitamin D there is reduced absorption of calcium from the gut, resulting in a decrease in the body pool of calcium. In order to maintain normal plasma calcium levels, parathyroid hormone is secreted and this mobilises calcium (and phosphate) from the skeleton. This leads to increased osteoclastic resorption, but osteoblastic activity also increases in an attempt to compensate. The pattern therefore is one of increased bone resorption and formation; but overall there is a negative balance so that there is insufficient calcium and phosphate properly to mineralise newly formed bone in the growing skeleton and for adequate maintenence of previously formed bone tissue (Mankin 1974a).

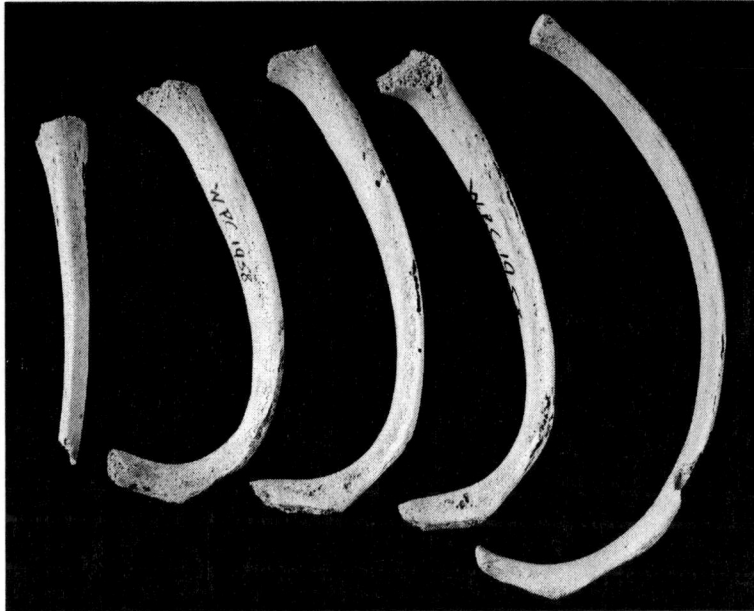

Figure 41. Ribs showing thickening, particularly towards their sternal ends, together with a rib or normal morphology (extreme right).

Rickets generally occurs during periods of rapid growth. However it is rare before about four months of age, as prior to this the infant generally retains adequate stores of vitamin D from foetal life (Ortner & Putschar 1985, 274). Rickets most often manifests at between 6 months and three years of age, although a few cases may occur at puberty, when it is known as late rickets (Stuart-Macadam 1988). In addition to skeletal lesions, individuals with rickets may show muscular weakness and poor muscle tone, gastro-intestinal upsets, retardation of growth, and anaemia (Mankin 1974a). Rickets is not a lethal disease, but it may nevertheless be a factor in infant and early childhood mortality, as those with rickets show a heightened susceptibility to infections, particularly of the respiratory tract (Hess 1930, 290).

THE SKELETAL CHANGES IN RICKETS

The bone changes associated with rickets enable its recognition in skeletal remains. Areas of rapid growth tend to show the most pronounced changes. Characteristic alterations may be visible at the sternal rib-ends, the metaphyses of long-bones, and in the pelvis, scapulae and skull; the smaller bones are often little affected (Mankin 1974a; Ortner & Putschar 1985, 274–280; Steinbock 1976, 262–272; Resnick & Niwayama 1988, 2096–2099; Ortner & Mays 1998). In the growing epiphysial plate, the normal cartilage structure is disrupted, with an increase in the number of cells in the maturation zone. There is an increase in the width of the growth plate and a widening of the

metaphysis (Fig. 41), and the bone immediately underlying the growth plate becomes roughened and irregular (Fig. 42). Since orderly cartilage formation, followed by calcification, must precede its replacement by mineralised osteoid, the cartilage abnormalities retard longitudinal growth (Aufderheide & Rodriguez-Martin 1998, 306) so that those with rickets tend to be short for their age. In rickets, bone turnover is increased, and the bone produced is poorly mineralised. In cortical bone, this may result in abnormal porosity, especially adjacent to the growth-plates (Fig. 43). The pores and other defects represent sites where un-mineralised osteoid was present *in vivo*. Cancellous bone may show a sparse, thinned trabecular structure. Bones may subsequently become thickened when osteoid deposits are mineralised (Ortner & Putschar 1985, 275). In the skull, deficient mineralisation may lead to thinning and softening of the calvarium, but thickening via deposition of porous bone on ectocranial surfaces may also occur.

The weakened rachitic bones frequently deform in response to weight-bearing and other mechanical forces. At the metaphysis, the characteristic mechanical deformity is collapse and spread of the bone end. Yielding of the bone immediately underlying the growth plate lends the bone end a concave profile, and the spreading of the bone here contributes to the flaring or widening of the metaphysis. These characteristic metaphysial changes are often referred to as 'cupping' (Mankin 1974a). In the diaphyses, the general pattern of deformation is for the natural curvatures of the long-bones to become exaggerated, so the femur tends to show increased anterio-lateral bending,

Figure 42. Sequence to illustrate porosis and roughening of the bone beneath the epiphysial plate in rickets. (a) Proximal end of a tibia from an infant showing normal morphology. (b) Distal femur in which the bone shows roughening. (c). Distal radius showing roughening and some pitting. (d) Distal radius showing extreme roughness and porosis.

and the tibia and fibula anterio-medial bowing. The arm bones may also become bowed (Fig. 44) in response to muscular forces or, in the crawling infant, to weight-bearing. The mandibular ramus may show deformation in response to chewing (Fig. 45). The severity of the bone changes may vary greatly, but as the child becomes sicker they may actually diminish: the epiphyseal plate lesions become milder as endochondral growth slows or stops, and the mechanical distortions become less as the child's activity level lessens.

In many instances, the skeletal changes caused by rickets in early life are subsequently removed by remodelling. However major deformities may become permanent. The most common residual deformities from rickets are the bending distortions of the leg bones. On X-ray, bowed bones show thickening of the cortex on the concave side (Ortner & Putschar 1985, 278), presumably as a response to altered biomechanical forces. There may also be persistence of pelvic deformities into adult life, and if severe these may lead to problems in childbirth in females

(Hess 1930). The frequency with which bone deformity is retained into adulthood will clearly depend upon the severity of the skeletal lesions suffered during childhood, but Hess (1930) cites sources which indicate that between 10 and 25% of cases of childhood rickets may retain noticable deformity in later life. In palaeopathological specimens in which the leg-bones show enhancement in their natural curvatures, it may be difficult when bending is slight to determine whether this denotes healed rickets, or whether it simply reflects normal morphological variation or alternative causes of increased bone curvature such as other metabolic diseases, trauma, congenital conditions or even post-depositional deformation (references in Stuart-Macadam *et al.* 1998). Some specimens, however, show marked and characteristic deformity, permitting unambiguous diagnosis of residual rickets (Fig. 46).

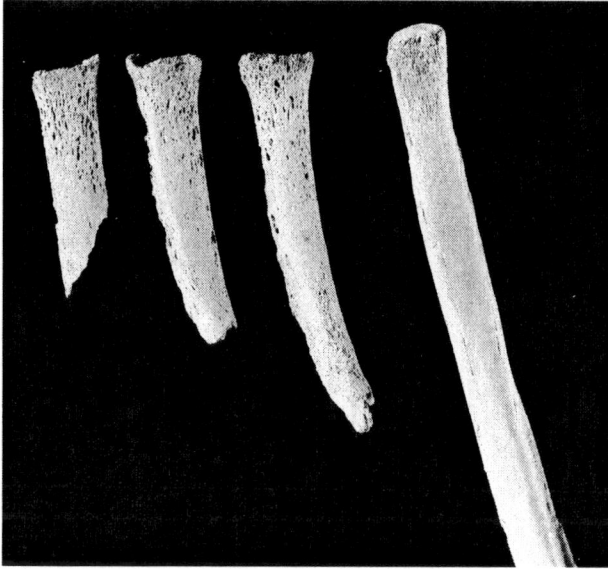

Figure 43. Three rib fragments showing pitting of their cortices and flaring of their sternal ends, together with a normal rib (extreme right) for comparison.

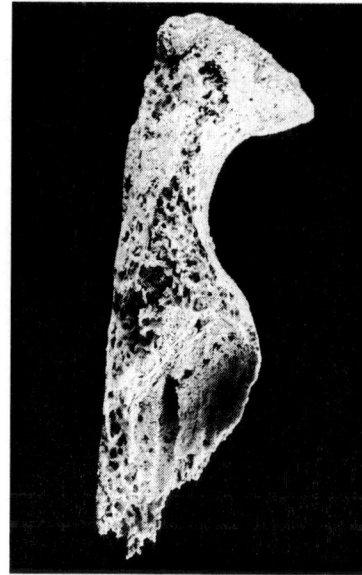

Figure 45. Superior view of part of a mandibular ramus showing abnormal medio-posterior bending.

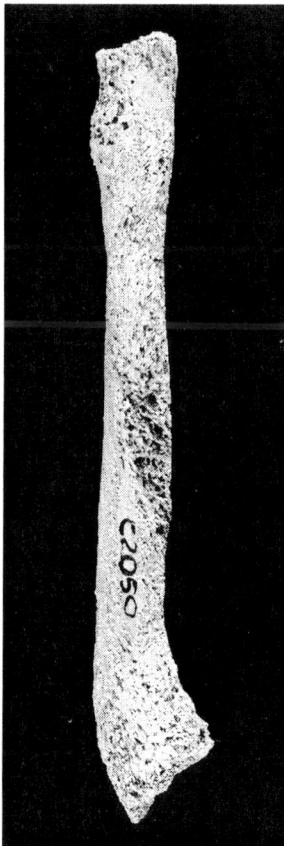

Figure 44. Radius showing abnormal angulation of its distal metaphysis

THE HISTORY OF RICKETS

Historical sources provide a rich body of evidence concerning rickets in earlier populations. Soranus of Ephesus (AD 98–138) provides us with the first convincing written description of the disease when he discusses a bow-legged condition of infants which, he claimed, was particularly common in Rome (Jackson 1988: 38). Slightly later, Galen (AD 129–?199) described the knock-knee, bow-leg, funnel-chest and pigeon-breast deformities of rickets (Steinbock 1993). The disease also seems to have been recognised by Chinese physicians at least as early as the eighth century AD (Lee 1967). Although there is some fairly dubious evidence, in the form of artistic depictions, for rickets in Europe in the 15th and 16th centuries (Foote 1927; Cone 1980), it is not until the 17th century that we have the first good clinical descriptions of the disease.

In 1645 Daniel Whistler described rickets in his dissertation, written when he was a 25 year old medical student at the University of Leiden, Holland. This volume, consisting of only 14 pages, was published (in Latin) in the same year. Despite the fact that it gives a good clinical description of the disease this work was not very influential: it was little read in Whistler's lifetime, nor thereafter even though he had it re-published in 1684, the year of his death (Clarke 1962).

Five years after Whistler wrote his dissertation, Francis Glisson, Regius Professor of Physic at the University of Cambridge, published a treatise on rickets. This Latin text was re-published in English in the following year. This was a much more substantial and mature work than that of Whistler. In addition to the clinical features, Glisson des-

Figure 46. The lower leg bones of an adult from Christ Church, Spitalfields, London, bowed as a result of childhood rickets. (Reproduced from Molleson & Cox 1993, fig. 3.9, with kind permission of Dr. T. Molleson).

cribed the morbid anatomy of the disease based upon his own post-mortem examinations, and he attempted to correlate the pathological findings with the clinical signs and symptoms (Dunn 1998). In contrast with Whistler's volume, Glisson's text was immediately popular and influential, and it was re-printed several times during the latter half of the 17th century (Clarke 1962).

Both Glisson and Whistler believed rickets to be a new disease in England which had first arisen during the early part of the 17th century, a view which was also held by other contemporary writers (discussion in Fildes 1986). The earliest reference to the disease by name occurs in 1630, and it is recorded in the London Bills of Mortality for the first time in 1634 (Clarke 1962). Although rickets is often regarded as the classic disease of the urban poor, this view is coloured by the late 19th century experience of the disease. When rickets was first recognised in the 17th and 18th centuries, it seems clear that it was not confined to urban areas. For example, Glisson himself noted that the disease was common in rural parts of western England (Gibbs 1994). Furthermore, he and other contemporary writers noted that it was the children of the more wealthy that tended to be affected (Fildes 1986; Kellett 1934; Dunn 1998). One possible reason for this

patterning in the occurrence of the disease by social class is that the wealthy tended to coddle their infants and children indoors (window panes effectively filter out ultra-violet rays, and indoor artificial lighting is of negligible health benefit), whereas the poor at this time were still bound to the land and hence retained the outdoor lifestyle of earlier generations (Gibbs 1994). The beginning of the transformation from an outdoor to an indoor lifestyle may have heralded the rise of rickets.

The frequency of rickets rose during the post-Mediaeval period, so that by the middle and later 19th century it was rife among the urban poor. This was demonstrated in, for example, a study of the social and geographical distibution of rickets in Britain carried out in the 1880s at the behest of the British Medical Association (Owen 1889). It was found to be common in large towns and cities, particularly those with heavy manufacturing industries. Its frequency was lower in smaller towns and it was rare in the country-side. In London, the data permitted analysis of rickets' distribution according to social class; it was rare in wealthy districts like Belgravia and Mayfair, but was common everywhere else. The prevalence of rickets reached its peak in the late 19th – early 20th centuries, when its frequency among infants and young children was over 90% in many industrial cities in Britain and northern Europe (Steinbock 1993).

Changes in general living conditions during the Industrial Revolution combined to limit severely the exposure to sunlight of many inhabitants of urban areas, particularly those of in the poorer social classes, and this was the factor responsible for the great epidemic of rickets seen at this time (Loomis 1970). In the teeming cities of the Industrial Revolution, sunlight failed to penetrate the narrow alleys which ran between the crowded tenements of the poor, and in any event air-pollution by industrial processes caused attenuation of solar ultra-violet, so that even when it did penetrate to ground-level it was of little potency (*ibid.*).

Seventeenth and eighteenth century physicians generally felt that rickets was a consequence of malnourishment, although other factors such as exposure to cold air, drinking cold fluids or eating "coarse foods" were also invoked (Hess 1930; Beck 1997). Another common fallacy at this time was that rickets was a manifestation of congenital syphilis (Hess 1930). However from about the end of the 19th century, lack of exposure of the skin to sunlight began to be appreciated as the true causal factor. Part of the evidence for this came from studies which had begun to look at the world-wide distribution of the disease. For example, in 1890 Theobald Palm, a Cumbrian General Practitioner, wrote to medical missionaries around the world concerning rickets and found that the disease was essentially confined to the large population centres of northern Europe, and there was evidence that European children suffering from rickets quickly recovered if moved to a tropical environment (Palm 1890). He deduced that the disease was caused by lack of exposure to sunlight. A number of other lines of evidence supported this. The frequency of rickets in northern Europe showed a seasonal pattern, it being more common in the sunless winter months (Schmorl 1909). Where rickets did occur outside Europe, it tended to be associated with cultural practices which limited the exposure of skin to sunlight (e.g. Hutchinson & Shah 1921).

As a result of his observations of the geographical distribution of rickets, Palm had recommended sun-baths for its treatment and prevention, but it was not until 1919 that there was experimental proof of the efficacy of ultraviolet rays, when Huldschinsky demonstrated the curative effects of irradiation with a mercury vapour lamp on several children with rickets. Two years later, work by Hess and Unger confirmed that natural sunlight had the same effect (discussion in Hess 1930).

At around the time that the value of ultra-violet light was becoming widely known, the efficacy of cod-liver oil also began to be conclusively demonstrated. The first indications of the value of cod-liver oil in cases of rickets emerged in continental Europe during the second and third decades of the 19th century. Some physicians then tried to encourage its use for rickets in Britain, but failed to make much headway against a sceptical medical establishment which favoured other remedies (such as administration of solutions containing phosphorus) and dismissed much of the evidence for the worth of cod-liver oil as anecdotal and circumstantial (Ihde 1975). However, in the early part of the 20th century, controlled experimental evidence (e.g. Hess & Unger 1917; Mellanby 1919; McCollum *et al.* 1922) indicating the specific value of cod-liver oil began to accumulate and eventually won over medical opinion, so that during the 1920s it became generally adopted as a remedy (Loomis 1970).

The active ingredient in cod-liver oil was of course, vitamin D, and this was discovered in the 1920s. In the following decade the actual isolation and characterisation of the compounds responsible for vitamin D activity was achieved (references in Boyle 1991 and Ihde 1975). It was at about this time that it became apparent that a small minority of cases of rickets were resistant to treatment with vitamin D. This paved the way for the discovery of the various forms vitamin D-resistant rickets associated with renal tubular disease (references in Mankin 1974b).

From the 1920s, the prevalence of rickets in Britain declined rapidly. The major factor was the use of cod-liver oil, both as treatment and prophylaxis. However the start of the vogue for sun-bathing and heliotherapy (Randle 1997), together with the gradual decline in air pollution in our cities also helped. By the 1940s rickets was almost unknown in Britain (Clements 1989). Since that time cod-liver oil has largely been replaced as a prophylactic by direct supplementation of foods (such as dried milk, margarines, breakfast cereals and baby foods) with vitamin D. Drops containing vitamin D also became available.

In the 1960s, however, a trickle of new cases of rickets began to appear in Britain. These were almost exclusively found in Asian immigrant communities, and included late rickets as well as the infantile form (Cooke *et al.* 1973; Swan & Cooke 1971). A number of factors have been implicated in the appearance of rickets among UK Asians, including lesser exposure to sunshine due to cultural practices, darker skin pigmentation meaning that longer exposure to the sun is needed for adequate vitamin D synthesis, and dietary factors (Clements 1989; Lawson *et al.* 1999). All are likely to play a part although many have emphasised the role of diet, in particular high intakes of cereal foods which appear to have an antagonistic effect on the action of vitamin D (Clements 1989). This serves to emphasise that when adequacy of exposure to sunlight is marginal, dietary factors may assume importance in the production of rickets. From an apparent peak in the early 1970s, rickets among UK Asians seems to have declined, with improved awareness of the problem and ready availability of vitamin supplements (Clements 1989).

THE ARCHAEOLOGY OF RICKETS

The palaeopathological study of rickets has a long history. As early as 1856, Dr E.P. Wilkins conducted an examination of the skeleton of Princess Elizabeth, daughter of Charles I, who died in 1650, and found clear signs of rickets (report reproduced in Burland 1918). Despite the fact that the condition has long been known about by palaeopathologists, few convincing cases from skeletal remains more than a few centuries old have been reported. To my knowledge, rickets has yet to be demonstrated in English prehistoric skeletal material. In continental Europe, a few reports of possible palaeopathological examples of prehistoric date have accumulated over the years (references in Grimm 1972). In general, however, these cases are unconvincing, although a Danish Neolithic specimen illustrated by Bennike (1985, 213–214) may represent a possible case, and a likely example of vitamin D-resistant rickets associated with renal tubular disease has recently been reported from Upper Palaeolithic Italy (Formicola 1995).

Given that simple exposure of the skin to natural light is sufficient to prevent rickets, it might be suggested that one would not expect to encounter it in prehistoric times, nor in other periods in which our ancestors enjoyed an outdoor, non-urban lifestyle. However this expectation may be misplaced. Ortner & Mays (1998) found eight cases of active rickets among infant and young child skeletons from the Mediaeval site at Wharram Percy, England. This was a rural farming community whose inhabitants would have led an outdoor lifestyle, and hence not a place where one might expect rickets to be encountered, yet this site has yielded a larger number of cases of the disease than any other published English site dating from before the rise of rickets in the Early Modern Age. Reasons why it was found at Wharram Percy were difficult to determine. However one hypothesis was that the cases encountered were infants and children who were otherwise sickly and for this reason were kept indoors in dark, smokey houses, and so developed rickets. This hypothesis is consistent with the observation that all these cases were individuals who had died in infancy with active rickets despite the fact that it is a non-lethal condition and with the finding that no individuals from this site who survived their early years showed any evidence of healed rickets. Whatever the reasons, the Wharram Percy results indicate that significant numbers of cases of rickets may be found in non-urban, agrarian communities, so there is no *a priori* reason to expect that it should be absent in prehistoric times.

It may be that biases in the skeletal record, and problems with palaeopathological diagnosis have led to under-enumeration of cases of infantile rickets. During many periods, the infant cohort is under-represented in British archaeological material, most probably due to differential burial practices. Secondly, although the deformities of healed rickets have long been known, the more subtle changes of active infantile disease have only recently been adequately collated for palaeopathologists (Ortner & Mays 1998), so infantile rickets may have been overlooked by earlier workers. Thirdly, although the changes described by Ortner & Mays (1998) in combination allow rickets to be recognised, many are not on their own diagnostic; this, given the fragmentary and incomplete nature of most archaeological infant skeletons, renders diagnosis of infantile rickets difficult in many assemblages. This is compounded by the fact that some of the changes, such as porosity and rugosity of the bone underlying the growth plates of the long-bones, require first class bone preservation for their recognition.

The earliest convincing cases of rickets of which I am aware in English material date from the late Saxon period (from Winchester (Ortner & Putschar 1985, 283) and Norwich (Stirland 1985)). The reported frequency of rickets in some large, published, late Saxon and Mediaeval assemblages is shown in Table 23. The frequency in the post-Mediaeval crypt assemblage from Christ Church Spitalfields, London is also shown.

During the Mediaeval period, there was significant air-

Table 23. *Frequency of rickets in some large collections of English human remains from Late Saxon/Mediaeval (10th–16th century AD) sites, and from Christ Church Spitalfields (18th–19th century AD)*

	With rickets	N	Reference
Carlisle Blackfriars	0	214	Henderson (1990)
Gloucester Blackfriars	1 (Ad)	129	Wiggins et al. (1993)
Guildford Blackfriars	0	113	Henderson (1984)
Hartlepool Greyfriars	0	150	Birkett and Marlow (1986)
Ipswich Blackfriars	0	250	Mays (1991)
Ipswich School Street	0	95	Mays (1989)
London, Merton Priory	0	74	Waldron (1985)
London, St Nicholas Shambles	0	234	White (1988)
North Elmham Park	0	206	Wells (1980)
Norwich Castle	4 (3J, 1Ad)	130	Stirland (1985)
Raunds	0	363	Powell (1996)
Taunton Priory	0	162	Rogers (1985)
Thetford Red Castle	0	85	Wells (1967)
Thetford St. Michaels	0	101	Stroud (1993)
Trowbridge Castle	0	293	Jenkins and Rogers (1993)
Wharram Percy	8 (all J)	687	Ortner and Mays (1998)
York Fishergate Gilbertine Priory	0	402	Stroud and Kemp (1993)
York Jewbury	0	476	Stroud et al. (1994)
York, St Helen's-on-the-Walls	2 (both J)	1041	Dawes (1980)
TOTAL MEDIEVAL/LATE SAXON	15 (13J, 2Ad)	5205	
POST-MEDIEVAL			
London, Christchurch Spitalfields	35 (20J, 15Ad)	968	Molleson and Cox (1993)

Note: N = total number of skeletons; J=sub-adult (aged 0 – 18 years); Ad=Adult (aged 18+).

Only sites where one can be reasonably confident rickets was looked for and scored reliably are included here.

born pollution in urban areas, particularly smoke from coal burning (Brimblecombe 1982). Nevertheless, the frequency of rickets in archaeological material of this date is very low (Table 23) and there is certainly no suggestion of a raised frequency in urban compared with rural groups. It would seem that during this period air pollution was as yet insufficient significantly to attenuate sunlight, and that even urban populations still enjoyed a largely outdoor lifestyle. The scarcity of Mediaeval and earlier cases is consistent with the views expressed by Glisson and others in the 17th century, that rickets had not been a problem for earlier generations. However it is clear from the archaeological evidence that, contrary to the beliefs of 17th century physicians, rickets was not in fact a completely new disease in England when they first recognised it.

Rickets is more than ten times as frequent at Spitalfields than in the Mediaeval/late Saxon groups listed in Table 23. In addition, Spitalfields is the only site to produce significant numbers of cases of healed rickets in adult skeletons. This may indicate that more protracted and severe disease was present here, causing permanent stigmata to remain on the bones. The elevated rate and greater severity of rickets at Spitalfields compared with earlier sites probably reflects a variety of factors.

Those interred in the Spitalfields crypt were born between 1646 and 1844. At this time London was a large urban centre suffering significant air-born pollution (Molleson & Cox 1993). Contemporary writers affirm that this was severe enough significantly to attenuate natural light (Brimblecombe 1982). The period of use of the crypt for burial spans part of the "Little Ice Age", with its generally lowered temperatures and increased precipitation. Gibbs (1994) speculates that this climatic dip may have contributed in some small way to the rise of rickets early in the post-Mediaeval period. Some of the Spitalfields coffins bore metal plates inscribed with the name of the occupant and his or her age and date of death. Of the skeletons of individuals with rickets whose year of birth could be ascertained from the information on their coffin plates, most were born in years where the following winter was particularly severe (Molleson & Cox 1993, 118). Many of those interred in the crypt came from fairly well-to-do families; perhaps they tended to keep their young offspring indoors in well-heated homes, especially in inclement weather.

It has been noted (Kellett 1934; Gibbs 1994) that a group who would have been particularly at risk from rickets was home-based textile workers. Whole families toiled long hours at home, and their infants and young children would have been kept indoors most of the time (*ibid.*). Kellett suggests that the rise of the home-based textile industry in the earlier post-Mediaeval period may have been a factor in the appearance of rickets at this time. This hypothesis would appear to be consistent with aspects of the distribution of rickets noted by 17th century physicians. For example, it was first recorded, according to Glisson, in the west of England, which Kellett points out was the most important textile producing area. Glisson also emphasised that here it was not among the children of 'the workless and the vagabonds' that the disease first arose, but among the offspring of the industrious and the somewhat better off (*ibid.*). Occupations are known for some of those buried at Spitalfields. The most frequent occupations listed (40%) are in the silk industry (Molleson & Cox 1993, 159). Although some of these were master weavers (who probably did little weaving once their 7–12 year apprenticeship was served), others were journeyman weavers; they and their families would have worked long hours indoors (*op. cit.* 166). In summary, it seems likely that the raised level of rickets at Spitalfields reflects a combination of occupational and climatic factors, and perhaps increasing industrial pollution.

CONCLUSIONS

More than 35 years ago, that pioneering palaeopathologist, Calvin Wells, emphasised that the pattern of disease which affects a population is never a matter of chance, but rather it is intimately bound up with their environment and general way of life (Wells 1964, 17). One could not wish for a better illustration of the truth of this contention than the history of rickets. It seems that the rise of rickets in 17th century England may have been associated with the start of a more indoor lifestyle at least for some sectors of society. Changes in labour practices meant that significant numbers of people (such as home-based textile workers and their families) began to spend long hours indoors. In addition, the general climatic deterioration which was underway at about this time may have helped encourage richer members of society to keep their infants inside.

In the later 19th century, there was an explosion in cases of rickets, together with a change in its social and geographical distribution so that it became primarily a disease of the poor in towns and cities. There is little doubt that the rise of the disease at this time reflected growing urbanisation and the massive increase in the involvement of the lower social classes in manufacturing industry. The poor, at least in urban areas, no longer had the outdoor lifestyle which the lower social classes, tied to the land, had pursued before. In addition, the pollution from the very industrial processes which the labour of the poor helped sustain, contributed to the suffering of their infants and children from rickets, as did their living conditions in tenements situated among narrow, dark alleyways in the hearts of large urban areas. Finally, the conquest of rickets in the first half of the 20th century is an early illustration of the power of increased scientific and medical knowledge to transform the disease experience of the general population.

So what palaeopathological work remains to be done in the study of rickets in past populations in England? The potential for finding cases of rickets (more especially active infantile disease rather than the healed form) in prehistoric times should not be under-estimated. Recent work has demonstrated the existence of the disease in the past in non-urban, agrarian communities. The palaeopathological signs of rickets in infants have until recently not been widely appreciated, so re-examination of existing skeletal collections may reveal further cases, and we should also be on the look-out for them when studying newly excavated material. In this way, palaeopathological investigation may help us extend our knowledge of the history of rickets back into the very remote past.

The majority of palaeopathological cases will, however, inevitably continue to come from post-Mediaeval assemblages. Given the richness of the written record, the cynic could be forgiven for questioning the need for palaeopathological study of the disease in this period. However we should not forget that documentary and archaeological evidence each suffer from their own shortcomings and biases; only by integrating the two sources will the best understanding of the history of disease be achieved. Skeletal evidence may help shed light upon some important questions concerning the history of rickets in the post-Mediaeval age, particularly where the written evidence is weak or ambiguous. For example, it would be interesting to determine whether the social and geographical patterning claimed by physicians for rickets when they first noted it in the 17th century can be substantiated archaeologically. It would also be useful to have an independent measure of the importance of the disease in the later 17th and 18th centuries, as the written evidence pertaining to these periods appears rather contradictory. A number of sources give the impression of a decline in the disease in the later part of the 17th century so that it became rare by the 18th century; others give the impression that the frequency continued to rise inexorably during this period so that it was very frequent in the 18th century (Kellett 1934; Gibbs 1994; Hess 1930). Whether these apparent contradictions reflect geographical or short-term temporal variations in the prevalence of the disease, or simply the inadequacy of the sources is unclear. Palaeopathological analysis has the potential to shed additional light on this, however because existing large post-Mediaeval skeletal collections are few, more are needed in order to fulfil this potential. Given the rapidity of social and technological change during the post-Mediaeval period, well-dated material is vital. The ideal is coffin-plated burials where dates of birth and death are known for individuals, but failing this assemblages dated to within tight limits are required. Given the pace of modern building development, especially in urban areas, and the fact that the value of post-Mediaeval human remains has become more widely appreciated within archaeology, it is likely that more post-Mediaeval assemblages will become available for study. It remains for us as osteologists to make the most of such research opportunities when they do arise.

References

Aufderheide, A.C. & Rodriguez-Martin, C. 1998. *The Cambridge Encyclopaedia of Human Palaeopathology.* Cambridge: Cambridge University Press.

Beck, S. 1997. Rickets: Where the Sun Doesn't Shine, pp. 130–135 in Kiple, K.F. (ed.) *Plague, Pox & Pestilence: Disease in History.* London: Weidenfeld & Nicolson.

Bennike, P. 1985. *Palaeopathology of Danish Skeletons.* Copenhagen: Akademisk Forlag.

Birkett, D.A. & Marlow, M. 1986. The Human Burials and Report on the Human Teeth. In (Daniels, R.) The Excavation of the Church of the Franciscans, Hartlepool, Cleveland. *The Archaeological Journal* **143**, 260–304.

Boyle, I.T. 1991. Bones for the Future. *Acta Paediatrica Scandinavica,* Supplement **373**, 58–65.

Brimblecombe, P. 1982. Early Urban Climate and Atmosphere, pp. 10–25 in Hall, A.R. & Kenward, H.K. (eds) *Environmental Archaeology in the Urban Context.* CBA Research Report No. **43**, London: Council for British Archaeology.

Burland, C. 1918. An Historical Case of Rickets. *The Practitioner* **100**, 391–5.

Clarke, E. 1962. Whistler and Glisson on Rickets. *Bulletin of the History of Medicine* **36**, 45–61.

Clements, M.R. 1989. The Problem of Rickets in UK Asians. *Journal of Human Nutrition & Dietetics* **2**, 105–16.

Cone, T.E. 1980. A Rachitic Infant Painted by Burgkmair 136 Years Before Dr Whistler Described Rickets. *Clinical Paediatrics* **19**, 194.

Cooke, W.T., Swan, C.H.J., Asquith, P., Melikian, V. & McFeely, W.E. 1973. Serum Alkaline Phosphatase and Rickets in Urban Schoolchildren. *British Medical Journal* **1**, 324–7.

Dawes, J.D. 1980. The Human Bones, pp 19–120 in Dawes, J.D. & Magilton, J.R. (eds) *The Cemetery of St Helen-on-the-Walls, Aldwark.* The Archaeology of York **12/1**. York: York Archaeological Trust.

Dunn, P.M. 1998. Francis Glisson (1597-1677) and the "Discovery" of Rickets. *Archives of Disease in Childhood* **78**, F154–F155.

Fildes, V. 1986. The English Disease: Infantile Rickets and Scurvy in Pre-Industrial England, pp. 121–34 in Cule, J. & Turner, T. (eds) *Child Care Through the Centuries.* Cardiff: British Society for the History of Medicine.

Foote, J.A. 1927. Evidence of Rickets Prior to 1650. *American Journal of Diseases of Children* **34**, 443–52.

Formicola, V. 1995. X-Linked Hypophosphatemic Rickets: A Probable Upper Palaeolithic Case. *American Journal of Physical Anthropology* **98**, 403–9.

Gibbs, D. 1994. Rickets and the Crippled Child: An Historical Perspective. *Journal of the Royal Society of Medicine* **87**, 729–32.

Grimm, H. 1972. Über Rachitis und Rachitis-Verdachtsfälle im ur- und frühgeschichtlichen Material. *Zeitschrift für die Gesamte Hygiene und ihre Grenzgebiete* **18**, 451–5.

Henderson, J. 1984. The Human Remains, pp. 58–71 in Poulton, R. & Woods, H. (eds) *Excavations on the Site of the Dominican Friary at Guildford in 1974 and 1978.* Research Volume of the Surrey Archaeological Society, No. 9. Guildford: Surrey Archaeological Society.

Henderson, J. 1990. The Human Remains (1983–4), pp. 330–55 in McCarthy, M.R. (ed.) *A Roman, Anglian and Mediaeval Site at Blackfriars Street.* Cumberland and Westmoreland Antiquarian and Archaeological Society Research Series No. 4. Kendal: Cumberland and Westmoreland Antiquarian and Archaeological Society.

Henry, H.L. & Norman, A.W. 1992. Metabolism of Vitamin D, pp. 149–62 in Coe, F.L. & Favus, M.J. (eds) *Disorders of Bone and Mineral Metabolism.* New York: Raven Press.

Hess, A.F. 1930. *Rickets, Including Osteomalacia and Tetany*. London: Kimpton.

Hess, A.F. & Unger, L.J. 1917. Prophylactic Therapy for Rickets in a Negro Community. *Journal of the American Medical Association* 69, 1583–1586.

Hutchinson, H.S. & Shah, S.J. 1921. The Aetiology of Rickets Early and Late. *Quarterly Journal of Medicine* 15, 167–94.

Ihde, A.J. 1975. Studies on the History of Rickets II. The Roles of Cod Liver Oil and Light. *Pharmacy in History* 17, 13–20.

Jackson, R. 1988. *Doctors and Diseases in the Roman Empire*. London: British Museum Press.

Jenkins, V. & Rogers, J. 1993. Human Bone, pp 120–7 in Graham, A.H. & Davies, S.M. (eds) *Excavations at Trowbridge, Wiltshire, 1977 and 1986–1988*. Wessex Archaeology Report No. 2. Salisbury: Trust for Wessex Archaeology.

Kellett, C.E. 1934. Glissonian Rickets. *Archives of Disease in Childhood* 9, 233–44.

Lawson, M., Thomas, M. & Hardiman, A. 1999. Dietary and Lifestyle Factors Affecting Plasma Vitamin D Levels in Asian Children Living in England. *European Journal of Clinical Nutrition* 53, 268–72.

Lee, T. 1967. Historical Notes on Some Vitamin Deficiency Diseases in China, pp. 417–422 in Brothwell, D.R. & Sandison, A.T. (eds) *Diseases in Antiquity*. Springfield: Charles C. Thomas.

Loomis, W.F. 1970. Rickets. *Scientific American* 223, 77–91.

Mankin, H. 1974a. Rickets, Osteomalacia and Renal Osteodystrophy. Part I. Journal of Bone and Joint Surgery 56A, 101–28.

Mankin, H. 1974b. Rickets, Osteomalacia and Renal Osteodystrophy. Part II. *Journal of Bone and Joint Surgery* 56A, 352–386.

Mays, S.A. 1989. *The Anglo-Saxon Human Bone From School Street, Ipswich, Suffolk*. Ancient Monuments Laboratory Report 115/89. London: English Heritage.

Mays, S.A. 1991. *The Mediaeval Burials From the Blackfriars Friary, School Street, Ipswich, Suffolk (Excavated 1983–85)*. Ancient Monuments Laboratory Report 16/91. London : English Heritage.

McCollum, E.V., Simmonds, N., Becker, J.E. & Shipley, P.G. 1922. Studies on Experimental Rickets. XXI An Experimental Demonstration of the Existence of a Vitamin Which Promotes Calcium Deposition. *Journal of Biological Chemistry* 53, 293–312.

Mellanby, E. 1919. An Experimental Investigation of Rickets. *The Lancet* 1, 407–12.

Molleson, T. & Cox, M. 1993. *The Spitalfields Project. Volume 2: The Anthropology*. CBA Research Report No. 86. York: Council for British Archaeology.

Ortner, D.J. & Mays, S. 1998. Dry-Bone Manifestations of Rickets in Infancy and Early Childhood. *International Journal of Osteoarchaeology* 8, 45–55.

Ortner, D.J. & Putschar W.G.J. 1985. *The Identification of Pathological Conditions in Human Skeletal Remains*. Washington: Smithsonian Institution Press.

Owen, I. 1889. Geographical Distribution of Rickets, Acute and Subacute Rheumatism, Chorea, Cancer and Urinary Calculus in the British Islands. *British Medical Journal* 1, 113–16.

Palm, T. 1890. Geographical Distribution and Aetiology of Rickets. *The Practitioner* 4, 270–342.

Powell, F. 1996. The Human Remains, pp. 113–24 in Boddington, A. (ed.) *Raunds Furnells*. English Heritage Archaeological Report No. 7. London: English Heritage.

Randle, H.W. 1997. Suntanning: Differences in Perception Throughout History. *Mayo Clinic Proceedings* 72, 461–6.

Resnick, D. & Niwayama, G. 1988. *Diagnosis of Bone and Joint Disorders* (2nd edition). London: W.B. Saunders.

Rogers, J. 1985. Skeletons From the Lay Cemetery at Taunton Priory, pp. 194–9 in Leach, P. (ed.) *The Archaeology of Taunton: Excavations and Fieldwork to 1980*. Western Archaeological Trust Excavation Monograph No. 8. Taunton: Western Archaeological Trust.

Schmorl, G. 1909. Die Pathologische Anatomie der Rachtischen Knochenerkrankung mit Besonder Berücksichtingung ihre Histologie und Pathogenese. *Ergebnisse der Inneren Medizin und Kinderheilkunde* 4, 403–454.

Steinbock, R.T. 1976. *Palaeopathological Diagnosis and Interpretation*. Springfield: Charles C. Thomas.

Steinbock, R.T. 1993. Rickets and Osteomalacia, pp. 978–80 in Kiple, K.F. (ed.) *The Cambridge World History of Human Disease*. Cambridge: Cambridge University Press.

Stirland, A. 1985. The Human Bones, pp. 49–57 in Ayers, B. (ed.) *Excavations Within the North-East Bailey of Norwich Castle, 1979*. East Anglian Archaeology No. 28. Gressenhall: Norfolk Museums Service.

Stroud, G. 1993. Human Skeletal Material, pp. 168–176 in Dallas, C. (ed.) *Excavations at Thetford by B.K. Davison Between 1964 and 1970*. East Anglian Archaeology No. 62. Gressenhall: Norfolk Museums Sevice.

Stroud, G., Brothwell, D.R., Brown, S., Watson, P. & Dobney, K. 1994. The Population, pp. 424–521 in Lilley, J.M., Stroud, G., Brothwell, D.R. & Williamson, M.H. (eds) *The Jewish Burial Ground at Jewbury*. The Archaeology of York 12/3. York: York Archaeological Trust.

Stroud, G. & Kemp, R. 1993. *Cemeteries at St Andrew, Fishergate*. The Archaeology of York 12/2. York: York Archaeological Trust.

Stuart-Macadam, P. 1988. Rickets as an Interpretive Tool. *Journal of Palaeopathology* 2, 33–42.

Stuart-Macadam, P., Glencross, B. & Kricun, M. 1998. Traumatic Bowing Deformities in Tubular Bones. *International Journal of Osteoarchaeology* 8, 252–62.

Swan, C.H.J. & Cooke, W.T. 1971. Nutritional Osteomalacia in Immigrants in an Urban Community. *Lancet* 1, 456–9.

Waldron, T. 1985. *A Report on the Human Bones From Merton Priory*. Ancient Monuments Laboratory Report 4483. London: English Heritage.

Wells, C. 1964. *Bones, Bodies and Diseases*. London: Thames & Hudson.

Wells, C. 1967. Report on the Human Skeletons From Red Castle, Thetford. *Norfolk Archaeology* 34, 155–86.

Wells, C. 1980. The Human Bones, pp. 247–374 in Wade-Martins, P. (ed.) *Excavations at North Elmham Park, 1967–72*. East Anglian Archaeology No. 9, Vol. II. Gressenhall: Norfolk Museums Service.

White, W. 1988. The Cemetery of St Nicholas Shambles, London. London: London and Middlesex Archaeology Society.

Wiggins, R., Boyleston, A. & Roberts, C. 1993. *Report on the Human Skeletal Remains From Blackfriars, Gloucester*. Report on File at the Calvin Wells Laboratory, University of Bradford.

17. A comparison of health in past rural, urban and industrial England

Mary Lewis

Investigations into the health of past populations making the transition from a hunter-gatherer to an agricultural subsistence have received much attention in biological anthropology. The majority of these studies suggest that sedentism and reliance on a less diverse food supply was detrimental to the health of early farmers. Recent studies have now begun to evaluate and compare the health status of past populations living in the rural, urban and industrial centres of Europe or North America, using human skeletal remains. It is likely that the inhabitants of these environments would have been exposed to a diverse range of pathogens, leading to contrasting patterns of morbidity and mortality. This paper discusses the environmental and cultural factors of rural, urban and industrial communities and uses documentary, environmental and skeletal evidence to assess the impact of these environments on the health of past populations in medieval and post-medieval England.

Keywords: Urban-rural, host-pathogen relationship, skeletal remains, environmental evidence, medieval and post-medieval England.

INTRODUCTION

The interaction of humans with their environment has been an issue in the anthropological and medical literature for many decades. More recently, archaeologists have begun to examine how people from past societies adapted to changing socio-economic circumstances and the impact these changes had on their surroundings and, subsequently, their health. These studies use a '*biocultural approach*' which combines biological and cultural data to investigate how cultural systems affect disease processes, and to measure the influence of disease on cultural change (Armelagos 1990; Fenner 1971; Larsen 1997).

Many factors within the environment influence our exposure and resistance to pathogens: from our climate, technology, water supply and large-scale disposal of waste, to individual domestic arrangements for food storage and preparation, sewage disposal and hygiene (Luckin 1980). In addition, our age, sex, genetic disposition and previous exposure to a disease, influence whether we recover from an infection, die during its acute stages, or survive long enough for the disease to become chronic or long-term. Cockburn (1977) has illustrated a change in this host-pathogen relationship through time as a result of shifting socio-economic circumstances. For example, Cockburn argued that in small hunter-gatherer communities the success of a pathogen relied on its ability to survive until new hosts appeared, causing chronic disease without it leading to death. More fatal (acute) diseases, such as measles, move rapidly through their hosts and rely on a large renewable population to survive. Hence, they only began to flourish with the establishment of larger agricultural and urban communities (Cockburn 1971).

Investigations into the health of past populations making the transition from a hunter-gatherer to an agricultural subsistence have been extensively studied in biological anthropology. The majority of these studies come from North America and suggest that sedentism and a less diverse food supply affected the health of early agriculturalists (Cohen and Armelagos 1984; Gilbert and Mielke 1985; Johansson and Horowitz 1986; Swedlund and Armelagos 1990). However, studies of the effects of urbanisation and industrialisation of past populations in Europe or North America, have only recently begun to be addressed. It is plausible that differences in housing, diet, sanitation, population density and trade relations would have exposed the inhabitants to a diverse range of environmental pathogens, leading to contrasting patterns of morbidity and mortality in urban and rural settlements.

DISEASE IN THE URBAN-RURAL ENVIRONMENT

Here, *rural* communities are understood to have small population numbers with the inhabitants being mainly involved in agricultural activities (Williams and Galley 1995). An *urban* settlement is defined as a large, dense population with a distinct and diverse range of economic functions, with established administration, politics and religion (Ottaway 1992). An *industrial* community is characterised as a large settlement where the majority of the population is engaged in mass-producing goods for trade.

The Rural Environment

Agricultural intensification in the Neolithic period had a detrimental effect on human health in many societies throughout the world (Cohen and Armelagos 1984). Although the transition from a hunter-gatherer to an agricultural subsistence removed some of the potential threats to human health, such as injury during hunting, or exposure to zoonoses during the butchery of wild animals, it led to the introduction of new health hazards (Boyden 1972). The development of agriculture meant people were dependent on a limited and less varied food supply, and crop failure could lead to pestilence and famine. Sedentism led to greater local environmental contamination, where permanent housing and attachment to land meant that people were no longer free to leave an area before pathogens could become established. An increase in population size resulted in closer contact with other humans and livestock, making the agricultural settlement an ideal place for disease transmission, as infections spread from person-to-person, or animal-to-person, via the respiratory tract (Cohen 1989; Manchester 1992). The domesticated cow, pig, sheep, cat and dog were accompanied by the rat, mouse, tick and flea, which acted as vectors for disease (Cockburn 1971). This closer contact of humans with livestock provided the opportunity for zoonoses to adapt to a human host and new diseases began to emerge (*ibid.*). For example, tuberculosis probably developed from the bovine form of the disease, transmitted through ingestion of infected meat and milk (Roberts and Manchester 1995). Contact with the milk, meat, skin and hair of domestic animals would also have exposed farmers to anthrax and

brucellosis (Armelagos 1990). Respiratory infections would have been spread in the confines of houses: during the winter wood and, later, coal fires would have exposed the inhabitants to the detrimental affects of smoke. Cultivation of fresh tracts of land for agricultural exploitation exposed people to new vectors and their pathogens. For example, mosquitoes would have had little contact with humans before deforestation and swamp drainage, which allowed for the transmission of yellow fever, dengue, scrub typhus and malaria (Cohen 1989; McGrath 1992). Contact with the soil exposed people to fungal diseases such as those caused by *Aspergillus fumigatus*, and the inhalation of silica-containing dust could cause silicosis, another persistent and damaging lung disease. The spreading of faeces on the land increased contact with pathogens, directly, or indirectly through the plants they fertilised, exposing the early farmers to typhoid, roundworm, hookworm and amoebic dysentery (Cockburn 1971).

The Urban Environment

After the decline of urban settlements in the Romano-British Period, urban areas did not become fully re-established in England until the eleventh century. Pre-industrial urban centres relied on the rural hinterland to provide the food for the increasing population of specialists inhabiting the urban areas (Storey 1992). Exploration and expansion into previously unexplored regions introduced new diseases to unprotected hosts, and an increase in trade and migration of people from other areas provided the means for new diseases to be introduced to the community. This constant supply of fresh hosts, in the form of new-borns and immigrants, provided the ideal breeding ground for infection. Respiratory and gastrointestinal infections, cholera, typhus, typhoid, pneumonic plague, measles and smallpox flourished in the unsanitary conditions where food, milk and the water supply were liable to contamination (Mims 1980; Woods and Woodward 1984). Population dependent diseases such as tuberculosis began to thrive with a ready accessibility to new hosts in overcrowded living quarters. As more hosts became immune to disease, infections became endemic (McGrath 1992). This change in the pattern of disease in the medieval period has been illustrated in the documentary evidence and skeletal material, where diseases such as leprosy, tuberculosis and treponematosis became more prevalent (Manchester 1992). Hudson (1965) argues that cultural and social changes in the urban environment resulted in increased sexual promiscuity and prostitution, which contributed to the development of the venereal form of treponemal disease, syphilis.

The Industrial Environment

The Industrial Revolution in the eighteenth century was characterised by rapid technological change, resulting in the establishment of new urban centres, population growth, rural-urban migration and subsequent rural depopulation (Storey 1992). Fully industrial centres were larger and more dependent on external food supplies and industrial advance resulted in an increase in environmental pollution. By the 1820s industrialisation had reached its peak and people complained about the effect of the urban and industrial environment on their health. There were concerns over the contamination of food and water supplies, which resulted in outbreaks of diseases such as cholera (Luckin 1980; Pelling 1983–4). In addition, the age of onset of menstruation increased, mortality rates rose (Williams and Galley 1995), children suffered from growth retardation (Meredith 1982) as rickets and scurvy became prevalent in the polluted industrial environment (Fildes 1986) and smallpox and measles were fatal childhood illnesses. Noise pollution, overcrowding, polluted air and the production of toxic chemicals would all have had an impact on both the psychological and physiological health of the individuals living in these rapidly expanding societies (Ekblad 1993). The proximity of rural settlements to urbanising centres, and the development of rural industry also had an effect on the health of rural dwellers as these areas became overcrowded as a result of immigration and the inhabitants were exposed to disease from neighbouring cities (King 1997).

ENVIRONMENTAL AND DOCUMENTARY EVIDENCE OF HEALTH

In the medieval period, statements about the nature of rural and urban lifestyles painted rural life as noble and natural with strong family values, compared to the degenerate life in the urban areas, full of vice, indulgence, disorder and debilitating conditions (Ericksen 1954). However, accounts about the real standard of living and health in rural areas are lacking. Some elements of the urban and rural environment were shared; rural areas provided urban centres with food, and crop failure would affect both groups. Despite having different microclimates, both areas experienced the same atmospheric conditions and were equally vulnerable to natural disasters. The interaction between urban and rural populations also provided the opportunity for similar diseases to become endemic.

Hygiene

Much of the documentary evidence for the management of English medieval towns comes from Winchester and London, where records of public concern for the odour and putrefaction of rubbish often coincided with outbreaks of the plague or a Royal visit. Piles of refuse, or 'muck piles', in the streets would have harboured pathogenic organisms and disease vectors such as lice, ticks, fleas and their hosts. The byways of towns and cities were notoriously filled with sewage (Cooper 1913) and cattle, goats and pigs were left to roam wild and were occasionally

reported to attack and injure small children (Keene 1982). Butchers and fishmongers regularly prepared their meat in the streets and blood was documented to flow down the narrow alleys (Sabine 1933). The level of personal hygiene and accumulation of domestic rubbish would have depended on individual households but, as Erasmus, the Dutch Christian humanist suggested, medieval English floors left a lot to be desired: "*...the bottom layer is left undisturbed, sometimes for 20 years, harbouring expectorations, vomitings, the leakages of dogs and men, ale-droppings, scraps of fish and other abominations not fit to be mentioned.*" (Keene 1982, 27).

Some researchers have taken official edicts on public health as evidence that medieval cities were not filthy, and that images of medieval 'squalor' were the creation of Victorian propaganda, designed to take attention away from the appalling conditions of the industrial cities (Lord 1997; Thorndike 1928). Complaints about the stench of open sewers, city cleaning and regulations controlling the dumping of butchers' offal, could be seen as evidence that medieval authorities were aware of the dangers that poor sanitation posed to the inhabitants. Butchers and fishmongers were given their own quarters of the city, principle streets were paved, and night carts removed sewage (Platt 1975). During the plague years, dogs and cats were killed and the streets cleaned, suggesting that the link between filth and disease was understood in medieval towns (Barnet 1968). However, documentary evidence from medieval London show that regulations controlling the disposal of waste permitted refuse to be dumped in the River Thames (Sabine 1933). In 1383, law also permitted the building of public and private latrines over streams, which acted as open sewers, polluted the water supply and carried filth away from the city (Sabine 1934).

Environmental evidence from archaeological sites, used to reconstruct the urban-rural conditions from insect and pollen remains is problematic, as confounding evidence may be carried onto a site on shoes, clothing, or in a slaughtered animal's gut (Green 1982; Kenward 1982). Nevertheless, Rackham (1982) found a higher concentration of pests and edible rodent species in the urban environment compared to the rural, including black and brown rats, domesticated ferrets, housemice, hares, rabbits and hedgehogs, and the remains of scavenging birds, which suggests the exposure of rubbish. At Blackfriargate in Hull, thirteenth and fourteenth century floor levels revealed parasites in rat and mice droppings (Schofield and Vince 1994). Documents related to the employment of rat-catchers in 1356 in Hull suggest the extent of the vermin problem (Armitage 1985). The analysis of a medieval cesspit from Worcester revealed that people were infected with both *Trichuris trichiura* (whipworm) and *Ascaris lumbricoides* (roundworm) (Greig 1981). The presence of both the human and pig species of whipworm in these cesspits suggests that humans may have also contracted the parasite from eating infected meat (Jones 1982). Not surprisingly, 'worms' were often cited as a cause of death in medieval children (Stone 1977), and parasitic infestation would have led to growth retardation and nutritional deficiencies (McGarvey 1998).

Diet

A balanced diet is essential in order to maintain a healthy immune system and prevent disease, and the synergistic effects of nutrition and infection are well-documented (Scrimshaw *et al.* 1959). Manual labour meant that the nutritional requirements of the rural inhabitants were greater than those living in the urban environment (Bogin 1988). However, although estates provided rations for their tenants, the need to produce a surplus to feed the growing urban population may have meant them going without (Schofield and Vince 1994). Nevertheless, the introduction of the mouldboard plough and three field crop rotation system in the seventh century had meant that more land could be cultivated and a wider variety of foods grown; and that animals could be reared on the fallow land (Tannahill 1973). This subsequent change in diet has been linked to increased longevity of women during the medieval period (Herlihy 1975), and Bullough and Campbell (1980) argue that the new availability of meat and therefore iron, led to a decrease in deaths in childbirth.

Medieval town populations were able to store food and had more variety in their diet due to trade, including access to imported meat and fish. However, overcrowding resulted in the division of land and the loss of many gardens (Tannahill 1973). The poor could no longer rely on their own plots to grow food, and became increasingly dependent on the cost and quality of the food provided by the rural hinterlands (Schofield and Vince 1994).

Climate

Between the tenth and thirteenth centuries, Northern Europe, the North Atlantic, Greenland and Iceland experienced a prolonged interval of warmth known as the *Medieval Warm Epoch* (AD 1000–1200) (Hughes and Diaz 1994). This period was characterised by warm springs and dry summers, allowing vineyards to be maintained in Britain (Goudie 1983). By the mid-fourteenth century, cold springs and wet summers predominated, and Britain entered another climatic period known as the *Little Ice Age* (AD 1400–1700) (Brimblecombe 1982). The Little Ice Age was characterised by extremes of weather causing an increase in storms and fluctuations in summer rainfall. Severe frosts, flooding and hailstorms caused serious loss of life and damage to property (Ingram *et al.* 1981). Lamb (1981) estimated that between the thirteenth and seventeenth centuries the growing season was shortened and crop production was reduced. The climate encouraged mould and rust to develop on grains and legumes, resulting in destruction of crops, increased grain prices, and human and animal diseases.

Landers and Mouzas (1988) and Galloway (1985) attribute variations in the pattern of disease in summer and winter in seventeenth and eighteenth century London to climatic changes associated with the Little Ice Age, which affected the life cycle of pathogens and left the population short of food. At Christ Church Spitalfields in London, Molleson and Cox (1993) found an association between severe winters and rickets, caused by a lack of sunlight.

Today, industrial areas are known to generate their own micro-climates, or *urban heat islands*, where furnaces, fires, population density, air pollution and trapped heat from high-rise buildings, generate excess heat. It has been estimated that medieval cities may have experienced temperatures of up to 4°C above the surrounding area (Brimblecombe 1982). Closer to the ground, artificial structures create an *urban canopy* resulting in an even greater increase in temperature. Howard (1833) was one of the first to notice London's '*artificial excess of heat*' (cited in Brimblecombe 1982, 14).

Air Pollution

As early as 1257, documents from the Priory of Dunstable mention the pollution of urban air, and between 1285 and 1310 air pollution levels were sufficient to warrant four commissions to investigate the problem (Brimblecombe 1975). The complaints about poor air quality in cities coincided with a change in fuel. Before the thirteenth century, charcoal, a relatively smokeless fuel, was in common use. However, owing to fuel pressures created by the Little Ice Age and increasing industrialisation, timber became scarce and was soon replaced by the introduction of cheaper more efficient *sea-coal* (Brimblecombe 1978). Coal was initially adopted by limeburners and blacksmiths, but by the sixteenth century was widely accepted as a domestic fuel (Brimblecombe 1982). Air pollution in the urban centres rose steadily until concern for public safety reached its height in 1661 when John Evelyn published '*Fumifugium*' (Brimblecombe and Ogden 1977). Increased levels of fog were responsible for a greater prevalence of diseases such as rickets (Fildes 1986; Foote 1927) and air pollution was blamed for high death rates in the city (Brimblecombe 1977).

Modern studies of rural areas have shown that internal air pollution, caused by slow cooking using unprocessed biomass fuels (crop residues, dung and wood) produce levels of air pollution of the same magnitude as industrialised countries (Albalak 1997). Evans and Jacobs (1982) argue that air pollution can have both physiological and psychological effects on those exposed to it. High levels of pollution have been linked to respiratory diseases such as asthma, bronchitis and eye irritations, which may lead to aggression, changes in activity patterns, decreased productivity, and memory and sensory loss. However, some research has shown that humans have the ability to adapt eventually to pollution after sustained exposure (Evans and Jacobs 1982).

Mortality

Much of the evidence for past urban and rural mortality comes from eighteenth and nineteenth century documents, concerned with social reforms and combating high levels of infant deaths in the cities. In 1900, a discrepancy in the life expectancy of urban and rural dwellers was apparent in England. In the rural areas, the average life expectancy at birth was around 55 years of age as opposed to 45 years in the towns (Woods and Woodward 1984). John Graunt (1662) was the first to study extensively the levels of infant and child mortality in London, using data from 1517–1519 (cited in Lancaster, 1990). He found that in non-plague years, 36% of urban children under six years of age could be expected to die, and urban deaths exceeded rural ones.

Williams and Galley (1995) examined infant mortality rates in urban and rural areas during the 1800s. They reported that, although there were lower levels of mortality in the rural areas, the peaks and troughs followed a similar pattern in both the towns and villages. However, the causes of infant mortality were slightly different. A report for 1891 found that the overall risk of death for infants born and reared in towns was more than double the rural picture. The majority of urban deaths were caused by diarrhoeal diseases, which killed eight times more in the urban area (39.61%) than in the rural (4.81%), and crowd diseases such as measles and scarlet fever were three times more prevalent, with tubercular diseases being double that of the rural areas (Williams and Galley 1995). Sanitation improvements in towns after the 1900s resulted in a reversal in urban-rural infant and child mortality rates, with rural areas now showing the highest rates of mortality (Bogin 1988).

Growth and Maturation

Studies of the differences in height between children in towns and villages have been carried out since the 1870s. During this period it was consistently found that the height of rural children surpassed that of their urban peers (Meredith 1982). For example in 1892, Schmidt (cited in Meredith 1982) studied the growth of German children and found that the urban group were on average 1.8 cm shorter than their rural peers. However, by the 1950s this situation had changed, and in Meredith's (1982) survey of studies carried out between 1950 and 1980, urban children between the ages of 7–10 years exceeded the height of rural children of the same age by 2.5 cm, and in weight by 1.1 kgs. This reversal in the trend is often attributed to improvements in sanitation, nutrition and health care in the cities after the 1900s (Bogin 1988).

Modern studies of growth in developing countries are complicated by numerous variables, (including different socio-economic status, genetic patterns, migration, altitude and feeding practices), that are difficult to control for and add confusion to the picture; particularly in the past, where many of these factors are impossible to account for. In fact, most studies have shown that poverty has a greater effect on growth, regardless of whether a person came from an urban and rural environment (Tanner and Eveleth 1976). For example, in nineteenth century London, male children from the urban slums were up to 20 cm shorter than children from the urban upper classes (Schell 1998).

SKELETAL EVIDENCE OF HEALTH

One of the first attempts to assess the impact of urbanisation using skeletal material was by Wells (1977). He examined the prevalence of maxillary sinusitis from the Bronze Age through to the later medieval period in Britain, and found an increase in the condition with time. Under-representation of the youngest members of these societies makes infant and child mortality rates difficult to assess. However, Storey (1988) examined the prevalence of prenatal defects in two samples from Mesoamerica. At Teotihuacan, a low-status densely populated urban centre, prenatal enamel defects were higher than at the high-status, low density site of Copan, reflecting the different stress patterns of the mothers in these two contrasting settlements. In the later periods of urbanisation at Teotihuacan (Tlajinga 33), Storey (1986) found an increase in perinatal, infant and child mortality, and attributed this to the worsening effects of urbanisation on the population. In 1987, Molleson compared the health of a Roman population living in the urban and rural sectors of Poundbury Camp, in Dorchester, England. Here, a decrease in female stature was noted in the urban sample and the urban quarter was made up of mainly young and middle aged adults, with the majority of neonates and older non-adults buried in the rural sector. However, studies into health and the urban environment were still rare in 1989, when Waldron outlined some of the conditions that may increase in skeletal samples with the onset of urbanisation, such as osteoarthritis, rickets, scurvy, lead exposure and growth retardation. However, he stressed that he was examining the potential of human skeletal remains as few data actually existed.

In the 1990s direct studies into the health of populations living in urban environments increased. In her study of skeletons from medieval York, Grauer (1991) found a higher percentage of women in the cemetery sample, possibly due to higher rates of female immigration. However, these women had a lower prevalence of chronic infection. Grauer suggested that, as part of the new migratory population, these women were less able to adjust to urban life and died in the acute stages of disease before any changes could be identified on the skeleton. The renewed interest in this area of research was reflected in the publication of 'Death in Towns' edited by Bassett (1992). This book drew together evidence for the health of populations living in urban centres from the Roman to later medieval periods in Britain. Nevertheless, none of the skeletal studies contained in this book set out to compare the health of the urban inhabitants with their rural counterparts but, instead, discussed the effects of urban living on human health in isolation. However in 1994, Brothwell began to redress this situation when he carried out a brief review of urban and rural cemetery sites in and around medieval York using published data. Brothwell (1994) examined seven sites at York to examine differences between urban and rural populations, in terms of stature, craniometrics and cribra orbitalia (a lesion thought to be indicative of iron deficiency anaemia). He calculated that at Wharram Percy (rural) the women were 2.1 cm taller than those at St. Helen-on-the-Walls (urban). However, in the adults from Wharram Percy the prevalence of cribra orbitalia was higher (53.1%) than at both Jewbury (urban: 21.7%) and Fishergate (urban: 21.0%). However, these results were not substantiated by any statistical tests and were inconclusive. Mays (1997; 1999) carried out a similar comparison between the adults of Wharram Percy and St. Helen-on-the-Walls and found levels of periostitis (indicative of infection and trauma) to be higher at St. Helen-on-the-Walls (Mays 1997). However, his data suggested that rates of porotic hyperostosis were lower in the rural sample (25%) compared to the urban (58%). This result is the opposite of Brothwell's (1994) but it is not clear whether Mays was referring to orbital (cribra orbitalia) or cranial lesions in his analysis. De la Rúa *et al.* (1995) also assessed human health in contrasting settlements by analysing the prevalence of skeletal markers in urban and industrialised centres, compared to agricultural and transitional populations, from published sites all over the world. They found an increase in cribra orbitalia and enamel hypoplasias in the urban and industrial groups compared to the rural groups.

Lewis *et al.* (1995) developed the work carried out by Wells (1977) and compared the prevalence of maxillary sinusitis in an urban and a rural community from later medieval Yorkshire. The results showed that 39% (106) of the individuals from Wharram Percy had evidence of sinusitis compared to 55% (134) of the individuals from St. Helen-on-the-Walls. It was suggested that this pattern could be attributed to occupation and industrial air pollution in the Medieval city of York. More recently, Judd and Roberts (1999) examined the patterns of trauma in urban and rural groups from Britain and concluded that an agricultural lifestyle contained more physical hazards than an urban one.

Despite documentary evidence for an increase in rickets with industrialisation, as a result of vitamin D deficiency through a lack of sunlight (Mankin 1974), skeletal evidence for rickets in the past is still lacking. However, diagnostic techniques are becoming more sophisticated and Ortner and Mays (1998) have recently described eight cases of rickets in rural Wharram Percy; one case was also discovered at Jewbury in York and at St. Helen-on-the-Walls (Dawes and Magilton 1980; Lilley *et al.* 1994), and around 20 cases were reported at Christ Church Spitalfields in London (Molleson and Cox 1993). The early changes of rickets are subtle and usually begin with an expansion and fraying of the rib ends and distal radius.

The extreme bowing deformities are later manifestations, and occur when the child applies weight to the affected limbs. However, the disease can render children immobile and, as they are susceptible to respiratory and gastro-intestinal infections as a result of the disease, they may not live long enough to develop the most obvious signs (Lewis 2000). These factors may explain why so few cases of the condition have been reported in the archaeological record.

Mays (1999) once again stressed the importance of human skeletal remains in the study of urbanisation and health, and included stable isotope analysis which suggested that the diet of rural Wharram Percy did not differ significantly from that of the city dwellers at Fishergate in York, suggesting that urban populations did not have greater access to non-local, imported foodstuffs. Recently, a more extensive study of non-adult remains from past urban, rural and industrial communities has shown that it was industrialisation, rather than urbanisation that had a detrimental effect on the health of the child populations (Lewis 1999). Weaning ages appeared to decline from two years in the Anglo-Saxon period to one year in the eighteenth and nineteenth centuries. Industrialisation was characterised by a lower mean age at death, growth retardation and an increase in the prevalence of rickets and scurvy. Although higher rates of dental disease and maternal stress were apparent in the urbanised samples, respiratory diseases were more common in the rural areas. However, growth profiles suggested that environmental factors were similar in the urban and rural communities in the later medieval period (*ibid.*).

CONCLUSIONS

This paper has outlined some of the environmental issues relating to urban and rural health in the past. Differences in pathogen exposure, environmental pollution, population density and diet have been shown to result in contrasting patterns of disease and mortality. However, the migration of people from rural to urban environments, shared macro-climates and the impact of social status on infant-feeding practices and growth, make straightforward comparisons between urban and rural environments challenging today and certainly when considering the past, where many of these factors cannot be accounted for.

Work into urban and industrial health in Britain, using human skeletal remains is still in its early stages. However, the recent availability of post-medieval material from crypt and cemetery clearances has begun to provide biological anthropologists with the data they need to address questions about health in industrial environments. As this research progresses it will become more important than ever to combine documentary, historical, environmental and skeletal evidence to provide a fuller picture of human health and adaptation in the past.

References

Albalak, R. 1997. Indoor air pollution in rural areas of the developing world: a review. *American Journal of Physical Anthropology* Suppl. **24**, 64.

Armelagos, G.J. 1990. Health and disease in prehistoric populations in transition, pp. 127–144 in Swedlund, A.C. and Armelagos G. (eds), *Diseases in Populations in Transition. Anthropological and Epidemiological Perspectives.* New York: Bergin and Garvey.

Armitage, P.L. 1985. Small mammal faunas in later medieval towns: a preliminary study in British urban biography. *Biologist* **32**, 65–71.

Barnet, M.C. 1968, The barber-surgeons of York. *Medical History* **12**,19–30.

Bassett, S, (ed.) 1992. *Death in Towns: Urban Responses to the Dying and the Dead, 100–1600.* Leicester: Leicester University Press.

Bogin, B. 1988. Rural-to-urban migration, pp. 90–129 in Mascie-Taylor, C.G.N. and Lasker, G.W. (eds), *Biological Aspects of Human Migration.* Cambridge: Cambridge University Press.

Boyden, S. 1972. Biological determinants of optimum health, pp. 3–11 in Vorster, D.J.M. (ed.), *Human Biology of Environmental Change.* Surrey: International Biological Programme.

Brimblecombe, P. 1975. Industrial air pollution in thirteenth century Britain. *Weather* **30**, 388–396.

Brimblecombe, P. 1977. London air pollution and climate 1200–1900. *Atmospheric Environment* **2**, 1157–1162.

Brimblecombe, P. 1978. Interest in air pollution among early Fellows of the Royal Society. *Notes and Records of the Royal Society of London* **32**, 123–129.

Brimblecombe, P. 1982. Early urban climate and atmosphere, pp. 10–25 in Hall, A.R. and Kenward, H.K. (eds), *Environmental Archaeology in the Urban Context.* London: Current British Archaeology Research Report 43.

Brimblecombe, P. and Ogden, C. 1977. Air pollution in art and literature. *Weather* **32**, 285–291.

Brothwell, D.R. 1994. On the possibility of urban-rural contrasts in human population palaeobiology, pp. 129–136 in Hall, A. and Kenward, H. (eds), *Urban -Rural Connections: Perspectives from Environmental Archaeology.* Oxford: Oxbow Monograph.

Bullough, V. and Campbell, C. 1980. Female longevity and diet in the Middle Ages. *Speculum* **55**, 317–325.

Cockburn, A.T. 1971. Infectious diseases in ancient populations. *Current Anthropology* **12**, 45–62.

Cockburn, A.T. 1977. Where did our infectious diseases come from? The evolution of infectious disease, pp. 103–113 in Elliot, K. and Whelan, J. (eds), *Health and Disease in Tribal Societies.* New York: Associated Scientific Publishers.

Cohen, M.N. 1989. *Health and the Rise of Civilization.* New Haven: Yale University Press.

Cohen, M.N. and Armelagos, G.J. (eds) 1984. *Paleopathology at the Origins of Agriculture.* New York: Academic Press, Inc.

Cooper, T.P. 1913. The medieval highways, streets, open ditches and sanitary conditions of the city of York. *Yorkshire Archaeological Journal* **22**, 270–286.

Dawes, J.D. and Magilton, J.R. 1980. *The Cemetery of St. Helen-on-the-Walls, Aldwark.* London: Council for British Archaeology.

De la Rúa, C., Izagirre, N. and Manzano, C. 1995. Environmental stress in a medieval population of the Basque country. *HOMO* **45**, 268–289.

Ekblad, S. 1993. Stressful environments and their effects on quality of life in Third World cities. *Environment and Urbanization* **5**, 125–134.

Ericksen, E.G. 1954. *Urban behavior.* New York: The Macmillan Company.

Evans, G.W. and Jacobs, S.V.J. 1982. Air pollution and human behavior, pp. 105–132 in Evans, G.W. (ed.), *Environmental Stress.* Cambridge: Cambridge University Press.

Evelyn, J. 1661. *Fumifugium.* London.

Fenner, F. 1971. Infectious disease and social change. *The Medical Journal of Australia.* **1**, 1–10.

Fildes, V.A. 1986. 'The English Disease': infantile rickets and scurvy in pre-industrial England, pp. 121–134 in Cule, J. and Turner, T. (eds), *Child Care Through the Centuries.* London: British Society for the History of Medicine.

Foote, J.A. 1927. Evidence of rickets prior to 1650. *American Journal of Diseases of Children* **34**, 443–452.

Galloway, P.R. 1985. Annual variations in deaths by age, deaths by cause, prices, and weather in London 1670–1830. *Population Studies* **39**, 487–505.

Gilbert, R.I. and Mielke, J.M. (eds) 1985. *The Analysis of Prehistoric Diets.* Florida: Academic Press, Inc.

Goudie, A. 1983. *Environmental Change.* Oxford: Oxford University Press.

Grauer, A.L. 1991. Life patterns of women from medieval York, pp. 407–413 in Walde, D. and Willows, N.D. (eds), *Proceedings of the 22nd Annual Chacmool Conference.* University of Calgary: Charcmool: The Archaeological Association of the University of Calgary.

Graunt, J. 1662. *Natural and Political Observations.* London: Tho. Roycroft.

Green, F.J. 1982. Problems of interpreting differentially preserved plant remains from excavations of medieval urban sites, pp. 40–46 in Hall, A.R. and Kenward, H.K. (eds), *Environmental Archaeology in the Urban Context.* York: The Council for British Archaeology.

Greig, J. 1981. The investigation of a medieval barrel-latrine from Worcester. *Journal of Archaeological Sciences* **8**, 265–282.

Herlihy, D. 1975. Life Expectancies for women in medieval society, pp. 1–22 in Morewedges, R.T. (ed.), *The Role of Women in the Middle Ages.* Albany: State University of New York Press.

Howard, L. 1833. *The Climate of London.* London.

Hudson, E.H. 1965. Treponematosis and man's social evolution. *American Anthropology* **67**, 885–901.

Hughes, M.K. and Diaz, H.F. 1994. Was there a 'medieval warm period' and if so, where and when? *Climatic Change* **26**, 109–142.

Ingram, M.J., Farmer, G. and Wigley, T.M.L. 1981. Past climates and their impact on man: a review, pp. 3–50 in Wigley, T.M.L., Ingram, M.J. and Farmer, G. (eds), *Climate and History: Studies in Past Climates and their Impact on Man.* Cambridge: Cambridge University Press.

Johansson, S.R. and Horowitz, S. 1986. Estimating mortality in skeletal populations: influence of the growth rate on the interpretation of levels and trends during the transition to agriculture. *American Journal of Physical Anthropology* **71**, 233–250.

Jones, A.K.G. (1982) Human parasite remains for a quantitative approach, pp. 66–70 in Hall, A.R. and Kenward, H.K. (eds), *Environmental Archaeology in the Urban Context.* York: The Council for British Archaeology.

Judd, M.A. and Roberts, C.A. 1999. Fracture trauma in a medieval British farming village. *American Journal of Physical Anthropology* **109**, 229–243.

Keene, D.J. 1982. Rubbish in medieval towns, pp. 26–30 in Hall, A.R. and Kenward, H.K. (eds), *Environmental Archaeology in the Urban Context.* London: Current British Archaeology Research Report.

Kenward, H. 1982. Insect communities and death assemblages, past and present, pp. 71–79 in Hall, A.R. and Kenward, H.K. (eds), *Environmental Archaeology in the Urban Context.* York: The Council for British Archaeology.

King, S. 1997. Dying with style: infant death and its context in a rural industrial township, 1650–1830. *Social History of Medicine* **10**, 3–24.

Lamb, H.H. 1981. An approach to the study of the development of climate and its impact in human affairs, pp. 291–309 in Wigley, T.M.L., Ingram, M.J. and Farmer, G. (eds), *Climate and History: Studies in Past Climates and their Impact on Man*. Cambridge: Cambridge University Press.

Lancaster, H.O. 1990. *Expectations of Life: A Study in the Demography, Statistics, and History of World Mortality*. London: Springer-Verlag.

Landers, J. and Mouzas, A. 1988. Burial seasonality and causes of death in London 1670–1819. *Population Studies* **42**, 59–83.

Larsen, C.S. 1997. *Bioarcheology: Interpreting Behavior from the Human Skeleton*. Cambridge: Cambridge University Press.

Lewis, M.E. 1999. *The Impact of Urbanisation and Industrialisation in Medieval and Post-medieval Britain. An assessment of the morbidity and mortality of non-adult skeletons from the cemeteries of two urban and two rural sites in England (AD 850–1859)*. Unpublished Ph.D. thesis, University of Bradford.

Lewis, M.E. 2000. Non-adult palaeopathology: current status and future potential, pp 39–57 in Cox, M. and Mays, S. (eds), *Human Osteology in Archaeology and Forensic Science*. London: Greenwich Medical Media.

Lewis, M.E., Roberts, C.A. and Manchester, K. 1995. Comparative study of the prevalence of maxillary sinusitis in later medieval urban and rural populations in northern England. *American Journal of Physical Anthropology* **98**, 497–506.

Lilley, S.M., Stroud, G., Brothwell, D.R. and Williamson, M.H. (eds) 1994. *The Jewish Burial Ground at Jewbury*. York: Current British Archaeology.

Lord, E. 1997. *Cleansing of the backsides: public health provisions in the medieval city*, paper presented at the Annual Conference of the Social History of Medicine, Health in the City: A History of Public Health, 4th–7th September, 1997.

Luckin, W. 1980. Death and survival in the city: approaches to the history of disease. *Urban History Yearbook* **24**, 53–62.

Manchester, K. 1992. The palaeopathology of urban infections, pp. 8–13 in Bassett, S. (ed.), *Death in Towns: Urban Responses to the Dying and the Dead, 100–1600*. Leicester: Leicester University Press.

Mankin, H.J. 1974. Rickets, osteomalacia, and renal osteodystrophy. *Journal of Bone and Joint Surgery* 56–A, 101–128 and 352–386.

Mays, S. 1997. Life and death in a medieval village, pp. 121–125 in De Boe, G. and Verhaeghe, F. (eds), *Death and Burial in Medieval Europe*. Papers of the 'Medieval Europe Brugge 1997' Conference, Volume 2. Brugge: I.A.P. Rapporten 2.

Mays, S. 1999. The archaeological study of medieval English human populations, AD 1066–1540, pp. 195–210 in Bayley, J. (ed.), *Science in Archaeology: An Agenda for the Future*. London: English Heritage.

McGarvey, S.T. 1998. Intestinal parasitism, pp. 337 in Ulijaszek, S., Johnston, F.E. and Preece, M.A. (eds), *The Cambridge Encyclopedia of Human Growth and Development*. Cambridge: Cambridge University Press.

McGrath, J.W. 1992. Behavioral change and the evolution of human host-pathogen systems. *MASCA: Research Papers in Science and Archaeology* **9**,13–22.

Meredith, H.V. 1982. Research between 1950 and 1980 on urban-rural differences in body size and growth rate of children and youths. *Advances in Child Development and Behavior* **17**, 83–138.

Mims, C. 1980. The Emergence of New Infectious Diseases, pp. 231–250 in Joske, S. (ed.), *Changing Disease Patterns and Human Behaviour*. London: Academic Press.

Molleson T. 1987. Urban bones: the skeletal evidence for environmental change, pp 143–158 in *Actes des 3èmes Journées Anthropologiques. Notes ei Monographies Techniques Number 24*. Éditions du CNRS: Paris.

Molleson, T. and Cox, M. 1993. *The Spitalfields Project, Volume II – The Middling Sort*. York: Council for British Archaeology Research Report 86.

Ortner, D.J. and Mays, S. 1998. Dry-bone manifestations of rickets in infancy and early childhood. *International Journal of Osteoarchaeology* **8**, 45–55.

Ottaway, P. 1992. *Archaeology in British towns: from the Emperor Claudius to the Black Death*. London: Routledge.

Pelling, M. 1983–4. Epidemics in nineteenth century towns: how important was cholera? Pp. 23–33 in Liverpool Medical Institution (ed.): *Transactions and Report*. Chester: The Bemrose Press Ltd.

Platt, C. 1975. The evolution of towns: natural growth, pp. 48–56 in Barley, M.W. (ed.), *The Plans and Topography of Medieval Towns in England and Wales*. York: The Council for British Archaeology.

Rackham, D.J. 1982. The smaller mammals in the urban environment: their recovery and interpretation from archaeological deposits, pp. 86–93 in Hall, A.R. and Kenward, H.K. (eds), *Environmental Archaeology in the Urban Context*. York: The Council for British Archaeology.

Roberts, C. and Manchester, K. 1995. *The Archaeology of Disease: Second Edition*. Gloucester: Alan Sutton Publishing Limited.

Sabine, E.L. 1933. Butchering in medieval London. *Speculum* **8**, 335–353.

Sabine, E.L. 1934. Latrines and cesspools of medieval London. *Speculum* **9**, 303–321.

Schell, L.M. 1998. Urbanisation and growth, pp. 408–409 in Ulijaszek, S., Johnston, F.E. and Preece, M.A. (eds), *The Cambridge Encyclopedia of Human Growth and Development*. Cambridge: Cambridge University Press.

Schmidt, E. 1892. Die körpergrösse und das gewicht der schulkinder des kreises saalfeld. *Archiv für Anthropologie* **21**, 385–434.

Schofield, J. and Vince, A. 1994. *Medieval Towns*. London: Leicester University Press.

Scrimshaw, N.S., Taylor, C.E. and Gordon, J.E. 1959. Interactions of nutrition and infection. *The American Journal of the Medical Sciences* **237**, 367–403.

Stone, L. 1977. *The Family, Sex and Marriage in England 1500–1800*. London: Weidenfeld and Nicolson.

Storey, R. 1986. Perinatal mortality at pre-Columbian Teotihuacan. *American Journal of Physical Anthropology* **69**, 541–548.

Storey, R. 1988. Prenatal enamel defects in Teotihuacan and Copan. *American Journal of Physical Anthropology* **75**, 275–276.

Storey, R. 1992. Preindustrial urban lifestyle and health. *MASCA: Research Papers in Science and Archaeology* **9**, 33–41.

Swedlund, A.C. and Armelagos, G.J. (eds) 1990. *Disease in Populations in Transition*. New York: Bergin & Garvey.

Tannahill, R. 1973. *Food in History*. London: Eyre Methuen.

Tanner, J.M. and Eveleth, P.B. 1976. Urbanization and growth, pp. 144–166 in Harrison, G.A. and Gibson, J.B. (eds), *Man in Urban Environments*. Oxford: Oxford University Press.

Thorndike, L. 1928. Sanitation, baths, and street cleaning in the Middle Ages and Renaissance. *Speculum* **3**, 192–203.

Waldron, T. 1989. The effects of urbanisation on human health: the evidence from skeletal remains, pp. 55–73 in Serjeantson, D. and Waldron, T. (eds), *Diet and Crafts in Towns: the Evidence of Animal Remains from the Roman to the Post-Medieval Periods*. Oxford: British Archaeological Research.

Wells, C. 1977. Disease of the maxillary sinus in antiquity. *Medical and Biological Illustration* **27**, 173–178.

Williams, N. and Galley, C. 1995. Urban-rural differentials in infant mortality in Victorian England. *Population Studies* **49**, 401–420.

Woods, R. and Woodward, J. 1984. Mortality, poverty and the environment, pp. 19–36 in Woods, R. and Woodward, J. (eds), *Urban Disease and Mortality in Nineteenth-Century England*. London: Batsford Academic and Educational Press.

18. Determining occupation from skeletal remains – is it possible?

Tony Waldron and Wendy Birch

From the condition of human skeletal remains in archaeological contexts, interpretations are often made about the individuals represented, including their lifestyle and occupation. When bone specialists attribute a previous occupation to a skeleton they usually do so on the basis of pathological changes: most often on the basis of the pattern of osteoarthritis. In this paper we discuss some of the assumptions made in the determination of occupation, and the reasoning behind these, as well as highlighting some of the dangers inherent in trying to make such interpretations. Findings from selected studies are used to emphasize these points, and recommendations are made for consideration in future work.

Keywords: Skeleton, occupation, osteoarthritis, pre-disposing factors, occupational activity.

Osteologists work with meagre resources, and they naturally wish to obtain as much information as possible about the populations whose skeletons they examine. The occupation of the individuals represented in the assemblage is always of interest. Many workers have made inferences about occupation: often, although not invariably, from the distribution of osteoarthritis throughout the skeleton. Osteoarthritis is a joint disease of great antiquity, having been found throughout most periods of the archaeological record. It is common and fairly easy to diagnose in skeletal remains. The basis for such deductions about occupation is the observation that repetitive activity is an important pre-disposing factor for the development of osteoarthritis, as shown below.

In Figure 47 it can be seen that activity is indeed related to joint failure, which produces appearances in the joint known as osteoarthritis: a joint that does not move does not develop osteoarthritis. A great deal of epidemiological work has been carried out to examine the relationships between osteoarthritis and occupation in modern populations, and some of those which have been found are listed in Table 24.

Precipitants of Osteoarthritis

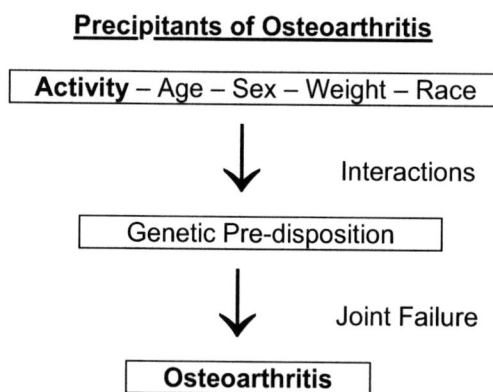

Figure 47. Model to show the precipitants of osteoarthritis. Interactions between the various precipitants act in those people with the genetic pre-disposition to produce joint failure, which is recognised as osteoarthritis.

Table 24. The relationship between different occupations and the site of development of osteoarthritis. Data from sources listed in Waldron (2001, 34).

Occupational Group	Site of Osteoarthritis
Miners	Knee, spine
Furnaceman	Elbow
Ballet dancers	Feet, ankles
Footballers	Knee
Mill workers	Hands
Farmers	Hips

Activity – Age – Sex – Weight – Race – Genetic Pre-disposition

↓

Interactions

↓

Joint Failure

↓

Osteoarthritis

Figure 48. Model to show the development of osteoarthritis.

The most compelling studies are those that have looked at osteoarthritis of the hands in mill workers, and osteoarthritis of the hips in farmers. The study of the mill workers was carried out by Hadler *et al.* (1978). These subjects were working in a cotton mill in the southern United States, and Hadler established that the type of work that they undertook determined which joints of the hands were affected with osteoarthritis. There have also been several studies of farmers in different countries. These all show that farmers are nine times more at risk of developing osteoarthritis of the hip than the rest of the population (Croft *et al.* 1992).

Although these data look impressive, some words of caution need to be expressed at this point. For example, none of the associations are *exclusive* to a particular occupation: those people who are not miners may develop osteoarthritis of the knee; and those who are not farmers may develop osteoarthritis of the hip. The development of osteoarthritis is also frequently the result of trauma to the joint, especially those involving impact loading. Therefore footballers who do *not* injure their knees are not more at risk of developing osteoarthritis at that site than the general population, whereas those who *do* sustain injuries are susceptible. There are also many studies in which no association between occupation and osteoarthritis could be demonstrated although these do not get quoted as frequently as the positive studies. It must be remembered that many individuals who engage in strenuous types of work for many years do develop osteoarthritis; conversely, many individuals whose work is not physically demanding, (university lecturers, for example), do develop osteoarthritis.

Nevertheless, despite these caveats, the notion that it is possible to predict occupation from the skeleton is still firmly established in the osteological literature. Many bone specialists feel content that they are able to do so.

Another way of examining the idea that it is possible to relate a skeleton of an individual to a particular occupation is to take, for an example, a modern rheumatology out-patients department. In a waiting room of about forty patients, all suffering from osteoarthritis, how accurate would the allocation of an occupation to each patient be here? The joints affected by osteoarthritis could be deter-

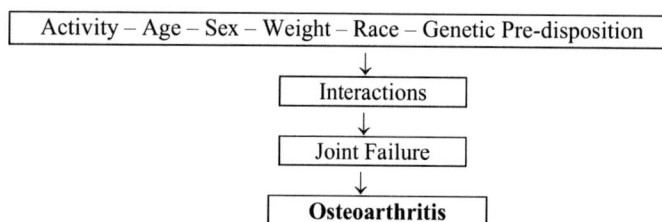

mined by examining each patient's radiographs, as well as asking each their medical history. From this information an occupation could then be assigned to each patient.

One difficulty encountered in this allocation of occupation is that the actual occupations which are represented amongst the patients differ markedly from hospital to hospital. In rural Gloucestershire, for example, it might be possible to identify correctly that one or two of the patients with osteoarthritis of the hip were actually farmers; but how many patients with osteoarthritis of the hip in the Royal London Hospital in the East End of London, would be likely to be farmers? On the other hand, in the London Foot Hospital it might be possible to correctly identify that a patient with osteoarthritis of the foot is actually a ballet dancer, but again this would be unlikely to be the case in Plymouth.

From this it should be clear that assigning an occupation correctly to an osteoarthritic patient has more to do with chance and probability than scientific inference. The reason for failure in this allocation of occupation is shown below (Figure 48). However, there is of course a very easy way of finding out what the occupation of each patient is and that is to ask each one of the patients directly; unfortunately this method is denied those whose patients are the dead and not the living!

Figure 48 shows a model for the development of osteoarthritis, which is widely accepted. In the top box are shown a number of factors that are known to influence the development of osteoarthritis. These include activity, (which has already been discussed as being important), age, sex, genetic predisposition, weight and race. Age is an extremely important factor and it is well known that the prevalence of osteoarthritis increases markedly with age. Osteoarthritis tends to be slightly more common in women than men and there are some differences in the expression of osteoarthritis in different countries and races. Weight is an interesting factor: it has been demonstrated many times that obesity is an important predisposing factor in the development of osteoarthritis of the knee and of the hand, but not of the hip (Felson 1995). A genetic predisposition is also extremely important and for some joints, such as the knee, it seems to be the most significant factor (Cicuttini and Spector 1997).

The second box in the diagram illustrates that the various predisposing factors interact to produce joint failure – osteoarthritis in other words. In individual cases it is not always possible to predict which factor or combination of factors is involved. The exception is when osteoarthritis follows damage to the joint. This might be sustained through a fracture of the ankle that goes into the ankle joint, and in this case it will be clear that osteoarthritis was a direct consequence of the trauma. In this instance one would refer to the joint changes as *secondary* osteoarthritis; here only *primary* osteoarthritis is discussed.

When attempting to assign an occupation to a skeleton from an archaeological context, the bone specialist is trying to follow the above model of development of osteoarthritis backwards. That is to say, starting with a skeleton, which has osteoarthritis in one or more joints, bone specialists attempt to follow the model from bottom to top and to establish the factor that was responsible for the disease. While they may not totally ignore the interactions, they are nevertheless trying to single out one predisposing factor, (this being the occupational activity), as being overwhelmingly more important than the rest. This is like starting with a bucket full of water into which five taps may drain and then trying to identify from which one of the taps, the water actually came. Trying to determine the occupation of an individual from the pattern of osteoarthritis in his or her skeleton is in our view a nonsensical premise. Even if the interpretation were to be correct, there is no possibility of being able to verify it, unless of course the actual occupation of the person involved was definitely known.

Two further points need to be made here. The first is that activity may determine those joints in which osteoarthritis is expressed in people genetically predisposed to develop it. This includes occupational activity. However, the second point is perhaps the more important. That is: the only way in which an occupation could accurately be determined from osteoarthritis in the skeleton is if the disease appeared at a particular site, or combination of sites, *only* in those following a single occupation. If osteoarthritis of the hip only occurred in farmers, then it would be safe to say that a skeleton with hip osteoarthritis was a farmer. However, the majority of people with osteoarthritis of the hip are not farmers and this fact invalidates the conclusion.

Collecting data about the distribution of osteoarthritis in a skeletal assemblage can be useful on a population basis, however. For example, consider two populations and suppose that in one population the sites most frequently affected by osteoarthritis were the hand, knee and shoulder whereas in the other, they were the cervical spine, hip and foot. To explain these differences, one would have to refer back to the model. Certainly one explanation which would account for these differences would be that the two populations had undertaken different types of activity. It is known that the pattern of osteoarthritis is different in medieval and post-medieval skeletons in this country: osteoarthritis of the hip was more common than osteoarthritis of the knee in the early period, whereas the converse is true in the later period, for example. Perhaps the explanation for this difference is to be found in different types of activity that were undertaken.

The reason that so many workers have been misled into thinking that they can deduce the occupation of an individual from pathology in the skeleton arises from a failure to recognise the multifactorial nature of osteoarthritis and by approaching the problem from the wrong direction; that is from the bottom up. Although it is doubtful that this paper will deter anyone from making incorrect and totally unverifiable assumptions in the future, it is hoped that it has instilled some doubt into the readers' minds, so that they will treat such predictions at least with scepticism if not downright disbelief.

References

Cicuttini, F.M., and Spector, T.D. 1997. What is the evidence that osteoarthritis is genetically determined? *Baillieres Clinical Rheumatology* **11**, 657–669.

Croft, P., Coggon, M., Cruddas, M., and Cooper, C. 1992. Osteoarthritis of the hip: an occupational disease in farmers. *British Medical Journal* **304**, 1269–1272.

Felson, D.T. 1995. Weight and Osteoarthritis. *Journal of Rheumatology Supplement* **43**, 7–9.

Hadler, N.M., Gillings, D.B., Imbus, H.R., Levitin, P.M., Makuc, D., Utsinger, P.D., Yount, W.J., Slusser, D. and Moskovitz, N. 1978. Hand structure and function in an industrial setting. Influence of three patterns of stereotyped repetitive usage. *Arthritis and Rheumatism* **21**, 10–20.

Waldron, T. 2001. *Shadows in the Soil – Human Bones and Archaeology*. Gloucestershire: Tempus Publishing Ltd.

19. The disposal and decomposition of human and animal remains: implications for health of people past and present

David W. Hopkins and Patricia E. J. Wiltshire

Data are presented to show that disposal of mammalian soft tissue by burial can result in a long-term persistence of coliform bacteria and the movement of decomposition products in seepage water. This has obvious implications for public health both today and in the past.

Keywords: Burial, soft tissue, coliforms, public health.

INTRODUCTION

Relatively little is known about the microbial processes involved in the break down of carcasses when buried. In this paper we discuss factors that affect the decomposition of human and animal remains and relate them to experimental investigations. Recent concerns about the disposal of animal carcasses as a result of health and economic crises in the farming industry, and the planning guidelines on the siting of new cemeteries, have highlighted the lack of detailed understanding of the processes of decay of human and animal remains.

Of what relevance is this to the theme of this volume - environmental archaeology of industry? The linkage is indirect. Burial of carcasses is a normal part of the agricultural industry, and burial of humans, particularly in large graveyards, has been a feature of large industrial cities for as long as they have been centres of population. Inhumation has, therefore, long been associated with human industrial and other economic activities.

The particular studies we focus on here are experiments involving investigation of processes in graves over relatively short periods (months and years) after burial. It is, of course, relevant to ask what can be learned by archaeo-logists from such short-term studies? The answer is that we do not know for certain. However, it is our contention that short-term experimental studies are useful because truly ancient things, whether they are in graves or not, do not *become* ancient without surviving the first few days, weeks, months and years. It is also reasonable, to suggest that during a biologically-driven process, such as decay of organic remains, the changes that occur early in the decay process affect the subsequent survival of remains. The primary purpose of this paper is to present and discuss experimental data on the microbiological processes that occur when mammalian soft tissues decay in soil.

FACTORS GOVERNING DECOMPOSITION

In their now-classic text on decomposition in terrestrial ecosystem, Swift *et al.* (1979) outline three broad groups of factors that govern decomposition of organic residues in soils. The organic residues with which these researchers were concerned were deposited by natural processes, and nearly all were of either plant or microbial origin. But Hopkins (2000) has argued that the principles outlined can be applied to the decomposition of animal and human corpses in archaeological contexts. The three groups of factors are (a) the resource or substrate quality of the organic residue, (*i.e.* the body), (b) ambient environmental factors, and (c) the decomposer organisms.

Factors intrinsic to the resource include its biochemical composition and accessibility to decomposer organisms. There are major differences in the biochemical composition of plant residues (*e.g.* between hardwood, softwood, and herbaceous litter), but mammalian and other carcasses are rather similar in composition. Major environmental factors which affect the efficiency of decomposition include water availability, pH, redox, temperature, and the degree of physical protection. The presence and activity of decomposer organisms clearly also affect the decomposition rate. It is widely presumed by environmental microbiologists that "all things are everywhere" and that microorganisms are collectively infallible when it comes to degrading organic materials. From this it follows that, given appropriate physical and chemical conditions, it is possible to find any known microorganism and many unknown ones. This suggests that, in any particular environment, the presence of organic remains will lead to the selection from the indigenous community of those organisms capable of decomposing the specific residues. Neither of these pieces of environmental microbiological dogma are actually accurate, but both are sufficiently close to being true that they can be adopted as safe working principles when considering the decomposition of all natural and many synthetic organic residues.

Extensive observations have been made of the decomposition of both buried and unburied human cadavers at the University of Tennessee's Department of Anthropology, and Mann *et al.* (1990) have summarised many years of observations. There are difficulties in interpreting rigorously some of the observations because of apparent lack of replication and experimental controls, but, based on their considerable experience and expertise, this group of researchers have attempted to rank the variables affecting decay of human remains. This ranking is summarised in Table 25, together with our assignment of these variables to one of the three sets of factors affecting decomposition (outlined by Swift *et al.* 1979).

The observations of Mann *et al.* (1990) were made on both buried and unburied bodies. This accounts, at least in part, for the high ranking of temperature and depth; in any case, these are linked factors since temperature decreases and becomes less variable with depth of burial. Similarly, it also accounts for the influence of animals (especially dipteran larvae) because access is easier for bodies left at the surface. Most of the emphasis of the observations summarised in Table 25 was on the effects of scavenging animals. But microbiological processes may predominate in the decomposition of soft tissue, especially where the body has been buried and all animals, including flies, have been excluded. However, the role or microorganisms does not appear to have been studied in the same detail.

CADAVERIC DECAY

Stages in cadaveric decay are summarised in Table 26 which includes information from several sources, most notably Gill-King (1997) and Trick *et al.* (2000). The time elapsed for each stage is probably highly variable and will reflect many factors, including those outlined in Table 25. Gill-King (1997) also lists the order in which organs and tissues decompose (Table 27), but there are many contradictory anecdotal and written reports of the sequence. This suggests that the interactions between the different factors affecting decomposition are not adequately understood.

After death, the soft tissues of the body begin to break down very rapidly through autolysis and putrefaction. Janaway (1996) reviews the microbial processes and intrinsic autolysis associated with cadaveric decay. Unless the body is mutilated or dismembered, **soil** microorganisms probably play a relatively minor role, at least at the outset. It is probable they have a major role in the biochemical processes of decay only in the later stages. Intra- and extracellular lytic enzymes released within the tissues start to break down cells while enteric microorganisms migrate from the gut to the rest of the body via the lymphatic and vascular system. Intense activity of aerobic coliform bacteria leads to oxygen depletion in the tissues, and anaerobes (particularly species of *Clostridium*) proliferate as putrefaction proceeds. It is important to note, however, that although decomposition of the corpse usually occurs under predominantly anaerobic conditions, (because of the large amount of decomposable organic carbon in a body), invertebrates that burrow into corpses can increase the rate of gas transfer and possibly facilitate decomposition by mixing, secretion of enzymes, and the introduction of microorganisms from the soil (see Janaway 1996).

Mammalian soft tissue is a rich source of fat, carbohydrate, and protein. Fats are usually hydrolyzed by both intrinsic lipases and those of microorganisms, and this leads to the production of adipocere. This is often rancid and contains a range of fatty acids including stearic, palmitic, and oleic acids. As conditions become increasingly anaerobic, bacterial fermentation of carbohydrates and proteolysis (particularly by *Clostridium*) result in the production of the foul smelling gases and compounds associated with rotting corpses and faeces. The accumulation of microbially-produced gases may leads to distension of the body cavity, and this can result in leakage of a solution rich in the soluble products of decay, initially via the natural orifices and subsequently via ruptures in the skin as it breaks down (Janaway 1996).

Soluble decomposition products can leach away from the corpse in ground water. In a recent criminal investigation being worked on by one of the authors (PEJW), police search teams used body dogs to try to locate dismembered human remains. The dogs gave a positive response to seepage water in a peaty, acidic soil 15.0 m

Table 25. Factors affecting the decomposition of bodies. Adapted from Mann et al. (1990).

Factor	Impact scale	Decomposition factor (Swift *et al.* 1979)
Temperature	5	Environment
Access by insects	5	Organism
Burial depth	5	Environment
Carnivores/rodents (scavengers)	4	Organism
Trauma (penetration/crushing/mutilation)	4	Resource
Humidity/aridity	4	Environment
Rainfall	3	Environment
Body size and weight	3	Resource
Embalming	3	Resource
Clothing	2	Resource
Substrate (little detailed information)	1	Environment

Impact scale: 1 = least effect and 5 = greatest effect

Table 26. Stages of cadaveric decay. After Gill-King (1997) and Trick et al. (2000).

Stage	Characteristics
Fresh body	Failure of metabolism and repair mechanisms
Early decay	Autolysis and bacterial decay characterised by methane, hydrogen sulphide, hydrogen and carbon dioxide production
Advanced decay	Liquefaction of soft tissues, saponification of lipids, adipocere formation
Skelenisation	Bones remains, fluids disperse

Table 27. Order of tissue/organ decomposition. After Gill-King (1997).

Order
Alimentary canal and associated organs
Cardiovascular system
Lungs and air passages
Urinogenital system
Brain and nervous system
Skeletal muscles
Connective tissues

down-slope of the cadaver. This shows that the products of microbial degradation, and possibly microbes themselves, can travel through soil. Such decomposition products, aided by percolation of water, lead to marked increases in the rate of microbial respiration and the size of the soil microbial community (Hopkins *et al.* 2000a). For a greater understanding of the rate at which liquid and gaseous products of decay disperse from a corpse, knowledge of the physical conditions of the soil is important.

A BURIAL EXPERIMENT

The opportunities to investigate microbiological processes at sites of human burial are obviously limited. Pigs are sometimes used as analogues of human bodies in forensic research and they are often buried in ways to simulate actual human disposal. This allows decomposition processes to be observed under comparable conditions (Turner & Wiltshire 1999). We have conducted microbiological analyses of samples in association with one such forensic experiment. The full reports of most of our findings will be published elsewhere (Hopkins *et al.* 2000a; 2000b), and here we summarise some of these data.

Burial Experiment and Soils

The carcasses of three 4–5 month old pigs were buried within 3 hours of death beneath 10 cm of soil in a hornbeam-dominated woodland in Hertfordshire, England in late December 1996. The soils were compacted stagnogleys derived from clayey drift and Tertiary clays of the Essenson soil association (Jarvis 1983). The pigs' graves were formed by removing the litter layer, excavating the soil, and then replacing most of it on top of the pigs' bodies, to leave an infilled grave level with the surrounding ground surface, which was then covered with leaf litter. The control soils were collected approximately 1.0 m from each of the graves. Scavengers (probably foxes or badgers) did not discover any of the graves until April 1997 but, subsequently, dug into all the graves at various times. Only one grave was disturbed to the extent that parts of the pig cadaver were dragged out of the hole. It was possible to repair the others by infilling with soil. Soil samples were collected on two occasions.

In February 1998, 14 months after burial, soil from all three graves and control sites was sampled, and in January 1999, just over 24 months after burial, only the grave of pig 1 (the least disturbed) and corresponding control were sampled. By the time the samples were taken, the pigs' bodies had lost their integrity and the graves contained intimate mixtures of decaying remains and soil. Samples from depths of 0–15 and 15–30 cm were taken by careful excavation at several locations close to the original position of the trunk of each pig, to give one composite sample at each depth for each pig. The first set of soil samples was used for the determination of soil microbial biomass and for counts of different groups of microorganisms; the second set of samples was used only for obtaining counts of different groups of microorganisms. Details of the methods used are reported in Hopkins *et al.* (2000a; 2000b).

Microbial biomass and activity

In every case (graves and controls), the microbial biomass C was greater for the 0–15 cm depth than for the 15–30 cm depth, although the difference with depth for the disturbed graves of pigs 2 and 3 was not significant (Table 28). For all three graves, the biomass C contents of the 15–30 cm samples were greater than the 15–30 cm samples of the controls. The observation that addition of a large amount of relatively decomposable organic resource led to an increase in microbial community size is not in itself surprising, but in the context of forensic and archaeological investigations, the information may be valuable.

Counts of microorganisms

The counts of culturable organisms in the control and grave soils (Table 29) indicate the broad differences between the samples. However, counts of culturable

Table 28. Microbial biomass of grave and control soils. Each value is the mean of two replicates and the standard deviations are shown in brackets. From Hopkins et al. (2000a).

		Depth (cm)	Microbial biomass C (μg C g^{-1} soil)
Pig 1	Grave	0–15	554 (231)
		15–30	308 (15.6)
	Control	0–15	204 (12.7)
		15–30	79 (20.5)
Pig 2	Grave	0–15	118 (11.3)
		15–30	113 (56.6)
	Control	0–15	598 (44.6)
		15–30	40 (25.5)
Pig 3	Grave	0–15	132 (32.5)
		15–30	129 (1.4)
	Control	0–15	204 (7.8)
		15–30	48 (9.9)

microorganisms in soil are not amenable to rigorous interpretation and are best used comparatively. In all cases, for the samples collected at the control sites in February 1998, there were more culturable microorganisms near the surface than at depth Conversely, in most cases for the soils collected from the graves, there were more microorganisms at depth than nearer the surface. The main observations from the samples collected in February 1998 were that there were larger total numbers of aerobic, anaerobic and coliform bacteria (indicative of enteric organisms or faecal contamination) in the soils from the graves than in the control soils. The most notable observation was the vast number of coliform bacteria in the soils at 15–30cm in the graves, compared with the controls. For pig 1 there were also more coliform bacteria at 0–15cm compared with the control soils. Comparison of the counts for total aerobic bacteria with those for coliform bacteria at 15–30cm in the graves indicates that the coliform bacteria were probably very heavily represented in the count of total aerobic bacteria.

The large number of coliform bacteria relative to total bacteria observed in the grave of pig 1 in February 1998 had declined by January 1999 (Table 30). This indicates that the phase in decomposition when the soil microbial community in the grave was dominated by coliform bacteria passed at some time between 14 and 24 months after burial. Presumably this was because the coliforms had flourished early in the decomposition of the carcass, but as the carcass decayed and conditions become less favourable, numbers of both total bacteria and coliforms declined.

Table 29. Counts of culturable microorganisms in soils sampled from the grave and control sites sampled in February 1998. Each value is the mean of two replicates and the standard deviations are shown in brackets. From Hopkins et al. (2000b).

		Depth (cm)	Aerobic bacteria (cfu g^{-1} soil)	Anaerobic bacteria (cfu g^{-1} soil)	Coliform bacteria (cfu g^{-1} soil)
Pig 1	Grave	0–15	5.4×10^6	1.2×10^6	6.3×10^6
			(1.06×10^6)	(0.25×10^6)	(0.28×10^6)
		15–30	7.3×10^8	7.5×10^5	1.9×10^8
			(0.14×10^8)	(2.54×10^5)	(0.42×10^8)
	Control	0–15	7.2×10^5	1.1×10^5	1.7×10^4
			(0.46×10^5)	(1.05×10^5)	(0.07×10^4)
		15–30	3.3×10^5	4.1×10^4	8.0×10^3
			(1.6×10^5)	(2.96×10^4)	(8.48×10^3)
Pig 2	Grave	0–15	6.0×10^8	4.7×10^5	1.4×10^3
			(4.1×10^8)	(3.42×10^5)	(0.42×10^3)
		15–30	2.7×10^8	3.5×10^5	1.9×10^7
			(0.14×10^8)	(4.21×10^5)	(0.78×10^7)
	Control	0–15	3.7×10^7	5.4×10^5	4.6×10^4
			(0.21×10^7)	(1.77×10^5)	(1.41×10^4)
		15–30	1.9×10^8	3.3×10^5	2.4×10^3
			(0.36×10^8)	(0.33×10^5)	(0.92×10^3)
Pig 3	Grave	0–15	3.6×10^9	1.4×10^6	8.0×10^4
			(0.42×10^9)	(0.59×10^6)	(0.71×10^4)
		15–30	3.8×10^9	3.3×10^5	1.6×10^8
			(1.27×10^9)	(0.28×10^5)	(0.71×10^8)
	Control	0–15	5.0×10^6	3.6×10^5	2.5×10^4
			(3.25×10^6)	(3.04×10^5)	(0.35×10^4)
		15–30	2.0×10^6	2.1×10^5	2.0×10^4
			(0.28×10^6)	(0.78×10^5)	(0.92×10^4)

Table 30. Counts of culturable microorganisms in soils sampled from the grave and control sites for pig 1 sampled in January 1999. Each value is the mean of two replicates and the standard deviations are shown in brackets. From Hopkins et al. (2000b).

	Depth (cm)	Aerobic bacteria (cfu g^{-1} soil)	Anaerobic bacteria (cfu g^{-1} soil)	Coliform bacteria (cfu g^{-1} soil)
Grave	0–15	4.4×10^6	2.0×10^6	1.8×10^6
		(4.44×10^6)	(0.14×10^6)	(0.49×10^6)
	15–30	4.5×10^6	3.9×10^5	1.5×10^4
		(1.82×10^6)	(0.35×10^5)	(0.71×10^4)
Control	0–15	2.0×10^6	4.3×10^5	1.2×10^5
		(0.19×10^6)	(0.64×10^5)	$(0.78 x 10^4)$
	15–30	2.3×10^5	1.3×10^5	2.6×10^4
		(0.21×10^5)	(0.26×10^5)	(0.85×10^4)

CONCLUSIONS

In the context of the investigation of the microbiological processes in graves, the data reported here can only be regarded as preliminary observations. They do, however, complement the work of Mann *et al.* (1990), by providing microbiological analyses to complement observations previously reported, which focused on the activities of soil animals. The presence of a large number of coliform bacteria in the grave is reasonable evidence that bacteria inhabiting the animals' bodies played a role in the decomposition process. This is not unexpected, although the fact that the culturable bacterial community of soils from the graves was dominated by coliforms over a year after burial raises questions about the persistence of bacterial pathogens at sites of body and carcass disposal – both in the past and following recent crises in the agricultural industry.

It is well known that, in the past, animal waste (both from industrial processing of hides, horn and bone, and from butchery) was disposed of by burial in pits and ditches (Albarella; Ervynck *et al.*, this volume). At urban sites, drinking water was commonly obtained from wells and water holes. These were often dug into the same aquifer as that penetrated by the refuse pits. We have shown that coliform bacteria can persist in soil for a considerable period after burial, and that seepage of decomposition products (and possibly, therefore, microorganisms) could occur into sources of drinking water by percolation. The implication for public health in the past seem plain. Furthermore, the recent mass burials of diseased farm animals as a result of foot and mouth disease might also have repercussion as yet unrealised.

Acknowledgements
We are grateful to Hertfordshire Constabulary, Bryan Turner of King's College University of London and Louise Dundee of the Queen's University Belfast.

References

Gill-King, H. 1997. Chemical and ultrastructral aspects of decomposition, pp. 93–108 in Haglund, W.D. and Sorg, M.H. (eds), *Forensic Taphonomy- The Postmortem Fate of Human Remains*. Boca Raton: CRC Press.

Hopkins, D.W. 2000. Interfaces of soil biology with archaeological investigations, pp. 483–512 in Bollag, J-M. and Stotzky, G. (eds) *Soil Biochemistry volume 10*. New York: Marcel Dekker.

Hopkins, D.W., Wiltshire, P.E.J. and Turner, B.D. 2000a. Microbial characteristics of soils from graves: an investigation at the interface of soil microbiology and forensic science. *Applied Soil Ecology* **14**, 283–288.

Hopkins, D.W., Dundee, L. and Wiltshire, P.E.J. 2000b. What ever happened to the three little pigs? Microorganisms in the soils from graves. *See Soil Journal* – in press.

Janaway, R.C. 1996. The decay of buried human remains and their associated materials, pp. 58–85 in Hunter, J., Roberts, C. and Martin, A. (eds), *Studies in Crime: An Introduction to Forensic Arcaheology*. London: B.T. Batsford Ltd.

Jarvis M.B. 1983. *Soils of England and Wales*. Sheet 6 SE England, Ordnance Survey, Southampton.

Mann, R.W., Bass, W.M., and Meadows, L. 1990. Time since death and decomposition of the human body: Variables and observations in case and experimental field studies. *Journal of Forensic Sciences* **35**, 103–111.

Swift, M.J., Heal, O.W. and Anderson, J.M. 1979. *Decomposition in Terrestrial Ecosystems*. Oxford: Blackwell Scientific Publications.

Trick, J.K., Williams, G.M., Noy, D.J., Moore, Y. and Reeder, S. 2000. Pollution potential of cemeteries: Impact of the 19th century Carter Gate cemetery, Nottingham. Presentation at the *British Society of Soil Science/ Society for Environmental Geochemistry and Health* joint meeting on *Soil, Environment and Health* at the University of Birmingham Medical School, 6–7 April 2000.

Turner B.D. and Wiltshire P.E.J. 1999. Experimental validation of forensic evidence: a study of the decomposition of buried pigs in a heavy clay soil. *Forensic Science International* **101**, 113–122.